Toward a Warless World

The Travail of the American Peace Movement

Toward a Warless World

The Travail of the
American Peace Movement
1887–1914

by DAVID S. PATTERSON

INDIANA UNIVERSITY PRESS
Bloomington / London

327.172
P317t

To Mary Margaret

Copyright © 1976 by Indiana University Press
ALL RIGHTS RESERVED

Published in Canada by Fitzhenry & Whiteside Limited, Don Mills, Ontario

Manufactured in the United States of America

Library of Congress Cataloging in Publication Data
Patterson, David S   1937–
Toward a warless world.
Bibliography
Includes index.
1. Peace—History.   I.   Title.
JX1961.U6P33 1976   327'.172'0973   75-28916
ISBN 0-253-36019-6   1 2 3 4 5 80 79 78 77 76

CONTENTS

PREFACE

THIS BOOK IS A HISTORY of the American peace movement in the generation before the First World War. It describes the growth of the peace cause from 1887 to 1914, the peace leaders' assumptions and programs, the difficulties the peace leadership encountered in promoting peace proposals, and the effects of the outbreak of the First World War on the movement. I have adopted a chronological format, for it is the peace movement as an evolving social movement through time that interests me. For the sake of clarity, the simultaneous development of several peace activities required occasional departures from a rigid chronological framework. Moreover, the first and tenth chapters attempt to provide a socio-cultural profile, or cross-sectional analysis, of the movement in the late nineteenth century and the last decade before the outbreak of the World War respectively. With these few exceptions I have tried to avoid back-tracking or overlapping of events.

Throughout this work I have emphasized the many frustrations and failures of the American peace movement—hence the word "travail" in the title. Both external and internal factors produced these frustrations and failures. The external factors were beyond the control of peace advocates. Some American peace proposals failed because of noncooperation of foreign states. Domestically, the American peace movement operated within the context of the pervasive nationalism of that era. Moreover, when Americans contemplated the prospects for international cooperation, few questioned the viability of their values and institutions for world politics; rather, Americans overwhelmingly assumed that they could extend them to the world. "Internationalism" for these people represented merely an extension of their national faith. It is probably true that people tend to embrace pacifism or internationalism in rough proportion to their revulsion against the massive destruction resulting from their nation's foreign policy excesses, as occurred in Japan and Germany following the Second World War, or among inhabitants of small states who perceive that their nation lacks the resources and manpower to defend its interests against more powerful and potentially hostile neighboring states. Neither of those conditions existed in the United States before the First World War. On the contrary, that period of relative peace and isolation witnessed no major or sustained crisis in foreign affairs.[1]

Thus, from 1887 to 1914, the general public in the United States showed little interest in peace questions, let alone commitment to genuine pacifism or internationalism. There were exceptions of course among pacifist sects and some secular pacifists and much discussion concerning proper approaches to world order, but the number of dedicated peace activists throughout that period was never sufficiently large to organize and develop a mass following. Historians have correctly emphasized that public revulsion against and memory of the devastation of the First and Second World Wars directly contributed to the growth of peace activities in the United States during and following these hostilities, though the near universal assumption among Americans of the righteousness of their nation's belligerency and the successful prosecution of these wars for total victory far from the continental shores of the United States again limited the size of the antiwar reaction and in consequence the growth of the peace movement.[2]

Another obstacle to the peace movement was the American Constitution. The constitutional provision requiring two-thirds majority in the United States Senate for consent to treaties with foreign states permitted a minority in the upper house to emasculate and defeat administrations' treaties contemplating even mild forays into the area of international cooperation. Unhappy memories of the harmful effects of executive-legislative and party battles on foreign policy issues along with the perceived threat to American security in the form of aggressive Russian communism led to bipartisan foreign policy consensus after 1945, but in the generation before 1914 factionalism predominated.

Those external factors were of fundamental importance in minimizing the potential effectiveness of the American peace movement. Internal factors, however, compounded those difficulties and further limited the effectiveness of the peace cause. The internal factors include the ambiguous motives, divided loyalties, flawed perceptions, misguided tactics and strategy, and ideological heterogeneity of peace spokesmen. I particularly explore their ideological diversity. In detailing their various approaches to world politics, I have employed the categories pacifist, generalist, world federationist (or federalist), and legalist, which Warren F. Kuehl developed in his study of the movement for international organization in the

United States before 1920.[3] In other respects, however, my approach diverges. On the one hand, I have not tried to supersede his exhaustively inclusive chronicle of American proposals for world order and have tried to interpret their essence. On the other, I have attempted to provide a more comprehensive treatment of the peace movement for the prewar generation by detailing peace advocates' responses to the entire spectrum of peace issues—specifically, diplomatic crises, wars, American interventions in foreign states, and the problem of armaments.

Pacifists, world federalists, generalists, and legalists did not sharply define their divisions before 1914, and individuals in one category flirted on occasion with blueprints for world peace advanced by individuals in other groupings. Moreover, variations developed within each group. The words "pacifist" and "internationalist," like "nationalist" and "isolationist," are tricky concepts and open to many interpretations.[4] Sectarian and nonsectarian pacifists appear in my study, and pacifists ranged from nonresistants on the extreme left wing who renounced all forms of military activity (though none resorted to complete noncooperation with the federal government) to selective pacifists on the right who abhorred violence but were willing to tolerate war for certain idealistic purposes such as the defense of small states against larger aggressors. I have tried to indicate the varieties of pacifist thought in my study but have not hesitated to use the words "pacifist," "pacific-minded," or "pacific-minded internationalist" to describe the basic outlook of those individuals. Similarly, since all peace spokesmen believed they were working for a more harmonious world order, they can be called "internationalists." I have employed that word in describing the peace leaders in my study, even though the solid nationalist biases of many of them severely qualified the "internationalist" label. I have preferred, however, to rely on the words pacifists, generalists, world federalists, and legalists to clarify the kind of internationalists in each case. I have also occasionally used the term "full-fledged internationalist" to differentiate the federalists' more radical vision of world order from the more limited conceptions of other international reformers.

In attempting to bring meaning to an extremely diverse, amorphous movement, I have focused on the most significant participants in the peace movement. Admittedly, this emphasis downgrades the role of individuals who were only marginally in the peace cause, but I have been willing to slight these people when I could find no evidence of any noticeable influence on peace counsels. The leadership of the peace movement set its tone. Admittedly, no clear criteria for defining active participation presently exists. My indices for including individuals in the peace movement were leadership of peace or internationalist organizations or fairly consistent participation at peace and arbitration conferences.

Peace movements are a controversial subject, and the historian's conclusions about them inevitably reflect his political biases. When I began,
I inclined to sympathize with the peace advocates. My own support for
the antiwar movement opposing American military intervention in Viet-
nam undoubtedly reinforced my initial predisposition to view with favor
the peace advocates before the First World War. As I delved more deeply
into my subject, however, I perceived that the American peace movement
before 1914 was quite different from its contemporary counterpart. Far
from radical, the movement before the First World War was quite moderate, even conservative, and I was increasingly struck by peace advocates' ambiguous attitudes and inconsistent actions. Other scholars reinforced these impressions. Michael A. Lutzker provided valuable information on the so-called "practical" peace movement in the two decades
following the Spanish-American war, and C. Roland Marchand related
participants in the American peace cause to other social and intellectual
currents during the progressive era.[5]

Though peace advocates often referred to themselves as "pacifists"
and "internationalists," I have not taken their definitions at face value
but have probed their rhetoric and looked at their actual behavior. To the
extent that I do not accept peace advocates on their own terms and
measure them against more absolute standards of pacifism and internationalism, I depart from conventional narrative history. If such departures can be called revisionism, so be it. My intention, however, has not
been to pillory the peace leaders as less than principled individuals but to
understand them as complex, fallible human personalities.

Many people helped me in the preparation of this study. Lawrence W.
Levine and Paul Seabury, both at the University of California, Berkeley,
and Armin Rappaport, now at the University of California, San Diego,
read my doctoral dissertation from which this study emerged and made
numerous suggestions. Warren F. Kuehl wrote a detailed critique of an
early draft, and I greatly profited from his stimulating conference for
peace researchers in history at the Center for Peace Studies, The University of Akron, in May 1974. Others who read and commented on selected chapters of my manuscript were Stanley L. Jones, Raymond
Wolters, Peter W. Stanley, J. Stanley Lemons, Hamilton Cravens, Harold
M. Hyman, Thomas L. Haskell, and my brother, James T. Patterson.
Of the many librarians and archivists who aided my research over the last
decade, I particularly am indebted to Claire Shetter, Ardith Emmons,
and Berenice Nichols, all at the Swarthmore College Peace Collection. I
also acknowledge Rice University for its financial contribution toward
the cost of publication. Linda Quaidy and Jeanette Waltham typed the
manuscript in various stages. I am grateful to the editors of the *Proceed-*

ings of the American Philosophical Society, Political Science Quarterly, and Schocken Books for permission to reproduce portions of my articles they have previously published. My greatest debt goes to my wife, Mary Margaret, for her many sacrifices, constant support, and informed editorial help. I am also indebted to Ralph M. Novak, Jr., who served as my research assistant on this project for one summer.

[1]

The Late
Nineteenth-Century Setting

IN THE POST–CIVIL WAR ERA the United States' growing interest in expansion beyond its continental shores culminated in a war with Spain and the acquisition of an extracontinental colonial empire. Starting with those dramatic events, historians of American foreign relations have looked backward to uncover the economic changes, expansionist theories of intellectuals, strategic factors, and political pressures that contributed to the eventual establishment of a new American empire. The territorial expansionists ultimately won but they were not the only individuals interested in influencing American diplomacy. Advocates of peace were among those Americans of this *fin de siècle* generation who attempted to persuade their government to adopt their proposals for a more pacific foreign policy.

Since the influence of American peace workers in the last decades of the nineteenth century was limited, it is not surprising that most historical accounts of that period of American history have relegated them to comparative oblivion. Yet the pacific-minded Americans who participated in the organized peace movement deserve attention for three reasons. First, they served as a healthy antidote to the accepted view that the American people were almost totally uninterested in international affairs immediately following the Civil War; and that when they did begin to express interest in international problems in the 1890s, they became overwhelmingly jingoistic and began to experience a "psychic crisis" that finally swept the nation into war with Spain in 1898.[1] Second, their numbers

1

gradually increased in the post–Civil War years. By the 1890s a modest contingent of peace advocates was promoting an Anglo-American arbitration treaty. Finally, and more important in the long run, before 1898 American advocates of peace had already organized several peace and arbitration societies that were to provide part of the foundation for expansion of the peace movement in the decade-and-a-half after the Spanish-American War.

Although not all friends of peace became dedicated members of peace organizations in closing decades of the nineteenth century, most willingly cooperated with those groups. Only a few peace societies received any notice from the nation's press or exerted much influence in the first two decades after the Civil War. The oldest peace organization, the American Peace Society, was the most prestigious. Organized in Boston in 1828, it quickly became and remained the best known of American peace groups in the antebellum period, mainly because of its dedicated leaders, among them William Ladd, William Jay, Elihu Burritt, and Senator Charles Sumner, and the scholarly merits of its monthly journal, *Advocate of Peace*. From its first days the society had a strong Christian emphasis. Protestant ministers always filled several directorships, and the constitution stated, "This Society, being founded on the principle that all war is contrary to the spirit of the gospel, shall have for its object to illustrate the inconsistency of war with Christianity."[2] The society also made profession of the Christian faith a prerequisite for membership until 1901, when this provision was dropped, although in practice it was apparently not enforced long before that date.

Despite the radical pacifist rhetoric of some of its leaders, the American Peace Society remained essentially a conservative organization. At times, indeed, it seemed more concerned with its image of respectability among the general public than with the abolition of war. Its support of almost all constructive alternatives to war reflected its moderate stance, but its leaders campaigned for treaties of international arbitration, periodic international conferences, and a world court. In promoting this program, they had worked closely with their transatlantic counterpart, the London Peace Society, in organizing a series of peace congresses from 1843 to 1853.

Badly divided by the Civil War and nearly bankrupted by the depression of the mid-1870s, the American Peace Society slowly recovered. In the 1870s and 1880s a new generation of intellectuals, reformers, businessmen, and professional people replaced the aged or now deceased leaders, but the orientation of the group remained moderately conservative. Among the new leaders were Edward S. Tobey, president (1873–1891); two energetic corresponding secretaries, James B. Miles (1871–

1875) and the Reverend Rowland B. Howard (1884–1892); Protestant ministers Charles G. Ames and Reuen Thomas; woman's rights advocates Mary A. Livermore and Julia Ward Howe; and the Boston clergyman Edward Everett Hale. Benefiting both from the widespread revulsion against the bloodshed of the Civil War and the moderate, middle-class orientation of the group's program, the American Peace Society underwent a modest revival. By the early 1890s the monthly circulation of the *Advocate of Peace* totaled 2,500, a twofold increase in twenty years.[3]

A second peace society was the Universal Peace Union. Several followers of William Lloyd Garrison's philosophy of nonresistance who had become disillusioned with the prowar stand of the American Peace Society during the Civil War founded the new group in early 1866. Fervently dedicated to the proposition that organized violence under any circumstances was un-Christian, the new group took an uncompromising antiwar position. The union's first president was the Quaker wool merchant Alfred H. Love, who believed that God had implanted peace principles in every human soul and that war therefore was an unnatural human institution resulting from ignorance, improper education, and misunderstanding. A devoted adherent of Garrisonianism, he had vigorously opposed and personally defied the military draft during the Civil War. Love, however, did not subscribe to the extreme no-government views of some Garrisonians. Although the society's activities centered around Love's home city of Philadelphia, its leaders also formed branches in several northeastern states, enrolled a few hundred active members and several thousand loosely affiliated sympathizers, cooperated with the Pennsylvania Peace Society (also founded in 1866), and began to fraternize with European pacifists and peace groups. Many supporters of the Universal Peace Union were Quakers, but members of smaller pacifist sects and religious liberals also joined the new group.

While supporting the principle of international arbitration treaties as one path to world peace, the new group also emphasized the armament problem. Believing preparation for war meant eventual war, its members championed immediate disarmament of all nations as the surest path to permanent world peace. Similarly, they attacked military training in the schools and colleges. Love even advocated the abolition of the armed forces of the United States and proposed a war referendum amendment to the United States Constitution that would have taken the war-making power out of the hands of Congress and given it to the people.

Unlike the American Peace Society's focus on international questions, the Universal Peace Union's propaganda activities also included the abolition of capital punishment, improvement of race relations, an end to the Indian wars, merciful treatment of captured Indians, arbitration of labor grievances, temperance, and women's rights. Although the legacy of Garrisonian radical individualism, along with the essentially middle-class backgrounds of its members, hindered the Universal Peace Union from identifying closely with labor unions and other collectivist movements in late nineteenth-century America, the breadth of its nonviolent philosophy nonetheless illustrated its commitment to Christian love and social justice. Alfred H. Love tirelessly expounded the Christian humanism of his peace group in letters and petitions to government officials, public addresses, and magazine articles.[4]

Among its many activities the Universal Peace Union sponsored four-day conventions each summer in Mystic, Connecticut, which at the zenith of their popularity in the 1890s drew more than 5,000 visitors. It also managed to publish a monthly journal, *The Peacemaker,* which Love edited from the mid-1890s until his death in 1913.[5] Both the Mystic gatherings and *The Peacemaker* helped publicize the peace group's program, but another promotional technique was the use of eye-catching symbols such as peace bells, flashy banners, and the peace plow. The last one dramatized the biblical prophecy of Isaiah: "They shall beat their swords into ploughshares and their spears into pruning hooks. Nation shall not lift up sword against nation, neither shall they learn war any more."[6] At the centennial celebration of the signing of the Declaration of Independence, a blacksmith forged a sword into a peace plow and a spear into a pruning hook; and the Universal Peace Union's exhibit of another peace plow at the Chicago World's Fair in 1893, depicting the same prophecy, won a grand prize. Many people, including some peace workers, ridiculed the union's tactics, which suggested its preference for the bizarre and superficial over more sophisticated analyses of the causes of war or new approaches to international cooperation that increasingly permeated the American peace movement after about 1900.[7]

Alfred H. Love remained the society's guiding inspiration, but a few dedicated disciples helped spread its pacifist message. Because of its commitment to women's rights and its emphasis on women's active role as peacemakers, about one-third of its membership as well as most of Love's closest helpers were women. These included the Quaker Arabella Carter, the Shaker minister Amanda Deyo, the venerable Quaker pacifist Lucretia Mott, and Belva Ann Lockwood. Mrs. Lockwood was the most active and forceful of these faithful supporters. An ardent suffragette, defender of the rights of organized labor, and in 1879 the first woman lawyer to argue a case before the Supreme Court of the United States, she was nominated for the presidency of the United States by the National Equal Rights party in 1884 and again in 1888.[8] In the previous decade Mrs. Lockwood, who lived in Washington, D.C., heard of the Universal Peace

Union and, strongly supporting its opposition to militarism, quickly became the union's main lobbyist on Capitol Hill. She also cooperated with Robert McMurdy and other pacifistic individuals in the nation's capital and many states in establishing the National Arbitration League in 1882 to muster support for arbitration and antimilitary resolutions in Congress.[9]

No less than Alfred H. Love, Mrs. Lockwood steadfastly promoted the peace cause. Her published articles and private letters to government officials documented her deep commitment to peace. A letter to Grover Cleveland at the onset of his first presidential term typified her idealistic internationalism. Endorsing the Universal Peace Union's and National Arbitration League's hopes for the new administration's negotiation of several arbitration treaties, she declared: "We beleive [*sic*] that war is a barbarism, legalized murder; abhorrent to the enlightened conscience of this age; and a condition that intelligent, christian nations should be educated out of. We declare our confidence in the better destiny of the human race, beleiving [*sic*] that in this industrial age intelligent educated people may be united on a common basis of mutual interest and equality of rights." [10]

The Peace Association of Friends in America completed the list of the most visible peace societies in the two decades after the Civil War. Founded by Orthodox Quakers' yearly meetings in the Middle West in 1867, the Peace Association of Friends established headquarters in New Vienna, Ohio, and twenty years later moved them to Richmond, Indiana. Although it remained exclusively a Quaker organization, it cooperated with other religious denominations in an attempt to mobilize the entire Christian church behind the peace cause. It also gave favorable attention to the work of the American Peace Society. The Peace Association's president for most of the years before the World War was William G. Hubbard, and Daniel Hill served as secretary until his death in 1899. Both also became officers of the American Peace Society, Hubbard eventually serving a total of forty-six consecutive years.

The Peace Association especially tried to proselytize ministers of the gospel in the hope that they would expound Christ's teachings of human brotherhood and nonviolence to their congregations. The group's journal, *Messenger of Peace,* edited by Hill, gained the largest circulation of any peace paper in the 1870s and 1880s, and in one year, 1871, reached as many as 12,000 ministers. The Peace Association of Friends reinforced the efforts of other pacifist agencies by financing traveling lectures and essay contests on peace for Quakers, reprinting and disseminating pacifist tracts, and frequently petitioning Congress against large armaments and in behalf of international arbitration.[11]

Other individuals expressed their abhorrence of war, although they were not actively associated with peace societies. These included disillusioned Civil War veterans like William Tecumseh Sherman and Ulysses S. Grant (whose indictments of war were frequently quoted by pacifists), Protestant ministers, and international lawyers. The lawyers were perhaps the most active nonpacifists who persistently searched for methods to substitute law for war. In cooperation with their professional counterparts in Europe as well as lay leaders of the American Peace Society, these judicially oriented individuals established two international law societies, the Institute of International Law and the Association for the Reform and Codification of the Law of Nations (renamed the International Law Association in 1895). The shock of the Franco-Prussian War and, more important, the enthusiasm generated by the Geneva arbitral award of 1872—which settled the thorny issue of American claims against Great Britain for the latter's building and outfitting of ships for the Confederacy during the Civil War— prompted lawyers to found these societies. They diligently drew up codes of international law in the hope that the major powers would endorse their work at some future international conference. Many of the discussions at the annual sessions of these two groups centered around David Dudley Field's pioneer work, *Draft Outlines for an International Code,* first published in 1872.[12]

Although pacifists placed more faith in the flexible provisions of arbitration treaties than in the precise legalism of an international code, many of them participated actively in the lawyers' conferences. Several members of the American Peace Society, including Field, were international lawyers and had played a major role in founding the Association for the Reform and Codification of the Law of Nations. Once the movement for international arbitration treaties began to grow in the late 1880s and 1890s, however, American pacifists' interests in international law societies declined, while their cooperation with less legalistic peace societies, both at home and abroad, revived. As a result, the impact of the international lawyers on the peace movement, which was never very pronounced from the start, slowly faded. Only after the First Hague Conference in 1899 did their legal expertise again begin to assume importance.[13]

Despite peace advocates' untiring efforts, as late as the mid-1880s their peace societies had little impact on American opinion. One sign of peace advocates' weak hold on the public imagination was their failure to arouse the support of Congress for international arbitration. Congressmen willingly introduced their petitions in behalf of international arbitration and a high court, but almost all these efforts died in the foreign relations committees. The lone exceptions occurred in 1874, when lobbyists of the Universal Peace Union persuaded New York Representative Stewart L. Woodford to introduce an arbitration resolution.[14] Temporarily steeped in the euphoric aftermath of the Geneva award, which had already resulted in the endorsement by the British House of Commons of a resolution advocating the "further improvement in International Law and the establishment of a general and permanent system of International Arbitration," the House of Representatives quickly endorsed Woodford's proposal and approved another later that same day, and the Senate endorsed a third one six days later.[15] Those actions, however, had no legal force, and the Grant administration never attempted to implement their sentiments.

So, too, the efforts of the Universal Peace Union and the American Peace Society before 1885 to induce the Republican administrations to negotiate arbitration treaties with foreign nations had little effect. All presidents paid lip service to the idea of international arbitration and on occasion negotiated treaties providing for arbitral tribunals for the resolution of specific controversies, but none gave it high priority. The chief executives responded sympathetically to the stream of American and European peace workers' requests for treaties establishing permanent machinery for the arbitration of future disputes or for the mediation of conflicts between other nations; in practice, however, they refrained from any such concerted diplomatic action that might jeopardize America's traditional isolationism.[16]

Another indication of the ineffectiveness of the movement was its static character. New societies appeared at this period, but many of them failed within a few years for lack of financial support and public interest. As a result, the total number of peace organizations (including local branches of the American Peace Society and the Universal Peace Union) fluctuated from twenty-five to thirty during the 1870s and 1880s, and as late as 1894 the secretary of the American Peace Society privately conceded, "Some of the peace societies exist only on paper."[17] Fewer than a dozen peace groups drew members outside their respective local communities, and even the overwhelming majority of members in the American Peace Society lived in the Boston area. Robert McMurdy, one observer in 1887, estimated, perhaps too conservatively, that loyal membership in peace groups totaled only four hundred.[18]

Moreover, the advanced age of the active leaders meant that the movement lacked vitality and had meager prospects for dynamic growth. Elderly survivors of peace, antislavery, temperance, and other early nineteenth-century reform movements predominated in the leading peace organizations. Though the groups managed to attract some younger members in the post–Civil War generation, there were not enough of them to reinvigorate the movement. During the 1890s successive deaths of the founders of the Universal Peace Union prompted Alfred H. Love to initiate a necrology section in *The Peacemaker.* Because the tiny majority of younger recruits to the group had little understanding of and still less sympathy for its Garrisonian nonresistant focus, they chafed under its uncompromising and, in their view, impractical peace principles. In consequence, some of the constructive energies that might have been devoted to the rejuvenation of the Universal Peace Union were diverted instead to two abortive efforts to oust Love from the presidency and turn the organization in new directions. In the long term, the American Peace Society proved more adjustable to new currents in the peace movement, but it never attracted enough young recruits to reduce its heavily weighted, superannuated leadership. In 1896 the average age of the board of directors was sixty.[19]

Further, all peace groups, including those with some semblance of a national or regional constituency, lacked the financial resources for effective work. The Universal Peace Union operated on a scant budget averaging only $1,500 a year, and *The Peacemaker,* reaching only a few hundred subscribers, consistently ran a deficit that had to be covered by a few wealthy donors. The annual income of the Peace Association of Friends totaled $5,000 in its first few years, exceeding the American Peace Society in comparative affluence, but by the late 1870s its receipts had fallen to one-third that amount. That decline continued into the following two decades, and financial stringencies forced the curtailment of peace work outside Indiana and suspension of publication of the *Messenger of Peace* for a time in the mid-1890s. The peace societies' penury also prevented the employment of any full-time peace worker. Even the zealous Alfred H. Love continued to rely on his woolen business for income. Peace work was not a profession.[20]

Several developments contributed to the societies' limited influence. A pervasive feeling throughout the Northern states that the Union forces had fought the Civil War for noble ends—the preservation of the Union and the abolition of Negro slavery—somewhat blunted the reaction to the horrors of war. Paradoxically, while the sectional conflict may have helped to mold or strengthen the antiwar attitudes of the most faithful pacifists, to a much larger number of American citizens the achievement of the Union's war aims served to justify the hostilities and reinforced their faith in self-confident nationalism.

Many antebellum pacifists also contributed to public discredit of pacifism. The American peace movement had centered almost entirely in the northeast before the war, and many pacifists from that section had renounced their antiwar loyalties when the prospect of sectional hostilities became imminent. Forced to choose between pacifism and abolitionism, many pacifists understandably abandoned the former at least for the war's duration. Even those northern friends of peace who believed that the Civil War was a repressible conflict assumed that only a stronger Southern willingness to free and resettle their Negro slaves could have prevented the armed clash between the sections. Beyond the Garrisonian founders of the Universal Peace Union and the remaining faithful among the pacifist sects, only a few others managed to resist the contradictory moral claims growing out of the war experience.[21]

Indeed, despite their high-minded principles several important postwar leaders of the American Peace Society were more infected by the nationalist feeling following the war than by authentic pacifist sentiments. One of the society's spokesmen, Senator Charles Sumner, Radical Republican from Massachusetts, inclined toward pacifism before the conflict, but he supported the Union cause during the hostilities; and in the following decade he was willing to contemplate war with Britain if that country did not acquiesce in his ultranationalist position on the question of arbitration of the Alabama claims. Another, Julia Ward Howe, who wrote the "Battle Hymn of the Republic," became more interested in involving European women in a peace crusade than in urging pacific policies by her own government.

Similarly, Edward Everett Hale had defended war in a college debate in 1838 and achieved notoriety for his authorship of *The Man Without a Country* (1862), a patriotic classic extolling the virtues of nationhood. After the war he seemed more interested in reforming Europe along American lines than in converting Americans to pacifism or internationalism. In 1871 he called for a United States of Europe, and his advocacy of a world court beginning in 1874, while demonstrating his growing interest in the ideal of international justice, was modeled after the United States Supreme Court. The president of the American Peace Society, Edward S. Tobey, promoted international arbitration at peace conferences and in his petitions to government officials, but also strongly endorsed a report by American admirals to the secretary of the navy stating, "the revival of American shipping interests by American *built* ships is indispensible to the rehabilitation of the U.S. Navy." These peace leaders were not deliberately hypocritical in advancing these opinions; rather, their views stemmed logically from their uncritical faith in American values and institutions. This national faith, much more than pacifism, molded their world view. They wanted to prevent conflict with foreign nations; but as their own nation's free security began to wither, they assumed that avoidance of war could come only if the rest of the world conformed to American standards.[22]

In addition, the peace movement had grown most rapidly during the so-called Romantic era of the 1830s and 1840s, when antislavery, educational, temperance, prison, and women's rights reforms flourished. By contrast, the post-Reconstruction era was not primarily a reform generation. Wearied of movements for human betterment, Americans turned to pecuniary ventures. Reform activity, however, was hardly dead, and the peace movement benefited from the enthusiasm of moral reformers' intent on purifying the American social order.[23] Nevertheless, in an emerging business culture, the few reformers of the utopian variety received little public attention. Fortunately for the most dedicated peace spokesmen, their incurable optimism helped conceal from their view the declining importance of religious and humanitarian values in a secular and materialistic age.

Finally, the peace movement had even less hold on the public imagination because of the dearth of important international issues. In the long run, the comparative absence of international crises and wars during the 1870s and 1880s increasingly encouraged peace workers' faith in progress toward a more peaceful world and provided them with an effective argument for involving in the cause several high-minded Americans who had little sympathy for pacifism but who instinctively supported humanitarian movements. During those post–Civil War decades, however, such an argument had little impact on the public mind. Once the arbitration of 1872 settled American Civil War claims against Britain, no questions of vital importance appeared on the international scene during the following two decades. Although certain businessmen were beginning to look outward for new markets for their agricultural and industrial surpluses in those years, they did not stimulate feelings of international consciousness among the American public. With the exception of those businessmen, the few advocates of peace and arbitration, international lawyers, and some governmental officials, the eyes of almost all Americans were turned on local and national issues or on the American West. Lands across the oceans still seemed remote. In terms of public interest in foreign affairs, that period constituted the nadir or at best the awkward years of American diplomatic history.[24]

The comparative absence of both external pressures and domestic factors devitalized the pacifist sects. Though the problems facing Quakers, Mennonites, Brethren, Shakers, and the other historic peace churches remained unique, the peace group within the Quakers, the Peace Association of Friends, illustrates tendencies present in all pacifist sects in the half century after Appomattox. The centrality of pacifism among Quakers began to decline in the Middle West as early as the 1870s and 1880s, partly because of the pervasive influence of religious revivalism on the sect's orientation. From the limited available evidence, it appears that almost all converts to Quakerism in those decades accepted it for reasons other than its peace testimony. To those new recruits, as Peter Brock has said, "the most important object appeared to be to bring Christ to the people as their Savior, to win souls for salvation. Mission work, not pacifism, was their major concern." As memories of the Civil War faded without any major new wars to test the faith's avowed commitment to conscientious objection (even the Spanish-American War was brief and required no conscription), the trend toward deemphasis of the Quaker peace testimony increased.

The growing split with Orthodox Friends in the East, who, the Westerners rightly suspected, were increasingly influenced by theological liberalism, intensified the tendency toward Protestant fundamentalism among western Quakers. Because a large proportion of eastern Quakers continued to take their faith's peace testimony seriously, the pacifism among their western counterparts may have suffered through guilt by association. The absence of major warfare even resulted in a declining emphasis on the peace testimony of eastern Quakers until the 1890s, when some of them began to cooperate with non-Quakers in promoting a revival of peace activity.

Related developments reinforced this disinterest in peace questions. One was the Quakers' general relaxation of membership standards, a phenomenon common to all Protestant churches in the late nineteenth century. That relaxation led inevitably to deemphasis or simply nonenforcement of the Quaker policy of disowning nonpacifists. Another was the erosion of pacifism growing out of the integration of rural as well as urban Quakers into the overwhelmingly predominant nonpacifist and more secular society. In the face of these countervailing influences, the dedication of that minority of pacifist Friends is the more remarkable. The major accomplishment of the Peace Association of Friends was its ability to keep the Quakers' peace testimony alive throughout that period. Nevertheless, in view of these new trends in the Quaker faith, it is hardly surprising that by 1890 the Peace Association of Friends had at best a modest impact on both the Society of Friends and the American peace movement.[25]

Although the American peace movement displayed little vitality in the first two decades following the Civil War, it was far from dead. In fact, just as it appeared moribund in the late 1880s, it began to show flickerings of new life. Slowly, but inexorably, new developments began to quicken interest in the peace cause. In the broadest sense, the growing interest in peace was an inevitable product of a shrinking world. By the end of the 1880s the perfection of new inventions such as the steamship, telegraph, and transatlantic cable had greatly facilitated contact and communication with foreign lands. The increasing frequency of American attendance in the 1870s and 1880s at international conferences on imperial claims and on scientific, marine, monetary, and postal matters was one index of a growing international consciousness among governmental leaders. Another was the tendency among American manufacturers and farmers to look outward. The more capitalists adapted scientific and technological innovations to expand industrial and agricultural production, the more their search for new markets abroad increased. All these developments, in turn, gradually induced many Americans to extend their intellectual horizons beyond the United States. Of course, America's growing involvement in the world convinced many industrialists, exporters, and politicians that business interest in foreign markets necessitated an expanded, modernized navy to protect American trade and to win commercial concessions from foreign nations. The nation's emergence on the world stage also increased the temptation to embark on imperial adventures and show the nation's physical might to the world. These changes in commerce, industry, transportation, and communications, however, simultaneously convinced pacific-minded Americans of the challenges and opportunities of trying to create a peaceful and stable world.

Actually, one internationalist idea that pervaded the peace movement was not really new, although it did not have any noticeable impact on the peace movement until the 1890s, when Americans began to look outward. This was the mid-nineteenth-century intellectual heritage of free trade. Many reformers in the Boston area—most notably Edward Atkinson, Raymond L. Bridgman, William Lloyd Garrison Jr., Edwin D. Mead, Moorfield Storey, and Congregationalist ministers Charles G. Ames and Adolph A. Berle—served simultaneously as members of the New England Free Trade League and the American Peace Society, and they equated free trade and peace. These Americans were devoted followers of British free-trade liberals Richard Cobden, John Bright, and William E. Gladstone, and they believed that universal free trade was a prerequisite, if not a panacea, for a harmonious world order. Like their English tutors, they viewed free trade as both an inviolable, natural economic law and a quasi-religious doctrine of all that was moral, just, and true. They confidently argued that the free exchange of goods in world commerce would produce an expanding, self-regulating, and increasingly interdependent world economy and rising material plenty for all peoples. The notion of unfettered exchange of goods in the world economy appealed to their lofty, reformist hopes for the triumph of cosmopolitanism, internationalism, humanitarianism, anticolonialism, anti-imperialism, and pacifism over protectionism, nationalism, militarism, imperialism, and war. Those optimistic people anticipated economic theorists like Joseph Schumpeter in arguing that capitalism was at heart rational, anti-imperialistic, and pacific. To be sure, unscrupulous financiers and businessmen, often in alliance with armament makers and the military, constantly attempted to overturn their sanguine expectations; but, to free traders, their acts constituted exceptions to the general rule of business pacifism.[26]

Other pacific-minded Americans apparently had no active association with free-trade groups, but whether confirmed pacifists or, like Andrew Carnegie, erratic, less-pacifistic peace spokesmen they likewise believed that free trade was conducive to international tranquility. Alfred H. Love might have been alone among peace spokesmen in dissenting from that consensus. Perhaps because of his woolen business, which was susceptible to the vicissitudes of fierce foreign competition, Love argued that tariffs provided domestic stability by giving industrialists the profits that were indispensable for higher wages. Emphasis on a stable home market, he believed, was less harmful to the cause of peace than the frantic competitive search for new foreign markets and the temptation to enlist the power of national governments to fight for them if necessary. He also correctly pointed out that England had frequently been at war during the period of its free-trade hegemony.[27]

American peace advocates' uncritical admiration of Britain's free-trade tradition nourished their desire for improved Anglo-American relations in the last decade of the century. Their main goal was the establishment of a system of arbitration between the two nations. As the movement for an arbitration treaty grew, it won the support of a wide variety of people. Only in the second half of that decade did the harsh realities of imperial rivalries and the Spanish-American controversy over Cuba starkly clarify basic differences between three broad groupings in the arbitration movement: pacifists who valued peace above other loyalties; nonpacifists who nonetheless espoused a benevolent or genuinely Christian Anglo-Saxonism and were receptive to suggestions calling for the extension of America's friendly contacts with other "Christian" or "civilized" nations; and those nonpacifists whose conception of "peace" consisted of ambiguous abstractions or was limited to an aggressive, power-oriented Anglo-Saxonism. Until then, however, international arbitration, especially Anglo-American arbitration, provided a fragile consensus.

The pacifists and, somewhat more cautiously, their pacific-minded allies viewed international arbitration as a panacea for the creation of a warless world. Create an interlocking web of such treaties, so it was thought, and peace would inevitably follow. In retrospect, this faith in arbitration treaties appears somewhat misplaced. Compared with twentieth-century efforts for world organization, arbitration expressed a very timid conception of internationalism. At most it provided only for a minimal sacrifice of national sovereignty by the contracting states and no sanctions for the enforcement of decisions against the recalcitrant nation.

Late nineteenth-century American peace advocates, however, did not see it that way. They had traditionally argued, and continued to do so into the first years of the twentieth century, that forceful sanctions were both undesirable and unnecessary. First, they pointed out that the use of coercion—an international police force or economic boycott, for example—even if practicable, was contrary to their "pacifist" principles. Second, they argued that arbitration was already a proven method for the settlement of international controversies because only in a tiny minority of cases had nations refused to accept the decisions of arbitral tribunals in the past century, and even in those exceptional arbitrations where nations had rejected the decision war had not followed. Third, they viewed arbitration treaties essentially as evolutionary extensions of legal contracts both among individuals and within individual states to the international sphere. They thus claimed that just as the fear of moral opprobrium in the local and national community sufficed as a sanction for carrying out the decisions of municipal judges and Supreme Court justices, respectively, so would the fear of worldwide, public disapproval of the lawbreaking nation serve as a sufficient international sanction in discouraging nations' rejection of arbitral awards.[28]

Those assumptions were of course idealistic. They would predominate in a world of dignified, self-restrained gentlemen and overwhelming public support for viable arbitral tribunals, but they might easily break down where this consensus gave way to human passions and surging nationalist sentiments. The pacifists usually ignored the fact that while individuals can be ethically upright in their dealings with their neighbors, nations as collective agencies usually place a higher priority on responsibility for the immediate security of their citizens than on morality. They also discounted possible megalomania of national leaders as another cause of international frictions.

Moreover, the pacifists' historical analogies were erroneous. They overlooked the frequent disregard of Supreme Court decisions by individuals and communities, and they failed to perceive that arbitration treaties had usually succeeded only because nations had limited their application to relatively minor disputes. From a more realistic perspective, in fact, the absence of economic or military sanctions meant that an arbitration agreement involved more of a symbolic moral pledge of the two governments' good intentions to negotiate stipulated categories of disputes than a binding legal commitment. If mutual goodwill persisted after a dispute arose, then it would be settled peacefully regardless of the existence of a treaty; if it did not persist, then the treaty might serve as a moral restraint on a nation only if the dispute did not appear to affect that nation's definition of its vital national interests.

Nevertheless, the peace advocates' emphasis on international arbitration benefited the late nineteenth-century peace movement. Since America's relative security still seemed to shield the nation from most foreign embroilments and wars, individuals easily made facile analogies between individual relationships in the local and national community and relations between nations. Just as many liberal nonpacifists took for granted the pacifists' general assumption, though not always with the same intense conviction, that mankind had virtually unlimited potentiality for good, so it was easy for them to extend the analogy by assuming that nations could behave rationally and decently toward one another. Besides attracting confirmed pacifists, that mode of reasoning particularly appealed to nonpacifist intellectuals and high-minded professional people who revered the Victorian values of good manners and gentlemanly behavior in both individual and international relationships.

Moreover, the peace workers' focus on international arbitration helped establish their moderation among the American public. In a society where traditional isolationism and self-assured nationalism predominated, bolder schemes for international organization or world government would have fallen on deaf ears. In that intellectual environment arbitration appealed to pacific-minded Americans who wanted their government to cooperate more actively with foreign states in the search for a peaceful world while avoiding the drawbacks of more utopian internationalist arrangements. Arbitration was also compatible with the muted, nonperfectionist quality of postbellum reform. While many people might wish to limit the scope of specific arbitration agreements, even many conservatives and ultranationalists would not reject those covering a small number of innocuous questions. Except perhaps for inveterate militarists, few people would publicly advocate the resort to arms over arbitration as an abstract principle in international relations.

Arbitration also had the advantage of historical precedent. Since it had been a cardinal principle of American foreign policy from the first years of the Republic and was successfully used on several occasions, it had the virtue of a proven method that would be extended in the future. It provided, in fact, a useful starting point for more adventuresome internationalist schemes in the following decades. The scope of bilateral arbitration treaties could be enlarged to include more important questions, could be made "obligatory" or "compulsory" on the parties, and could be linked with mediatory functions for prevention of war. They could also provide for a permanent tribunal of judges, which in turn might be gradually expanded to include other nations and judges. Eventually, perhaps, a genuine world court—composed of renowned jurists from different nations, sitting in continuous session, and with an enlarged authority —would evolve. Such at least would be their hopes as they began to perceive the possibilities for the creation of permanent international institutions in the early twentieth century.

[2]

Toward Anglo-American Understanding

TODAY AMITY BETWEEN the United States and Great Britain is assumed, but few people in the late nineteenth century took Anglo-American relations for granted. The two nations had been enemies in the War of Independence and the War of 1812 and had nearly resorted to hostilities during the American Civil War. Disputes between the United States and Canada over fishing rights off the Newfoundland coast and the Bering Sea seals continued to plague Anglo-American relations after 1865. The Irish immigrants in the United States further embittered their relations. Intensely anti-English, many Irish joined an Irish-American organization, the Fenians, which in the 1870s used the United States as a base for armed raids on Canada. Many other Irishmen returned to Ireland to inflame anti-English sentiment. Yet the Irish constituted an important political force in the United States, and both major political parties carefully cultivated their votes. As late as 1900 many politicians recognized that twisting the lion's tail was still good politics.[1]

The leaders of the arbitration movement, however, believed that such obstacles to Anglo-American understanding were surmountable. Both nations had led the way in the negotiation and ratification of arbitration treaties. Either the United States or Great Britain had been a party in 102 out of a total of 147 arbitration agreements before 1886, and beginning with the Jay Treaty in 1794 (the first international agreement with arbitral features in the modern world) the United States had concluded more than a third of its arbitrations with Great Britain.[2] The Geneva arbitration, peace leaders justly claimed, was not only the most recent but also the most important Anglo-American arbitration treaty, and therefore was a promising sign for the negotiation of a more permanent treaty.

Furthermore, though Quakers talked in terms of the two nations' Christian heritage, secular peace advocates also emphasized their common language and shared traditions in law, literature, and politics. The British Quaker John Bright, long-time advocate of Anglo-American friendship, summarized the humanitarianism of this growing sentiment: "England and . . . United States are two nations, but I always like to regard them as one people. On them the growth of all that is good in the world greatly depends."[3] For those reasons alone, peace workers argued persuasively that the United States should begin negotiations for an arbitration treaty with Great Britain.

Moreover, in the late nineteenth century Social Darwinism enhanced the idea of Anglo-American understanding by stimulating the notion of racial affinity. Especially popular among the white intelligentsia and upper classes of both nations, "Anglo-Saxonism" or "race patriotism" increasingly became the rationale for closer transatlantic ties.[4] In the long run, those whose conception of international friendship was limited to Anglo-Saxonism had little in common with the broader Christian and humanitarian concerns of the most dedicated peace workers, but in the decade after 1887 the latter also genuinely supported the concept of an Anglo-American rapprochement. Only a few of the most humanistic pacifists failed to advance racial arguments in support of an Anglo-American arbitration treaty, and all friends of peace used the racial rhetoric of that day to explain the cultural affinity of the two peoples. All agreed such a treaty was the first, most logical step toward a peaceful world order.[5]

Little came of the peace advocates' first attempts to promote a permanent Anglo-American arbitration treaty, but their efforts exemplified the many barriers that lay in the path of Anglo-American understanding. The first move for such a treaty came from Britain in 1887. Randal Cremer, a British labor leader, provided the catalyst for a brief flurry of peace activity in both nations. A fervent believer in arbitration of both industrial and international disputes, he attempted to promote the latter with the founding of the International Arbitration League in 1871. Unlike the predominantly religious or upper-class membership of other peace groups on both sides of the Atlantic, this group comprised mainly skilled laborers, many of whom were also members of Cremer's labor organization, the Workingman's Association. Elected to the House of Commons in 1885, Cremer began soliciting his colleagues to sign a memorial addressed to the president of the United States pledging support for an Anglo-American arbitration treaty. By the spring of 1887 he had gained the signatures of 234 members of Commons and 38 members of the House of Lords.[6]

Before bringing the memorial to the United States, Cremer secured the aid of an influential ally, the Scottish-born Andrew Carnegie. Though Carnegie had championed the Federal cause in the Civil War and never espoused absolute pacifism, his interest in the cause of peace was genuine. He had inherited a hatred of war and militarism from an uncle who inclined toward pacifism. He had also admired John Bright—"my favorite living hero in public life," Carnegie later called him—and closely followed Bright's efforts on behalf of peace. His reading of Herbert Spencer's theory of evolution in the late 1870s convinced him that the world was evolving away from primitive violence toward a more civilized and peaceful world order. "All is well since all grows better" became his motto, and it served not only as a good rationalization of his fabulously successful career in the iron and steel business but as an explanation of international relations as well.[7]

Such a simplistic philosophy led to a vulgar pragmatism; the end, so long as it could be rationalized in terms of benevolent "progress," justified the means. Carnegie thus overlooked the obvious anomaly between his faith in the sanctity of international arbitration agreements and his repeated willingness to break pooling agreements with rivals in the steel business whenever he found a competitive advantage. The simplicity of that view actually reinforced his optimistic faith in evolutionary progress toward a peaceful world order and his willingness to cooperate with friends of peace in promotion of that cause. As dueling and religious hatred had disappeared in the Western world, he thought, so eventually would national rivalries and wars. Carnegie's faith in civilization's continued progress comforted him in times of international tension and sustained his interest in the cause of world peace, no matter how remote.

Until about 1900, however, his involvement in movements for international amity extended mainly to American-British relations, and even on that issue he relied on informal cooperation with like-minded individuals rather than active membership in American peace organizations. Carnegie perhaps best expressed the racial rhetoric that provided much of the intellectual cement for Anglo-American understanding. Carnegie's annual summer sojourns in his native Scotland deepened his love for and identity with both nations, and he publicized his dual affection by sewing together the Union Jack and the Stars and Stripes and flying this unique flag from his summer castle. Moreover, for all his talk about the racial unity and common interests of the Anglo-American people, his primary loyalty rested with his adopted country. He delighted in unfavorably comparing

England's monarchy, established church, and privileged aristocracy with America's equal opportunity, republican institutions, and political democracy. The ironmaster hoped that the Liberal party, guided by his hero William Gladstone, would reform and abolish Britain's feudal vestiges, but his allegiance was always to America.[8]

In 1887, however, when Cremer approached him with the memorial, Carnegie was enthusiastic. Carnegie viewed Cremer's campaign as a favorable sign of growing British acceptance of this enshrined American ideal, and upon his return to the United States he arranged an interview with President Cleveland for the British delegation.[9]

Meanwhile, William Jones, an English Quaker and member of the London Peace Society, secured an interview with President Cleveland a few weeks in advance of Cremer's arrival. Jones used the meeting to endorse the Cremer mission and to urge the President to express publicly his support for the arbitration principle. When the President replied that he had to speak cautiously because he knew so little about the subject, he may have been sincere; but his later interviews with arbitration advocates suggested that he was also aware of the political hazards of any hasty endorsement of an Anglo-American treaty.[10]

Cremer's delegation included nine members of Commons, three representatives of the Trades Union Congress, and Lyon Playfair of the House of Lords. All were Gladstone Liberals.[11] When they met with Cleveland on October 31, 1887, he was noncommittal and in fact stated that practical difficulties would probably interfere with their proposal. Though Cleveland did not specify those difficulties, they were fairly obvious to peace workers. Senatorial opposition to a pending fisheries treaty with Great Britain and Irish antipathy toward England undoubtedly induced Cleveland's caution. With a national election only a year away and Anglophobia still rampant among large portions of the electorate, Cleveland probably reasoned that his formal endorsement of the Cremer proposal would be politically unwise.[12]

If the Cremer group had any illusions concerning the absence of virulent Anglophobia in the United States, they were dispelled by the Irish-Americans. Following their interview with the President, the British visitors appeared at public meetings in Boston, New York, Philadelphia, and Camden, New Jersey, which local peace societies and civic leaders sponsored to mobilize public support for the memorial. Irish agitators, however, interrupted the meetings with cries of "Remember the Alabama!" "Home Rule for Ireland!" "We want no peace with England!" "Give us arbitration for Ireland!" "We won't listen to English assassins!" The Irish were so disorderly that they nearly broke up the Camden meeting. The adoption of a resolution urging Britain's arbitration of its difficulties with

Ireland pacified the demonstrators, who then allowed the assemblage to pass a resolution endorsing an Anglo-American treaty.[13]

Though considerably sobered by the Irish demonstrations, Cremer did not abandon the effort. He and two other British delegates returned to Washington, where several American congressmen told them that they would support an Anglo-American convention. Perhaps, Cremer now reasoned, congressional endorsement of the British proposal might influence the President to begin treaty negotiations eventually. Cremer found an ally in Senator John Sherman of Ohio, chairman of the Foreign Relations Committee, a steadfast advocate of international arbitration and a world court, and a vice-president of the American Peace Society and the Universal Peace Union. He gave the British visitors a hearing before his committee, and Anglophile congressmen responded by introducing arbitration resolutions in both houses.[14]

Nor did American friends of arbitration lose hope. Several state and local yearly meetings of the Society of Friends as well as scattered groups of idealistic citizens petitioned Congress in support of the Cremer proposal. Moreover, Samuel Gompers arranged for his British labor counterpart to address a convention in Baltimore of the fledgling American Federation of Labor, which responded by passing a resolution endorsing Cremer's objectives. In Boston, peace, business, educational, and civic leaders drafted a petition urging presidential action on the British memorial; and Edwin D. Mead, a member of the American Peace Society, presented it to Cleveland in January 1888. Further, a meeting in New York City authorized the mayor to appoint a committee, which persuaded the New York state congressional delegation to introduce a petition requesting that the President initiate formal negotiations for an Anglo-American treaty.[15]

Although Cremer wished to extend the arbitration agreement to all disputes between the two nations, in practice he as well as American arbitrationists were willing to limit the scope of such a treaty in order to accommodate American and British nationalist sentiments. The New York memorial, for instance, specifically excepted questions "respecting independence or sovereignty of either nation, its equality with other nations, its form of government, its internal affairs, or its continental policy."[16] The primary objective, all arbitration proponents agreed, was the establishment of the principle of arbitration as a starting point, for once the two nations successfully arbitrated a few minor disputes the application of the principle would widen and result in the negotiation of treaties with other nations.

The House failed to take any action on the arbitrationists' resolutions, but in June 1888, the Senate Foreign Relations Committee reported a concurrent resolution endorsing the principle of international arbitration, and upon Senator Sherman's urging it passed. Framed in general terms, the Senate resolution "requested the President to invite, from time to time as fit occasions may arise, negotiations with any government with which the United States has or may have diplomatic relations, to the end that any differences or disputes arising between the two governments which cannot be adjusted by diplomatic agency may be referred to arbitration, and be peaceably adjusted by such means."[17] The House did not act on that resolution, but in January 1890, when Sherman introduced an identical concurrent resolution, it passed both houses without objection.[18] The State Department dutifully communicated the resolution to foreign governments but three years would elapse before any government responded.

Meanwhile, an arbitration scheme for the Americas also held peace advocates' attention. In fact, the growing interest in inter-American cooperation facilitated the easy passage of Sherman's resolution. The pan-American arbitration proposal evolved out of the movement for a pan-American conference. President Cleveland issued the formal invitations for the conference, but by the time the delegates convened on October 2, 1889, the Harrison administration had assumed office.[19]

President Harrison's appointment of James G. Blaine as secretary of state was favorably received by arbitration proponents. Blaine had long urged more cordial relations with the American republics, and as secretary of state in 1881 had issued invitations to a pan-American convention. Blaine's plan had collapsed shortly after the assassination of President Garfield, however, when the new President, Chester Arthur, removed Blaine from the cabinet and withdrew the invitations. In 1889, however, Blaine had a second chance. When the International American Conference, as it was officially called, convened in Washington, Blaine personally presided over the sessions. As his frequent remarks on pan-Americanism testified, he believed the prerequisite for commercial prosperity throughout the hemisphere was peace and the means for stimulating the desired peace was an inter-American arbitration treaty.[20]

Harrison's appointment of Andrew Carnegie as an American delegate to the Pan-American Conference gave Blaine an ally in his promotion of an arbitration treaty. Though the steel magnate's notions of Anglo-Saxon superiority as well as his realistic appreciation of the United States' predominant power in the hemisphere tempered his potential instincts for full inter-American equality, his paternalistic attitude toward the Latins was benevolent. He spoke in favor of the arbitration convention that a committee of the conference had painstakingly formulated; and when various delegations began to squabble over it, Blaine left the dais, assumed the role of an American delegate, and vigorously defended the convention.[21] The conference finally approved a multinational arbitration accord for disputes that diplomacy could not settle, except for questions imperiling a nation's "independence."

President Harrison warmly praised the arbitration treaty but delayed submitting it to the Senate. Whatever enthusiasm he may have initially felt for the treaty soon disappeared with rapidly deteriorating Chilean-American relations culminating in a barroom brawl between Chileans and American sailors in Valparaiso. That incident, resulting in the loss of two American lives, convinced Harrison, if he was not convinced already, that the provisions of the treaty were too inclusive. As he remarked the day after the incident, "It is quite possible to apply arbitration to a dispute as to a boundary-line; it is quite impossible, it seems to me, to apply it to a case of international feud." Without presidential backing the convention died before the deadline fixed for the exchange of ratifications.[22]

The Latin American governments also helped deliver the fatal blow to the arbitration scheme. Suspicious of any comprehensive arbitration plan that might allow their northern Big Sister to foment controversies and then demand arbitration as a means of wresting commercial and diplomatic concessions from their countries, six of the sixteen Latin American delegations refused to sign the convention, and the home governments of all the rest except Brazil failed to approve the treaty. The Harrison administration's unsuccessful employment of diplomatic and naval pressure against a rebel faction in Chile and then its humiliating ultimatum, which coerced the new regime into accepting American demands following the Valparaiso incident, confirmed the Latin American governments' deep distrust of the Colossus of the North.[23]

Nevertheless, some correlation existed between peace advocates' approval of the pan-American idea and their unfavorable reactions to Harrison's handling of the Chilean crisis. Shortly after the Valparaiso slayings, Andrew Carnegie, fearing American overreaction to the incident, cabled Harrison from his summer residence in Scotland: "Chile very weak and sorely tried. Her giant sister should be patient and forebearing. Why Americans are unpopular in any sister republic needs inquiry."[24] Of Harrison's cabinet, only Blaine, ailing and indisposed throughout much of the crisis, urged arbitration of the controversy, although his appeals were too sporadic to make any noticeable impression on the President. Edwin D. Mead, an admirer of Blaine's pan-Americanism, correctly perceived Harrison's exploitation of the latent jingoism in the American public. Now editor of the *New England Magazine,* Mead editorialized that the issues were really "petty" but had nonetheless revealed "an insane itching to get out our new navy and spank this little South

American republic, [and] kill a few thousand Chilians [*sic*] to avenge our ruffled 'honor.' "[25]

It is doubtful whether American advocates of peace had any marked influence on the American political leadership between 1887 and 1893. Despite their enthusiastic support of the Cremer mission, President Cleveland had failed to endorse an Anglo-American treaty, and Blaine required no encouragement from peace spokesmen to promote his arbitration scheme for the Americas. Except for Sherman's concurrent resolution of 1890, the peace advocates could point to no concrete accomplishments by their government in the arbitration movement. Yet simultaneously with the interest in international arbitration on the governmental level came signs of modest growth and expansion of the peace movement. The number of peace societies did not increase appreciably from 1887 to 1893,[26] but a few reform organizations now included international peace among their aims. The existing peace societies also added new leaders and broadened their contacts to include other peace agencies both at home and abroad.

One indication of an awakening of peace interest came from two women's organizations, the National Woman's Christian Temperance Union (WCTU) and the National Council of Women. In 1887 the WCTU, founded more than a decade earlier, established a department of peace and arbitration. The Ohio WCTU had added the subject of peace to its list of departments in 1885 and at its state convention in 1887 voted to request the forthcoming WCTU national convention to add a peace department. Frances E. Willard, inspirational president of the national organization and a supporter of the Universal Peace Union, attended the Ohio convention and warmly endorsed the resolution. In introducing the Ohio resolution at the WCTU national convention in Nashville in late November 1887, she linked the peace and temperance movements. The creation of a peace department, she insisted, was "strictly germane to our work for nothing increases intemperance like war, and nothing tends toward war like intemperance."[27] To bolster support for the Ohio proposal, she invited the English Quaker William Jones to address the convention. On the strength of Willard's and Jones's appeals, the WCTU established a department of peace and arbitration.[28]

Hannah J. Bailey, a Quaker, was appointed superintendent of the new peace department. Although Mrs. Bailey remained active in suffrage, temperance, and other reform movements, the peace department was her major interest for the next twenty-seven years.[29] She believed that the women of America, especially the mothers and schoolteachers among them, could most effectively educate the youth of America in moral and religious principles that lay at the heart of international friendship. "It is early training," she stressed, "that exerts the greater influence. Mothers should not allow their children to have military toys, to practice warlike games, or anything that makes them familiar with taking life, as a pastime. They should be early taught the divine law as to the sacredness of human life, and also the golden rule."[30]

Operating out of her residence in Winthrop Centre, Maine, Mrs. Bailey advanced these ideas in her two monthly peace publications, *The Acorn* for children and *Pacific Banner* for adults. She also issued a stream of peace tracts. In 1888 her department distributed 4,500 Bible readings, 2,500 leaflets on peace, and 16,000 more for children, and a year later it sent out 5,000 calendars depicting the blessings of peace and the horrors of war.[31] With Frances Willard's encouragement and loyal support, she enlisted the services of ten women lecturers to spread the gospel of peace and antimilitarism and to promote the organization of peace bureaus on the state and local level. By 1893 the WCTU had established departments of peace and arbitration in twenty-five states and the District of Columbia. Many of the state departments even managed to foster the establishment of peace committees on the county and town level.

Furthermore, in 1890 the World's WCTU, its international arm, created a peace department, which Mrs. Bailey also headed. The state and local departments particularly lobbied in legislatures and school boards against military training in the public schools and spoke out against Sunday schools' sponsorship of Boys' Brigades, an organization composed of young males who wore uniforms and carried rifles owned and supplied by the churches. The departments also cooperated in supporting international arbitration and resisting militant nationalism. In January 1892, for instance, at the height of war talk over the Valparaiso incident, members of WCTU peace departments presented President Harrison with a petition from the World's WCTU urging him to submit the Chilean dispute to arbitration.[32]

How effective were these peace departments? Mrs. Bailey consistently extolled the successes of their lobbying activities, and the decline of the Boys' Brigades by the late 1890s may have stemmed in part from their efforts. One should not exaggerate their significance. The membership was never large, and even within the WCTU structure peace and arbitration was only one of forty-one departments on the national level and one of seven on its international counterpart. Moreover, because woman's suffrage only began to be realized in a few locales by 1900, these peace departments could at the most exert a moral influence on male lawmakers. Whatever its actual impact on governmental policy, the comparatively limited influence of the other peace organizations helped highlight the significance of the rapid emergence of the WCTU peace departments in the eyes of American peace workers. Their phenomenal growth prompted Alfred H. Love to declare without exaggeration, "The peace department of the National Woman's Temperance Union, though only one of the phases of the work carried on by this great organization of women, is really one of the strongest and most influential of our peace organizations."[33]

A year after the founding of the WCTU's peace department, a group of women reformers organized the National Council of Women. Mrs. May Wright Sewall, a dedicated suffragette and pacifist from Indianapolis, Indiana, was the driving force in the new organization, though other pacifistic women including Frances Willard, Mrs. Lockwood, and Mrs. Bailey joined at its founding and became active members and officers. Women pacifists in the Universal Peace Union, WCTU, and National Council of Women cooperated so closely in their peace work that the three bodies seemed to act more as sister organizations than as separate reform groups. In addition, Mrs. Sewall's cooperation with National Women's Councils in Europe led to the formation of the International Council of Women in 1889.[34]

While pacific-minded women were organizing two pacifist agencies, the older peace organizations began to show new signs of life. In 1889 leaders of American peace organizations, responding to an appeal by European pacifists, attended a Universal Peace Congress in Paris. Pacifists had held international peace congresses in 1843, 1848 to 1851, and 1878, but these meetings had neither been widely attended nor attracted much attention. More than 500 friends of peace, including a few delegates from the American Peace Society, Universal Peace Union, and WCTU peace bureau, participated in the 1889 congress, however, and peace workers assembled annually thereafter (excepting 1895, 1898, 1899, 1909, and 1911) in European and American cities until the First World War.

While the wide-ranging discussions of those congresses seemed to indicate an inability to focus on a specific program, there was a consensus on the many valid approaches for reducing international tensions. Above all, they agreed that peace workers should no longer merely condemn the inhumanity of warfare but should also cooperate in promoting practical alternatives for reducing the chances of international bloodshed. The first three conferences generated so much enthusiasm for further cooperation that the pacifists decided to establish a permanent organization, the International Peace Bureau, in Berne, Switzerland, to handle the administrative work for future conferences and to serve as a worldwide clearing house for peace proposals.[35]

During these same years the American Peace Society also added two new leaders, Robert Treat Paine, Boston philanthropist, who served as its president from 1891 until his death in 1910, and the Quaker pacifist Benjamin F. Trueblood, who held the position of secretary from 1892 until 1915. Paine was no full-fledged pacifist. Rather his interest in peace was an outgrowth of his high-minded Mugwump background and his philanthropic and charitable work, and his participation in the peace movement represented an extension of his emphasis on individual good will and benevolence to the international sphere.[36] Paine's presence gave the American Peace Society a prestigious name, but Trueblood's influence was more important. As a devout Quaker, the new secretary was thoroughly familiar with peace questions but had spent his early manhood as a professor of Greek and Latin and then as president of two Quaker colleges. In 1890, however, he had given up the presidency of Penn College, Iowa, to spread the Quaker faith in Europe. Sponsored by the Christian Arbitration and Peace Society, a Quaker group founded in the Philadelphia area in 1886, Trueblood had devoted much of his missionary activity to the spread of the Quaker peace testimony. Though he had found his European work personally rewarding, he had regretted the long periods of separation from his family. The offer of the secretariat of the American Peace Society in late 1891 allowed him to resettle his family and continue his peace work in Boston.[37]

The new secretary brought a rare combination of administrative ability and missionary zeal to the American Peace Society. His careful editing of the *Advocate of Peace* immeasurably enhanced its respectability without sacrificing its high moral tone. Moreover, no other American peace worker rivaled his mastery of French, German, and Italian or his historical knowledge of the peace movement. While Quakerism inspired his pacifism, he was also tempered by the Christian humanistic writings of Erasmus and the moral rationalism of Kant. Although his editorials criticized military education in the schools, unthinking patriotism, and the temptations and debasing consequences of imperialism, his pacifism was almost entirely intellectual and rhetorical. Because he accepted the undoubted truth of the Quaker peace testimony, he assumed that pacifist tracts and formal lectures would suffice as a long-range educational process in which the number of peace converts would increasingly swell in numbers.

In his personal relationships Trueblood was gentlemanly and scholarly, as befitted the respectable image of the American Peace Society. He sympathized neither with the Universal Peace Union's flamboyant and radical tactics nor with Leo Tolstoy's doctrine of nonresistance as the ultimate antidote to the war system, but he cheerfully cooperated with almost all attempts at broadening public exposure to peace questions. He was a personal friend of Mrs. Bailey's and maintained contact with Quaker peace groups, but he also assiduously encouraged those friends of peace who eschewed antimilitarism and nonresistance in favor of the more modest aim of international arbitration.[38] Not surprisingly, Trueblood quickly gained the respect of almost all participants in the peace movement. Perhaps his most important contribution was later suggested by his friend Edwin Mead: "it is right to say that he was the only professional peace worker in the United States, the only man who made service of the peace cause his vocation."[39]

The additional pacifist agencies, individuals, and international contacts encouraged American workers for arbitration to believe that their promotional efforts might bring success. In 1893 they undertook a new campaign for an Anglo-American arbitration agreement—a campaign that, after many temporary disappointments, ultimately resulted in the negotiation of the Olney-Pauncefote treaty of 1897. Again the initiative came from Randal Cremer. In 1893 he introduced a resolution in the House of Commons asking for the government's official endorsement of an arbitration treaty with the United States, and on June 16, 1893, the Gladstone ministry pushed an amended version of Cremer's proposal through Commons. While not specifically promising British initiation of negotiations for such a treaty, as Cremer had wished, it recommended that both the British and American governments use the Sherman formula as the basis for an arbitration agreement.[40]

The British resolution fell on fertile ground in the United States. Robert Treat Paine urged Secretary of State Walter Q. Gresham to secure some favorable mention of the British proposal in President Cleveland's annual message to Congress.[41] Whether Paine's interview influenced Gresham is not known, but on December 4, 1893, the secretary wrote Sir Julian Pauncefote, the British ambassador to Washington, praising the House of Commons' endorsement of the Sherman resolution. The same day Cleveland informed Congress of the British resolution and commended the growing sentiment for an Anglo-American arbitration treaty. He had at last expressed his mind on a subject he had increasingly favored privately.[42]

Yet the President still hedged. He did not specifically promise to open negotiations for a treaty but probably hoped his message would induce Congress to authorize him to take formal steps in negotiating a treaty with Britain. If that was his intention, he soon discovered that Congress was not very interested in the matter. Only one resolution proposing an arbitration treaty between the United States and Great Britain was introduced in each house, and both were immediately buried in committee.[43] Trueblood and Paine interviewed members of the respective foreign affairs committees but received little encouragement. Unwilling to take the initiative, committeemen lamely pointed out that even a congressional resolution would probably have little effect because the constitutional power for negotiating treaties rested in the hands of the chief executive.[44]

With the movement coming to an apparent standstill in the United States, Cremer again seized the initiative. In 1894 he circulated a petition among the members of the House of Commons endorsing a treaty of arbitration with the United States. The British labor leader was rewarded for his efforts, for he received the signatures of 354 members of Commons, 120 more than signed the memorial of 1887. Bearing the new petition, Cremer sailed for the United States in early January 1895.[45] As far as Cremer was concerned, his second American visit was a complete success. Of his interview with Secretary Gresham, he wrote: "My first conference with Mr. Gresham lasted nearly an hour, and, although I am not at liberty to repeat what transpired, I can say that no more earnest, enthusiastic supporter of our cause could be found on either side of the Atlantic, and the impression I then formed was fully confirmed at two subsequent meetings I had with the hon. gentleman." Cremer's optimism was justified, for Gresham had indicated two weeks before Cremer's arrival in the United States that he soon expected to begin negotiations with the British government and have a treaty signed within six months. Cremer believed his interview with President Cleveland was "equally gratifying."[46]

Cremer forwarded a copy of the British memorial to every member of Congress, and Congressman William J. Coombs of New York followed by introducing a resolution calling for an Anglo-American arbitration treaty.[47] In the next few weeks, more than twenty representatives and senators introduced resolutions endorsing such a treaty. Cremer helped stimulate this activity when he made personal appearances on the floor of the House and Senate and testified before the foreign relations committees of both houses. Although he realized that Congress would probably not find time to act on the resolutions before adjournment in 1895, he returned to England in a sanguine mood. "If the present Government is in office when the treaty is prepared," he predicted, "there will probably be little difficulty in the way of its being ratified."[48]

At the same time Cremer was exuding optimism, however, a boundary dispute between Venezuela and British Guinea was complicating Anglo-American relations.[49] The dispute had existed since the 1820s and had worsened in the late 1880s, but in 1894 and the first months of 1895 it increased to the extent that British military intervention in defense of its

territorial claim seemed imminent. Believing intervention would provoke
a serious crisis in Anglo-American relations, Gresham tried throughout
1894 to persuade Great Britain and Venezuela to arbitrate the dispute.
His efforts were unsuccessful, for Venezuela had already broken off diplomatic relations with Great Britain and refused Gresham's entreaties to
resume them. But if Gresham was annoyed by Venezuela's intransigence,
he believed the threat of British incursions on American commercial and
strategic interests in the New World was much more serious. Indeed,
Britain actually extended its boundary claim westward in the first months
of 1895.

In the face of Britain's obstinacy, the suspicion increasingly grew in
American governmental circles that Britain's professed interest in negotiating an Anglo-American treaty concealed sinister motives. Some skeptical Americans argued that the British interest was really a clever design
to hoodwink the United States into acceptance of a position from which
Britain could challenge and ultimately emasculate the authority of the
Monroe Doctrine whenever it became involved in disputes with Latin
American states. Opponents of arbitration delighted in presenting that
view to the Cleveland administration.[50]

Yet Gresham also realized that the dispute as well as other unresolved
issues between Britain and the United States only made some kind of
permanent system of arbitration between the two nations more desirable
as an additional safeguard against war. Although he became increasingly
annoyed at Britain's intransigence in early 1895, he may have hoped to
promote an amicable settlement of the Venezuelan controversy and then
proceed apace with discussions on a permanent arbitration agreement.
Whether Gresham could have successfully steered a moderate course of
patience and persuasion until the British government came to accept his
position is unanswerable, for he fell ill and died on May 28, 1895.[51]

Gresham's death brought only a momentary pause to the hopes of the
arbitration workers. Only a week following his demise, thirty-five prominent supporters of the arbitration movement responded to the invitation
of the Quaker businessman Albert K. Smiley, to meet at his hotel-resort
in the Catskill Mountains of New York for a three-day conference on
international arbitration. Isolated from the outside world, surrounded by
beautiful scenery, and with no liquor or card playing permitted on the
premises, Lake Mohonk was a suitable location for high-minded discussions on important reform proposals. Smiley had long dedicated himself
to benevolent causes. In 1883 he had started annual conferences at Lake
Mohonk on the Indian problem and seven years later had begun similar
meetings on Negro affairs. While he did not immediately abandon these
interests, his conference on international arbitration indicated his con-

version to a new cause.[52]

Though a member of the Society of Friends, Smiley was not a nonresistant; and without altogether prohibiting discussion on the armament question, he wanted to limit the scope of the conferences as much as possible to the subject of international arbitration.[53] The 1895 conference had far-reaching effects on the peace movement, for it proved the first of twenty-two annual spring meetings on peace and arbitration. These regular conferences represented the initial departure from the ad hoc meetings that had previously characterized the American peace movement. As a common meeting place for all peace workers in the Northeast and Middle West, the Mohonk sessions served in succeeding years as a spawning ground for organizational schemes that would broaden the appeal of the American peace movement.

Smiley invited the leaders of the peace movement as well as prominent businessmen, educators, lawyers, and ministers to his first arbitration conference. Peace advocates delivered lofty speeches on the merits and advantages of international arbitration in general and an Anglo-American arbitration treaty in particular. All of these speeches obscured the harsher realities of world politics and America's growing involvement with them. Indeed, neither the speakers nor the platform so much as mentioned the growing tension between the United States and Great Britain over the Venezuelan situation. With both President Cleveland and the British Parliament on record in favor of international arbitration, they trusted implicitly the good faith of the American and British statesmen to solve what seemed to them only a minor irritant on the way to a more positive relationship between the two nations.[54]

The myopic optimism of the peace leaders was revealed only a month later when Gresham's successor as secretary of state, Richard Olney, with President Cleveland's full approval, sent a bombshell message to England demanding arbitration of the Venezuelan boundary. In effect, Olney's note demanded Britain's recognition of United States' supremacy in the Western Hemisphere. When the Salisbury government at first ignored and finally brusquely rejected Olney's sweeping contention that the Guinea-Venezuela dispute required any deference to the Monroe Doctrine, Cleveland reiterated America's uncompromising position in a special message to Congress on December 17, 1895, which he concluded with the hint of impending war.

Friends of peace reacted with alarm to the upsurge of virulent jingoism and its deliberate exploitation by the President. Some had previously shown slight interest in the questions of war and peace, but only after the Venezuelan crisis did they begin to assail forcefully both jingoism and war in principle.

In Boston, Charles G. Ames, a Unitarian minister, William Lloyd Garrison, Jr., a son of the noted nonresistant abolitionist, and Edward Atkinson, an amateur economist and businessman-inventor, condemned the war talk. An admirer of the British free trade Liberals, Richard Cobden and John Bright, Atkinson believed that lower tariffs would promote international trade, which in turn would foster benign notions of an interdependent world. He had already written an article pointing out the harm of wars and war scares to domestic industry and foreign commerce. If Atkinson opposed war for materialistic reasons, he abhorred it just as strongly as un-Christian and immoral. He had denounced the Mexican War as a young man and never entirely forgot the temptation of the American government for military adventures. It was the jingoistic outburst following Cleveland's message that prompted him, in his words, "to use every effort in my power to prevent the spread of any desire for war with any country or any light discussion of the possibility of it." He immediately sent cables and letters to several prominent Englishmen urging the submission of the Monroe Doctrine to arbitration for proper definition of its authority. The implausibility of the Cleveland administration's acceptance of that suggestion did not discourage him. He also sent off letters to local newspapers, President Cleveland, and several cabinet officers deploring the President's appeal to the jingoistic spirit and confidently predicting that the sober sense of the nation would condemn Cleveland's course.[55]

Although Garrison inherited his father's nonresistance, he had earlier expressed as much interest in other reforms, particularly free trade and single taxism. In an address to the Universal Peace Union's Mystic gathering the previous summer, he had emphasized the importance of worldwide adoption of free trade and the single tax as panaceas in eliminating the monopoly of land, absentee landlordism, and trade discrimination, which in his view created the social injustices and resentments out of which domestic and international hatreds arose. The Venezuelan episode so startled him that henceforth he began to devote much more of his time expounding nonresistance as an antidote to jingoism. As he later observed, following the Civil War Americans had "fostered the belief that foreign war was impossible because no nation would desire to attack us. The idea of our taking the part of the aggressor seemed beyond reach of probability until the Venezuelan message of President Cleveland developed the unsuspected savagery latent in the American people." Garrison and Ames used their influence in the New England Free Trade League to pass a resolution by an overwhelming margin urging a peaceful resolution of the dispute.[56]

Meanwhile, in New York City, Ernest H. Crosby, a recent convert to

Tolstoyan nonresistance, joined the founder of the single-tax movement, Henry George, and moderate reformers like Lyman Abbott, Congregationalist minister and editor of the influential weekly *Outlook,* in organizing a large peace meeting.[57] After characterizing the war talk as "an epidemic of froth and hysteria," Crosby sarcastically remarked that "the Monroe Doctrine means that we Americans don't allow anybody to steal but us." Crosby's irreverent comments only aroused the ire of large numbers of war-minded workingmen, including many Irish, in the audience, but Abbott helped to calm them in a temperate speech.[58]

Of these Boston and New York critics of American policy, only Abbott's hatred of war was skin-deep. A Christian desire for peace as well as staunch Republican loyalties in part motivated his criticism of the Cleveland administration; much more decisive, however, was his commitment to an aggressive Anglo-Saxonism. In a sermon immediately following the President's December message, Abbott declared, "In another hundred years we will make the American people the greatest, most potent empire in the world," and he went on to characterize Venezuela as a government ruled by a reactionary, barbaric Catholic church and to urge Britain, which he assumed had spread enlightened ideals wherever it expanded, to absorb all the South American Republics except Brazil. "Together," he concluded, "England and American [*sic*] may wrap the world round with liberty and fill it with peace."[59]

Because Abbott had vigorously castigated warlike expressions against Britain and began to urge the creation of a permanent Anglo-American arbitral tribunal, he attracted the attention of directors of the American Peace Society, who quickly elected him a vice-president of their organization. Possibly the directors were unaware of Abbott's brand of Anglo-Saxon imperialism, but more likely their decision indicated their own uncritical Anglophile orientation and their preoccupation with attracting men of influence and prestige rather than of genuine pacifism or internationalism to their organization. In any event, Abbott's support of war and imperialism at the turn of the century would prove embarrassing to the more confirmed pacifists in the American Peace Society and intensify internal divisions within the organization.

Wholly committed to the rule of morality over expediency in international life, those already prominently associated with the peace movement viewed international arbitration as the best and most humane expedient for allowing nations to resolve their controversies in a civilized fashion. They had thus unthinkingly supported the American President's initial call for arbitration of the Venezuelan dispute and could never quite understand why England, presumably a law-abiding nation, would refuse to act rationally by accepting arbitration of its claims, nor why a weak

Venezuela had no alternative recourse but to propose arbitration. In November 1895, Alfred H. Love had written, "If Great Britain really desires a treaty of Arbitration with the U.S., let her set a good example in Venezuela."[60] Yet Love as well as most other peace workers were shocked by Cleveland's December message, and they launched a modest campaign to defuse the war enthusiasm. While the WCTU, Quaker bodies, and the Universal Peace Union petitioned Congress to delay hasty action and heed the growing expressions of sentiment in the nation for a permanent system of arbitration to settle this and future disputes with Britain, the union also sent an appeal for restraint to Lord Salisbury, dispatched one of its vice-presidents to Caracas to ascertain the Venezuelan government's position on arbitration, sent delegations to the White House, and organized a mass antiwar demonstration in Philadelphia.[61]

In Boston, Edwin Mead and his colleagues in the Twentieth Century Club, a discussion group devoted to social and political reform, unanimously passed a resolution registering its whole-hearted protest against Cleveland's course. Mead also lashed out against the administration's "reckless appeal to the war spirit" in the editorial columns of *New England Magazine*.[62] Trumpeting a similar message were the directors of the American Peace Society, who issued a statement to the press deploring the possibility of war and urging both sides to recede from their extreme positions. Trueblood and Paine cabled Lord Salisbury and telegraphed Senate leaders imploring them to exercise restraint in the crisis and to seek arbitration of the boundary dispute.[63]

Of the long-standing arbitration advocates, Andrew Carnegie seemed most willing to support the administration's position. He wrote an article that concluded with a bellicosity toward Britain as fervent as that of the most confirmed American jingo.[64] Carnegie's patriotic outburst seemed to represent a sudden betrayal of both his pacifist inclinations and his promotion of Anglo-American amity. Actually, though, it constituted an especially forceful expression of his strong national feelings. Throughout the previous decade he had exhibited an unquestioned faith in America's pristine purity. At heart, Carnegie was an anti-imperialist; as early as the 1880s he had opposed American overseas expansion and advocated a small American navy because he wanted the United States to avoid imperial rivalries outside the Western Hemisphere. "If you have ships of war you will have naval contests," he had said.[65] Consistent with those beliefs, he had refused to manufacture armor plate for the American navy. But by the end of the decade he had begun to allow his steelworks to fill large orders for armor plate for the building of an enlarged and modernized United States Navy.

As he reneged on his pacifist sentiments, he rationalized that armor plate constituted only "defensive" armament and thus amounted to only a minor compromise of his pacifist principles; much later he claimed that he had initially agreed to manufacture the armor plate only after President Harrison asked him to provide it and then not because of the lucrative profits involved (he claimed he could have made more money by producing pig iron instead) but because of his sense of patriotic duty. In view of Carnegie's national pride, his explanation of deference to presidential authority is understandable, but the fantastic profits in the production of this armament was another real motive in Carnegie's decision. Indeed, the lure of new contracts in the depressed mid-1880s prompted Carnegie to urge his partners to produce gun forgings, or "offensive" armament, but they spared the ironmaster complete renunciation of his antimilitarism when they rejected his proposition as economically unsound. In any event, the *Advocate of Peace* bluntly pointed out that regardless of his motives Carnegie's acceptance of government armament contracts was tortured and inconsistent with his professed love of peace.[66]

If Carnegie had any guilt feelings about these compromises, he easily repressed them. Compared with his grandiose vision of inevitable progress, such inconsistencies were quickly reduced to trifles. He possessed in truth a simplicity of mind that blurred the contradictory implications of specific ideas and actions. When he wrote the article on the Venezuelan crisis, he assumed that only England was contemplating the initiation of hostilities and that "the peace-loving people of the United States" would fight only as a last resort in defense of the noble principle of arbitration; but he neither pondered the possibility of American aggressive military action nor realized that historically wars had always undermined the good will and trust that were indispensable elements for successful utilization of the arbitration principle. Benjamin F. Trueblood probably had Carnegie in mind when he wrote mockingly:

> So great and enthusiastic has our attachment to it [arbitration] become, that our government, inspired by the extraordinary virtue of some of its citizens, has already decided that in certain eventualities it will go to war and employ the whole military power of the nation, on land and sea, in order to enforce this *peaceful* system on a sister nation.[67]

Fortunately for Anglo-American understanding, Great Britain had no intention of going to war over the Venezuelan question. Lord Salisbury might have remained firm in his earlier refutation of the American position but for a diplomatic crisis between England and Germany that followed closely on the heels of Cleveland's message. The new crisis with Germany over South Africa, which was much closer to Britain's main interests than British Guinea in South America, frightened members of

Salisbury's cabinet and induced the Prime Minister to adopt a more flexible position on the Venezuelan question. Whatever they had thought earlier, the possibility of a war with the United States now seemed the height of folly. Gradually, and grudgingly, Salisbury accepted Olney's position of American interest in the boundary dispute and agreed to conduct further discussions on the issue in Washington, where the pliant Pauncefote could work personally with Olney. By April 1896, the two nations had agreed on the principles for arbitration of the Anglo-Venezuelan boundary dispute. They then used diplomatic pressure on Venezuela to bring about an Anglo-Venezuelan treaty binding the parties to arbitration in early 1897.

When the two nations' peace leaders realized that neither the United States nor Great Britain seemed anxious to go to war, they began to appraise Cleveland's message, though a colossal diplomatic blunder in the short run, as a distinct long-range benefit to Anglo-American understanding. In expounding the points of agreement as well as disagreement between the two nations, Cleveland's message had cleared the air for an Anglo-American rapproachement and was really a "blessing in disguise."[68] Though friends of arbitration had no solid reasons beyond their own compulsive optimism for predicting a thaw in the frigid diplomatic climate between the two nations, their analyses were correct. While Olney and Pauncefote were exchanging notes on the arbitration of the Venezuelan boundary in January 1896, they were simultaneously discussing the possibility of establishing a permanent Anglo-American arbitration treaty.

Events surrounding the Olney-Pauncefote arbitration treaty reaffirmed peace leaders' firm acceptance of the inviolability of the nation-state as the starting point for discussion of peace questions and confirmed their rising interest in the establishment of permanent international machinery for the peaceful resolution of international disputes. Peace advocates' rather sporadic protests against American jingoism received a short period of renewed life during the Cuban crisis and the imperialistic outburst at the end of the century, but the campaign for the Olney-Pauncefote accord foreshadowed a definite long-run trend away from absolute pacifism. Related to the emphasis on practicality was the growing elitism in the peace movement. New participants in the peace movement were usually moderate or conservative in outlook and consequently expressed little faith in the common man or in social democracy. They were much more inclined to trust the political leadership and various functional elites —businessmen, lawyers, educators, and other professional people—for the maintenance and promotion of peace.

The Olney-Pauncefote negotiations were secret and very tentative until early March 1896, but in the meantime friends of arbitration had already taken the first steps toward promotion of a general arbitration treaty. Thirty-seven prominent Chicago citizens, none of whom were peace workers, initiated the campaign on February 5, 1896, by issuing a circular calling for the cities and towns of the nation to launch "a movement for cementing all the English-speaking people of the world in peace and fraternal unity." The circular particularly called for public meetings to discuss the question of establishing "arbitration as the method of concluding all differences between the two powers which diplomacy could not settle."[69] Citizens in several cities responded by holding public meetings at which they endorsed an Anglo-American arbitration treaty. Representatives from these cities formed a committee, which invited a thousand prominent men to a two-day National Arbitration Conference in Washington, D.C., in late April. About three hundred came, and another two hundred endorsed the meeting in their letters of regret. The delegates approved resolutions urging the United States government to negotiate a treaty with Britain "providing for the widest practicable application of the method of arbitration to international controversies" and "the earliest possible extension of such a system to embrace all civilized nations." The conference also appointed a delegation to present the resolutions to President Cleveland and established a National Arbitration Committee to awaken and educate the public in favor of a permanent system of Anglo-American arbitration.[70]

The dominant tone of the conference was moderation. Some speakers stated that they wished to exclude from arbitration all questions of national honor, territory, and independence and in no way wished to compromise their fundamental patriotism or their faith in the sanctity of the nation-state. Several affirmed that war was in many instances fully justified, and a few even exulted in the prospect of using an Anglo-American arbitration agreement, together with the two nations' naval forces, to promote Anglo-Saxon global commercial and political supremacy. When the noted anti-imperialist Carl Schurz stressed the unpleasant consequences of navalism and imperialism, even the antimilitarist peace workers, eager to win over moderate and practical men to the arbitration movement, either remained silent or openly opposed the broadening of the scope of peace questions at the conference. One of the leading promoters of the meeting, the Reverend Leander T. Chamberlain, summarized this cautious approach when he talked about "the sane, conservative purpose of this conference."[71]

The participants' elitist assumptions also dominated the proceedings and foreshadowed the limited effectiveness of the arbitration campaign.

The promoters' efforts to involve opinion leaders in their movement was undoubtedly sound, but their conception of this elite was limited to former Mugwumps, professional people, and successful businessmen. Their failure to encourage the attendance of United States senators or to invite spokesmen of labor, immigrant, or moderate reform groups, or other segments of American society to the conference or to include any of them on the National Arbitration Committee indicated their narrow and essentially apolitical approach to propaganda work. Although many members of peace societies and clergymen had journeyed to Washington anticipating their participation in the proceedings, they found to their chagrin that those promoting the meeting had limited the invitations to only a selected few among the peace leaders. The admission of more pacifists and the inclusion of a few representatives from these other groups might have jeopardized the underlying harmony of the discussions, but the organizers did not so much as risk a gesture to these other elements in the American social order. One speaker perhaps best depicted the participants' faith in enlightened leadership and their corresponding neglect of mass opinion when he bluntly remarked, "At the service of those in authority, we place our present and our future efforts."[72]

The conference even excluded women entirely from the proceedings, and Mrs. Lockwood vainly protested this insult to her sex. "The managers of the conference," she charged, "had ignored the fact that this gathering was the result of an uprising of the people, of whom the women had formed a large component." Not surprisingly, she found the delegates believing "they were distinguished men—that their eloquence and appearance then and there would move the world," while in reality "they represented nobody but themselves."[73]

The wisdom of the exclusive leadership seemed apparent when a deputation of the conference headed by George Edmunds took the resolutions to the White House. Both President Cleveland and Secretary Olney cordially recognized "the personal dignity and influence represented in the members of the Conference." Such support did not convert Olney to international arbitration since he had quietly begun formal negotiations with Pauncefote two months earlier, but it probably increased his determination to press on with the negotiations and surely strengthened his belief that an Anglo-American arbitration treaty was popular among influential professional and business people in the United States and would receive their strong backing.[74] The secretary's later active encouragement of these arbitration proponents would further suggest his reliance on this elite for mobilizing popular support behind the treaty. Throughout the remaining months of 1896, Olney conducted formal negotiations with Pauncefote, which culminated in a treaty providing for a system of permanent arbitration between the United States and Great Britain that covered a variety of disputes.[75]

Although the promoters of Anglo-American understanding hailed the Olney-Pauncefote accord as "one of the greatest events of modern history,"[76] the mood of the Senate was hostile from the outset, and backers of the treaty failed to make a favorable impression on the lawmakers. Their limited appeal stemmed in large part from factors beyond their immediate control. Senators, elected by state legislatures every six years, were relatively isolated from public pressure. Moreover, senators, fiercely jealous of their prerogatives in the treaty-making process, tended to resent public pressures during their deliberations on the treaty. In fact, while the National Arbitration Committee was launching its campaign, some senators, including a few nominal friends of Anglo-American understanding, openly deplored the growing volume of letters and petitions urging speedy consent to the agreement. Entreaties favoring the treaties did not amount to a massive public outcry, but they were sufficiently numerous to prevent senators from ignoring them.[77] George F. Hoar, Republican senator from Massachusetts, had been a proponent of international arbitration, but he complained bitterly about public statements and letters urging the Senate's quick consent to the treaty while it was "still in progress of negotiation" in that body, and he unfairly charged that "earnest, eloquent, heated, impatient utterances coming from the pulpit, the press, and the colleges" for immediate consent to the treaty constituted "meddling with important diplomacy by angry and impassioned utterances." At one point he complained to Atkinson: "It is one thing to approve this treaty. It is quite another thing to be a natural born fool, like many of the gentlemen who are so ready with their sage advice and their conceited criticism."[78]

Hoar was exceptional among senators only for his thin-skinned reactions to public pressures, for his colleagues in the upper house almost universally agreed with his statements emphasizing the necessity for the Senate's careful study of the treaty provisions. They denied any deliberate policy of procrastination but argued that the Senate constituted an integral part of the treaty-making process, and they rightly feared that widespread public clamor for an unamended treaty might undercut the credibility of the Senate in any changes it wished to make. Rigorous defense of the authority of that august body was occasionally labeled "undemocratic" by the treaty's more liberal proponents but failed to make senators more responsive to its supporters. The conservative Democrat George Gray, a staunch friend of international arbitration, was virtually alone among senators in welcoming expressions of public sentiment on the treaty.[79]

The failure of Olney and Pauncefote to provide for a senate voice in the arbitral process strengthened the upper house's determination to protect its constitutional prerogatives. A substantial majority of senators reacted negatively to the articles allowing the President and then the arbiters to decide whether a dispute fell within the provisions of the treaty and omitting any mention of Senate confirmation of arbitrators or its consent to their decisions. Handing over all authority to the President and an arbitration tribunal seemed to many senators to smack of an unwarranted and potentially dangerous abdication of their traditionally important position in the conduct of American foreign policy. Later developments in the arbitration movement would confirm that the Senate's desire to maintain some control over foreign policy was an imposing obstacle to successful completion of any arbitration agreement.[80]

Further, many senators feared that the treaty would tie the hands of future executives in securing concessions from Great Britain on the construction and fortification of a canal across Central America. Moreover, the potential enthusiasm of many senators was dampened by a new anti-English issue, the irritation of the Western silverites in the Senate. Frustrated by their defeat at the polls in 1896, they found revenge in attacking the agreement with Britain, symbol of the hated gold standard. Contemporary press reports of Britain's inaction against Turkey during the Armenian massacres, its acquiescence in Turkey's suppression of the struggle of Greek subjects for liberation from Ottoman domination, and its evident designs on the Transvaal reinforced their unfavorable image of a self-interested and imperialistic Britain. A few senate opponents also appealed to undiscriminating anti-British prejudices by charging that Lord Salisbury and the Conservatives had to have ulterior purposes in authorizing the treaty because they represented the imperial ambitions and cupidity of the British aristocracy. All these arguments suggested that the lawmakers' hostility toward England was still widespread, if no longer so deep seated.

These anti-British sentiments reflected a deeper nationalist bias against all Europeans. Many objected to the provision for selection of a final arbitrator by the king of Sweden and Norway if the United States and Great Britain could not agree on the appointment. They asserted that European leaders, particularly monarchs, were suspicious or jealous of the American republic and that appointments by this European king would ipso facto result in decisions unfavorable to the United States. Related to those nationalist prejudices were the fears of many isolationist senators that the many obligatory features of the treaty might lead to unexpected and embarrassing contingencies in the future, and they consequently favored a more restricted agreement excluding from arbitration traditional American principles like the Monroe Doctrine.

The arbitrationists further had to contend with sporadic public antago-nism directed against the pending accord. Predictably, many protests came from Irish-American organizations, but others came from American ultranationalists who were not so interested in staring John Bull in the eye on all international issues as they were concerned about the possible implications of the agreement for American foreign policy. One organiza-tion with some following in eastern cities, the Monroe Doctrine League, was especially active in pointing out that in future disputes Great Britain might use the treaty machinery to undermine the traditionally sacred con-cepts of Monroe's 1823 message. Foes of the accord also included influ-ential jingoistic newspapers like the *Chicago Tribune, New York Journal,* and *New York Sun,* which savagely attacked the treaty.[81] While all those expressions did not numerically equal those in favor of the arbitration agreement, they served to neutralize the boasts of arbitration proponents that American public opinion overwhelmingly favored the treaty.

The National Arbitration Committee, headed by New York business-man-philanthropist William E. Dodge, perceived the strong Senate oppo-sition from the start and undertook a campaign to arouse public support for the treaty. Though Dodge was a grandson of David Low Dodge, founder of the first American peace society, and son of William E. Dodge, Sr., who had helped to formulate plans for a world court and the codifi-cation of international law in the 1870s, he was (unlike his grandfather but much like his father) no pacifist. Rather, his interest in peace ques-tions was limited mainly to Anglo-American friendship and initially stemmed from his position as Presbyterian president of the Evangelical Alliance, a Protestant missionary group dominated by British and Ameri-can clergy and laymen.[82] Only five days after the announcement of the Olney-Pauncefote accord, Dodge warned its most influential friends about strong Senate opposition to the treaty, urged them to write their senators, encourage others to do likewise, "use your best efforts with the press, [and] promote the calling of public meetings if you deem it advisable." A few days later his assistant, the Reverend Leander Chamberlain, wrote that he and Dodge, just back from the nation's capital, had "learned that nothing but the most decided public opinion, and the most earnest, rig-orous *expression* of that opinion, will save the noble treaty."[83]

The arbitrationists concluded that only widespread expressions of pub-lic opinion could soften the Senate opposition. Secretary Olney worked behind the scenes in the arbitrationists' promotional campaign. He co-operated with railroad promoter James J. McCook in encouraging Prot-estant mission boards to pass resolutions endorsing the agreement at their interdenominational meetings and relied upon his lawyer and business acquaintances around the nation to mobilize support among state bar associations and local chambers of commerce.[84]

He also helped to formulate the strategy of the Arbitration Committee.[85] With Olney's assent Dodge's committee issued statements to the press rebutting senators' reservations on the treaty. The committee interpreted the phrase in the accord whereby the two nations agreed to arbitrate all questions in which either party had "rights against the other under treaty or otherwise" to mean only legal rights as recognized under existing international law and therefore clearly to exclude all questions of domestic and foreign policy like the Monroe Doctrine, tariff, and monetary standards. Though that interpretation was plausible, it was also debatable because of the absence of codified law on the subject. In any case it failed to convince a substantial number of senators who deplored the general and indefinite language of that provision and demanded the right to approve arbitration of each question as it arose. The committee also correctly pointed out that it had been common precedent in American-European arbitral tribunals to allow for the appointment of judges by disinterested European governments. The committee further argued that the matter was not crucial because the treaty provided that only a special court composed of three American and three British jurists could decide territorial claims and all questions "of grave general importance affecting the national rights" of either party. Even this court required at least a five-to-one majority before making the award unless both governments accepted the decision of a lesser majority. They advanced these arguments to support their conclusion that the treaty had been drawn "with unusual caution and precision, so as to protect the just rights of each country."[86]

The National Arbitration Committee also sent out 50,000 circular letters, endorsed by leaders of eleven Protestant denominations, to ministers encouraging them to urge their congregations to write their senators, circulate petitions, and hold public meetings in behalf of the accord. It sent 3,000 more to prominent people in other professions, many editors, and every United States senator, asking them to support the treaty and to state their opinions publicly. During the next two months the committee received replies from more than two-thirds of the 3,000 circulars, and 93 percent of the replies favored ratification without amendment. In a separate survey the *New York World,* a Democratic party mouthpiece, found that the bishops and archbishops of every church and more than 400 presidents of colleges and universities endorsed the treaty without qualification, while the mayors of 54 cities, 361 of 400 daily newspapers, and the presidents of the boards of trade and chambers of commerce of more than 50 cities also supported it.[87] Many peace, business, law, church, and women's organizations, college students, professors, and other interested citizens supported this campaign by sending letters and petitions to senators urging prompt ratification of the agreement.[88] Moreover, several state legislatures from Maine to Alabama passed resolutions endorsing the treaty.[89]

Those associated with peace groups played an important part in promoting many of these resolutions. In Boston, Trueblood wrote Senator Hoar protesting his objections to public expressions of support for the treaty, defending citizens' rights to petition their senators, and reminding him of his long-standing support of the principle of international arbitration. In the *Advocate of Peace* he accused the senators of delay and obstructionism, vigorously rebutted their criticisms and grudgingly accepted their minor refinements of the treaty's wording while deploring their more restrictive amendments.[90] Trueblood's role was exceptional only for the large volume of words supporting the treaty. Several other members of the American Peace Society—Robert Treat Paine, Moorfield Storey, and the Reverends Reuen Thomas, Philip S. Moxom, Edward Everett Hale, Charles F. Dole, and Adolph A. Berle—also made forceful statements in favor of the treaty and successfully used their influence in their church congregations or various civic groups like the Mugwump-dominated Massachusetts Reform Club to sponsor petitions to their senators.[91]

Arbitration proponents were also active in New York and Philadelphia. Dodge, Schurz, John Bassett Moore, Crosby, Josiah Strong, and others obtained the endorsements of 250 prominent New Yorkers representing a wide variety of civic and occupational interests and organized a mass meeting attended by some 2,500 people; while Love, Edmunds, and Herbert Welsh, pacifistic editor of the Philadelphia weekly *City and State,* wrote articles upholding the treaty and organized a public meeting in Philadelphia.[92]

But those most committed to Anglo-American understanding came almost entirely from the Northeast and to a lesser extent the Middle West and thus were handicapped from the start in their desire for a nationwide movement. Padding of the National Arbitration Committee with names outside the Northeast could not conceal that one-half of its thirty members came from eastern urban centers and that New Yorkers alone constituted a majority of its executive committee. Senators from the West and Southwest were especially hostile toward the accord, but there were few peace and arbitration groups in those sections to counteract those prejudices. Another indication of the meager support for the treaty outside these sections was that all but 35 of the 266 petitions to the Senate favoring ratification came from New England, Middle Atlantic, and North Central states.[93]

The arbitrationists' promotional effort did not change the minds of any senators on the original treaty, but it eventually caused several skeptics among them from eastern and middle western states to vote for the final emasculated version of the agreement. Samuel Gompers, the one prominent labor leader outspokenly in favor of the treaty, later reported that the *New York World*'s survey of civic leaders showed "an expression of general opinion in favor of the treaty . . . so emphatically and so convincingly that even the Senate took notice of the extraordinary poll."[94] It may also be that the many expressions of support for the treaty in Massachusetts, including resolutions passed by the Massachusetts legislature, caused Senator Lodge to refrain from public opposition, though he was really hostile to it.[95] The paucity of vocal approval for the treaty in the South and trans-Mississippi West, however, permitted senators from these regions to denounce any kind of arbitration agreement with England. Unfortunately for arbitration proponents, equality of state representation in the upper chamber gave senators from those less-populous states sufficient votes to deny a two-thirds majority for almost any treaty.[96]

Limitations of the arbitration campaign compounded those imposing difficulties. Peace workers' recent allies in the movement—educators, businessmen, ministers, and lawyers—helped to win over certain like-minded individuals in the professional and business establishments but showed little interest in mobilizing a larger cross section of the populace. An elitist approach to peace work was certainly wise where only foreign policy initiatives by the executive branch were involved, but a broader public involvement was necessary on agreements requiring senate approval. More important, almost all groups supporting the accord undertook no concerted campaign to marshal opinion behind it. Besides the religious conventions' endorsements, the New York and Philadelphia meetings appear to have been the sole attempts to muster mass support for the accord, and even the peace societies failed to follow up their original resolutions with petitions or other pleas for public support.

Because the issue was removed from the immediate, mundane concerns of most Americans, it is doubtful whether the arbitrationists could have forged intimate working relationships with more than church groups and certain civic organizations. Besides the most dedicated peace workers only a few of the most zealous individuals on the National Arbitration Committee bothered to campaign actively for the treaty. The fundamental weakness of the arbitration campaign was its shortage of dedicated activists. The campaign revealed that many prominent people were willing to lend their names to the cause, but too few were sufficiently zealous to organize mass meetings and circulate petitions that might have resulted in the involvement of a larger and more committed citizenry for the success of the treaty.[97]

When William McKinley assumed the presidency on March 4, 1897, the Senate still had not voted on the treaty. Cleveland and Olney were disappointed and feared the new administration would let the matter die. In his inaugural address McKinley strongly urged the Senate to approve the agreement "not merely as a matter of policy, but as a duty to mankind."[98] His endorsement of the accord, however, failed to deter the Senate from deleting the article allowing for the appointment of an arbitrator by the king of Sweden and Norway. It also passed an amendment exempting questions that in the judgment of either power materially affected its honor, its territorial integrity, or its foreign or domestic policy except by special agreement. Another amendment provided for Senate confirmation of arbitrators in each case and its consent to all decisions made under the treaty machinery. Those changes effectively effaced the treaty beyond all recognition. Even then, however, a diehard group of senators opposed the weakened version and defeated it by three votes.[99]

The defeat of the Olney-Pauncefote treaty was a bitter blow to the arbitrationists. Conservatives in the campaign attempted to understand the Senate's reasoning, but even they assumed overwhelming public support for the treaty and joined more liberal participants in placing blame for its defeat entirely on a recalcitrant and provincial Senate. Frances E. Willard forcefully expressed this sentiment when she charged that the few opposing senators, "dressed in a little brief authority, do not represent the great kind-hearted 70,000,000 of our people. They do not represent the pulpit or the press."[100]

Yet all arbitration proponents managed to remain sanguine in defeat. Minimizing the importance of the drastic Senate amendments before the final vote, they pointed out that the treaty had almost obtained the two-thirds majority. They found other encouraging signs. Had not their campaign demonstrated that the public strongly favored an arbitration agreement? And might not this public sentiment induce the Senate to reconsider its action? Moreover, did not McKinley seem interested in the matter? And would not his appointment of John Sherman as secretary of state facilitate the negotiation of a new treaty?[101]

Those assumptions were unduly optimistic. They underestimated the self-confident nationalism of the decade that increasingly threatened to undercut even the most modest efforts at international cooperation, senatorial jealousy of executive encroachments, Secretary Sherman's senility, and President McKinley's preoccupation with other issues at the outset of his administration. Despite the arbitrationists' recognition of the importance of public opinion for ultimate success, the predominant elitism pervading much of the arbitration movement hindered their consideration of new strategies for broadening their public appeal. Only Trueblood dimly perceived the arbitrationists' genteel predelictions accounting for the restricted political impact of their campaign when he remarked, "We have looked too much, possibly, at the heads of government rather than to the cultivation of public sentiment among the people, and among the representatives of the people in both houses of Congress."[102]

Nevertheless, friends of arbitration, disregarding or deemphasizing those obstacles, decided to resume their campaign for a treaty. A month after the Senate rejected the Olney-Pauncefote accord, the Lake Mohonk Conference appointed a committee to see the President about reopening negotiations on the subject. Long before the interview McKinley intimated that he did not give high priority to international arbitration, but the fact that he had allowed Sherman to begin informal negotiations with Pauncefote on a new treaty raised the committee's hopes for a satisfactory interview.[103] McKinley, claiming the Senate was tired of arbitration, promised no definite action. He merely consented to mention international arbitration in his first annual message to Congress and wrote out the substance of his remarks on the subject in the presence of the delegation. If McKinley meant to dampen the delegates' enthusiasm for a new treaty, he apparently did not succeed. One delegate, Benjamin F. Trueblood, at any rate, optimistically concluded that the chief executive had assured them that he would "promote permanent arbitration with other nations as fast as it may be found practicable to do so." Senator Sherman in no way discouraged that view. On the contrary, he assured them that he had reopened negotiations with Britain.[104]

At that point the American workers for arbitration once again received further encouragement from the indefatigable Randal Cremer. Other British peace leaders wrote McKinley praising his interest in an Anglo-American accord, but Cremer also relied on personal diplomacy. Five days before the Mohonk deputation's interview with the President, Cremer arrived in the United States on his third visit in ten years. Narrowly defeated for reelection to the House of Commons in July 1895, he did not bring another memorial from Parliament but one signed by 7,432 English trade union officials, who, Cremer claimed, represented some 2,750,000 workingmen. The British labor leader hoped that circulation of the memorial would dispel the belief in some American circles that the arbitration movement in Britain was supported only by the aristocratic and ruling classes.[105]

Shortly after Cremer's arrival, McKinley's first annual message briefly reaffirmed the President's support for arbitration agreements that did not imperil the nation's interests or honor. The *Advocate of Peace* thought

McKinley's statement might be a prelude to a later special message proposing a new Anglo-American treaty, but Cremer realized that his remarks were too general and cautious to be taken seriously. McKinley confirmed that impression on February 2, 1898, when he personally asked the British peace leader to defer presentation of his memorial until the administration decided the time for a treaty was opportune.[106] After seeing John Sherman, Cremer also perceived that the secretary, now old, feeble, "and with a very defective memory," was without influence in the administration. Sherman did have difficulty in managing even routine business in the State Department, and McKinley soon persuaded him to resign.[107]

The McKinley administration's rather evasive posture on international arbitration was prompted not only by the President's instinctive caution at the onset of his presidential term or the secretary's senility; it was even more the result of their nearly total preoccupation with other matters: the Dingley tariff, revival of the Hawaiian annexation issue, and the controversy with Spain over the revolutionary turmoil in Cuba. The Cuban imbroglio particularly vexed him. With jingoistic politicians in Congress clamoring for American military intervention on the island, he found that the diplomatic crisis with Spain demanded his constant attention. Advocates of peace too began to realize that the Cuban crisis took precedence over Anglo-American arbitration. The threat of hostilities would starkly reveal the fragility of the American peace movement.

[3]

The Cuban Crisis

THE SPANISH-AMERICAN controversy over Cuba had waxed and waned since the 1820s and had grown in intensity after February 1895, but as late as 1897 the leading pacifists were the only peace advocates to display much interest in the problem. Through their peace journals they regularly reported the course of events in Cuba and in occasional editorials deplored the rising tide of national emotion that threatened to precipitate American military intervention. While strongly in favor of Cuban independence, they urged the withholding of belligerent rights to the Cuban rebels as one way to restrain interventionist sentiment until the United States could devise a diplomatic solution. Otherwise, even the pacifists did not display special interest in the problem.[1]

The peace workers' inattention continued into early 1898 when the publication of the De Lôme letter, in which the Spanish minister in Washington criticized McKinley's handling of the Cuban situation, and the explosion of the American battleship *Maine* inflamed American passions in favor of intervention to stop the inhumanities in Cuba and to obtain revenge for the alleged Spanish challenge to American honor. Following those incidents, cries of "Cuba Libre" and "Remember the *Maine*" began to fill street demonstrations.[2]

In the nine weeks between the *Maine* disaster and the American declaration of war on Spain, the ineffectiveness of the peace forces became strikingly evident. To be sure, several people attempted to persuade the McKinley administration to avert hostilities, but significantly many of those efforts came from individuals who had no official connection with peace societies and in direct response to McKinley himself who solicited the advice of influential individuals for feasible alternatives to war. Oscar Straus who had played a small part in organizing the 1896 National Arbitration Conference was one of the few friends of peace to gain the ear of the President in the final crisis. A former minister to Turkey, Straus told McKinley in mid-March that the United States should ask Spain to deal with Cuba as Turkey had much earlier dealt with Egypt; that would give self-government to Cuba in domestic affairs and require only an annual tribute to Spain. The latter could not intervene militarily in Cuba but would retain nominal sovereignty over the island. In essence, Straus proposed dominion status to meet most of the special demands of Cuba, Spain, and the United States without recourse to further bloodshed. In his diary Straus noted that McKinley praised his ingenious plan as "the most practical of any that have been brought to his attention, but intimated, not in so many words, but by the general drift of the conversation, such a plan would not stop the Jingoes."[3] When McKinley submitted an outline of the plan to the Cuban junta, however, the Cubans, sensing the popular clamor for war—a war that more than likely would result in their full independence—immediately rejected any such complex arrangement for the future political system of their homeland.[4]

The Society of Friends in several states and the WCTU petitioned the President and Congress imploring a peaceful resolution of the Cuban imbroglio. May Wright Sewall was especially active. She drew up a statement arguing that just as the defense of honor among individuals no longer justified the killing of one's adversary, so should consideration of honor be no casus belli among "sister nations" like the United States and Spain. She managed to obtain the signatures of seventeen women leaders of the National Council of Women and affiliated groups before sending it to President McKinley in late March. Anna Garlin Spencer, minister of a liberal, nondenominational church in Providence, Rhode Island, had already participated in the WCTU's protests against military education in the schools; she signed Mrs. Sewall's appeal and also prevailed upon the local branch of the National Council of Women to address an antiwar resolution to the Rhode Island delegations in Congress. Meanwhile, New Yorkers Ernest H. Crosby and George Foster Peabody, a pacifistic philanthropist, unequivocally opposed American military intervention in Cuba.[5]

Of all locales, however, Boston easily predominated as the center of antiwar activity. Several ministers in the Boston area persuaded their congregations to send resolutions opposing intervention to their congressmen, senators, and the President. Edward Atkinson supported that activity and wrote McKinley imploring him "to avoid the hell of war."[6] He also used the Massachusetts Reform Club as a forum for vigorously denouncing a Spanish-American conflict. Virtually unanimous in their opposition to such a war, the Club's members applauded when Atkinson and Moorfield Storey sardonically remarked that they would abandon their objections to hostilities if all the jingos could be drafted into the army and sent to the front lines.[7]

In addition, the Boston carpet manufacturer Samuel Capen and Edwin D. Mead successfully promoted resolutions endorsing the President's peace efforts in the Boston Chamber of Commerce and the Twentieth Century Club, and the two cooperated in pushing a similar resolution through the Boston Municipal League. The millionaire text book publisher Edwin Ginn joined other leading residents of suburban Winchester in dispatching an antiwar resolution to their congressman.[8] All three wrote the Commonwealth's former governor, Secretary of the Navy John D. Long, to bolster his sagging resistance to interventionist pressures. The pleas of Ginn and Capen linked their previous involvement in the arbitration movement with their present hopes for peace. As Ginn argued, "the men that are doing the best work in the world are no more in favor of war now than they were last year, when almost to a man they petitioned Congress to enter into negotiations with England and the other great powers for treaties of arbitration to settle all disputes," while Capen, a devout Congregationalist, concurred that "[t]he feeling is very strong here that a Christian nation ought to find some way to settle this difficulty without resort to arms. The country is on trial before the civilized world to see how much our talk of the past few years with regard to Arbitration is worth."[9]

Charles F. Dole, Unitarian minister, went one step further. He traveled to Washington, D.C., to see the Republican congressman from his district, Samuel June Barrows. Formerly editor of *Christian Register,* Barrows had actively supported liberal and humanitarian causes and favored a pacific solution to Spanish-American difficulties. Together the two obtained an interview with House Speaker Thomas B. Reed and President McKinley on April 2. Reed promised to hold off the interventionists in Congress for as long as the administration stood firm, while McKinley expressed his gratitude for the peace forces and assured them that these forces during the previous week had helped to neutralize the influence of the jingos.[10]

Such antiwar activities indicated that the peace advocates were not inactive during the Cuban crisis, but their influence was, of course, brief. The few personal interviews with McKinley appeared to have little lasting effect; and besides those letters and petitions sent directly to him, it is doubtful how many of the peace advocates' written pleas actually found their way to his desk. Even if he was aware of most of them, his gradual acceptance of intervention indicated that they failed to convince him of widespread and deep-seated opposition to the war spirit. The church groups' petitions might have appealed to his penchant for Christian forbearance and tolerance toward Spain, and the business resolutions might have cheered him since he identified easily with conservative business interests and would not move precipitately toward war without their tacit or open support. But much of that opinion came from Boston and was more than counter-balanced by prowar sentiment throughout the East and on a more virulent scale throughout the trans–Appalachian West. Even the Boston Chamber of Commerce nullified the impact of its antiwar resolutions by passing two amendments pledging the group's continued allegiance to the President if war ultimately resulted.[11]

Nor could McKinley derive much comfort from the assertions of peace loving Bostonians that "men of repute and influence" as well as the "best," "thinking" people opposed war when this high-minded elite neither furnished any solid evidence of broader popular support nor with the possible exception of Atkinson tried actively to cultivate such support outside their narrow constituency.[12] The closest Boston came to an antiwar mass meeting occurred shortly before the President's April 11 war message when a handful of its citizens, none of whom was associated with the peace movement, began to organize such a gathering but abandoned it when they could not obtain leading Republicans as speakers.[13]

In truth, while friends of peace exerted their influence in various voluntary associations against war, they did not attempt to mobilize larger segments of society against intervention. In consequence, the opposition to hostilities never had a chance to develop into the semblance of a mass protest movement. There is no evidence to suggest that they even seriously contemplated such a large remonstrance even though rumors in the press persisted into early April that the McKinley administration was quietly attempting to spark a back-fire in the form of vocal business and public protests against the interventionists in Congress.[14]

One logical rallying point for opposition to war, especially in the Boston area, was the American Peace Society, but the peace group gave little direction to antiwar opinion. Indeed, the organization starkly epitomized the prevailing irresolution of the peace forces. From the beginning of the hysterical aftermath of the *Maine* tragedy, the *Advocate of Peace* expressed deep concern over the volatile state of public opinion but relied entirely on the President's personal diplomacy, patience, and good will to avert war.[15] The society's leadership failed, however, to give McKinley much encouragement in resisting the interventionist temper of Congress. The most the directors of the peace group offered was a resolution dispatched to the President urging him to use "every influence short of war" to end the Spanish injustices to the Cuban population.[16] When McKinley's private secretary thanked them for their "cordial words of approval of the course pursued by the administration," the society made no further effort to bolster the President's pacific pretensions and failed to protest his gradual capitulation to the interventionists. Indeed, the leadership of the American Peace Society circulated no petitions, held no mass rallies, or otherwise demonstrated against the prowar forces.[17]

Part of the peace advocates' irresolution stemmed from their underestimation of the interventionist pressures on President McKinley. Though aware of the pervasive jingoism in Congress, they optimistically assumed that the chief executive steadfastly opposed war and that their few pleas for a peaceful resolution of the Cuban problem would suffice to sustain his resistance to the interventionists. Beginning in late February 1898, Edward Atkinson spent a month of frantic correspondence in an unsuccessful attempt to redirect the activities of the moribund National Arbitration Committee into support of his proposal for neutralization of the Hawaiian Islands (the proposal also indicating his optimistic belief in international cooperation). It never occurred to him to query his correspondents on the prospect of mobilizing the committee against the war-minded Congress on the Cuban issue.[18] Such an effort undoubtedly would have failed for several reasons, not the least of which was the prowar or at best tepid antiwar sympathies of many of its members, but Atkinson's earlier and later emphasis on cooperative efforts for peace indicates that his underestimation of the war danger more than fear of failure explains his behavior.[19] When he finally perceived the imminent possibility of war in late March, it was too late to do more than to protest as an individual and to appeal to the churches against intervention.

Moreover, McKinley's friendly replies to peace advocates' antiwar appeals may have helped to convince them that no further exertions were necessary to bolster his position. The rapid successes of the Spanish premier Praxedes Mateo Sagasta in revoking the *reconcentrado* order, promising a greater measure of Cuban self-government, and announcing an unconditional armistice further lulled them into false hopes.[20] Peace advocates refused, however, to believe that McKinley's message to Congress of April 11 asking for authorization to use American military and naval forces "to secure a full and final termination of hostilities between the government of Spain and the people of Cuba" signified his capitulation to the war hawks in Congress. McKinley further demonstrated the exhaustion of his patience when he refused to substitute a new and more conciliatory message and merely tacked on a noncommittal postscript requesting "just and careful attention" to the eleventh hour Spanish concessions.[21] Those advocates of peace who commented on the message, however, naively interpreted his reasoned view of Spain's capitulation to American demands and his concluding statement as a pacific message designed to delay any war resolution until passions cooled.[22]

But in general the timidity of peace advocates in the final crisis stemmed much less from absentmindedness or intellectual error than from their elitist assumptions. Since several of them believed that proper education could convert a large majority of the general public to peace principles, their elitism did not constitute deliberate snobbery. Edwin Ginn expressed their faith in the beneficent effects of liberal education when he remarked that "people are honest and mean to treat each other fairly, and the only reason they do not is because they do not have sufficient knowledge of each other's position."[23] Because they were steeped in the Mugwump traditions and teachings that were common among many moderate reformers of that era, they assumed that the man in the street constituted an important ally only in proportion to his ability to absorb their high-minded faith in reason, moral rectitude, and gentlemanly conduct. Since the numerous and passionate demands for war seemed to indicate that the masses had not yet been uplifted to acceptance of these principles, the peace leaders concluded that for the present they alone were the proper custodians of the peace cause. Their reliance on self-restraint of course resulted in a marked deemphasis on emotion and spontaneity. Accordingly, they eschewed mass rallies and petitions because they might arouse the public passions they abjured.

Shortly after the De Lôme letter and the *Maine* explosion, Trueblood advised friends of peace to oppose the interventionists "in a quiet way. Refusing to give ear to floating rumors, they should keep themselves in a calm, self-possessed attitude, which will have a direct restraining effect on others."[24] Trueblood thus defended the Society's inaction with the assertion that the chief aim of peace societies was not to demonstrate against war when the people were carried away with emotion but to conduct a long-range educational campaign that would eventually "bring about such a change in public sentiment in reference to the whole subject of war and the methods of administering international justice as will ultimately render all war impossible."[25]

Although Trueblood's writings during and after the war clearly reaffirmed his uncompromising pacifism, in the crucial days before American military intervention he was sincere in advocating this cautious strategy. Then and later he displayed a marked preference for the well-reasoned lecture on pacifism or internationalism over rousing antiwar street demonstrations or emotional appeals to mass opinion. If he ever contemplated more active opposition to the war hawks, two factors undoubtedly helped to reinforce his timidity. First, he probably realized that appeals to anti-war sentiment would be exercises in futility. Considering the small number of peace societies, the difficulty in stirring up opposition to a war which was championed as a humanitarian crusade to liberate the Cubans from their Spanish oppressors, and the absence of close contacts with anti-interventionists in Congress, such appeals undoubtedly would have failed to prevent war and more likely would have been widely denounced as unpatriotic. Second, he surely reasoned that his more active opposition to intervention would vividly contrast with Paine's and the American Peace Society directors' preference for formal, orderly antiwar procedures and perhaps create a rupture in its leadership.

Trueblood's reticent behavior typified Boston peace workers' avoidance of radical antiwar tactics. The virtual silence of these friends of peace in the final crisis revealed more clearly than during the campaign for the Olney-Pauncefote treaty the gap between their own peaceful intentions and the vocal masses who now seemed determined to go to war.

Moreover, those who had opposed war during the Venezuelan boundary dispute and had supported Anglo-American arbitration were unquestionably sincere, but most of them did not advocate peace-at-any-price. Humanitarian and racial sympathies rather than religious doctrines of nonresistance motivated their interest in peace questions, and they would have needed considerably more courage consistently to profess a policy of nonintervention in the face of long-standing suffering in neighboring Cuba. Much as many of these nonpacifists hoped for a peaceful resolution of the Spanish-Cuban imbroglio, they rather easily acquiesced in America's forceful intervention once McKinley's pacific policies had failed. Assuming the sincerity of the administration's motives, these nonpacifists believed that American military intervention would restore order on the island, promote justice and social progress, and serve the cause of humanity.[26] Congressman Barrows could claim, "I deplore war considered as war," but rationalize that his vote authorizing the administration's military intervention in Cuba did not constitute an endorsement of war since Spain still had the alternative of compliance with the American ultimatum. In any event, he sincerely believed that intervention in the name of freedom and humanity for the Cubans was laudable.[27]

Further, for all their talk about international harmony, most friends of peace had strong national loyalties, and they admired other nations in rough proportion to their conformity to American ideals and institutions. Great Britain and France came closest to their conception of progressive and democratic nations in the civilized and Christianized community, and they assumed that other nations rarely measured up to their standards. Earlier, their reactions to the Turkish massacres of Armenian Christians and persecution of American citizens and destruction of American property in the Ottoman Empire provided a foretaste of their attitudes toward less "civilized" nations including Spain. The responses of Capen, Mead, Dole, Garrison, and Paine to Turkey and Spain from 1895 to 1898 indicate that no exact parallels necessarily existed between peace advocates' perceptions of and reactions to the inhumane deeds of the two nations. Capen and Mead had publicly endorsed the Greek subjects' struggle for "liberty" from Turkish "tyranny" in Crete without urging any specific action by the American government, while Garrison and Paine had condemned the Turkish regime during the Armenian difficulties and were willing quietly to acquiesce, if not openly advocate, joint military action of the United States and the European powers against Turkey. Only Dole openly came close to avowing an absolute pacifist position in opposing any military intervention in these lands. Yet all five resisted the demands for military intervention in Cuba, although Paine's outrage at Spanish inhumanities in Cuba qualified his hopes for a peaceful solution and contributed to the paralysis of the American Peace Society in the final crisis.[28]

Several Protestant spokesmen associated with the peace and arbitration movements, however, did not distinguish between the Turkish and Spanish difficulties but judged both by their unquestioned standards of the superiority of Anglo-Saxon Protestantism. Their well-intentioned talk about serving humanity really amounted to an uncritical mixture of Americanism, Anglo-Saxonism, and Protestantism. William Dodge's and Josiah Strong's eloquent talk about Anglo-American friendship derived from their positions of leadership in American missionary bodies, the Evangelical Alliance and the American Board of Commissioners for Foreign Missions, and they were understandably willing to use American military force to protect American missionaries and missions abroad. When Turkey had begun to persecute American Protestant missionaries, they had twice petitioned President Cleveland in behalf of these organizations, urging "the prompt sending of a guard-ship to Constantinople" and "the strengthening of our naval force in the eastern Mediterranean" to prevent further infringements on American rights and interests.[29] Dodge renewed that plea for American governmental action in early 1898.[30] Those appeals assumed that the mere show of American force would suffice to stop the persecutions but allowed the President discretionary authority in selecting the "specific means" necessary to assure the missionaries' safety. While their entreaties were unsuccessful, they revealed not only the two men's contempt for the Turkish Sultan and his autocratic government but their preoccupation with the concerns of American evangelical Protestantism. Only their first petition mentioned the plight of the Armenian

Christians as a secondary reason for American intervention, and their names were conspicuously absent from the many ad hoc committees in the United States that had been created for the relief of the refugees. Not surprisingly, they offered no protest against the extension of a bellicose version of America's humanitarian and racial mission against a decadent, autocratic, and Catholic Spain on the Cuban issue. If they never publicly approved the jingoistic rhetoric of ultranationalists—such as Theodore Roosevelt when he wrote just before rushing off to the Cuban hostilities, "Spain and Turkey are the two powers I would rather smash than any in the world"[31]—they were willing to accept the consequences of American military action against both nations.

Though Lyman Abbott was not an active member of the American Board of Commissioners for Foreign Missions, he shared many Protestant clerics' disdain for Turkey and Spain. Following the Turks' destruction of some American missions, he had declared, "Now is a good time to send over one or two of our White Squadron to Turkish waters with a demand for the instant payment of our delayed claims."[32] As the controversy over Cuba intensified, he deplored the sensational journalism and urged public support for McKinley's struggle for a peaceful solution, but he never wavered in his belief in the essential righteousness of the American position if McKinley chose war. On the eve of American military intervention, he expounded that the crisis was one "between a benighted and dwarfing despotism on the one side, represented by Spain, and a popular intelligence and a rapid human development on the other, represented by the United States. The issue does not differ in essential character from that represented by Spain under Philip II and England under Elizabeth." He logically concluded that the "spirit of justice and humanity demands intervention."[33]

Edward Everett Hale and Philip Moxom apparently never advocated American action in Turkey, but they both endorsed the decision for war against Spain. Hale believed that the United States was God's agent of human progress and thus had "certain duties in defense of the civilization of the world." In sanctioning America's declaration of war against Spain, he even remarked quite seriously: "There is cause enough for war in saying that we will not have a fever-bed of yellow fever directly to windward of us, against the poison of which we must struggle every year."[34] Indeed, the faith of all five—Dodge, Strong, Abbott, Moxom, and Hale—in America's unrivaled virtue was so deep that they rather easily accepted McKinley's decisions during and after the war to extend American hegemony over the peoples of Hawaii, Puerto Rico, and the Philippines.[35]

The secular Andrew Carnegie vacillated in the final crisis, but his firm patriotism ultimately resulted in his open support of the American war effort. The ironmaster at first feared that the congressional proponents of the annexation of Hawaii might exploit the Cuban crisis to their own advantage, but once the United States entered the war his patriotic fervor fully emerged. He now reasoned that America's complaints against Spanish actions in Cuba were just, that its sole aim was full independence for Cuba and Puerto Rico, and that it would be a short war which would not only rid the New World of Spanish colonialism but strengthen republicanism. He even cabled the commander of American forces in Cuba, General Nelson Miles, urging him to proceed "full force" to capture Puerto Rico, and Miles later acknowledged that he presented the steel magnate's proposal to McKinley who then authorized the Puerto Rican campaign.[36]

Carnegie's racial outlook also qualified his latent antiwar sympathies. Conceivably, if England had strenuously objected to the McKinley administration's polite rejection of European nations' overtures for mediation of the dispute, Carnegie might have hesitated before openly endorsing the war, but the Salisbury government's lukewarm response to this *démarche* and its full acquiescence in American belligerency resulted in a widespread belief in British sympathy for the American cause.[37] Carnegie thought that the outbreak of the war clearly exposed "the genuine attachment of Britain to the American people and its Government" and helped to solidify "the two branches of our English-speaking race." In dramatizing the European continental powers' resentment of Britain's world dominance, the war helped to convince British leaders that "[h]er only secure and permanent home is with her own race." It did not seem to trouble him that fear of European embroilments rather than genuine friendship for the United States should motivate the British government's desire for closer American ties.[38]

Finally, women associated with peace societies demonstrated that they were far from one mind on the Cuban crisis. Standing apart from the several women resisting a Spanish-American confrontation were many women who consented to the conflict by their silence, and a vocal minority who openly endorsed the war. Given the septuagenarian Julia Ward Howe's ardent national loyalties, it was readily predictable that her love of peace would easily give way to humanitarian expressions of sympathy for the victims of Spanish cruelties and finally for war. It was not that she had repudiated her earlier professions of peace but that she had always valued more highly an amalgam of other American values—freedom and democracy in particular—and was willing to endorse the use of the nation's military forces to extend their realization in international life. More than peace, she believed in justice but from the start of the crisis assumed that the American position was just. Moreover, like many others she linked together the Armenian and Cuban situations. Shortly after the war began, she remarked, "I am glad that we have taken the first step towards righting the wrongs of other nations. At a little meeting two years ago, I said I thought that a few warships and a dose of iron might be good for Turkey. We have not gone there—I wish we had—but we have sent our warships to Cuba. We must feel that all are brothers, and that none can be wronged, even at the ends of the world, without our being wronged."[39]

Other suffragists who had offered some support to the peace cause were less unequivocal but shared Mrs. Howe's attitude. The *Woman's Journal,* the leading suffragist magazine, had occasionally asserted that "Men are the belligerent sex" and that the United States would never become a truly peace loving nation until women obtained the right to vote. "Woman suffrage means peace" became the monotonous motto of several articles and editorials on this theme.[40] The editors had condemned the male politicians for their jingoistic speeches on the Venezuelan crisis, and shortly after the defeat of the Olney-Pauncefote treaty the magazine editorialized, "women, who are by nature the less belligerent sex, and who make up a large part of the active membership of the peace societies, have especial reason to regret that the United States should refuse to take this advanced step in civilization."[41] Occasionally they even came close to espousing an absolute pacifist position. For example, editor Henry B. Blackwell wrote in 1896, "War is always and everywhere an evil; almost always a mistake. It is legalized murder and organized barbarism."[42]

These scattered utterances for peace and arbitration could not obscure the magazine's overriding preoccupation with woman's suffrage and the consistent subordination of other reforms to that primary issue. The tendency among feminists to focus their attention almost exclusively on the suffrage question, a common phenomenon after 1900, had begun to appear with increasing frequency in the last decades of the nineteenth century. As early as 1895, the *Woman's Journal* gave full summaries of Garrison's and other pacifists' speeches at the Universal Peace Union's Mystic meeting mainly as a pretext for publicizing its own critique of traditional pacifist arguments. "[T]he fundamental reform," the journal editorialized, "without which peace principles can never prevail, does not seem to have been emphasized by the speakers. That reform is impartial suffrage for women."[43] During the Venezuelan dispute the only comment of the *Woman's Journal* appeared in print several weeks after the danger of war had subsided, and even then the editors revealed that the primary purpose of their attack on jingoistic politicians was not so much hatred of war as an argument for the ballot. "All this is an object lesson in the need of woman suffrage," editor Henry B. Blackwell wrote. "It proves that a political society of men alone cannot be trusted to keep the peace."[44] Similarly, the magazine remained curiously silent during the difficult months of senate debate on the Olney-Pauncefote treaty. The editors' tardy comments on both episodes indicated their reluctance to associate closely with a potentially controversial cause like peace which might divide the suffragists on a side issue and tarnish the suffrage movement's quest for respectibility.

As the Spanish-American controversy hurtled toward war, the *Woman's Journal* seemed no more eager to take a position on the crisis, "because," Henry Blackwell weakly explained, "women, as yet, are not recognized as having any responsibility in the matter, and because there is no way of making their opinions respected."[45] William Lloyd Garrison, Jr.'s letter after the onset of hostilities sharply criticizing the magazine's evasion of the Cuban question finally brought a reply. Determined to justify his silence, Blackwell claimed that his gradual awakening to the real suffering in Cuba and the destruction of the *Maine* made war palatable. He speculated that if women had been voters, their pacific actions might have exerted sufficient influence to prevent war, but, he concluded, "as the world goes [now], our intervention between Spain and her victims marks an advance, not a retrogression, in national methods."[46]

Alice Stone Blackwell supported her father's arguments. She plausibly claimed that "women constitute the bulk of the membership in the peace and arbitration societies" and that they were much less unanimous for war than the exclusively male United States Congress. She was also willing to concede that "when the cause of a war appeals to the maternal instinct in women, to their hatred of cruelty, their disposition to defend the weak and oppressed, many women become as keen for war as men, if not keener."

Both Blackwells argued that the moral appeal for Cuban intervention had its antecedents in the American Civil War. Alice Stone Blackwell pointed out that the "maternal instinct" had motivated Northern women to support the appeal to arms for the freedom of "the suffering slaves" and had prompted Southern white women to defend the peculiar institution as vital for the well-being of their children. Henry Blackwell concurred, arguing that the Spanish General Valeriano "the Butcher" Weyler had organized "Andersonvilles" in Cuba for civilians, and the present conflict would "make an end of absolutism and political slavery in the West Indies, just as the North rose with a similar impulse, 37 years ago, to make an end of chattel slavery in the Southern Confederacy."[47]

Garrison, however, refused to accept their moral and humanitarian justifications of the war. To Alice Blackwell's endorsement of a war "to defend the weak and oppressed," Garrison hotly replied that there was nothing defensive about a powerful nation invading the territory of a much weaker neighbor. Quite apart from his nonresistant views, Garrison denounced American intervention "absolutely upon the common ethical ground of my indignant critics. . . . The United States is the aggressor," he concluded dogmatically.[48]

The most notable exception to the uncoordinated or half-hearted antiwar efforts of the peace forces in the final crisis was the Universal Peace Union. Radical pacifists to the core, Alfred Love, Belva Lockwood, and a few of their coworkers in the union labored incessantly for peace from the first days of the Cuban crisis. Until February 1898, their proposals paralleled Cleveland's and McKinley's policies for avoiding a showdown with Spain on the Cuban situation: the withholding of belligerent rights to the Cuban rebels, diplomatic moves to secure the withdrawal of General Weyler, end of the reconcentration orders, political reforms granting the Cuban landholders and taxpayers greater autonomy in administering and governing the island, and the retention of the American consul general in Havana to maintain contact with both the Spanish and Cuban authorities there and to receive clothing, food, medicine, and other necessities of life for the relief of suffering among the Cubans.[49] So anxious were they to prevent war that they endorsed any presidential move that seemed to dampen the public's enthusiasm for intervention. Thus the *Peacemaker* at first naively applauded McKinley's decision to send the *Maine* to Havana on a "pacific" visit, though after the sinking of the battleship it immediately realized its mistake and now charged that the battleship had been "armed to the teeth" and "under certain circumstances . . . was prepared to sink other vessels or bombard a city, to destroy, maim or kill."[50]

In the final few weeks before the American war declaration, Alfred Love and Belva Lockwood intensified their peace efforts. Only a week after the *Maine* disaster, the Universal Peace Union passed resolutions praising President McKinley's calmness and moderation, and Love sent several letters to President McKinley's moderate cabinet officers and anti-interventionists in Congress commending their restraint and attempting to bolster their sagging spirits.

Fearing the rising demands in Congress for military intervention in Cuba, however, these same union leaders also tried to avert war by persuading the Spanish government to make additional concessions and encouraging the European powers to offer their good offices for mediating the Spanish-American difficulties. In early March, they sent an appeal to Pope Leo XIII to mediate the Spanish-American controversy and urged Cardinal James Gibbons to serve as a mediator between the Pontiff and the President. They also used the International Peace Bureau at Berne to channel their proposals for mediation to the major European powers. Further, Belva Lockwood and Love dispatched letters to the Spanish premier Sagasta urging further concessions to the Cubans and appealed to one of the union's Spanish supporters, Don Arturo de Marcoartu, a member of the Spanish Cortes, requesting him to use his influence among Spanish political leaders to grant Cuba autonomy as a step toward its eventual full independence. Since autonomy would be a major Spanish concession, Love wrote the Cuban leaders asking them to accept the same proposal as a test of the Spanish good faith.[51]

None of these efforts restrained the war tide. Senator de Marcoartu either did not grasp the rapid deterioration in Spanish-American relations, as Lockwood believed, or had no influence in Spanish ruling circles, for he did not affect Spanish policy. In any case, the absence of strong peace sentiment in Spain distinctly limited the impact of individual Spaniards' antiwar appeals. Similarly, when the Holy See offered mediation, it came to President McKinley through Archbishop John Ireland, not Cardinal Gibbons, and the European powers advanced awkward and hesitant mediation proposals but not because of any urgent entreaties from the International Peace Bureau. The bureau in Berne encouraged its members in the United States to work for a pacific solution and forwarded an appeal by the noted Austrian pacifist, Baroness Bertha von Suttner, to President McKinley and the Queen Regent of Spain for outside mediation of the dispute. Those initiatives were too sporadic, however, to have any influence on Spanish-American relations. Moreover, the Berne Bureau had insufficient funds to run a well-oiled propaganda machine for promoting and coordinating the mediation proposals of the European nations.[52]

Meanwhile, Love undertook a personal antiwar campaign. When George Edmunds, who had recently had an interview with President McKinley, told Love that only a barrage of letters to congressmen could sustain the chief executive's anti-interventionist efforts, he wrote several Senators and Congressmen and dispatched 150 written appeals to union colleagues and other friends of peace urging them to do likewise. He also wired John W. Hoyt, former governor of Wyoming and a union representative in Washington, advocating two pacific alternatives: arbitration or a special commission dispatched to Cuba and Madrid to delay war declarations until the parties could try peaceful methods. Although a union meeting appointed a delegation to take these proposals to the White House, McKinley apparently failed to receive it.[53]

Alfred Love's most persistent efforts for averting war, however, rested with Stewart L. Woodford, the American minister in Madrid. Woodford

had successfully sponsored the Universal Peace Union's arbitration resolution in the House of Representatives in 1874. Consequently, when
Woodford went to Spain, Love hoped that the minister would be receptive to his peace appeals. In the last two months before the outbreak of
war, Love wrote him on several occasions, and each time Woodford replied promptly and courteously and encouraged his peace efforts.[54] In a
letter of late March, Woodford reassured Love: "I have done, am doing
and shall, to the last, try to do all that I can to keep peace between Spain
and the United States, with justice to Cuba and with protection to American interests." While Woodford's hopes for peace were sincere, his qualifications about "justice" and "American interests" barely concealed the irreconcilable differences between the American and Spanish governments.[55]

Love's appeals to Woodford did not influence the latter's diplomatic
efforts, but in the final crisis both suggested nearly all the policies McKinley considered to avert war. A striking illustration of their similar viewpoints existed on a military armistice in Cuba. Love cabled Woodford on
April 9: "Urge Queen concede unconditional armistice." But Woodford,
who had already been working for this Spanish concession, learned only
hours before the arrival of Love's message that the Sagasta ministry had
granted a temporary cease-fire. The American minister revealed his ela-
tion when he wrote back to Love that this Spanish action "may be the
beginning of permanent peace in Cuba."[56] Yet Woodford's joy was premature, for McKinley decided that time had run out. Believing that only
an immediate Spanish guarantee of full Cuban independence could prevent American intervention, McKinley yielded to the war hawks in his
message to Congress on April 11.

Like other firm friends of peace, Love deemphasized the ultimatum to
Spain in the President's message and eagerly grasped at its few conciliatory remarks; unlike them, he refused to concede defeat when the prospect of hostilities appeared inevitable. He continued to implore cabinet
officials and congressmen to support the President's search for peace. He
also cooperated with peace loving Philadelphians in planning an antiwar
mass meeting and abandoned the effort only after Edmunds and Hoyt
independently reported that their recent interviews with the President and
members of Congress had convinced them that it was too late to stop the
unmistakable drift toward war.[57]

Though discouraged, Love initiated three final efforts to prevent war.
First, he tried to persuade Luis Polo de Bernabe, De Lôme's replacement
in Washington, to grant full independence to Cuba, the American sine
qua non for avoiding hostilities. But Polo's reply to Love on April 13
reaffirmed what he had told officials in the McKinley administration three
days earlier. Spanish concessions, he wrote, had "reached the limit of
what a nation can give without detriment to her honor and self-respect,"

and he indicated that his government was unwilling at that moment to make the one final concession of full independence which might have appeased the jingoes in Congress.[58]

Love made his second last plea on April 19, the eve of the final vote on the congressional joint resolution authorizing American military intervention in Cuba. Hearing rumors of further mediation overtures by the European powers, he wrote Sir Julian Pauncefote, doyen of the diplomatic corps in Washington, urging him to request his government to offer mediation. He was too late. The reply from the British Embassy two days later intimated that mediation would have no hope of success. Realizing that the United States was determined to go to war, the British government showed less enthusiasm than the other European powers for exerting strong moral pressure on the United States to draw back from the brink. In a sense, the arbitrationists' campaign had worked too well. Having promoted Anglo-American friendship over the previous decade, they now found that Great Britain was averse to any policy that might contribute to ill feeling between the two governments. The irony of Britain's acquiescence in an American war of conquest in 1898, just as it had supported the peaceful policy of the Olney-Pauncefote treaty a year earlier, was not lost to many American peace workers.[59]

Finally, on April 21, the day after McKinley signed the congressional declaration authorizing military intervention in Cuba but before war had been formally declared or hostilities had actually commenced, Love sent a letter to the queen regent of Spain begging her to abandon Cuba. The letter, which in the face of Spain's determination to fight would have failed in its purpose anyway, was intercepted by postal authorities in New York and three weeks later returned unopened with the words: "Dispatch to Spain or colonies prohibited on account of war." Although the course of hostilities indicated that the defeat of Spain was virtually certain, on May 17 Love sent the letter to Hoyt, asking him to obtain permission from the State Department to forward the letter to Spain. Unwilling to flout the government's war effort, Love still hoped that if his appeal could reach the queen, it might persuade her to abandon a lost cause and perhaps hasten the end of the conflict. The State Department allowed the union to send the letter to the International Peace Bureau at Berne where it was relayed to Madrid, but this effort, like all the union's previous ones, failed to alter the course of events.[60]

The total frustration of the peace proposals of Love and his coworkers in the Universal Peace Union would have had all the makings of an opera bouffe, if the onset of hostilities did not have its tragic aspects. As it was, their inability to influence events and the timidity of the other peace societies indicated that the American peace movement had much work to perform if it was to have any influence in averting future wars.

[4]

Reaction:
War and Imperialism

THE SPANISH-AMERICAN WAR proved an unpleasant, if happily brief, experience for pacific-minded Americans. With the surge of the martial spirit, further criticism of the administrations' foreign policies was widely denounced as treasonous. Pacifists' fears of reprisals and their realization of their status as a tiny minority convinced them that antiwar protests would serve no practical purpose.[1] Charles Dole, speaking for many Boston peace advocates, later wrote, "We surmised that it was useless to say any more" once hostilities commenced.[2]

Albert Smiley remained silent on the war for somewhat different reasons. Because his primary concern was harmony at the Mohonk Conferences, he advised the conferees to limit their discussions to the subject of international arbitration, which always had been the primary purpose of the conferences. Smiley never publicly expressed strong approval or disapproval of the war or, for that matter, of the imperialistic aftermath, but these events apparently did not make him more than mildly uncomfortable. In any event, since he was particularly interested in influencing the McKinley administration on international arbitration, he requested that "nothing would be said that would in any way convey to the outside world an impression of disloyalty to the government."[3] Nor did he attempt to restrain those participants who lauded certain "benefits" of the war, such as the hastening of the reconciliation between North and South in the United States and further nourishment of Anglo-American understanding. Several speakers in fact advanced grandiose visions of an Anglo-Saxon global mastery.[4]

Some Mohonk participants, however, refused to refrain from criticism of the war and its imperialistic consequences. Even the temperate George Edmunds complained at the 1899 Conference that it was impossible to separate the nation's past decisions for war and imperialism and its future intentions in the area of international arbitration. When George Mercer finally criticised Lyman Abbott and other defenders of the war, Smiley rejoined sharply, "this is an arbitration conference and not a peace conference."[5] Smiley's narrow focus on arbitration was well calculated to discourage the attendance of antiwar and anti-imperialist people, some of whom thereafter bypassed his Mohonk Conferences. In view of the small number of zealous peace advocates, those secessions meant that more conservative and nationalistic Americans would dominate the conferences. It is not known whether more pacific-minded absentees withdrew voluntarily, but Smiley achieved the same result by deciding the topics and speakers in advance, and, as a last resort, denying invitations to unreformed antiwar people.[6]

Even during the hostilities, however, a few peace advocates, especially Garrison, Love, and Trueblood, publicly espoused conscientious objection.[7] Because of Trueblood's and Garrison's uncompromising antiwar statements, ultrapatriotic Americans sent them vituperative letters accusing them of disloyalty. They escaped widespread public abuse partly because they confined their remarks to sympathetic journals, many of whose readers gave lukewarm support at best to the American war effort.

Though Alfred Love continued to defend his opposition to the war, he became the target of sensational journalism. Concerning an innocent flag exhibition in the offices of the Universal Peace Union, the *Philadelphia Evening Bulletin's* reporter wrote that the Spanish flag was "flaunted defiantly" until the objections of visitors prompted the secretary to take it down. He added a rumor that was probably untrue but appealed to ultrapatriotic minds: "It is said it was unceremoniously thrown upon the floor and trampled upon by several men who were in the sales-room at the time." More damaging, however, was the newspaper's account of Love's letter to the queen regent that omitted Love's entreaties for full independence for Cuba and his professions of loyalty to his nation and gave the false impression that Love had sent her a "letter of sympathy."[8] Following publication of that newspaper story, threats on Love's life were made, and a mob numbering several hundred persons in nearby Chester, Pennsylvania, burned him in effigy, after which the "corpse" was riddled with bullets and dragged through the streets while the marchers sang patriotic songs and yelled, "Down with Love and his brand of traitors."[9] As a final insult, the city of Philadelphia ordered the Universal Peace Union immediately to evacuate its offices in Independence Hall which it had leased to the peace group rent-free in 1895, and the union members managed with great difficulty to relocate elsewhere.[10]

The experience of the Universal Peace Union in the early months of the war furnishes additional evidence that the press, so often irresponsible in its reporting before the war, continued to provide the sensational news that a large segment of the American public apparently wanted. Such news stories undoubtedly helped to sustain the war fever during the course of hostilities and helped to drown out what little dissent against the administration's war policy still existed.

With the annexation of Hawaii during the war, and, after the ratification of the treaty formally ending the war, the Spanish cession of Puerto Rico, Guam, and the Philippines, it was clear that the United States had become an imperial power. Given the new fact of insular imperialism, the demands became irresistible for an even larger, modernized American navy to defend these possessions from possible aggressive actions of foreign powers.

The most loyal peace advocates reacted negatively to America's emergence as a great power. Wedded to arbitration and antimilitarism they responded adversely to the harsh realities of world politics facing the United States after 1898. Their opposition to the war with Spain and their denunciations of imperialism and navalism that followed seemed to suggest a profound pessimism toward the dominant thrust of world politics at the turn of the century. Nor were they a lonely minority in this pessimism for others found it difficult to adjust to the far-reaching implications of America's new position in international affairs. Some of these individuals reacted so strongly to the Spanish-American War, imperialism, and navalism that they began to ponder seriously the problem of war and readily cooperated with the peace forces. Their activity gave new life and strength to the American peace movement.

Of the individuals who began earnest involvement in the movement largely because of the war and imperialistic experiences, three of the most dedicated were David Starr Jordan, president of Stanford University; and two Boston reformers, Edwin D. Mead and Lucia True Ames. The war itself was not such a shock to these three since they recognized that the United States could not indefinitely tolerate Spanish inhumanities in Cuba, but they were alarmed by the jingoistic pressures that resulted in President McKinley's capitulation to the prowar camp. They were particularly disturbed by the growing indications that a peaceful settlement of the issues with Spain over Cuba was possible and in fact on the verge of success when McKinley broke off negotiations and Congress overwhelmingly approved the joint resolution for American military intervention.

Edwin Mead's distaste for the Spanish-American War acted as a catalyst for his already emerging pacifist sympathies.[11] It will be recalled that he had presented the American Peace Society's resolution on behalf of Anglo-American arbitration to President Cleveland in 1888, had participated in a few arbitration conferences, and had assisted the Twentieth Century Club and the Boston Municipal League in opposing American military intervention in the Venezuelan and Cuban crises. Born and raised in New Hampshire, Mead developed literary and scholarly interests and as a young man moved to Boston. He was fascinated by the intellectual heritage of his native New England. He admired both the early Puritan settlers for their fervent quest for truth and fearless dedication to moral principle and their nineteenth-century descendents, the Transcendentalists. His graduate training in England and Germany— the latter further nourished his philosophical idealism—intensified his interest in inspirational statesmen in history, and his literary works unabashedly glorified Ralph Waldo Emerson, Thomas Carlyle, Martin Luther, and the American Puritans.[12] He recalled that his interest in peace first began to crystallize when he was challenged to a friendly debate on international arbitration while studying at Cambridge in 1875. Defending the principle, Mead won that oratorical contest and in succeeding years became a strong admirer of Gladstone's idealistic internationalism. After assuming the editorship of *New England Magazine* in 1889 from his friend Edward Everett Hale, he had written editorials attacking the growing jingoism in the nation. He had also written short studies of previous prophets of international organization, Dante, Henry of Navarre, William Penn, and Immanuel Kant. All these outpourings revealed Mead's contempt for ultranationalist sympathies. His preoccupation with peace prophets also foreshadowed his life-long search for a new Luther, Emerson, or Gladstone, who would rejuvenate mankind's spiritual strivings and direct them toward the creation of a world unscarred by war.[13]

Nevertheless, until the outbreak of the Spanish-American War, Mead's name rarely appeared in peace journals, and his writings on international peace were more scholarly exercises than calls to organized peace efforts. Fully devoted to his literary and journalistic interests and various civic reform causes in Boston, he even allowed his membership in the American Peace Society to lapse in the 1890s and did not rejoin until the end of that decade. With so many commitments to domestic reform groups, it is not surprising that Mead found little time for active peace work.[14]

While Mead was never an absolute pacifist, he nevertheless hated war and antiwar equivocators. "If there is any one whom he hates, so far as his kindly nature lets him hate anyone," his wife later said, "it is a trimmer."[15] Yet just as he had already cooperated with people of different beliefs in various reform groups on the municipal level, he recognized that if work for peace was ever to be successful, it would require his active cooperation with more timid, nonpacifist friends of peace and systematic attempts to organize them behind movements for world amity. One of his late colleagues in the peace movement aptly depicted Mead's blend of personal pacifism and cooperative internationalism when he labeled him "a constructive radical."[16]

No individual had more influence on Edwin Mead's interest in world peace than Lucia True Ames, Boston school teacher and social reformer, whom he married in September, 1898. Like her future husband, Lucia Ames was born in New Hampshire and was a child of the New England antislavery tradition. She heard and read much in her youth about Transcendentalists and abolitionists, and her writings contained numerous favorable comments about them. For several years she gave lectures to adult classes in Boston on nineteenth-century intellectual history. By the age of forty she had published three books on literary and educational topics, including a semi-autobiographical story, *Memoirs of a Millionaire* (1889), apparently modeled after Edward Bellamy's utopian novel, *Looking Backward, 2000–1887*. She also championed municipal reform and wrote essays depicting the growing ugliness and poverty in Boston, advocating urban renewal projects, and popularizing the nascent settlement-house movement. In addition, her interest in the franchise for women soon resulted in her election to the presidency of the Massachusetts Woman's Suffrage Association.[17]

Despite her reformist zeal Lucia Ames showed no interest in the peace movement until she accompanied her future husband to the 1897 Lake Mohonk Conference. Her address to this gathering outlined the philosophical foundations of her approach to peace. In view of her intellectual heritage, it is not surprising that a transcendental humanism formed the core of her peace ideas. "We are not, first of all, Americans," she emphasized; "we are, first of all, human beings; we are, first of all, God's children, and we have identical interests with all God's children all over the face of the earth."[18] Her application of transcendentalism to international affairs naively downgraded national self-interest in international relations, but she truly reflected the other leading peace workers' cardinal assumption that nations like individuals could be selfless in their dealings with their neighbors.

Whatever the limitations of her philosophy, she believed that she was realistic and would later talk of her participation in the "practical" peace movement. She readily accepted the reality of the nation state system and in succeeding years fully cooperated with political internationalists who wanted to erect permanent international institutions for deterrence of

war. In some ways she was less effusive, emotional, and backward looking than her husband. Despite her idealism she harbored few romantic
illusions about human nature. In 1897 she remarked that "the natural
child is a natural bigot,"[19] and her later writings indicated her awareness
of the selfish and irrational motives of large segments of society. As an
educator she hoped that school teachers would instill a sense of idealistic
internationalism in the minds of American youth. She recognized, however, that teachers lacking her faith in international friendship could reinforce perverse notions of nationalism and patriotism. The most learned
could turn out to be the most wicked. As she said in 1902, "The men
who are most responsible for the Boer war are university graduates."[20]

If her awareness of human depravity discouraged her at times, her faith
in the organic unity of mankind sustained her hopes for a more harmonious world order. She continued to believe that her own writings as well
as persistent education would help people to perceive this unity. In
addition, her writings expressed an unquestioned faith in moral progress, which helped to convince her that human nature was inexorably
improving.

Lucia Ames was no beauty and in fact was forty-two when she married
Edwin Mead. Their marriage signified not only an emotional union and
common intellectual interests, but also their mutual pledge to devote the
rest of their lives together as activists in the quest for world peace. The
Meads immediately involved themselves in the anti-imperialist movement
against America's acquisition of the Philippines and, after that agitation
subsided, in the American peace movement. Her husband even resigned
his editorship in 1901 so that he could join his wife in full-time commitment to peace work. They quickly became two of the most prolific writers
and most forceful and inspirational speakers in the peace movement.

Like the Meads, David Starr Jordan had given attention to the issues
of war and peace prior to 1898, but as president of Stanford he lived far
away from the major peace organizations on the eastern seaboard. He
became a good friend of May Wright Sewall during his service as president of Indiana University from 1885 to 1891 and surely knew about her
peace work.[21] His first direct contact with this problem of international
peace did not come until 1896 when President Cleveland, hearing of his
extensive research on marine life, appointed him to serve as an American
delegate on a joint commission with Great Britain to investigate the fur
seal problem in the Bering Sea. The experience started Jordan thinking
seriously about international arbitration and made him an enthusiastic
advocate of joint commissions and arbitration treaties for the pacific
settlement of international disputes. The signing of the Olney-Pauncefote
treaty, which Jordan endorsed, also evidenced that interest.[22] Following

the last session of the British-American Commission, Jordan made "the first of . . . many addresses . . . in behalf of arbitration, a society of nations, and the abolition of military force as an argument in economics or politics."[23] The eleventh-hour breakdown in diplomatic negotiations preceding the Spanish-American War only deepened his resolve to take a more active role in the peace movement.

Those experiences quickened Jordan's knowledge of international problems and his awareness of the possibilities of international cooperation, but two elements deeply rooted in his background underlay this growing interest in peace. The first was the death of his older brother, whom he idolized, while fighting for the Union cause during the Civil War; thereafter Jordan began to question whether the potential and actual gains of that war—and by extension all wars—were worth the human costs. The second was his uncompromising sense of moral rectitude, which he had absorbed from his Puritanical parents, his favorable adolescent memories of abolitionists and radical Republicans in his native upstate New York, and his reading of Transcendentalists. Of all the authors who influenced him while a student at Cornell, for example, he "put Thoreau first." Jordan of course never adopted Thoreau's philosophical anarchism and was never an absolute pacifist. He in fact demonstrated considerable skills both as a prolific scholar and as a practical-minded (if sometimes erratic) college administrator, but he continued to admire Thoreau's commitment to personal freedom and ethical principle.[24] That intellectual heritage motivated Jordan's sense of duty to protest immoral and unjust actions in international affairs and to search for pacific alternatives. Because warfare involved regimentation and the use of brute force, it contradicted those fundamental principles and was rarely justifiable. During the Spanish-American War he confirmed those beliefs. "War is killing, brutal, barbarous killing and its direct effects are mostly evil," he wrote.[25]

As the United States moved toward war in 1898, Jordan was at first willing to admit the possibility of justice in America's desire to free the Cubans from their Spanish yoke, but in succeeding years he regretted his acceptance of the war and came to believe that the yellow press, the Cuban Junta, and certain capitalists who foresaw investment opportunities on the island had deliberately inflamed public opinion and thereby foisted war upon the nation.[26] Jordan received first-hand confirmation of his belief that the Spanish-American War was a repressible conflict from Minister Woodford who shortly after his return from Spain in May 1898 candidly discussed with him the diplomacy leading to hostilities. Seventeen years later Jordan recalled that the ex-minister was "extremely distressed and humiliated" because he believed his delicate negotiations had verged on success only to be undercut by the domestic pressures that precipitated McKinley's surrender to the jingoes. Woodford's words undoubtedly helped Jordan believe that the war was a terrible aberration in the American experience.[27]

In a larger sense, the Spanish-American War was only a prelude to a more extensive problem for the American Republic, for once Admiral Dewey's fleet had demolished the Spanish squadron in Manila Bay the prospect immediately loomed of American acquisition of the Philippines. In fact, Dewey's exploits were just as important as the onset of the war in pushing pacific-minded individuals more deeply into active cooperation with the peace forces. Only two days after the battle of Manila Bay, Jordan discarded his prepared speech on "Anglophobia" to a women's meeting and instead lectured on the baneful consequences of imperialism.[28] His address was only a minor event in the peace movement, but to Jordan it "marked a turning point in my life." As he elaborated these remarks in succeeding weeks, he became a prominent spokesman of the anti-imperialist viewpoint.[29]

Jordan's metamorphosis brought him into closer contact with other peace advocates, who, with the few exceptions noted earlier, were virtually unanimous in their opposition to imperialism. Edward Atkinson was one of the founders of the Anti-Imperialist League in the autumn of 1898, which by early 1899 had grown to include Jordan, Andrew Carnegie, George Mercer, Herbert Welsh, George Edmunds, and John Sherman among its fifty-two vice-presidents. Ernest Crosby headed the New York branch of the League, and Edwin D. Mead, Edwin Ginn, William Lloyd Garrison, Jr., and the Reverends Charles Dole and A. A. Berle served as officers of the New England branch. Even those self-professed peace workers who did not hold positions of leadership in the anti-imperialist movement endorsed the league's program and occasionally appeared on the same platform with its leaders. In addition, some others who had previously shown no institutional affiliation with the American peace movement—social reformer Jane Addams; Congregationalist clerics Charles E. Jefferson and Herbert S. Bigelow; the Unitarian minister and editor of the liberal weekly *Unity,* Jenkin Lloyd Jones; Texas congressman James L. Slayden; and journalist-author Raymond L. Bridgman—joined the anti-imperialist movement and, after that agitation subsided, became participants in the peace movement.[30]

As might be expected in such a large group, the intensity of these individuals' commitment to anti-imperialism markedly varied. The public stances of Edmunds, Sherman, Ginn, and Capen, for instance, were either so perfunctory or self-contradictory as to neutralize their moral qualms about American territorial expansion. The political loyalties of Edmunds and Sherman, both life-long Republicans, constrained the vehemence of their outspoken criticism of the McKinley administration throughout the debate. Ginn and Capen signed petitions to Congress opposing the annexation of the Philippines but backed off from full support of the anti-imperialists.[31] Though strongly opposed to imperialism in principle, Ginn worried that the United States' renunciation of its conquests in the Spanish war might alienate Great Britain, whose leaders had welcomed America's entrance into the imperial game and whose friendship and close cooperation he valued for the promotion of permanent international institutions for the peaceful settlement of disputes.[32]

Samuel Capen's election in early 1899 to the presidency of the American Board of Commissioners for Foreign Missions, the largest Protestant missionary group, severely circumscribed his mildly anti-imperialist and pacifistic instincts. Not only did many members of the American Board openly advocate United States' retention of the Philippines, but the Boxers' assault on American missionaries and missions in 1900 cast a dark cloud over the future of the entire Christian commitment. Capen, never questioning his ideal of a Christianized world, refused to turn back: "We hear discussion about taking down the flag after it has been unfurled, something which we have done in the past and doubtless will do again, but we must never consent to taking down the cross." It is difficult to believe that Capen could conceive of a total missionary effort in China without desiring American or European nations' military protection as a last resort against future anti-Western outbreaks, and it is doubtful whether he opposed the Western nations' collective suppression of the Boxer revolt. Nevertheless, Capen devoutly believed in his vision of *pax Christiana* and, fearing that the bellicose implications of his statement might be misconstrued, he reaffirmed his commitment to peace. "Let no one suppose that there is anything in this statement which hints at jingoism, so-called," he declared.[33]

Despite such deviations in actual behavior, the ideological outlook of the friends of peace and those anti-imperialists not associated with the peace cause was in most respects similar. Although the individuals in the two groups were not all of one mind on the questions of Hawaii and Puerto Rico, their rhetoric on the issue of the Philippines shows a certain consensus.

A key word for understanding the position of peace advocates, as well as anti-imperialists, in the debate over the future disposition of the Philippines is "tradition." Whatever arguments they advanced against imperialism, they invariably invoked that word or its equivalent to express their satisfaction with America's relatively stable and secure position in world affairs before 1898 and their profound dissatisfaction with the administration's foreign policies between 1898 and 1900, which seemed to them to repudiate the basic principles on which the Republic had been founded and had accepted for more than a century. They believed American imperial expansion obviously signified a drastic departure from America's traditional isolationism. Again and again they repeated the solemn admonition of George Washington's Farewell Address against permanent entangling alliances or other foreign commitments far away from the Western Hemisphere, and they believed that the planting of the American flag in the Philippines would repudiate that principle.[34]

The peace advocates' premonitions were not entirely unfounded. Since Japan and the territorial possessions of several European powers strategically surrounded the Philippines, it was inconceivable that the United States could govern the islands without becoming embroiled in East Asian problems. If the United States decided to retain the Philippines, it could no longer ignore the diplomatic intrigue, suspicion, and the recurring dangers, rumors, and threats of war that pervaded the area. As Carnegie warned, "The Far East is a mine of dynamite, always liable to explode."[35] Since the United States did not have sufficient military strength to resist aggression of another major power or combination of powers in the area, the decision to remain in the Philippines would require the building of a large navy and the expansion of the army or the reliance on the support of a friendly Great Britain in maintaining American influence. Even with a formal or informal rapprochement with Britain, however, it was probable that the United States would have to increase substantially its military establishment to neutralize the military strength of the other powers in the area.

Pacific-minded individuals disliked those options. They immediately rejected increases in the army and navy as antithetic to their antimilitary prejudices, and they were also repelled by the idea of a formal Anglo-American alliance. While they admired the British tradition of liberty and British achievements in literature, commerce, and industry, they had little sympathy with British imperialism and no desire to play Britain's game in world politics. Carnegie, Mead, Jordan, Atkinson, and Trueblood wrote extensively on England between 1898 and 1900, but they carefully distinguished between its "false" imperialistic tradition of Benjamin Disraeli, Joseph Chamberlain, and Cecil Rhodes and the "true" England of Richard Cobden, John Bright, John Morley, and William Gladstone, all anti-imperialist Liberals.[36]

Similarly, those pacific-minded Americans desired to preserve a relatively compact, continental America with a minimum of binding foreign commitments. Since Britain was experiencing increasing difficulties in extending its colonial possessions in China and Africa, while simultaneously defending its vast holdings, they believed that British leaders would use any Anglo-American alliance covering Far Eastern matters to their own selfish advantage or even draw the United States into any Far Eastern war. At the same time, however, the United States would run the risk of being deserted by its ally whenever it needed diplomatic or military support in the area. American peace advocates minimized the possibility of carefully defining the mutual obligations of any agreement between the two powers. Rather, they assumed that Britain was only slightly less perfidious than the other colonial powers and, therefore, a poor risk for the future security of America's territories in the western Pacific.[73]

When those imperial critics did not recall the memory of George Washington and the self-contained Republic, they still looked to the past for their arguments. They upheld, for example, the free trade theories of Cobden, Bright, and the Manchester School which had influenced American economic thought in the mid-nineteenth century. Those British theorists had opposed colonialism in part because they thought it was economically unsound and ultimately ruinous to the financial health of the homeland. American friends of peace frequently argued that colonial expansion would erode the age-old laissez-faire liberalism, notably the "natural" law of free trade, which in their view had stimulated business initiative, promoted commerce, and raised the level of material plenty for the American people.[38] If the United States annexed the Philippines, they predicted ominously, the creation of a colonial bureaucracy and increases in administrative expenses of the federal government would inevitably follow, to say nothing of the spiraling costs of an enlarged army and navy. In politics the tendency, if not the immediate result, would be a powerful executive branch which would upset the constitutional checks and balances and ultimately destroy democracy.[39] Concerning colonial administration, for example, Jordan postulated a simplified precursor of Parkinson's Law: "The more it had to do, the more effective such a colonial bureau would become. Every governmental department tends to aggrandize itself. Colonies would demand more colonies."[40] Economically, annexation would gradually lead to the enslavement of the masses in taxes and debt. They rejected out of hand the contention of territorial expansionists that American financial and commercial interests would exploit the economic potential of the Philippines and bring increased trade and other economic rewards that would more than compensate for the administrative expenses of the government. As for opportunities for private investment, Edwin Mead wrote, "No man of common sense can believe that a hundred million dollars put into the Philippines would yield half the returns of the same millions put into Oregon and Texas."[41]

Most frequently, however, the annexationists cited the old imperial maxim that trade followed the flag, and therefore the United States should remain in the Philippines not only for the trade of those islands but for their value as stepping stones to larger commercial opportunities in the Orient. Several peace participants attempted to disprove that "fallacy." Carnegie, for example, claimed that Canada bought its Union Jacks in New York rather than from the mother country because they were cheaper in the former.[42]

Such anti-expansionist remarks might seem to suggest that those pacific-minded individuals were rigidly opposed to any extension of American political or economic influence outside the Western Hemisphere. They were, however, far from inflexible isolationists. Just as the term "little Englanders" is not entirely adequate in depicting the followers of Gladstone's foreign policies in Great Britain, so is the term "little Americans" inappropriate for the friends of peace during the debate over imperialism.[43] To be sure, they wanted to preserve America's innocence and virtue by remaining aloof from the "corruptions" of European power politics. However, those Americans' earlier advocacy of international cooperation in general and arbitration treaties in particular qualifies the isolationist label. Nor did they protest commercial expansion as long as it was undertaken honestly and peaceably. The free trade theories of the Manchester School, after all, were not only a negative economic argument against imperialism but also an affirmative appeal for the free flow of goods in world commerce. Just as important to these participants in the peace cause were the political implications of free trade, for they believed that the unfettered international exchange of goods would stimulate the growth of commerce, and this growth, by multiplying contacts between nations and creating mutual, dependent interests, would "weave the web of concord among nations."

Several friends of peace were even willing to modify the doctrinaire aspects of free trade to adjust to the changing commercial and geopolitical realities stemming from America's recent involvements in the Caribbean and Pacific. Edwin Mead conceded that "[t]he proper limits of 'expansion' for any nation are hard to define; the sagacious practical statesmanship of each time has got to determine them for that time as best it can," and he endorsed the notion that "this republic will in due time be coextensive with North America."[44] All peace advocates had opposed American rule over the Hawaiian islands and saw no particular economic benefits to annexation; but because they recognized their potential strategic value for the defense of the West Coast, they rather easily acquiesced in the decision of Congress to annex them. Only a few of the more radical peace workers denounced the annexation for its denial of self-government and suffrage rights, and even their opposition was subdued.[45] Benjamin Trueblood voiced suspicions of the American military government's purpose in Cuba, but he gradually accepted the administration's promises of "independence" at face value and by December 1900 rationalized that its Cuban policy was undertaken "peacefully and with the confidence and affection of the [Cuban] people."[46]

A few went even further. Carnegie had no objection to the retention of Puerto Rico and predicted that the Cuban sugar interests would control the new government there and desire annexation to the United States. In the early stages of the debate, he, Jordan, Straus, and Mrs. Lockwood separately indicated their willingness to accept the retention of a coaling station in the Philippines for the benefit of American business and shipping interests in the Far East.[47] Though Jordan opposed outright annexation of Cuba and Puerto Rico, he believed that the peoples of these tropical areas were unfit for self-government and would require frequent intervention by the United States to assure stable governments and prevent possible European violations of the Monroe Doctrine. A firm adherent of the "open door" concept, he also praised the "peaceful conquest of Mexico" by American capitalists. Such economic penetration can be labeled the imperialism of free trade, anti-colonial imperialism, neocolonialism, open door imperialism, or informal empire, but Jordan succinctly called it "permeation."[48]

Of all the anti-imperialists, Atkinson was the most vigorous proponent of an American informal empire. An open door ideologue, he had supported the Olney-Pauncefote arbitration treaty in part because he believed the accord would allow the two nations to divert much more of their human energies and financial resources from war preparations into agricultural and industrial development and then to penetrate foreign markets for the disposal of surplus goods. Though he did not believe that the annexation of territory in Asia and Africa was necessary for the profitable sale of American exports, he viewed the exploitation of foreign markets in those areas as crucial to the nation's economic future. On the eve of war with Spain he had expounded, "Every port in China and everywhere else shall be kept open, on equal terms, to the commerce of all nations."[49] In the following months he hoped that the United States would avoid the annexation of Hawaii and the Philippines, but as a concession to America's obvious predominance in the Caribbean he privately admitted that American protection or annexation of Cuba and Puerto Rico would give the United States "the command of the Gulf of Mexico and the coast of South America." Moreover, as an alternative plan for the Philippines, he proposed the neutralization of the islands by agreement among the great powers, a scheme whereby the archipelago would be demilitarized and "all nations might buy coaling stations, land commodities and enjoy commerce under the same system of collecting the revenue, called the open door."[50]

Far from suggesting isolationism, those views point to expansionism. Indeed, they seem to lend support to the interpretative framework of certain recent historians who have emphasized that the so-called Great Debate over imperialism between 1898 and 1900 was fought out not between two diametrically polar groups of expansionists and anti-expansionists, since both groups assumed America's exceptional values and institutions and justified some measure of commercial and territorial expansion, but between annexationists and anti-annexationists on the "narrow and limited" question of the future status of the Philippine archipelago.[51] Because these friends of the peace cause acquiesced in the annexation of Hawaii, approved the retention of coaling stations, and either urged or tolerated American dominance of the Caribbean, they seemed much more concerned with the future strategic and economic position of the United States than with the aspirations of the native inhabitants of those areas. Certainly their willingness to compromise the abstract political principle of the right of self-government for those peoples demonstrated that they were neither moral absolutists nor democratic ideologues. In fact, the infectious character of the imperialist mania throughout the late nineteenth-century Western world, together with the increasing awareness of America's growing export requirements, had strongly tempted if not altogether seduced these anti-imperialists. That they only sporadically protested later American military interventions in the Caribbean area carried out by the Roosevelt, Taft, and Wilson administrations also indicates the fragility of the anti-imperialist viewpoint.[52]

Moreover, Slayden, Carnegie and Jordan further confused the moral issue because they shared the expansionists' pseudo-Darwinian argument that these alien peoples were "inferior." They accepted the imperialists' paternalistic and patronizing attitude toward the Caribbean peoples and differed only in their conclusions over the probable consequences of American rule over brown-skinned Filipinos. Whereas fervent expansionists like Albert Beveridge or Lyman Abbott argued that the annexation of the Philippines provided a God-given opportunity to regenerate and civilize the Filipino natives, some supporters of the peace movement claimed that American rule of these natives would inevitably result in the mental, moral, and physical degeneration of both rulers and ruled.[53] Such attitudes helped to blur differences between anti-annexationists and annexationists and weakened the force of the anti-annexationists' position among the uncommitted middle classes who followed the debate on the Philippines.

However, the debate over imperialism was no narrow disagreement over degrees of expansion. Emphasis on the consensual aspect of the debate tends to slight the chauvinistic nationalism, racial pride, worship of martial values, and synical disdain for "sentimental" liberalism and humanitarianism that typified the individuals most responsible for foisting imperialism on the nation. Jingo psychology was anathema to anti-imperialists. A deemphasis of the differences between imperialists and anti-imperialists simultaneously underestimates the ethical underpinnings of the anti-imperialists' protest. The more pacific-minded anti-imperialists in particular emphasized that the debate involved irreconcilable differences over political morality. Whether drawing upon the uncompromising moralism of the British anti-imperialist, Christian pacifist, or antislavery traditions, or some combination of the three, the thrust of their argument was clear: the rule of subject peoples without their consent was fundamentally wrong.

Not surprisingly, the Quaker peace advocates took the "high" pacifist position, and their petitions, editorials, and articles consistently emphasized that America's governance of unconsenting foreigners was un-Christian and should be abandoned.[54] Other American friends of the peace cause wrestled with the prospect of their government ruling unwilling peoples with varying degrees of uneasiness, but almost without exception came out in favor of self-determination. Edward Atkinson, perhaps aware of the inconsistency between his anticolonial position and his private acquiescence in American formal control over Cuba and Puerto Rico, never publicly advocated their takeover; and when he perceived the McKinley administration's growing appetite for overseas areas in late 1898, he came out firmly against the takeover of any territory. While that position was consistent with his preference for an informal over a formal empire, he most forcefully denounced the proposed annexations because they contradicted the fundamental principle of the consent of the governed.[55] Drawing on his abolitionist inheritance, he wrote President McKinley, "I venture to present my protest against any longer occupation of the Phillipine [sic] Islands, of Cuba and Porto Rico, or the use of any larger forces than are needed to enable the people of these islands to frame and form a method of government under which personal liberty and individual rights may be established, and to enter upon this undertaking." Forcible extension of American sovereignty thus amounted to "criminal aggression" and a "national crime."[56]

Just as important, when ardent imperialists began vigorously to advance trade-follows-the-flag rhetoric as an economic argument for America's retention of the Philippines, Atkinson jettisoned his emphasis on America's global export needs and began to cite recent trade figures demonstrating that less than one-hundredth of one percent of American exports went to the Philippines and only slightly more than three percent went to all the non-British areas of Africa and Oceania. Unlike annexationists, he assumed that American takeover of coaling stations or other land in the Philippines would not appreciably change the situation and in any case would not be worth the additional burdens and dangers. While the relative insignificance of Pacific and Asian trade for America's economic well-being increasingly impressed him, he also began to stress that the United States should harness its brains, manpower, and capital to the further exploitation of the nation's vast, untapped resources. He did not categorically repudiate his free trade views and continued to reason that domestic prosperity would depend on foreign trade; but he emphasized trade with the developed nations of Europe, which had the necessary purchasing power for absorbing ever increasing quantities of American goods, and with Europe's colonies, especially those of Great Britain, which already practiced the open door.[57]

Throughout the winter of 1898–1899 Atkinson was confused. On the one hand, he urged the great powers to cooperate in imposing peace and purchasing free ports in the Philippines without much regard for the inhabitants' aspirations; on the other hand, he defended the right of the Filipinos to decide their own destiny. As late as a year later Reverend Dole felt he had to remind Atkinson that it was "dangerous" for him to encourage businessmen to believe that free trade would automatically compel them to be "just, humane and Christian," when it might instead create easier opportunities for unscrupulous individuals to take advantage of the unregulated market for their own selfish purposes, or at least lead the average businessman to ignore the needs and aspirations of ordinary citizens. Dole in effect stated what should have been (but never was to Atkinson) an obvious truism: non-regulated international trade might help to create a peaceful atmosphere, but it could not ensure peace unless the concerned parties also had a peaceful disposition and really worked for it.[58]

The other participants in the peace movement emphasized the wishes of the native inhabitants. All but Carnegie regretted the annexation of Puerto Rico and Hawaii, and even Carnegie felt it necessary to rationalize their annexation in terms of the will of the inhabitants. He reasoned that the populations of both had "no aspirations" and concluded, despite some contrary evidence, that the natives overwhelmingly opposed independence because they docilely accepted American occupation. Along with Belva Lockwood, he even mistakenly claimed that the Hawaiian people had voted for annexation to the United States.[59] Carnegie would have done better to approve those annexations solely on strategic grounds

which had been the consistent thrust of his anti-imperialist ideas throughout the previous decade, but he apparently felt he had to justify them in
terms of the inhabitants' desires.

Moreover, no advocate of peace wobbled on the question of self-
determination for the eight million Filipinos. Conceivably, if the Filipinos
had meekly submitted to American occupation of their archipelago,
spokesmen in the peace movement would not have mounted a sustained
protest against the takeover, although their geopolitical, economic, constitutional, racial, and cultural arguments would have provided sufficient ammunition to carry on the opposition. Long before the Spanish-
American War a strong independence movement had existed in the
islands, and American friends of peace assumed that the islanders were
freedom-loving people who were asking for the same self-government
that had long been a cardinal principle of the American political system.
The growing prospect of the McKinley administration attempting to sup-
press these aspirations led them to perceive imperialism almost entirely
in human terms. They began to point out that because imperialism above
all else meant the subjugation of foreign peoples without their consent, it
was at heart immoral. Although the Filipinos' initiatives in establishing
their own government and then attempting to defend it against American
troops would strengthen the peace advocates' confidence in the universal
relevance of the self-determination principle, several friends of peace
stressed that ideal from the start of the debate. They were usually careful
to explain that their economic and other arguments, while not unimportant, were always secondary to the ethical issue. Imperialism, they agreed,
was wicked. With burning indignation they called it "the ambition of
power, mingled with the greed of gain," "the lust for gold," "tyranny,"
"the devil's gospel," "conscienceless brigandage," "stealing," "robbery."[60]

In the same way, much as the proponents of peace praised Cobden,
Bright, Morley, and Gladstone for their opposition to permanent foreign
entanglements and for their free trade theories, they revered them more
fundamentally as moralists who had preached the brotherhood of man
and the peaceful mission of Anglo-Saxon peoples. A few condemned the
British imperialists not so much for their expansionist beliefs, pernicious
though they were, but for the deviously clever rationalizations of their
colonial policies. More often than not, those policies resulted in the
"brutal" and "rapacious" subjugation and exploitation of foreign peoples.
Over the years, they claimed, the rationalizations of territorial expansionists had blurred the central moral question and had seriously eroded the
Christian humanistic strain in the British character. Small wonder, therefore, that they found the British heart "hardened" and the British blood
"poisoned" from many imperialistic adventures.[61]

American peace advocates often cited the example of British moral decline to predict that the American annexation of the Philippines would prove but the first fatal step on the way to a similar fall for their own nation. They feared that the American people now faced the possibility of prostituting the nation's past anticolonial record and might repudiate entirely the very foundation of its political morality. They believed that the Spanish-American War was one sign of that tendency, but the imperialistic aftermath seemed an even more drastic departure from America's cherished ethical heritage, a deplorable shift from self-denying morality to national self-glory, from idealism to vulgarity, from high principle to opportunism. The Filipinos reminded them of America's own struggle for independence. How could Americans uphold the principles of the Declaration of Independence, they asked, and yet prevent the Filipinos from attaining the same freedom for which the Seventy-Sixers had fought and died?[62] As Garrison wrote:

> What a spectacle for gods and men is that of the countrymen of Thomas Jefferson, Samuel Adams, and Joseph Warren attempting to impose a foreign yoke upon a people struggling for liberty and self-government! ... Let the exercise of your benevolence begin at home. Do justice to Indians in your own domain whom you have cheated, robbed and slaughtered through a century of dishonor. ... Before you can persuade us of your kindly purpose, wipe from your garments the freshly spilled blood of your own negro citizens in the South.[63]

Garrison's extension of those principles to non-whites was derived, of course, from his abolitionist inheritance, but many other peace spokesmen also drew upon their past involvement in Indian reform and antislavery movements. Often they referred to Abraham Lincoln's "half-slave" "half-free" speech, making the analogy that in the present age the nation could not long endure half-Republic and half-Empire.[64]

Slayden's, Jordan's, and Carnegie's notions of the Filipinos' racial inferiority, of course, contradicted that humanistic faith, and in the eyes of indiscriminating Americans their racial views may have appeared little different from the annexationists. Those three can be blamed for inconsistent and confused thinking, but unlike the blatant racism of many imperialists they used the words "inferior," "superior," "uncivilized," and "civilized" more in a cultural (or geographical) than in a biological sense. Jordan and Carnegie even showed an understanding of cultural relativism. It was the torrid heat, Jordan asserted, more than inferior blood that made the Filipinos "degenerate" and "sensuous," and he was willing to give them the benefit of the doubt in their struggle for independence against American troops. The leader of the Filipinos, Emilio Aguinaldo, might be a poor imitation of George Washington as a liberator, but he was comparable and was as fully "right" in wishing self-government for his people.[65] Further, Carnegie's earlier round-the-world travels, particularly his unfavorable observations of the deleterious effects of British control over India, softened his judgments about "inferior" peoples. He thought the Indian people preferred their own rulers, regardless of any resulting administrative efficiency, political corruption, and social tumult. He also assumed that the Filipinos should be the best judges of their political future: "If left to themselves they will make mistakes, but what nation does not? Riot and bloodshed may break out—in which nation are these absent?"[66]

All these peace leaders' arguments were common and widespread before the Filipino insurrection. Once hostilities commenced, however, the peace advocates' moral argument pushed all others more deeply into the background. From November 1898 to January 1899 participants in the peace movement vainly warned the McKinley administration of an imminent clash between American occupation troops and Aguinaldo's supporters.[67] The first skirmish resulting in the loss of a few American lives on February 5, 1899 was erroneously depicted in the American press as a deliberate Filipino assault on United States' forces. Because this news reached Washington only hours before the Senate vote on the treaty providing for the Spanish cession of the Philippines to the United States, it probably persuaded a few anti-annexationist Senators, angered at this affront to the nation's honor, to vote for the treaty which gained the necessary two-thirds approval by only one vote.[68]

After the Senate consented to the treaty, the peace proponents did not immediately abandon the fight against imperialism, which they hoped would become the major issue of the 1900 election. In preparation for that campaign, they unleashed verbal barrages against the McKinley administration for its determination to crush the Filipino insurgents. They recognized that McKinley had unpleasant alternatives in dealing with the rebellious Filipinos, especially after ratification of the treaty legalized American sovereignty over the islands, yet they still believed that regardless of his motives the consistent thrust of his Philippine policy revealed a remarkable insensitivity to the human costs. Andrew Carnegie charged that the administration's policy, if resolutely applied, would kill half the Filipinos in order to civilize the rest. Jordan, Dole, Mercer, and Jane Addams agreed that the outbreak of guerrilla warfare in the Philippines subordinated the expansionist issue to the question of peace.[69] "Good intentions lie at the bottom of the greatest crimes of history," Jordan stated bluntly, and concluded angrily:

Do what you will with the Philippines, if you do it in peace—but *stop this war*. It is our fault and ours alone that this war began. It is our crime that it continues.[70]

While pacific-minded Americans found the war of conquest against the Filipinos a degrading experience, the outbreak of hostilities between the British and Boer settlers in South Africa seemed to presage the final capitulation of Great Britain to the most selfish and brutal aspects of imperialism. They cited Britain's vigorous prosecution of the Boer War as a parallel to the logical consequences of America's conquest of the Philippines. If the United States and Great Britain, both of which they assumed to be in the vanguard of civilization, could trample on the rights and liberties of others, then the future course of world history would be very grim indeed.[71] Andrew Carnegie assailed the promoters of the Boer War for their sordid motives. "It was brought on by Great Britain in her desire for the gold fields and for race supremacy in South Africa," he exclaimed, and he specifically linked this "infamous and unjust" war to the American attack on "the poor Filipinos. These two attacks are a disgrace to both branches of our race."[72] Both of those imperialistic adventures confirmed their belief in the moral degeneracy of the times.

Despite the ideological similarities between the anti-imperialists and the peace workers, the two movements began to diverge somewhat even before the election of 1900. None of the fifty-two officers of the Anti-Imperialist League who had remained aloof from the peace and arbitration causes before 1898 expressed any active interest in them after 1900, although the peace movement grew rapidly afterwards and became respectable in the eyes of many more Americans. Nor did most of those identified with the campaigns for peace and arbitration before the Spanish-American War participate more than marginally in the anti-imperialist movement after the turn of the century, even though the Anti-Imperialist League continued to exist and agitate for the independence of the Philippines as late as 1920.

There were two reasons for the divergence of the two movements. First, those already firmly committed to the peace cause found other important foreign policy questions demanding their close attention. Even during the height of the debate over imperialism, they directed their attention to the Russian Czar Nicholas II's invitation to an international disarmament conference at The Hague in the early summer of 1899. The call for this conference, which also created interest in possible agreement on arbitration and mediation procedures and a world court, prompted several friends of peace to popularize the upcoming meeting and in a few cases even to journey to The Hague to lobby for their objectives. The proposed conference especially attracted the attention of the officers of leading peace societies who had most vigorously promoted disarmament or arbitration. Those people never turned their backs on the anti-imperialists and continued to cooperate with them in denouncing the war in the Philippines, but they left the major decisions of this campaign to the leaders of the Anti-Imperialist League.[73] The limited achievements of the First Hague Peace Conference merely intensified their interest in conference diplomacy in the first years of the twentieth century as the most promising antidote to international strife.

At the same time, the failure of the conference to reach any agreement on limitation of armaments, together with the large navy programs of the McKinley and Roosevelt administration, motivated their greater emphasis on the naval preparedness issue. With the passing of the danger of future extension of a formal colonial empire, antimilitarism rather than anti-imperialism concerned them, although they recognized the connection between the two. By contrast, some of the leading anti-imperialists had strong obligations to the Anti-Imperialist League and found time to direct their organizational and propaganda efforts only toward the single issue of independence of the Philippines. David G. Haskins, Jr., and Moorfield Storey, two of the League's most energetic officers after 1900, were members (though never officers) of the American Peace Society. They shared the society's interest in international questions but were so committed to their own anti-imperialist work that they took only passing interest in the activities of the peace group.[74]

A second, more inclusive reason for the divergence of the two movements was the differences in the temperaments of their leadership. A closer look at the anti-imperialist and peace leadership will provide a better understanding of that dichotomy.

A profile of the Anti-Imperialist League's fifty-two officers from 1898 to 1900 reveals a hodgepodge of political loyalties, but the overwhelming majority were profoundly conservative on economic and social questions, and they remained conservatives into the twentieth century. Whether nominal Republicans, independent Republicans (Mugwumps), true independents, or conservative Democrats, these anti-imperialist leaders viewed with distinct caution any attempts to use the state and national governments to legislate reforms in American social, political, and economic life. Mugwump anti-imperialists were crabbed and essentially backward looking individuals, and their opposition to imperialism represented a culmination of their rising disillusionment with the dominant political, economic, and social forces of late nineteenth-century urban-industrial America, which had undermined the ethical verities associated with the older, comparatively pre-industrial America of their youthful years. Specifically, the imperialist mania in the last years of the century became "the last straw" in the development of the Mugwumps' "bleak pessimism" over the wave of "new" immigration from eastern and southern Europe; the rise of gigantic corporations and dirty, depersonalized cities; clashes between labor and capital; growing signs of a popular or "vulgar" culture; and paternalistic government.[75] Depicting these Mugwump anti-imperialists as an aged, displaced, and a politically irrelevant elite appears more plausible because they failed to defeat both the peace treaty in the Senate and McKinley's reelection.[76]

Moreover, Mugwump anti-imperialists carried their cautious views into the area of international reform. These anti-imperialists were fundamentally pessimistic about the future course of their nation. If they all did not yearn for a full-scale retreat into its nineteenth-century isolationist shell, they espoused no missionary role for the United States as a promoter of world amity. In effect, they retained the same "skittish" attitude toward American foreign policy after 1900 that had first prompted their participation in the anti-imperialist movement.[77] While not altogether denying their "idealism and selflessness," one can agree that "the anti-imperialists failed to offer an alternative vision of the nation's future."[78]

That composite profile of conservative, disillusioned anti-imperialists also can be applied to certain peace leaders. Evidence exists linking their misgivings about trends in domestic society with their own opposition to imperialism. Among the American Peace Society's officers, for example, Samuel Capen and Robert Treat Paine were active members of the Immigration Restriction League, which sought to curtail the "new" immigration, and both never really adjusted to the progressive reform movement after the turn of the century. Capen, though president of the Boston Municipal League, did not view the organization as a democratizing force; on the contrary, he attempted to use it as a vehicle for promoting the extension of the number of appointive offices in order to increase their distance from the newer immigrants. The continuing influx of foreigners led him to complain in 1899 "that Massachusetts is not in the character of its population what it once was."[79]

Even the liberal Reverend Charles Ames occasionally expressed displeasure with contemporary society. In 1897 he lamented "the collecting of population in slumming masses," "the degradation of politics," "excess of legislation," "excess in administration," and the increasingly popular notion that "we shall all feed at the public crib," and he concluded, "Citizenship is becoming sad." All these participants in the peace movement would have readily agreed with Reuen Thomas when he complained during the imperialistic debate that the upsurge of "wild-goose patriotism reveals all but too surely the degenerate condition of our time."[80] Charles Jefferson carried this mentality into the twentieth century. As a leading critic of American navalism, he charged in 1904 that aside from self-interested naval officers the large navy sentiment emanated most directly from "the great crowds of barbarians in all our cities."[81] Since the average age of the directors of the American Peace Society was sixty-one in 1900, it would further tend to confirm the similarities between the archaic character of the peace and anti-imperialist movements.[82]

Other peace advocates displayed similar reluctance to come to terms with twentieth-century realities. One can plausibly argue, for instance, that the nonresistance of Love, Crosby, and Garrison was out of step with their nation's new role as a major power in a smaller, more interdependent world. The seeming remoteness of Love from the mainstream of American life has prompted his biographer to write that he "was isolated from the twentieth century. He continued to see and think as a Garrisonian."[83] Allowing for degrees of maladjustment, we can say that all peace leaders who became caustic critics of McKinley's foreign policies were alienated from international reality.

One can, however, advance certain reservations to that unflattering interpretation. It tends to accept a "realist" view of international developments: because the anti-imperialists failed politically, their criticisms were either unrealistic, unreasonable, or both. That view also assumes a kind of logical inevitability to the course of events and depreciates the timeless and universal appeal of the anti-imperialists' utterances. It also devalues the impact of their criticisms. Granting the political shortcomings of the anti-imperialist movement, one can still ask whether the anti-imperialists failed as moralists. As moral critics the anti-imperialists reminded Americans of their complicity in acquiescing silently in their nation's reprehensible actions in the Philippines, caused many zealous imperialists to moderate their expansionist rhetoric, and helped to restore a widespread anticolonial consensus (excepting perhaps the Caribbean area) in the United States after 1900. In a broader sense, their skepticism, firmly rooted in an appreciation of human weaknesses and the blunders of nation-states throughout recent history, served as a healthy antidote to the unthinking optimism and boosterism of those American expansionists who talked and acted as though the destiny of the United States was divinely inspired, exceptional, and beyond the judgments of history.[84]

Moreover, research on any social movement depends on the individuals profiled. While it may be roughly accurate to depict most officers of the Anti-Imperialist League as well as certain peace leaders as rather narrow-minded men of little faith in the future, it is less true as a general description of many of the most prolific peace spokesmen. Although these pacific-minded individuals' attacks on the administration's expansionist policies made them sound like gloomy prophets of the Last Judgment, they felt rather uncomfortable in their narrow, peevish, and essentially negative posture during the debate over imperialism, and they held out hope for the return of national sanity in the near future. The peace advocates' hopeful expressions ranged from pious, mechanical, and uninspired reaffirmations of America's peaceful mission to bold, unalloyed visions of a warless future. Compared with anti-imperialists outside the peace movement, the outlook of peace spokesmen as a whole was at once more liberal, optimistic, affirmative, idealistic, and adjustable to new conditions in both domestic and international life.

One might expect a more expansive, optimistic world view from individuals who expressed interest in international cooperation before 1898, but that faith survived the debate over expansion and in many instances would even lead them to join the burgeoning movement for world organization in the first years of the new century. After 1900 certain foreign and domestic developments facilitated their active involvement in the peace movement. The gradual suppression of the Filipino rebellion, for instance, helped to save them from prolonged anguish, while the limited achievements of the First Hague Peace Conference offered hopeful prospects for a more orderly world in an otherwise difficult time. Moreover, the optimistic overtones of the progressive reform movement helped to soften the most pessimistic views. Essentially, their confidence in international cooperation stemmed from their sturdy liberal faith in the potential aptitude of men and nations for moral improvement.[85]

Several friends of peace expressed a more confident outlook during and after the imperialistic debate. Mead, despite his scathing anti-imperialistic prose, did not despair. Indeed, he indicated that a major weakness of the anti-imperialist movement was its underlying pessimism. Mead did not deny the American capability to rule the Filipinos as honestly and fairly as circumstances allowed until they were given self-government; he opposed American rule there simply because he thought it stupid, unnecessary, and a travesty to the highest, noblest ideals of the Republic.[86] Similarly, the Reverend Dole, claiming to express the views of countless anti-imperialistic Americans, penned a forceful statement of the nation's peaceful mission:

> We are not pessimists; we are not mere conservatives; we never despair of the Republic. We believe that the advancement of the national welfare is not in the path of military glory, of territorial aggrandizement, or of arbitrary protectorates over half-civilized peoples. Our real welfare must

be in perfecting our free institutions, in realizing our splendid democratic ideals, in doing justice to our own people, of different colors and
races, who heartily call our flag their own in directly promoting international good will, and finally in creating national happiness that other
nations seeing what freedom, law, enlightenment, and peace do for us,
shall follow our beneficent lead.[87]

David Starr Jordan was less sanguine during the debate over imperialism, and he could say shortly after the first clash of arms between Filipinos and American troops that "there are occasions when optimism is
treason. Only an accomplice is cheerful in presence of a crime." Perhaps
because of that pessimism, Jordan often seemed interested only in preventing future American military interventions in foreign lands and responded more slowly to other peace advocates' faith in international
cooperation. His gloom, however, was essentially limited to time and
place, for his deeper convictions were at once more affirmative, optimistic, even utopian. A decade later he said, "Unless your soul dwells in
Utopia, life is not worth the keeping. Your windows should look toward
heaven, not into the gutter."[88]

Thirty-two liberal and radical clergymen, including Jenkin Lloyd Jones
and Herbert S. Bigelow, expressed the same idealistic faith in a campaign statement urging voters to repudiate President McKinley. Though
their appeal deplored the administration's "criminal aggression" and increases in military spending, both of which signified the nation's capitulation to the more sordid realities of European power politics, it also
stated, "We desire to see America exercise her influence as a 'world
power' in a new rather than in the old way. . . . We desire to see her
become the supreme moral factor in the world's progress."[89] That last
sentence, taken almost verbatim from William Jennings Bryan's speech
accepting the Democratic party's presidential nomination in 1900, not
only depicted their confidence in the righteous example of America's
peaceful conduct in foreign affairs but also foreshadowed the basic outlines of Bryan's own thoughts on peace that would mature during the
next decade. Even the skeptical Jefferson, while certain that "the brute
is ahead of the lamb," and continuing to deplore the American public's
dangerous flirtation with "the delusion of militarism," affirmed in 1900,
"I will keep on dreaming" for peace.[90]

Another indication of the different temperaments between those anti-
imperialists who actively participated in the peace movement and those
who shunned such involvement can be seen in their divergent reactions
to the presidential election of 1900. Almost without exception those anti-
imperialists unaligned with the peace movement had deep reservations

about supporting Bryan's candidacy, for they did not care for his flamboyant political style and could not understand his behavior in asking Democratic Senators to consent to the peace treaty with Spain. They strongly disagreed with his dubious argument that ratification of the treaty would bring legal peace and give the United States government freedom of action in solving the Philippine question. Even more distasteful to them was his "radical" domestic program, especially his revival of the free silver issue as equal in importance to the question of imperialism. Although the Democratic party platform of 1900 declared that imperialism was the "paramount issue" in the campaign, Bryan refused to abandon the money question or the rest of his domestic reform program, but made them co-equal issues with imperialism.[91] By contrast, the pacific-minded critics of empire were on the whole much more sympathetic to Bryan's candidacy. They were far from united in their choice of presidential candidates, but a much higher proportion of peace proponents than other anti-imperialists rejected McKinley's candidacy and supported Bryan.

Edwin Mead was one of the few anti-imperialists who put himself in the Bryan camp from the onset of the campaign. In his wide friendships among Boston Mugwumps, his distrust of the "spirit of party," his belief in honest and efficient government ruled by men of social position and intellect, his commitment to tariff reform, and his opposition to the free silver agitation of the mid-1890s, Mead seemed to share the Mugwump political philosophy, but he never joined their ranks and never sympathized with their underlying conservatism. Throughout that decade his persistent campaign for many political, social, and economic reforms in Boston contrasted vividly with the Boston Mugwumps who offered no remedy for the problem of poverty in an industrial society and viewed with alarm any attempts to redistribute wealth. Mead was, in sum, an advanced progressive long before progressivism began to make headway on the national scene, while his growing commitment to the peace movement after 1898 represented an extension of his crusading zeal into the area of international reform.[92] By 1900 he still worried about Bryan's silver views, but he strongly supported his presidential candidacy both because of his anti-imperialism and his domestic reform program. The local Democratic organization even asked him to run for Congress, and he refused only because the Republican candidate from his district, the incumbent Samuel W. McCall, was also an anti-imperialist.[93]

Other Boston friends of peace—Bridgman, Dole, Ames, Garrison, Haskins, and Storey—were less enthusiastic about Bryan but endorsed him nonetheless.[94] Those Bostonians made up part of the "large majority" of like-minded members of the New England Anti-Imperialist League who voted for him mainly because of his stand against imperialism.[95] Trueblood and Love, true to the nonpolitical orientation of their peace societies, did not formally support any presidential candidate, but their uncompromising opposition to the imperialistic policy of the McKinley administration and their favorable references to Bryan's anti-imperialistic statements in their journals clearly indicated that they too submerged their reservations about Bryan's "financial errors" to the foreign policy question.[96] Similarly, Crosby, Bigelow, Jones, and two leading Philadelphia anti-imperialists, Herbert Welsh and George Mercer, endorsed Bryan.[97]

Jordan, Carnegie, and Atkinson were among the few leading peace spokesmen who failed to support Bryan. They rejected him in part because he refused to heed their strong pleas for outspoken opposition to ratification of the peace treaty. Referring to Bryan's support of ratification, Atkinson, who refused to vote for a president in 1900, remarked that he could not cast his ballot "either for the robber or for the receiver of stolen goods," while Jordan and Carnegie concluded that the Nebraska Democrat's peculiar behavior on the treaty issue suggested that he lacked the proper judgment to be President. More important were their lingering doubts about his domestic views, which conflicted with their conservative notions of domestic stability. It is not surprising perhaps that those three, all of whom had been most tempted by expansionist notions of expanding foreign markets for future business prosperity, should perceive Bryan's continuing attacks on the gold standard as a threat both to domestic prosperity and the stability of international trade exchanges.[98]

Nevertheless, even they retained a confident faith that nourished their future interest in the peace movement. While Jordan's optimism was serious, Carnegie's and Atkinson's was superficial and compulsive. Predisposed to look on the bright side of every issue, Atkinson was ready to believe before the start of the presidential campaign that Bryan would abandon free silver and that such a stance would result in his election,[99] and shortly before the election he convinced himself that McKinley in his search for votes would find an excuse to withdraw American forces from the Philippines and thereby prove that the entire question had been only a "temporary aberration" in the American experience. McKinley's reelection failed to discourage his exuberant hopes. In the closing days of 1900 he wrote, "I think the world is more interesting that it ever was before, and I have greater confidence in progressive human welfare."[100] Carnegie prophesied more rhapsodically, "All goes well upward and onward. I believe that as the twentieth Century closes the earth will be purged of its foulest stain, the Killing of Men by Men in battle under the name of war and that the profession of Arms, hitherto the most and until recently the only profession thought worthy of a gentleman, will be held the most dishonorable of all and unworthy of any being in human form."[101]

Although the ironmaster continued to value his personal friendships with influential conservatives, he easily adjusted to the progressive reform impulse permeating American political life after 1900. The sale of his steel business in 1901 facilitated his commitment to "progressive" causes, for he then spent more of his time and money on philanthropic projects including the peace movement. In succeeding years he demonstrated a remarkable capacity to work closely with almost all peace advocates regardless of age and temperament. He became more idealistic and in the following decade channelled that idealism into more active cooperation with the peace forces.

[5]

To The First Hague
Peace Conference

ON AUGUST 24, 1898, Czar Nicholas II invited the nations of the world to attend an international disarmament conference. That invitation was of particular importance to the American peace movement. In the short run, it rekindled peace advocates' interest in the possibilities of international amity. Those individuals continued to cooperate with anti-imperialists after the first news of the Czar's rescript, but the prospect of a disarmament conference gradually diverted their attention from the expansionist to the armament issue. By the spring of 1899, with the Spanish treaty ratified, it was relatively easy for peace workers to channel their reform energies into the imminent convocation of the peace conference. The Czar's decree also had long-range impact on the American peace movement. When the peace conference actually took place and the delegations agreed to create an international court of arbitration and to improve arbitration and mediation procedures, interest in peace questions in the United States received a major boost.

American peace workers reacted enthusiastically to the Czar's invitation. Immediately following its announcement, Ernest Crosby wrote in his characteristically poetic prose, "God bless the Czar! . . . From the heart of the Northern Bear at last we may gather honey. The armed hordes of Muscovy and Tartary cry 'Peace'!"[1] The journals of the American Peace Society and Universal Peace Union as well as the nonpacifist *Woman's Journal* signified their approval of the Czar's note by publishing it in full, and the union also dispatched a laudatory message to the Russian Emperor

92

imploring him to persevere in his efforts for a disarmament conference.[2]

At first friends of peace showed no interest in organizing a campaign to rally public opinion behind a disarmament conference such as they had earlier tried to mobilize behind the Olney-Pauncefote arbitration treaty. Instead, they refrained from any specific suggestions until they received tangible manifestations of interest from the various governments. A month after the Czar's invitation, the *Advocate of Peace* emphasized that his proposal had "tremendous significance" for the future but recognized that the lukewarm reaction of the American government was a discouraging sign.[3] Despite McKinley's promises of American support for the Czar's proposal, he indicated that the armament problem was basically a European question, not an American one. During the hostilities with Spain, McKinley had announced his intention to enlarge the nation's armed forces, but keeping them smaller than those of the major European powers. Unhappy with the American position, the directors of the Boston society in late September voted to send a petition to President McKinley opposing increases in armaments "except for police purposes." Reflecting their ambivalence, however, they simultaneously congratulated McKinley on his prompt approval of the Czar's proposal and asked him to instruct the American delegation to promote discussions on other peacekeeping measures at the conference, especially the framing of a model arbitration treaty and the creation of an international tribunal. They also sent a resolution to the Russian ambassador in Washington, Count Arthur Cassini, praising the Czar for his invitation.[4]

Others endorsed the conference. A convention of the Episcopal churches overwhelmingly agreed to send the Czar a letter "hailing with joy the great peace manifesto." The letter supported reduction in armaments and expressed the hope that the Czar's conference would result "in the establishment of some method of judicial arbitration for the settlement of international difficulties."[5] The latter resolve, if not the former, might have come at the urging of Robert Treat Paine, who attended the conference. A delegation of ministers personally communicated those resolutions to the President in late December, but McKinley, though claiming sympathy for a disarmament conference, made clear that he had not wavered in his position that the tangled question of armaments did not apply to the United States.[6] Meanwhile, Lucia Mead addressed a public appeal to wealthy people asking them to contribute money to create a fund of $300,000 or more to finance a nationwide propaganda campaign for the Czar's disarmament proposal.[7] When her suggestion received no encouraging response (even the pacifist journals failed to mention it), she quietly dropped the idea. In retrospect, her proposal was interesting both for reaffirming her genteel faith in moral uplift and education and in prefiguring the greater value friends of peace would place on enlisting the financial support of wealthy capitalists and philanthropists.

Despite the support for the Czar's proposal, peace societies and individual peace advocates made little attempt to educate the public on the potential importance of a peace conference in the four months following the Czar's invitation. There were several reasons for their gingerly approach to the Czar's proposal. In the case of the Universal Peace Union, the lack of aggressive activity stemmed not from lack of interest in the subject since its leaders had always believed that disarmament was the only sure path to world peace, but from the union's defensive position after its recent attempts to avert the Spanish war. The union's journal was so obsessed with detailed explanations of its unpopular actions before and during the recent war that other subjects received comparatively little attention.

The expansionist issue further weakened the pacifists' initial interest in the Czar's proposal. Much as they wanted to support international disarmament, many leading peace workers saw imperialism as the pressing question of the moment. Imperialism, they reasoned, was a real issue which would be decided in the near future, and the final result would have an extensive effect on the future course of American and world history; the Czar's offer, on the other hand, was only an invitation to a disarmament conference and still required the cooperation of the major powers before the conference could convene. Even if they succeeded in persuading the American government to champion the disarmament conference and perhaps modify its position on the armament question, there was no absolute guarantee that the other nations would agree to a conference.

Another matter helped to divert their attention from disarmament. When they were not promoting the anti-imperialist movement, they lobbied for an Anglo-American arbitration treaty. British friendship for the United States flourished during the Spanish-American War, and most peace workers believed that the prospects for an arbitration treaty had improved since the Olney-Pauncefote debacle. The American Peace Society and the Episcopal Church convention recognized Anglo-American amity and in their petitions to the President included requests for an arbitration treaty. When Paine attended the Episcopal Church convention in Washington, he called upon the new secretary of state, John Hay, who recently had returned from a successful tour as the American ambassador to the Court of St. James'. One might have expected that Paine would have raised the question of the Czar's invitation (or perhaps of the administration's territorial aspirations); but he later recounted that he had urged Secretary Hay only to revive the abortive arbitration treaty between Great Britain and the United States. Anglophile though he was, Secretary Hay managed to convince the deferential Paine that it was unwise at present to renegotiate the treaty and thus risk another rejection by the Senate. Hay and McKinley did not entirely shut the door on an Anglo-American arbitration treaty, and it is not surprising therefore that some peace leaders thought arbitration was as important as a disarmament conference.[8]

Finally, talk about the allegedly darker motives behind the Czar's circular was so widespread that the peace advocates were at first cautious not to champion the conference until they received some confirmation of the Russian monarch's sincerity. Had not the autocratic Russian government always been noted for its duplicity in diplomacy, its insatiable land hunger, and its intolerance of minority groups and dissenting opinions? How could Nicholas II, a despot, pose as the mouthpiece of the world's most enlightened ideals? Peace advocates' suspicions reflected not only the antimonarchical biases of Western liberals but also their knowledge of the Czar's proclamation revoking the constitution of Finland and the Russian government's recent persecution of the Doukhobors, a nonresistant sect, for their refusal to bear arms and proclaim loyalty to the government. Despite Ernest Crosby's paean of praise for the Czar's invitation, even he noted this skepticism, and Trueblood and Mary Livermore early admitted that Russia's autocracy and tyranny troubled them, though they refused to believe that the Czar was as insincere and villainous as others pictured him.[9] Whatever peace workers thought, by December 1898 a rumor circulated that the leading powers were so suspicious of the Russian motives that the conference would consist only of a meeting of the foreign ministers already assigned to St. Petersburg.[10]

The underlying purposes of the invitation were more self-interested than altruistic. The idea for the invitation originated with his most intimate advisors, who informed the autocrat that unless the European powers concluded some kind of international disarmament agreement in the immediate future, Russia would have to allocate enormous sums of money to make up for its deficiencies in military technology. Once Nicholas saw the Russian predicament, he and his ministers perceived that a conference would reach a satisfactory agreement on armaments, which would give Russia a breathing spell to recover from its financial and military difficulties. Given such sober, even cynical reasoning, the Czar's rescript was far from a disinterested document. As one historian has succinctly concluded, "The truth was that the peace rescript had been conceived in fear, brought forth in deceit, and swaddled in humanitarian ideals."[11]

American peace spokesmen of course were ignorant of the self-interest of the Czar's note; and while widespread suspicion of his motives in official diplomatic circles and among American and foreign newspaper press contributed to the peace advocates' initial caution, they naturally hoped for the best and were temperamentally inclined to accept the Czar's word. Gradually they came to overlook the possibilities of Russian duplicity and to champion the Czar's invitation as a supreme opportunity to negotiate agreements on disarmament as well as other international matters.

The favorable reactions of European peace workers to the Czar's invitation bolstered their American cohorts' hopes for such a conference. Shortly after the publication of the rescript, the more militant and radical pacifists on the European continent heralded the Czar's initiative as a supreme opportunity to check the armament craze, which had assumed an increasing financial burden on the European powers and helped to foster the growing feeling of insecurity throughout Europe.[12] Even more encouraging were the favorable newspaper reports of their interviews with Russian leaders. The Austrian pacifist Baroness von Suttner had an interview with Count Muraviev during his visit to Vienna in November 1898, and he convinced her that the Czar's intentions were wholly idealistic. In addition, the Czar met two months later with Count Leo Tolstoy, whose uncompromising opposition to armaments and his disdain for Russian despotism were already well known, and according to press reports the youthful ruler convinced the Count of his sincere belief in and genuine enthusiasm for a disarmament agreement.[13] The *Advocate of Peace,* reassured by that news, remarked, "this interview, if it occurred as the dispatches declare, is of much significance in showing that the Czar is not only in earnest, but also determined to enlist every influence possible in support of his purpose."[14]

Even more encouraging was the resurgence of peace interest that the Czar's proposal generated in Great Britain. A few days after the announcement of the invitation, Randal Cremer sent a circular to 218 members of Parliament asking them to sign a telegram to the Czar expressing their approval for a disarmament conference. Although Parliament had adjourned for the summer, Cremer received 126 replies, of which 104 were favorable. At the same time, the International Arbitration League worked with the London Peace Society and other British peace groups to plan public meetings throughout Britain to mobilize opinion in support of the conference. By the end of the year, those peace organizations, with the support of many industrial, trade union, and religious bodies, held more than one hundred meetings throughout Britain endorsing the conference.[15] Those meetings were not well publicized in the United States, but peace workers read the reports of them in the British newspapers and peace journels.[16]

The actions of William T. Stead, the dynamic but erratic editor of the British *Review of Reviews,* impressed American peace workers even more and ultimately were to convince even the most skeptical among them. No pacifist, Stead had previously promoted a variety of causes: a large British navy, defense of the British empire, various urban reforms, and spiritualism. He had also desired more friendly relations between Great Britain and the United States, and in the aftermath of the Anglo-Venezuelan boundary dispute of the mid-1890s had published a penny pamphlet, *Always Arbitrate before You Fight: An Appeal to All English-speaking Folk*, which supported an Anglo-American arbitration treaty.[17]

Most important, Stead had long favored closer ties with Russia. With relations between the two nations deteriorating in the summer of 1898, Stead planned a visit to Nicholas II. When he heard of Nicholas' invitation, he broadened his itinerary to include interviews with European statesmen and learn their reactions to the Czar's invitation and after his arrival in Russia to find out from the Russian leaders themselves their true motives in promoting a disarmament conference. All his requests for interviews with political leaders in Belgium, France, and Germany were refused, and Stead arrived in St. Petersburg a disappointed man.[18] His hopes revived, however, after talking to the Russian leaders. Concealing the real motives behind the invitation, the Russian officials who saw him, including the Czar, received Stead courteously and convinced him completely of the sincerity and conviction that stood behind the document. Fully rejuvenated by those interviews, Stead returned to England with great enthusiasm for a disarmament conference.[19]

Since Stead had seen the Russian leaders face to face, it is small wonder that American pacifists were willing to take him at his word when he hailed the Russians' devotion to the Czar's initiative. Stead's account of his Russian visit, the *Advocate of Peace* stated optimistically, "has been able to remove from the mind of the civilized world all doubt as to the real and earnest wish of the young Emperor to accomplish what he has proposed in his rescript."[20]

Stead realized that his own words alone would not induce the major world powers to unite behind the Russian appeal and frame a disarmament agreement. If these ends were to be attained, he believed, tangible manifestations of public support would be necessary. He surmised that the success of a disarmament conference depended on the strong support that the governments of the United States and Great Britain gave to the Czar's invitation. He thus announced the formation of an international peace crusade to arouse Americans and Britons behind the conference. He proposed mass meetings in every town and city in the two nations to rally support for disarmament. As an integral part of this grass roots approach, he planned a pilgrimage starting with a deputation of peace-loving Americans in San Francisco who would journey to the nation's capital where they would receive the blessing of President McKinley. Thereupon they would depart for England, join the British crusaders, and journey to Paris, Berlin, Vienna, Budapest, and Rome. Everywhere the pilgrimage went, Stead envisaged receptions and public demonstrations. By the time the pilgrims arrived in St. Petersburg, they could relate personally to the Czar "how passionately the people desire peace, how enthusiastically they have responded to his [the Czar's] initiative, and how emphatically they bid him stand firm in the name of 'God and the people' and achieve this great good for humanity."[21]

Although Stead's peace crusade aroused the interest, if not the respect, of the British public, it received no support in the United States. American peace workers approved of Stead's grandiose plan but made no attempt to organize a pilgrimage. Andrew Carnegie praised Stead's proposal but contributed neither time nor money to its promotion.[22] Besides, Stead's motives were suspect. When the British publicist first announced his peace crusade, he blithely related the Czar's disarmament proposal to his own prejudices for a dominant British navy. Stead believed that a disarmament conference was in Britain's best interest since any disarmament agreement would more than likely freeze the armaments of the contracting parties at their present levels and thereby recognize the status quo. As Stead bluntly remarked, the Czar's invitation "is equivalent to a proposal that for a term of five or ten years the naval supremacy of England should be recognized as a fundamental principle of the world's balance of power."[23] When Trueblood learned of Stead's erratic reasoning, he sharply rebuked him and wondered how Stead could believe that the conference could have the remotest chance of success if the British delegation at the conference would approve only those disarmament proposals perpetuating British naval supremacy.[24]

The eccentric Stead did not worry about those suspicions or the generally muted response of American peace leaders, for he hoped to appeal directly to the American people. Yet even his many letters to government officials and prominent Americans who were not members of peace societies but had worked for the Olney-Pauncefote treaty fell on deaf ears. The recipients of his letters soon became annoyed at his persistence. William E. Dodge, for instance, convinced himself that some increases in the American armed forces were necessary, and he rankled at the stream of Stead's letters promoting the disarmament conference.[25]

Lacking the necessary American support, Stead reluctantly abandoned his plans for a peace pilgrimage in the United States. The lackluster response to Stead's pleas did not mean, however, that American peace advocates were not interested in promoting a disarmament conference, for at about the same time they began to warm to the Czar's invitation. The catalyst that fully awakened them from their earlier lethargy was the news that the Russian Emperor had release a second circular on January 11, 1899, that reiterated his earlier disarmament proposal but also urged discussion of other international matters at the conference. It was now entirely obvious, as it had not been earlier, that the Russian government was determined to promote the conference. As the *Advocate of Peace* remarked, "It is clear that the Czar means serious business."[26] The Czar did indeed, for within a few weeks after his second note the Russian government arranged with the Netherlands to hold the conference at The Hague. The Dutch Foreign Office immediately sent out formal invitations to all nations having diplomatic representatives in St. Petersburg as well as to three other states, Luxembourg, Montenegro, and Siam. All those governments except Brazil, a total of twenty-six, accepted the invitation, and the Dutch government set May 18, 1899, for the opening session of the conference.[27]

Among the new topics added to the second circular were specific proposals on the prohibition of new military weapons, restrictions on the use of certain ones already developed, revision of the laws and customs of war, and improvement of mediation and arbitration procedures. The last proposal particularly appealed to American peace leaders. Realizing that chances for a disarmament agreement seemed slim, they still hoped that the conference could agree to improve and add to the existing conventions for the arbitration of international controversies. They also realized that they would avoid working at cross purposes with their own government and perhaps influence its position at the conference. However lukewarm the American government's position on disarmament, they remembered President McKinley's endorsement of the Olney-Pauncefote treaty two years earlier. Moreover, since they believed the United States was the "mother of arbitration" and had an exemplary record in that area, they were eager to have the American delegation again assume leadership.[28]

Many American peace leaders wanted the United States to take one important step beyond arbitration by promoting the establishment of a permanent international arbitration court at the conference. As we have seen, some of the petitions to President McKinley immediately following the Czar's initial invitation had urged the American government to promote an international tribunal; after the Czar's second circular, however, peace advocates' interest centered on that subject. Indeed, if one had read only their petitions and their peace journals in the four months between the Czar's second circular and the opening of the First Hague Peace Conference, one would have assumed that an arbitration court was the primary subject for discussion at the conference, although the Czar had never included a court as part of his program.[29]

In part, the peace participants' growing preoccupation with a permanent court of arbitration seemed to represent another desperate attempt to save the conference from the inevitable stalemate that would result if it discussed only armaments. There is some truth in that view, although it was never admitted by advocates of peace. Instead, they sincerely believed, and with considerable justification, that they were acting in the mainstream of the peace movement which had always promoted an international tribunal.

The dream of a permanent arbitration court was not new in 1899 or even wholly a creature of the nineteenth century. A French official had proposed such a court for European states in the fourteenth century, and in succeeding centuries it had appeared in the peace plans of several European sovereigns and philosophers.[30] In the United States the American Peace Society had advanced plans for an international court almost from the date of its founding. One of its early leaders was William Ladd. His lengthy treatise, *An Essay on a Congress of Nations,* published in 1840, contained a detailed formula for creation of periodic international congresses of nations. One of the main duties of this international body would be the creation of a court of nations to decide cases that disputing governments voluntarily submitted. The court would judge existing cases involving the "true interpretation" of existing treaties and international laws passed by the congress of nations; in the absence of treaties and laws the court would render decisions according to the principles of equity and justice.[31] The Treaty of Washington of 1871, which established the special tribunals to adjudicate the *Alabama* claims and other Anglo-American differences, had further stimulated interest in an international court. David Dudley Field's draft code published in the following year had stipulated that nations failing to settle their differences by diplomacy or joint commissions would be obligated to submit the case to an international tribunal. Each of the governments agreeing to the code would recommend four of their nationals for the court, and the disputants by a process of elimination would settle on seven of them. Like most blueprints for the establishment of international institutions, none of those proposals provided for economic or military sanctions against recalcitrant states.[32]

In the 1880s American peace workers' growing interest in a permanent tribunal had paralleled their government's hesitant endorsement of the principle of international arbitration with European and Latin American states. As early as 1882, in the aftermath of the stillborn conference of American states, the Universal Peace Union had petitioned Congress to promote an international arbitration court, and in the next decade resolutions from other peace organizations, religious bodies, and interested private citizens were occasionally introduced in Congress as a supplementary aim of the arbitration movement. Some of these petitions had specified a tribunal of arbitration between the United States and Great Britain while others had envisaged a more general arbitral body composed of leading powers.[33] With the revival of the Universal Peace Congresses in 1889, American and European pacifists had occasionally discussed the advantages of an international court, and the 1893 Congress in Chicago had devoted a session for discussion of several plans. The American Peace Society presented a proposal, and the delegates authorized Trueblood, Love, and W. Evans Darby (representing the London Peace Society) to appoint a committee of jurists and publicists to formulate a plan for the creation of an arbitration tribunal among the so-called civilized nations.[34]

Perhaps the most influential organization to promote an international court was the Interparliamentary Union. Formally established in Paris by Randal Cremer and a few other British and European legislators on June 29, 1889, only two days after the conclusion of the Universal Peace Congress in that city, the Interparliamentary Union met annually in different European cities to discuss and formulate proposals for the peaceful settlement of international disputes. The Interparliamentary Union was composed entirely of lawmakers and ex-lawmakers from every European nation (except Russia which participated after the creation of the Duma in 1905). Since most of those men were elected and responsible to their constituents at home, their programs were more practical and carried more weight with their governments than the agitation of idealistic pacifists. The Interparliamentary Conferences discussed many measures designed to stimulate more cordial diplomatic relations among all the European nations. The first conferences passed resolutions endorsing the extension of arbitration treaties and revisions of some established principles of international law, but the Interparliamentary Conference at Rome in 1891 voted to discuss the subject of an international tribunal at its sessions the following year. After three years of serious debate, the 1895 Conference at Brussels passed a resolution formally endorsing the draft of an international arbitral court.[35]

Those European developments occurred simultaneously with the gathering momentum for an Anglo-American arbitration treaty. When the Venezuelan crisis temporarily disrupted the movement, some friends of peace emphasized that it was not sufficient in times of excitement to trust the good will of the contesting powers to resolve their differences through the establishment of a temporary tribunal or through normal diplomatic channels. More naively, they also pointed out that if a permanent court had existed, it was probable that the two nations would have submitted the dispute to the court and thereby prevented the crisis from reaching the critical stage. In the aftermath of the Venezuelan debate, those peace advocates interpreted the negotiations for an Anglo-American arbitration treaty as a transitional stage in the progress toward a permanent tribunal;[36] the main difference between the resulting Olney-Pauncefote accord and a permanent Anglo-American tribunal was that the former provided for the appointment of a new set of arbitrators for each dispute instead of a court of permanent judges. Despite the defeat of the Olney-Pauncefote accord, it constituted another small step toward formal institutionalization of the arbitral process between two leading powers.

One group began to envision bolder ideas. Only a month after Cleveland's inflammatory message to Great Britain had aggravated the Venezuelan crisis, the New York State Bar Association established a committee of eleven attorneys to formulate a plan for a permanent international tribunal representing nine nations—United States, Great Britain, France, Germany, Russia, the Netherlands, Mexico, Brazil, and Argentina. Dissatisfaction with the selection of arbitrators animated their discussions. Arbitrators picked by their respective governments were almost always partisans and thus lacked the detachment necessary for impartial judgment. As a possible remedy for that shortcoming, the committee recommended a plan authorizing each of the highest judicial bodies of the nine participating governments to select one of its members to sit on the court. The proposal attempted to insure greater impartiality in at least two ways. First, it would enable the greater majority of judges whose nations were not parties to particular disputes to hear the cases more dispassionately; and second, the members of the court would likely be eminent jurists and would presumably render decisions more faithful to international law than arbiters untrained in the law.[37] The New York plan did not require nations to submit disputes to the court but allowed them voluntarily to conclude a special agreement in each instance which would define the dispute and, presumably, the extent of the court's authority. It was important, one member of the committee stressed, to persuade governments to create the court; then statesmen could watch its progress and decide how much its jurisdiction could be extended.

On April 21, 1896, a delegation of the Bar Association presented the plan to President Cleveland. Cleveland was his usual noncommittal self, though he reportedly conceded, "There is one fact about this matter: you have a *plan*; nobody else has given us a plan."[38] Subsequently, one of the New York lawyers discussed the proposal with the British ambassador, Sir Julian Pauncefote, and still later with President McKinley. About the time the Czar issued his second circular of January 1899, the Bar Association adopted a resolution praising his proposed disarmament conference and appointed a committee to draft an address to the Czar and President McKinley praising the movement to limit armaments. The committee eventually sent that address and their 1896 court proposal to the delegates of every nation at the Hague Peace Conference. The New Yorkers' plan had some influence on the State Department personnel who drafted the American proposal for a permanent court, but it was too advanced to receive the Hague delegates' serious attention. It nonetheless represented another sign of the growing awareness among international reformers of the possibility of transforming the idea of a court into a living reality.[39]

By the mid-1890s many participants in the peace movement were urging the creation of a permanent arbitration court, but the single most persistent promoter was the Boston clergyman, Edward Everett Hale. As early as March, 1885, Hale had preached a sermon in Washington, D.C., predicting the establishment of an international court for the twentieth century, and in 1889 he had reiterated that view in another sermon at the centennial celebration of the inauguration of President George Washington.[40] When the First Pan-American Conference convened in Washington, Hale had seen an opportunity to promote a tribunal for the Americas and published his first article on the subject. If his own testimony can be believed, he had even managed to persuade James G. Blaine to sound out informally the opinions of the Latin American delegates on the feasibility of raising the question of a high court at the conference. Although a few delegates had expressed interest in the subject, Blaine decided that the time was not ripe and did not raise the subject.[41]

Hale, undiscouraged, continued throughout the 1890s to conduct a virtual one-man crusade for a tribunal composed of the American and European nations. At the Chicago meeting of the Universal Peace Congress in 1893, he submitted an outline for an international tribunal, and a year later he pointed out that the deterioration in the Pan-American spirit resulting from America's unpleasant relations with Chile and Brazil made some kind of permanent tribunal all the more desirable.[42] At the first three Lake Mohonk Conferences, Hale reiterated his interest in an international court and good-naturedly attempted to persuade his colleagues there that they should subordinate the more limited aim of international arbitration to the more far-reaching goal of such a court. He frequently expressed his support for the New York State Bar Association plan and played a leading role in cajoling the 1896 and 1897 Mohonk meetings to adopt resolutions endorsing establishment of an international tribunal.[43]

Hale derived his ideas for an international court from his fundamental faith in American institutions. He believed that the genius of American political life could be directly traced back to the framers of the United States Constitution who had wisely provided for a Supreme Court. He admired the ability of that judicial agency to settle peaceably the many boundary disputes and other controversies between the separate states and among individuals. He even intimated that the Supreme Court could have averted the Civil War if slavery had not been so thoroughly enmeshed in the Constitution. With the exception of that one failure, which Hale minimized, he marveled that the high court had settled amicably the many controversies that had threatened the peaceful development of the American nation.[44]

In explaining the genius of Americans in terms of their Constitution, Hale ignored the cultural and intellectual consensus among Americans that had facilitated the creation and widespread acceptance of its political institutions. In the same way his unthinking glorification of the Constitution led him to believe that it could function effectively on an international scale. He minimized the national, religious, and geopolitical differences between nation states that had long served as obstacles to the establishment of any permanent institutional machinery for the peaceful settlement of international disputes. Far from accepting the deep-seated rivalries among the European powers, by the 1890s Hale believed that the European states were so commercially and culturally interdependent that a closer political union was entirely feasible. Much like John Fiske who may have reinforced his views, Hale naively compared the present situation in Europe with the condition of the thirteen American states on the eve of the Constitutional Convention of 1787. Just as the American states had earlier submerged their particularisms and agreed to form a more perfect union, so would an agreement among the European states to establish an international court provide the first major step in the development of a united Europe. As early as 1871, he had prophesied a "United States of Europe," and in the 1890s he began to emphasize that an international tribunal was the proper starting point for the confederation of European states. By this time, too, he was convinced that once the European states could make some progress toward the establishment of a court, then it would be a relatively easy task to broaden its membership and include the several American nations. He assumed that it was the mission of the United States to persuade the reluctant Europeans to accept some kind of institutional plan which might lead to a fuller integration of the Western world, and the world court was the most obvious first step in that direction.[45]

Hale's single-minded efforts on behalf of an international tribunal help explain his comparative silence during the agitation for an Anglo-American arbitration treaty, the *idée fixe* of almost all participants in the peace movement in the 1890s. Calling himself an "edge-of-the-wedge-man," he worked for the Olney-Pauncefote treaty mainly because he believed that ratification of the accord would quicken public interest in his own dream of a world court; and he viewed the defeat of the treaty less as a setback to the arbitration movement than a blow to his own hopes for the creation of a permanent international tribunal.[46]

More than peace, Hale believed in international justice. Because neither an international court nor a comprehensive system of rules and procedures of international conduct yet existed, he saw no compelling reason to oppose the Spanish-American War and despite some mental reservations acquiesced in America's imperialistic venture. His firm patriotism hindered his ability to question the justice of the American position on those issues. Moreover, because his cherished court proposal urged only the voluntary submission of disputes to the court, it involved no sacrifice of America's freedom of action in the world arena. Nevertheless, Hale's liberal faith in the essential goodness of man and inevitable progress convinced him that once the court was established, governments would begin to submit cases to it, and gradually it would gain the necessary prestige to expand its authority. This same faith underlay his conviction that the Czar was sincere in his disarmament proposal. Even before the Czar's second circular added the subject of arbitration to his list of proposals for discussion, the Boston clergyman began to champion the conference for the work it could accomplish in creating an international tribunal. He hoped for "some partial disarmament" but added, "Whatever the conference may do about present armaments, it can certainly determine on a tribunal whose dignity and prestige and power shall make such armaments unnecessary."[47]

Though he was seventy-six in 1899, Hale, with the energy of one more than a generation younger, promoted the conference. His boosterism originally had no direct relationship to Stead's international peace crusade but became the closest approximation to any transatlantic cooperation on behalf of the conference. Early in 1899 Hale addressed about fifty public meetings in thirteen states in the Northeast, Middle West, and South in support of the conference; during his visit to Philadelphia he prevailed upon the Universal Peace Union, as well as George Edmunds, George Mercer, Herbert Welsh, and other Philadelphians to organize a citizens' committee to publicize the Czar's proposal.[48] In late March he arrived in the nation's capital and had interviews with Secretary of State John Hay, Assistant Secretary of State David Jayne Hill, and the Russian ambassador, Count Cassini. Hale was satisfied that those officials were eager to do all they could to make the conference a success.[49]

Meanwhile, Hale had not neglected his home city. Shortly before embarking on his speaking tour, he called a meeting in Boston to initiate a peace crusade. Acting under the auspices of the Massachusetts Good Citizenship Society, Edwin D. Mead, its president, organized five noon meetings on consecutive Mondays in March and April to promote the conference. The assumption of America's regenerative influence in this movement for international harmony allowed imperialists, including Hale and Lyman Abbott, to join anti-imperialists in extolling the lofty purposes of the conference. One meeting devoted to women heard speeches by Lucia Mead, Julia Ward Howe, and Mary A. Livermore.[50] With the assistance of the Meads, Dole, Ames, and other Boston peace advocates, Hale also started a fortnightly magazine *The Peace Crusade,* which served as a mouthpiece for his own ideas and included articles on local movements supporting the Hague Peace Conference. By the time the conference adjourned, Hale had published twelve issues of this journal.

May Wright Sewall organized the only comparable peace crusade. At the triennial convention of the National Council of Women in February, 1899, Mrs. Sewall obtained that body's endorsement of the upcoming Hague Conference; and when a peace committee of the International Council of Women selected her as the American head of planned worldwide demonstrations for peace at the opening of the Conference, she sent telegrams to the presidents of all affiliated women's organizations in the United States asking them to support this international event. Hannah J. Bailey and Anna Garlin Spencer actively promoted Mrs. Sewall's appeal. On the appointed day, 163 meetings in about twenty states, attended by more than 71,000 women, and representing groups with a total membership of over 175,000, passed resolutions endorsing both a permanent arbitration court and the efforts of women throughout the world who desired more public recognition from governments for their peace efforts. In a separate petition the septuagenarian reformer Carolina M. Severance, who had supported Julia Ward Howe's peace efforts in the 1870s, obtained the signatures of seventy-five opinion leaders in the women's movement.[51]

That activity had little lasting effect except among scattered individuals in the Boston area and among women activists, most of whom were already sympathetic to the peace cause. It is doubtful whether the promoters of the conference could have done much more to arouse public concern, for even after the Spanish-American War a deep isolationist feeling persisted in the nation and presented an insuperable barrier to their efforts to arouse Americans to the immediate relevance of a disarmament conference far away in Europe. Public interest in foreign developments was limited almost entirely to stories of American heroism in the Spanish War or to the Filipino insurrection. One pundit captured the incongruity between those realities and Nicholas II's "idealistic" proposal: "The visionary and under present conditions impractical peace manifesto of the Czar has no more effect in the universe than a dog barking at the moon."[52] Though most American newspapers were not so openly scornful, they sensed a lack of public concern in disarmament and gave little attention to the conference until its actual convocation; even then the coverage was inconsistent. At the outset of Hale's peace crusade, Trueblood lamented that the Czar's invitation "has produced scarcely a ripple on the surface of American life."[53] Hale had undertaken his peace crusade to remedy that defect, but his zealous activities, even when combined with those of his Boston friends and pacific-minded women, were simply insufficient to convert large numbers of people into true believers. Hale's journal, for example, probably had no more than a few hundred subscribers outside Boston.[54] Belva Lockwood summarized their frustration on the eve of the Hague meeting when she admitted, "We are working against the tide, for the press are [*sic*] not with us."[55]

Despite Hale's abiding faith in public opinion, he gradually realized that only a few Americans really cared about the Hague Conference. Two weeks after the opening of the conference, he attended the Lake Mohonk sessions and quickly discovered that most of the participants had only a superficial understanding of the proposals before the Hague Conference, although presumably they were the American private citizens best informed on the Hague assemblage. "The general run of the people here," he sadly reported, "are as ignorant of the subject as average school boys would be."[56]

If peace spokesmen failed to arouse much public interest in the Hague proceedings, they found that Andrew D. White, American ambassador in Berlin, and the New York attorney Frederick W. Holls, chairman and secretary respectively of the American delegation, strongly sympathized with their campaign for a permanent international tribunal. White in particular wished success for the conference. No pacifist, he was sufficiently realistic to concur with the other delegations' profound pessimism concerning the prospects for a disarmament agreement. Nor did he show any appreciation of pacifists' propaganda efforts. Because the American delegation voted at the outset to direct Holls to receive and acknowledge all private correspondence from the United States, White may not have been aware of the many letters and cables from WCTU peace departments, churches, and other voluntary associations in support of firm international agreements on the armament and arbitration questions.[57] Nor did Trueblood and Howard D. Jenkins, Quaker editor of the *Friends' Intelligencer,* the only two American peace advocates who witnessed the proceedings at The Hague, attempt to impose their ideas on the American delegation. Trueblood was so impressed with the difficulties of the delegates in overcoming the aura of suspicion and in reconciling the many different propositions that, aside from polite interviews with certain American and foreign delegates, he was content to leave the delegates alone so that they could work out these difficulties with a minimum of outside interference.[58] European peace activists were more visible, but White quickly discounted their lobbying activities. As he wrote during the early stages of the conference, "we are greatly bothered with all kinds of enthusiasts, dreamers and cranks presenting every kind of scheme, plan, whimsy, etc. from a statue of 'Peace' to cost millions of francs, in Paris, . . . down to suggestions in behalf of a badge on a hospital nurse's dress."[59]

White continued to believe that conference diplomacy could advance international law and arbitration. If a good plan for arbitration could be agreed upon, then disarmament might soon follow; "in fact," he wrote, "that is the logical sequence—Arbitration first and Disarmament afterward." Moreover, he revered the seventeenth century Dutch jurist Hugo Grotius for his classic treatise on international law, *De jure belli et pacis,* which had attempted to humanize warfare as well as develop arbitral and mediatory machinery for war prevention. "I have always felt," White wrote a friend, "that of all books not claiming divine inspiration his work on 'War and Peace' has done most good to mankind." White had visited Grotius' tomb at Delft outside The Hague as a young man and had bought two portraits of him, which he hung in the Cornell Law Library and his office. He viewed the Hague Conference as a renewal of Grotius' dream of a more peaceful, humane world and during the conference took special pride in holding a ceremony in memory of the Dutch jurist at Delft.[60]

Despite White's good intentions the First Hague Peace Conference accomplished little. The delegates from the twenty-six participating nations earnestly discussed world problems but concluded no substantive agreements on controversial questions like disarmament. Their failure resulted in part from the restrictive rule requiring unanimous consent to all conventions, but much more from national suspicions permeating world politics. Even the United States, thanks mainly to the important role played by its military delegates Alfred Thayer Mahan and William R. Crozier, helped to tone down or reject the few conventions even mildly initiating reform of the anarchic international system. In consequence, diplomatic history textbooks have treated the 1899 Conference as a minor episode in international history.

Yet the Hague assemblage did agree on conventions defining procedures for the establishment of commissions of inquiry, arbitration, and mediation among nations; another reiterating generally accepted rules of warfare; and an innocuous declaration urging nations to limit armaments as "extremely desirable for the increase of the material and moral welfare of mankind." Most significant for the future of the peace movement, however, was the creation of the Permanent Court of Arbitration at The Hague, the first international tribunal in history. Actually, the Hague Court was hardly permanent or a court at all, for it established neither permanent judges nor compulsory arbitral features, but only a panel of arbiters from which nations could voluntarily select their adjudicators. In other words, nations were not legally bound to refer any disputes to the Hague Court.[61]

Nevertheless, Hale, Dodge, and other peace advocates helped to prod the McKinley administration and an uninterested Senate into ratification of the Hague conventions.[62] Predisposed to magnify even the most superficial signs of progress toward international cooperation, the most optimistic friends of the peace cause proceeded to hail the founding of the Court as "the beginning of the Parliament of Man," the "Magna Charta of International Law," "the most wonderful court the world ever dreamed of," "one of the greatest events in the history of human society," and certainly "the great event" of the century. Oscar Straus even claimed that the establishment of the Court marked "not only the crowning glory of the nineteenth century, but, with God's blessing, the most enduring humanitarian achievement of the ages." Along with the provisions for commissions of inquiry, mediation, and arbitration, he exulted, the Hague Court represented "an International Covenant on the Mount." At last, those optimistic liberals believed, the peace movement had entered its "practical" or "political" phase. Henceforth, the nations of the world would not have to rely entirely upon haphazard and involved diplomatic negotiations but could turn to this tangible institution to settle international differences.[63]

While peace spokesmen assumed that the nations of the world would feel a strong moral obligation to submit their international disputes to the new court, they realized that it was an embryo which could develop into full maturity only through the actual adjudication of international controversies. European and American pacifists thus urged their governments to submit their controversies with other nations to the Hague Court. They particularly wanted the United States to assume the world's leadership in making the new tribunal a living institution by offering to submit the Alaska boundary question, which a joint high commission had failed to resolve, or some other dispute to the new international agency.[64] Although Trueblood and other friends of peace could not persuade President McKinley to submit an outstanding dispute to the court, they continued their efforts with his successor, Theodore Roosevelt.[65] The leading French peace worker, Baron D'Estournelles de Constant, was particularly active in trying to win the interest and support of the new President. In the first months of 1902 he wrote several letters to and had an interview with Roosevelt on the subject, and the chief executive responded sympathetically.

Roosevelt's favorable replies to D'Estournelles' appeals derived in part from his realization that the Court posed no danger to America's vital interests, but they also coincided with his tendency to act more responsibly on foreign policy issues as President than when out of power. Just as he began to tone down his ultranationalist rhetoric after assuming the presidency, so did he come to sympathize with the general purposes of the Hague Court; and he realized that unless the major powers agreed to submit some disputes to the tribunal, it would become a paper institution. He therefore asked Secretary of State John Hay to propose the settlement of the Pious Fund controversy, a politically innocuous but nonetheless long-standing dispute between the United States and Mexico over the latter's obligations to Franciscan missions in California, at the Hague tribunal. Since Mexico had already agreed to arbitration, the Hague Court received and decided its first case in 1902.[66] Shortly thereafter, other nations also turned to the Court for the settlement of their international differences. Most significant of the dozen cases settled by the Court before the First World War was the second one, the Venezuelan debt controversy. After considerable pressure from President Roosevelt, the creditor nations of Great Britain, Germany, and Italy (and eventually eight other nations) on the one side, and defaulting Venezuela on the other, agreed in 1903 to arbitrate the dispute before the Court.[67] This arbitration was particularly gratifying to many peace workers, because Roosevelt, though asked by both sides to mediate the dispute himself, refused and instead convinced them to submit it to the new Court.[68]

[6]

Toward World Organization

THE FIRST HAGUE PEACE CONFERENCE induced a handful of individuals to develop programs for the creation of additional international institutions. They were optimistic liberals who believed that the United States should lead the world community in the establishment of permanent institutions for war prevention. Temperamentally and ideologically, they were forerunners of Woodrow Wilson's vision of a league of nations as the cornerstone for a liberal international order, although Wilson later developed his ideas on world organization largely independently.

Among the first to sketch the outlines of a full-fledged organization was the Massachusetts publicist Raymond L. Bridgman. Bridgman was an extreme example of an anti-imperialist whose enthusiasm for future international cooperation resulted in bold suggestions for creation of a new world order. As early as 1899 he had argued that the Hague Conference was but the first step in an inevitable trend toward a world constitution consisting of judicial, executive, and legislative branches. In the next few years Bridgman elaborated details of his dream in several articles, which he shortly collected and published in a book entitled *World Organization*. While he hoped that the Hague Court would become a truly judicial body and that an executive agency would gradually evolve to administer the international organization, he emphasized the creation of an international legislature as the first step. He dramatized his interest by petitioning the Massachusetts legislature in 1902 to ask Congress to call an international meeting to begin discussions on the creation of a world congress.

Like other liberal internationalists in early twentieth-century America, Bridgman believed that a world legislature should be patterned after the

American federal system. Although he claimed that his peace structure provided a reasonable blueprint for world politics, his transcendental faith in humanity—what he called the "sovereignty of man"—suggested that the evolutionary development toward international institutions would logically culminate in world government. He was one of the few internationalists in the American peace movement in the first decades of the twentieth century to envision the eventual obliteration of national boundaries. Bridgman's petition specifically requested nations to relinquish lawful authority over matters clearly related to international commerce, monetary systems, and sanitation to the world legislature. His writings, while vague on the enforcement powers of his international organization, contemplated some kind of interference even in the internal affairs of nations when individual and human rights were involved.[1]

Bridgman's petition interested the Meads and Trueblood, and they soon persuaded the American Peace Society to sponsor one of its own. The petition of the Boston peace group advanced the more modest aim of periodic congresses meeting every five or seven years to consider questions of common interest and to make recommendations to their governments. The change reflected Paine's and Trueblood's more traditional views on international organization. In a short book, *The Federation of the World* (1899), Trueblood had portrayed federation as a slowly accelerating development leading inevitably to the unity of the human race. At least for the immediate future he showed little enthusiasm for authoritative international institutions, and he perceived an international congress as an advisory rather than as a lawmaking body.[2] Paine fully agreed, arguing that "[t]he time is not yet ripe when a congress can meet with power to legislate for the world."[3] The memorial of the American Peace Society provided that all actions of the international congress "would require ratification by the governments before becoming public law, and thus it would not encroach in any way upon the sovereignty and autonomy of the different countries."[4] Trueblood and Paine in effect desired above all else to put the Hague Conferences on a permanent footing. The First Hague Peace Conference had written a vague declaration suggesting a second conference at some point in the future, but the two perceived that Bridgman's amended petition could provide an opportunity to publicize the Hague idea.

When the Massachusetts legislature considered Bridgman's and the American Peace Society's petitions in early 1903, they showed a distinct preference for the latter. They unanimously approved the society's petition, which was then endorsed by the governor and sent to Congress. The peace group circulated copies of the memorial to the press and prominent citizens, and soon it had received favorable mention in several periodicals. Peace, church, and other voluntary associations unleashed a flurry of supporting petitions to Congress; one, promoted by the Peace Association of Friends of Philadelphia, received the endorsements of the governor, attorney general, and all seven justices of the supreme court of Pennsylvania, and a number of well-known clergymen, businessmen, and lawyers. But Congress remained unresponsive to proposed innovations in world politics. Although the backers of the memorial received a sympathetic hearing in the House Foreign Affairs Committee, their petition languished and finally died in its Senate counterpart.[5]

Meanwhile, enthusiasm for the Hague Court in particular and international institutions in general had begun to attract newcomers to the American peace movement. One was Richard Bartholdt. A German by birth and a popular Republican congressman from a German-American district in St. Louis from 1893 to 1915, Bartholdt had shown no interest in the peace movement in the 1890s. Party loyalty as well as strong interventionist pressures from his constituents resulted in his endorsement of the war with Spain and his vigorous defense of America's annexation of the Philippines as "the law of nature" and "the invisible momentum of progress and civilization."[6] Yet he responded enthusiastically after the First Hague Peace Conference. Echoing peace advocates' exhilaration at the accomplishments of that conference, he claimed that the creation of the Hague Court was "by far the greatest achievement of the nineteenth century."[7]

Thereafter Bartholdt's commitment to the peace cause developed rapidly. He regretted voting for war in 1898 and became so dedicated to the peace movement that he eventually was known as "the peace apostle" in the House. But he was never a complete pacifist.[8] Rather, his pacifist proclivities were a curious amalgam of Germanophilism and American idealism.

A close observer of international events, Bartholdt feared with good reason the anti-German direction of American foreign policy. Recurrent press rumors of the Germany navy's alleged attempt to interfere with Admiral Dewey's conquest of the Spanish fleet in Manila Bay as well as rising Anglophilia suggested that the United States might abandon its traditionally benevolent attitude toward all European nations. Because he began to sense, if he did not yet fully perceive, that the United States' emergence as a major world power might be the decisive factor in European politics, he was uneasy about the anti-German (or pro-British) thrust of American policy.[9] He saw that the real danger to world peace existed in Europe where Germany, encircled by the Franco-Russian alliance (and after 1904 by the Anglo-French *entente cordiale*) had increased its armaments and assumed a suspicious attitude toward the major powers. Europe, he repeatedly argued, was at the crossroad, one leading its people "in the future, as in the past, in [to] the fires of hell and war, . . . the other leading them through the open portals of The Hague to heavenly peace."[10] He feared war unless the United States pursued an active and friendly policy toward both major European power blocs. His ultimate goal was the abolition of German militarism. Once amicable European relations existed, then, and only then, would Germany throw off its military harness.[11]

In pursuit of his dream of a European detente, Bartholdt argued that the American government could most immediately improve the chances for European amity by calling a second international conference at The Hague. Assuming the good will of the Kaiser and his advisors, he thought Germany would prove receptive to the proposal. Even if a second conference did not immediately dampen the suspicions between the European power blocs, he believed that the reservoir of American good will, if persistently and patiently applied, would defuse European hatreds.

Bartholdt attempted to implement his proposal for another Hague meeting through the Interparliamentary Union. Before Bartholdt's participation in the Interparliamentary Union, most American congressmen had never heard of it.[12] Even in American peace circles the union was known before 1900 only to those peace workers who had regularly attended the Lake Mohonk and international peace congresses. Bartholdt, in fact, discovered the union by chance. During one of his regular trips abroad, he visited the First Hague Peace Conference and then journeyed to Berlin where a friend invited him to attend a meeting of the union at Christiania (later Oslo), Norway. The dedication and the politically practical nature of the European legislators immediately impressed him. Overestimating the union's potential influence in ameliorating nationalistic rivalries in Europe, he believed that more active American participation in its deliberations would greatly improve the chances for world peace.[13]

Bartholdt formulated a plan to popularize the activities of the union in the United States. At the 1903 meeting of the union in Vienna, he, without the approval of the American government, persuaded the delegates to hold the 1904 congress in St. Louis. Returning to the United States, he called on President Roosevelt. To Bartholdt's relief, Roosevelt agreed to request that Congress extend the customary invitation to the union. Roosevelt also agreed to ask for and soon obtained a congressional appropriation of $50,000 to defray the expenses of the foreign visitors.

Heartened by that support, Bartholdt called a meeting of congressmen who were interested in forming an American group of the Interparliamentary Union. Trueblood delivered an address to the forty-odd members of Congress at the meeting.[14] In the next decade that group grew to over two hundred senators and representatives. Although almost all of those legislators expressed only passing interest in the union, a handful regularly attended its later meetings in various European cities. Two in particular,

Ohio Republican Theodore Burton and Texas Democrat James J. Slayden, both opposed to Roosevelt's large navy programs, actively participated in the union. Burton had already attended one of its meetings in
Paris in 1900. They gradually drew closer to the inner circle of peace
workers. Elected officers of the American group of the union, they soon
became active in the American Peace Society, Burton serving as president
of the Boston group from 1911 to 1915 and Slayden as director from 1913
to 1917 and president from 1917 to 1921.[15]

Meanwhile, Bartholdt's peace efforts did not go unnoticed outside pacifist and congressional circles. Hayne Davis from North Carolina was an
aspiring young attorney in New York City when he was attracted to the
peace cause. Responding to United States' participation in the First Hague
Peace Conference, he began in 1903 to publish articles on the future development of international organization, and the following year he proposed
a supplement to Bartholdt's program for the Interparliamentary Union.[16]

Davis' program for world organization derived from his faith in American institutions. Like Edward Everett Hale, he believed that the early
formative period of the American nation should serve as the model. "The
idea of a Union of Nations," he said, "must go thru [*sic*] substantially the
same development as the idea of a Union of our States." Stretching the
analogy between the development of national and international institutions, Davis claimed that the First Hague Conference was "really the first
Constitution of the United Nations, as the Articles of Confederation was
the first constitution of our Union." While the establishment of the Hague
Court was a significant accomplishment, he perceived that it represented
only a "feeble" beginning and by itself was "hopelessly inadequate to the
needs of the people of the world," just as the union of American states
under the Articles of Confederation had proven inadequate to the needs
of the American people in the 1780s. Although he wanted to strengthen
the Hague Court and believed its public acceptance was indispensable for
progress toward internationalism, he recognized that without powers of
enforcement it "was manifestly incapable of preserving the world's peace."

To remedy that defect, Davis urged the establishment of an international
legislature. Such an assembly might not immediately prevent armed outbreaks, but it would bind the nations of the world and strengthen their collective responsibilities in working for a peaceful world order. The international parliament would have authority to develop rules of international
law for the jurisdiction of the Hague Court and generally serve as the
proper forum for the discussion of all important international questions.
Davis was vague on the enforcement powers of this international congress
but apparently thought that nations would adhere to the principles of international law declared by the international congress and applied by the

Hague Court without the necessity of establishing any police machinery. But the problem of sanctions was not a matter of immediate importance to Davis. He was interested solely in elaborating the logic of an international legislature as the next step toward world organization.[17]

Davis originally presented his ideas in a series of articles in *The Independent,* but in 1904 he found an opportunity to introduce them directly into the peace movement. In June of that year he met Richard Bartholdt at the Lake Mohonk Conference. Bartholdt had previously shown no interest in an international congress, and his address to the Mohonk delegates made no mention of a congress. He predicted in fact that the discussions at the forthcoming meeting of the union in St. Louis would focus on arbitration and disarmament.[18] Nevertheless, Davis was impressed by Bartholdt's address on the union as a forum for discussion and dissemination of proposals for world organization. Believing that the union could promote his own proposal of an international legislature, he conferred with Bartholdt on a few occasions and apparently won him over to the merits of an international legislature, for at the St. Louis meeting Bartholdt included it on his list of proposals.[19]

The St. Louis meeting of the Interparliamentary Union, attended for the first time by several American congressmen, unanimously passed a resolution endorsing Bartholdt's entire program. That resolution requested the president of the United States to call a second conference at The Hague. Furthermore, it declared that this conference should formulate international arbitration treaties for the jurisdiction of the Hague Court and consider the establishment of a world legislature which would convene periodically to discuss international questions.[20] Following the St. Louis meeting the delegates attended a reception at the White House at which President Roosevelt accepted the resolution and cautiously promised to promote a second peace congress.[21]

Roosevelt kept his word. Less than a month later he ordered the State Department to send out a circular note to the American diplomatic representatives accredited to the governments' signatory to the final acts of the First Hague Peace Conference asking them to communicate to these governments the American interest in a second conference.[22] Formal invitations were delayed until the conclusion of the Russo-Japanese War and still further by a question of protocol. The Russian government assumed that since Nicholas II was the acknowledged initiator of the First Hague Conference, he should have the honor of calling the second one. When Roosevelt learned of Nicholas' interest in a second conference, he deferred to the Russian Emperor who in 1906 summoned it for the following year.

As the Second Hague Peace Conference approached, many flocked to the peace movement. Of the new promoters of the fledgling movement for an authoritative internationalist organization, the most important was Hamilton Holt, managing editor of *The Independent,* which had already published several of Hayne Davis' articles on world organization. Before Davis approached Holt in 1903 with his internationalist proposals, Holt had expressed no personal interest in the movement.[23] He had in fact fully approved America's imperialistic adventures at the turn of the century. Davis soon convinced him that the subject of international organization was the most promising and important reform movement in the United States, even more important than the various domestic reforms Holt favored. Holt's initial motivation seemed to be a facile optimism in the ability of the United States to reform world politics, and the opportunity to perform more than his share of good works as a vigorous promoter of an embryonic movement. Nevertheless, his commitment was sincere and intensified with each passing year. The youthful and energetic Holt, who was thirty-two in 1904, began attending the Lake Mohonk Conferences and wrote several articles on international aspects of the peace movement. Peace workers found him a valuable ally, both in the favorable publicity he gave to their movement and in his active participation in its daily operations.[24]

Foreshadowing his later campaign for Wilson's League of Nations, Holt was mainly interested in the machinery of international organization. Like Davis, Holt used the American Constitution as the model for the future federation of the world. Also like Davis, he believed that the Hague Court alone could not bring about permanent peace (which would become a reality only after the development of international peacekeeping machinery), and he strongly endorsed Davis' plan for an international legislature as the next logical step in the international peace movement. In one respect Holt went further. Realizing that Davis' conception of an international legislature stopped short of a truly authoritative body, Holt argued that if a world congress were to have any lasting influence, it would require an executive body to enforce the legislature's acts. As he wrote in an editorial commenting on one of Davis' articles for a world congress, "without an executive agent and organization, the acts and resolves of a world legislature would have a merely advisory force."[25]

In an article published in April 1907, Holt advanced a ten point plan for "A Constitution of the World." It proposed that the Hague Conferences —what he called a General Assembly of Nations—should meet a third time in 1915 and thereafter every fifth year. That assembly would apply the principles of international law framed by an executive council of the Interparliamentary Union that would be called the international house of representatives. The most important section of Holt's "Constitution" involved the enforcement of the assembly's decisions. While it recognized the right of nations to maintain and use their armed forces whenever not specifically prohibited by treaties, it added that "the armed forces of all the nations represented in the Assembly shall be at the service of the Assembly for the enforcement of decrees rendered by the International Court at The Hague according to recognized principles of law and under the provisions of treaties of arbitration."[26]

While the movement for the Second Hague Peace Conference was gathering momentum in the United States, Bartholdt attempted to persuade his European colleagues in the Interparliamentary Union to endorse his specific proposals as the union's official recommendations for the forthcoming international conference at The Hague. Supported by seventeen other American congressmen at the Brussels meeting of the union in 1905 and by ten congressmen at the London meeting the following year, Bartholdt presented an advanced program. Of the many provisions in what became known as the American plan, Bartholdt particularly urged two: a permanent international legislature and a model arbitration treaty obligating nations to refer specific categories of disputes arising out of the interpretation or enforcement of treaties to the Hague Court. Acceptance of the model treaty, he thought, would facilitate the negotiation of more arbitration treaties which would enlarge the jurisdiction and strengthen the authority of the Hague Court; acceptance of the international legislature would provide a forum for making laws for the Hague Court to administer and stimulate the movement toward world organization.[27]

After some deletions, amendments, and refinements of language, the union completed its recommendations for the forthcoming Hague assemblage. They called for periodic and automatic meetings of the Hague Conference; a general arbitration treaty obligating signatory nations to refer nineteen specified cases relating to treaties and conventions to the Hague Court, including a code of law guiding its deliberations; mediation by one or more friendly powers or an international commission of inquiry to undertake an investigation of all other disputes before the nations resorted to war; and the establishment of a permanent consultative council to codify international law for the approval of later meetings at The Hague. Thus the union endorsed Bartholdt's proposal for a model arbitration treaty but severely restricted its scope and for his proposal of an international legislative assembly substituted an advisory body. Union delegates were perfectly willing to discuss an authoritative international organization but offered many objections as soon as specific proposals were brought forward. Nor did the union make any specific recommendation on the tangled question of armaments, although it urged full and serious discussion of the issue at the Hague Conference. Finally, it advocated measures designed to "humanize" warfare by imposing technical restrictions on belligerents: prohibitions on the use of new types of weapons and the bombardment of unfortified ports and towns, the immunity of private property, and broad definitions of the rights of neutrals.[28]

When the Second Hague Peace Conference convened in the summer of 1907, American peace spokesmen had high hopes that their efforts would induce the delegates to adopt many of their proposals. But the conference failed to live up to those expectations. The delegations did not agree to any concrete measures for the improvement of the machinery of international organization. While they discussed all the recommendations of the union, they made only minor improvements in the wording of the existing conventions relating to the Hague Court and mediation procedures. The ten new conventions governed the rules and techniques of warfare. Since the delegates could not agree on the limitation of armaments, the selection of judges for a newly designed judicial arbitration court, or compulsory mediation or arbitration of any cases, it simply recognized them as desirable principles but deferred positive action on them to a future conference.[29] In light of these meager accomplishments, even the "practical" peace proposals of the union were much too sanguine. After the Second Conference, in fact, the rival alliance systems in Europe hardened so rapidly that the union became more a debating society than a constructive sounding board for international reform proposals.[30]

The immediate reaction of most peace workers to the Second Hague Conference ranged from mild discouragement to outright scorn. Trueblood gently scolded the nations for allowing their delegations to make only half-hearted and dilatory proposals on armament limitation and obligatory arbitration treaties while dissipating their energies on the war conventions. The excessive talk on the laws of warfare, he lamented, was "a disgrace to our civilization."[31] Belva Lockwood and Alfred Love of the Universal Peace Union agreed.[32]

But the peace spokesmen's pessimism was only skin deep. The longer they reflected on the Second Hague Conference, the more they considered it beneficial. Because they could claim very little in the way of concrete achievements at the Second Conference, they pointed out its indirect benefits. As they had argued after the First Conference, though then with more justification, the actual meeting of nations in a recognized conference and the delegates' careful consideration of complex international problems were significant accomplishments. Living in a generation that accepted the idea of progress as an article of faith, they confidently pointed out that great movements often had small beginnings.[33] Compared with the First Peace Conference, for example, eighteen more nations (mostly from Latin America) attended the second. Edwin Mead claimed that on the basis of that increased representation the Second Hague Conference "was the most pregnant and significant gathering in human history," while Trueblood hailed it as "the first general representative assembly of the world."[34]

Even more significant from the same perspective, the Second Peace Conference, unlike its predecessor, recommended a third meeting after a lapse analogous to the one between the first two, or about 1915. Periodic congresses thus seemed definitely established. It also recommended the appointment of an international preparatory committee two years before the third conference to draw up a program and a system of organization and procedure for that conference. Susceptible to words and gestures which provided more than a glimmer of hope for the future, friends of peace looked to the day when their programs which had won the formal approval of most nations in 1907 would be achieved. Even the more cautious peace participants were optimistic. John W. Foster, former secretary of state and delegate representing China at the Second Hague Conference, argued that the conference was "the most important event in the history of the human race."[35]

Peace advocates also noted that the modest American proposal for a general treaty obligating nations to arbitrate legal questions provided they did not involve the vital interests, independence, or honor of the contracting powers, stimulated much interest and prolonged debate. The proposal foundered on the unanimity principle; but since only nine nations (four of which abstained) failed to approve it, pacifists and world federalists reasoned that unanimity on such a measure was surely possible and even probable at a future conference. The Second Conference's adoption of a resolution approving "the principle of obligatory arbitration," particularly for the interpretation of treaties and other legal questions, seemed to confirm progress toward international reform. The conference also approved in principle the establishment of a new international institution, a court of arbitral justice. The failure of the larger and smaller nations to agree on a formula for the selection of the comparatively small number of judges prevented implementation of the plan, but peace leaders predictably minimized the difficulty. If future negotiations could not break the impasse, the major powers could devise a suitable formula for their own governments and proceed to establish the court, which would gradually win the support of all nations.[36]

It is impossible to measure exactly how much the Hague Peace Conference forwarded the American peace movement. The conference, however, triggered a surge of speeches and writings. Moreover, many who were uninterested in peace prior to 1899 now joined the movement. Whether old or new, peace advocates optimistically interpreted the conference as a turn from "idealistic" to "practical" proposals.[37] Frederick Lynch, a leading liberal clergyman who joined the peace forces in the early twentieth century, recalled, "We felt . . . a new era had dawned . . . the peace problem was being brought down out of the world of idealism . . . and was becoming a practical, political question."[38]

The dichotomy of "ideal" and "practical," however, is misleading. That generation's intellectual elite considered themselves practical people even though they couched their ideals in the vague phrase "practical idealism."[39] Spokesmen in the peace movement also used the words "practical idealism" and "practical idealists" to explain their approach to peace work.[40] They were correct in believing that their institutional approach to peace was practical in comparison with the nineteenth-century peace movement's more negative antigovernment doctrines like individual nonresistance. In view of the public's indifference to foreign policy, they were certainly more realistic to work through government officials and established institutions. The prospect of a Second Hague Peace Conference prompted even the Lake Mohonk Conferences after 1904 to add the concept of periodic international congresses to its arbitration emphasis. The peace movement had come a long way in trying to keep abreast of America's increasingly important role in international politics.

The growing interest in a permanent legislature and executive branch inevitably stimulated debate on sanctions. Edwin Ginn, Lucia Mead, and Andrew Carnegie in particular argued that a permanent international body should be given limited powers such as the employment of an economic boycott, and, as a last resort, the use of an international army to coerce recalcitrant nations.[41] The movement also became increasingly "practical" in selection of its personnel, and after 1905 the support of prominent business and professional people accelerated rapidly. As we shall see in the following chapters, the increasing domination of the peace movement by these practical-minded men seemed to confirm the movement's growing respectability among governmental leaders and reinforced the elitist predelictions of the movement's more active participants.

Yet many of those who expressed considerable interest in the peace cause before 1905 remained at heart idealistic. Their concern for the procedures of arbitration and mediation and the details of world organization could not obscure their buoyant optimism, and their emphasis on the "practical" nature of their internationalist proposals often seemed more an affirmation of their own hopes than an accurate assessment of the chances for realization of their proposals.

In their more honest moments participants in the peace movement freely admitted that they were more idealistic than realistic; but even when they did not specifically affirm their idealism, it was revealed in their rhetoric. Shortly after his return from the Second Hague Peace Conference, Hamilton Holt prepared a stereoptican lecture entitled "The Federation of the World," which he delivered to university, school, and public gatherings. His lecture was an enthusiastic peroration of the achievements of the two Hague Conferences. The two meetings at The Hague, he emphasized, foretold the inevitable founding of an international judiciary and legislature. Then, he continued, "it will be possible to add an International Executive & when that golden period is at hand—and it cannot be very far distant— we shall have in very truth Tennyson's dream of 'The Parliament of Man, The Federation of the World,' and for the first time since the Prince of Peace died on Calvary, we shall have 'Peace on Earth and Good Will to men.' "[42] Another new recruit to the peace movement, William I. Hull, a Quaker pacifist and professor of history at Swarthmore College, and writer of sober accounts of the two Hague Conferences, could boldly claim, "the Hague Conferences are to international law what the industrial revolution of the eighteenth and nineteenth century [sic] was to human industry or what the rise of the American Republic was to human government."[43] That rhetoric was not exceptional; others emphatically hailed the cumulative achievements of the two conferences as harbingers of a warless world.[44]

Peace workers resorted to exuberant rhetoric to uplift their audiences and hopefully convert some to active service in the movement, but they were also affirming their own quasi-religious devotion to the cause. It is also likely that their exultant statements served certain psychological needs; bold reaffirmations of their faith, for instance, helped to purge whatever nagging self-doubts still existed concerning the wisdom of their deepening commitment to idealistic internationalism.

Although the two Hague Conferences greatly stimulated interest in world organization, peace advocates did not abandon their traditional emphasis on arbitration treaties. The two meetings at The Hague in fact helped to promote international arbitration as had no previous efforts of peace workers. The establishment of the Hague Court in particular stimulated renewed interest in arbitral accords, which despite the efforts of pacifists, nonpacifist supporters of international understanding, and diplomats had just begun to flourish before the First Hague Peace Conference. Between 1901 and 1910, however, more than 130 arbitration treaties, double the number of the previous decade, were ratified. Furthermore, one of the conventions of the 1899 Hague assemblage stipulated that nations could conclude agreements obligating nations to submit certain disputes to arbitration. In succeeding years arbitral agreements specifically provided for automatic referral of certain classes of technical and legal cases (such as the interpretation of treaties) to the Permanent Court of Arbitration.

Arbitration treaties between Chile and Argentina and the Netherlands and Belgium went further in specifying that all controversies were to be referred to arbitration for settlement, the latter explicitly naming the Hague Court as the tribunal.[45]

Good reasons existed, however, for viewing these developments with some skepticism. In actuality governments signed those treaties not because they were converted to international friendships, but because they sought security in an unstable world. Moreover, the overwhelming majority of those treaties covered only minor legal questions unlikely to lead to war. In any case, because the total number of actual arbitrations of disputes undertaken by the contracting parties declined slightly after 1900, most arbitration accords remained symbolic gestures of good intentions.[46] Perhaps most important, almost all were negotiated between nations possessing comparable physical power, but the great powers displayed virtually no interest in arbitrating important questions with smaller nations.

The realities of international politics, especially the problem of asymmetrical power relationships, received some attention in American peace circles after the Roosevelt administration's successful military support of a secessionist revolt in Panama in early 1904 against Colombia had led the grateful Panamanian leaders to give the United States absolute control over the Panama Canal Zone. One anonymous critic in the *Advocate of Peace* said that the American military's successful obstruction of Colombian troops from the isthmus during the revolt had flouted clauses of a United States treaty of 1846 with New Granada (later Colombia) in which the United States had guaranteed "the rights of sovereignty and of property" as well as "free transit" on the isthmus. The writer demonstrated that these clauses legally prohibited any United States aggressive action against Colombia. Even if one accepted the Roosevelt administration's reference to Secretary of State Seward's earlier claim that the guarantees applied only to foreign powers, the administration's willingness to employ force to aid the Panamanian revolt clearly violated Seward's assertion in the same declaration that the United States should uphold the clause guaranteeing the "perfect neutrality" of the isthmus during internal revolutions.[47]

A few months later, Moorfield Storey asserted in an address to the American Peace Society that the United States had rejected Colombia's request to submit the 1846 treaty to the Hague Court—though the interpretation of treaties was a subject for arbitration under almost all existing arbitral agreements—because the Roosevelt administration realized that it could coerce hapless Colombia without fear of reprisals and felt, with good reason, that the tribunal would decide against the United States. Secretary Hay had correctly claimed that Colombia's grievances were political and therefore not subject to judicial decision, but his and Roosevelt's statements that the administration's military and political actions were legally justified under the 1846 treaty only strengthened Colombia's contention that the real issue involved the correct interpretation of that treaty.[48] Anti-imperialist peace advocates Charles F. Dole and Ernest H. Crosby seconded those criticisms of the Roosevelt administration, also attacked its "unlawful" intervention in the Dominican Republic, and succeeded in passing resolutions in the New England Anti-Imperialist League protesting "the rape of Panama" and the establishment of a protectorate in the Dominican Republic.[49]

Trueblood joined the anti-imperialists both in his specific condemnation of the administration's "indecently hasty paramountcy" in the Panamanian affair and in his general critique of the great powers' disdain for the integrity of smaller nations. He lamented that the larger powers had recently destroyed independence movements in the Philippines, South Africa, and Finland, and ominous signs existed of their imminent intent to bring about the political death of Tibet, Korea, Siam, and Persia. He even concluded that "we are in considerable danger of seeing at no remote day the disappearance of all the small states of Western Europe."[50]

The impressive successes of President Roosevelt and other avowed imperialistic politicians at the polls in Massachusetts and elsewhere in the 1904 elections, however, indicated that the voters either approved America's imperial exploits or brushed them aside as politically irrelevant when public attention focused on domestic problems. Even the anti-imperialists' moral influence declined considerably as advancing years and deaths sapped the vitality of the anti-imperialist movement. Newcomers to the peace movement between 1900 and 1914 rarely spoke in defense of the rights of small states. Because several of the newcomers were as old as their predecessors, the different views on international reform of additions to the peace movement before and after 1900 did not constitute a "generation gap;" but almost without exception the latter was much less affected by the humanistic rhetoric of "freedom," "equality," and "democracy" of the Civil War era. Instead, their outlook was molded by a variety of subtle influences that will be explored in succeeding chapters. Suffice it to say here that those joining the peace movement after 1900 adjusted more easily than earlier recruits to the emergence of the United States as a major world power. Not surprisingly, therefore, they accepted at face value the large powers' moralistic rhetoric professing their sincere interest in peace and arbitration while ignoring or excusing their subjugation of foreign peoples.

One exception was Oscar Straus who joined the arbitration and anti-imperialist movements before 1900 yet managed to supply the Roosevelt administration with a rationalization of its high-handed actions following the Panamanian secession. When Roosevelt began to search for some legal justification for his support of the Panamanian revolution, he asked Straus, a member of his "Kitchen Cabinet," whether the United States was still bound to its 1846 treaty with Colombia, and Straus replied that the American government's obligation remained in force because the treaty was "a covenant running with the land."[51] Roosevelt seized upon the remark and instructed Secretary Hay to incorporate Straus' argument into the administration's defense of its decision to guarantee to the new state of Panama all the 1846 treaty rights against possible "foreign" (*i.e.,* Colombian) incursions. Straus' legal sophistry was too much for John Bassett Moore who wrote Straus that his advice to Roosevelt really amounted to a "covenant running (away!) with the land!!"[52]

Straus' awareness of Roosevelt's determination to keep Panama as well as his warm personal regard for the President predisposed him to search for some legal sanction for the administration's *fait accompli.* Moreover, he apparently never wavered in believing in the essential legality of America's actions during the revolt, for he regretted Roosevelt's frank admission in 1911 that his own determination to secure a canal in Panama rather than concern for legal niceties had prompted his actions. As Straus later commented, "Instead of saying, 'I took it,' he (Roosevelt) might better have said, 'I exercised our rights under the treaty.' "[53] Because of the complicated legal questions and the imprecision of international law, Straus' legal argument was perhaps plausible. Yet he was well aware of the forceful arguments of certain Democratic politicians and peace advocates that the American government's position was indefensible even under a generous interpretation of the 1846 treaty, and his continued desire to justify the American position suggests his unconscious nationalism.

Straus in fact never really challenged the notion of the leading imperial powers' dominance of the international system. Although his two terms as American minister in Turkey sharpened his disapproval of the big powers' more flagrant imperial excesses, it also schooled him to accept their resort to expediency, including the use of force, as indispensable, if unfortunate parts of the diplomatic game. If Straus, one of the more idealistic peace advocates, could defend the Roosevelt administration's meddling in Panama, it is not surprising that more "practical" peace spokesmen repressed whatever moral qualms they might have had and remained silent.

Most Americans who first participated actively in the peace movement after 1900 were so preoccupied with the powerful or "civilized" nations that they never bothered to ask whether the system of power politics itself might be a root cause of war. Another newcomer to the peace movement Theodore Marburg, an independently wealthy and self-trained political economist, believed that almost all peoples except the Americans and

Europeans were "backward," and he had strongly endorsed the war with Spain and the takeover of the Philippines. Thereafter he became increasingly interested in the problem of large nations' violations of small states' sovereignty but believed that the major problems of peace and order were global and had to be solved by cooperative action between the United States and the major European powers. Marburg remarked in 1910, "Many of the South and Central American states are backward states. We must face the facts. . . . Our civilization is European. The geographical view of this question is the narrow view. . . . It is the great powers of the world that determine the world's peace on a great scale."[54] In view of their great power mentality, Marburg and others joining the movement after 1900 consistently expressed less concern over the moral and legal questions of Roosevelt's "Big Stick" policy in the Caribbean than in arbitration treaties and other institutional arrangements for moderating potential conflicts between the larger powers.

They were in truth already absorbed in a new campaign to encourage the United States to assume leadership of the arbitration movement. The rapid rapprochement between the United States and Great Britain from 1898 to 1903 helped advance the arbitration movement in the United States by reviving enthusiasm for an arbitral accord between the two nations. Most of the same proponents of the Olney-Pauncefote treaty of 1897 decided in 1903 that the time was ripe for renewed activity in support of an Anglo-American arbitration accord.[55] The promoters of the 1896 Conference on International Arbitration called a second conference in Washington, D.C., in January 1904 to initiate another campaign for such a treaty. In addition to "Old Guard" peace and arbitration advocates, more recent proponents were among the 150 participants. The conference passed resolutions urging the United States to conclude an Anglo-American treaty covering all disputes and including mutual promises not to resort to hostilities in any controversy until it was submitted to the Hague Court or a commission composed of an equal number of competent jurists from each side. A final resolution urged the negotiation of agreements "to the same effect, as soon as practicable, with other powers."[56]

Partly in response to these appeals and partly because of Secretary Hay's sympathetic support for arbitration, Roosevelt approved the negotiation of arbitration treaties with several powers in late 1904 and early 1905. Since Hay's treaties covered only differences of a legal nature and excepted questions involving "vital interests," "independence," and "honor" of either party, or "the interests of third parties," and had to be renegotiated every five years, they did not go as far as many arbitrationists desired.[57] John Bassett Moore argued that they constituted "a step backward" because they fell short of the Hague conventions in extending the scope of arbitration. All agreed, however, to support their ratification. The predominant view among the arbitration leadership, Moore noted rather disconsolately, seemed to be that it was "better to accumulate treaties, no matter how poor they may be, than to rest upon those that have already been made."[58] Those like Foster who arranged public meetings in several cities in support of the treaties stressed their few positive features. For one thing, they emphasized that because the treaties provided that those disputes covered by the agreements would be referred to the Hague Court, it would enhance the usefulness and prestige of the institution. Moreover, they suggested that even their limitations appeared to be an advantage in that they avoided the sweeping and indefinite provisions that had earlier led to the Senate's rejection of the Olney-Pauncefote accord.[59]

A majority in the Senate still remained skeptical. Arbitration proponents received a foretaste of the Senate position when the Foreign Relations Committee indifferently received a delegation of the Washington Arbitration Conference. Few Senators objected to the reservations in the treaties, which safely protected the nation's freedom of action on important foreign policy questions, but many expressed displeasure with the clause allowing the governments to sign a "special agreement" whenever they needed to interpret the provisions of the treaty before beginning arbitration of a given dispute. Believing that clause gave the executive branch undue powers, the Senate Foreign Relations Committee proceeded to change the words "special agreement" to "treaty," thereby requiring Senate consent to an additional treaty specifying the issues in each dispute before arbitration could commence. Roosevelt correctly perceived that if the Senate approved this amended version, his treaties would be rendered innocuous. In that event, he warned, he might refuse to allow their ratification.[60]

Agreeing with Roosevelt's outspoken opposition to the Senate amendment, Trueblood and Straus advised Roosevelt to withdraw the treaties from the Senate if it passed the nullifying amendment. Straus even urged the President to appeal to public opinion in the hope that an aroused public sentiment would undermine Senate intransigence. Never an enthusiastic convert to international arbitration, Roosevelt was unwilling to follow that course that surely would have intensified legislative-executive tensions. Once the Senate passed the amendment, however, he agreed with Straus' denunciation of that body's action as a mockery of the arbitration principle and pigeon-holed the accords.[61]

Though temporarily sobered by the upper house's jealous regard for its prerogatives, arbitration proponents did not abandon the effort. Richard Bartholdt sought a compromise. When he prepared his model arbitration treaty for the Interparliamentary Union, he tried to avoid the indefinite language that had prompted the Senate amendment. His model treaty stated that the Senate would relinquish its prior consent to clearly defined and limited categories while retaining its constitutional authority over all other arbitral arrangements. Since his treaty won the tacit support of many senators sympathetic to the Interparliamentary Union as well as the Democratic party's titular leader William Jennings Bryan, it was just barely possible that the Roosevelt administration could have successfully incorporated that compromise formula into new arbitration treaties with foreign governments. The controversy between the President and Senate over an executive agreement with the Dominican Republic, however, exacerbated the Senate's concern for its prerogatives and made a compromise unlikely. In any event, although Bartholdt and Hayne Davis suggested this remedy in an interview with the President, he never attempted to implement it.[62]

Instead, Roosevelt relied on Hay's successor, Elihu Root, for guidance. Though a friend of arbitration, Root was decidedly cautious in his approach to international reform proposals. Root persuaded Roosevelt to accept the Senate amendment and then negotiated twenty-five arbitration treaties in 1908 and early 1909, twenty-four of which were ratified. Arbitration proponents were comforted in the belief that these limited treaties marked the beginning of real leadership in the arbitration movement by the United States. They also attempted to put the best possible face on the accords by stressing their obligatory features while overlooking their extraordinarily narrow jurisdiction and the Senate amendments, which virtually nullified general application of the arbitration principle.[63]

Even though arbitration advocates magnified appearances at the expense of reality, they were somewhat justified in their hopes for more aggressive United States' action. Roosevelt had assumed the activist role without enthusiasm, but William Howard Taft's election to the presidency in 1908 signified an even greater awakening of the movement. A firm friend of international arbitration, he would soon advance the most extensive arbitration scheme yet proposed by any American President. After Taft committed himself to the arbitration cause, the dedicated workers for international arbitration began to predict that in a few swift years a network of arbitration treaties would span the globe, bind nation states closer together, and bring their dream of the federation of the world closer to fulfillment.

[7]

Toward a
"Practical" Peace Movement

FROM ABOUT 1905 TO 1912 the American peace movement expanded
rapidly. One indication of the growing interest in peace and arbitration
among professional people and businessmen was the attendance figures at
the Lake Mohonk Conference. The thirty-five attending the first 1895
meeting reached about 100 in 1900, and 169 by 1904. The numbers at
the 1905, 1906, and 1907 Mohonk Conferences swelled to 190, the most
the hotel could accommodate.[1]

Moreover, the 1907 National Arbitration and Peace Conference in New
York strikingly demonstrated the growing enthusiasm of functional elites
for the movement. Organized by Boston and New York peace leaders,
this four-day gathering met in a packed Carnegie Hall. President Roosevelt sent the conference a letter cautiously approving its objectives and
Secretary Root addressed the opening session. Among its supporters were
eight cabinet officers, two former presidential candidates (William Jennings Bryan and Alton B. Parker), ten United States Senators, four justices
of the United States Supreme Court, nine state governors, ten mayors,
twenty-seven millionaires, eighteen college and university presidents,
thirty labor leaders, forty bishops, and sixty newspaper editors. Several
political and professional leaders gave speeches lauding the lofty purposes of the movement toward world amity. There were also a large number of businessmen representing some 166 commercial and manufacturing organizations. Many had earlier been uninterested in the peace

movement and would participate only perfunctorily thereafter, but they were willing to share its present popularity by making a public appearance on the platform. In all, more than 1,200 people from thirty-nine states and seventeen foreign nations registered for the sessions. The congress, one reporter claimed, was "the greatest gathering ever held in advocacy of the abolition of war . . . and the most important non-political gathering ever held in this country for any purpose."[2] The public's warm response to this meeting so encouraged peace leaders that they held similar congresses biennially until 1915 in other American cities.

Interspersed between these national congresses were state and regional peace conventions in Texas, Pennsylvania, and Connecticut, which likewise attracted much public interest, won the endorsements of numerous political, civic, and municipal leaders, and featured a wide array of veteran peace speakers.[3] Another barometer of enthusiasm was the proliferation of organizations devoted to world peace. Between the fall of 1904 and the Senate vote on President Taft's arbitration treaties in March 1912, the rising interest in the peace cause resulted in the establishment of about twenty-five peace and internationalist societies, most notably the American Society of International Law, New York Peace Society, American School Peace League, Chicago Peace Society, Massachusetts Peace Society, and American Society for the Judicial Settlement of International Disputes, and two richly endowed institutions, the World Peace Foundation and Carnegie Endowment for International Peace.[4]

Why the sudden interest in peace? One might expect heightened concern for peace during a war crisis, but these were years of international tranquility for the United States. American fears of the increasing military rivalries among the major powers perhaps stimulated rising interest in international reform proposals. A general uneasiness about militarism may have partly prompted involvement in the peace movement. Some, however, had earlier supported American territorial expansion; others had expressed little interest in it and thereafter indicated no marked concern for halting the large navy programs of their own nation. A few were willing to sign petitions protesting the further expansion of the American navy, but the anti-preparedness agitation among peace spokesmen continued to emanate largely from the anti-imperialists active in the peace movement since at least the turn of the century. Unlike pacifists or idealistic internationalists involved in the organized peace cause before about 1905, almost all of the later arrivals were much more cautious in their approach to international reform and in fact prided themselves on their "practical" approach to the problem of world peace.

Veteran peace workers, eager to increase the respectability and practicality of the movement, helped to attract newcomers to the peace movement. They assiduously cultivated persons prominent in legal, educational, diplomatic, and business elites and eventually prevailed upon many to participate in the peace cause. As the peace movement absorbed increasing numbers of establishment figures, its own membership became increasingly conservative and nationalist. More like-minded individuals joined the cause when they perceived its conservative orientation. While mutual reinforcement resulted in the addition of professional and business people to casual or indifferent membership in specific peace groups, it fails to explain why several newcomers became active participants and in some instances even assumed important administrative positions in the movement. Other motives were surely involved in pushing them toward leadership in the cause.

Since the post-1905 arrivals rarely articulated their reasons for joining, any attempt to explain their motives involves some speculation. Certainly their motivations were complex and perhaps often unconscious. This much is certain: no sudden revelations or conversions induced their involvement in the peace cause, nor did they operate in a cultural vacuum in which purely rational calculations governed their decisions. On the contrary, they were products of their social and intellectual environment, and their entrance into the peace movement stemmed from forces simultaneously affecting American social life and foreign policy in those years.

Some of the newcomers were motivated by little more than genuine interest in American foreign relations. If they did not give anti-preparedness high priority, they nonetheless wanted to influence American foreign policy in constructive directions. They perceived America's entrance into world politics at the turn of the century as an essentially positive development. As the peace movement acquired a nationalist cast, they increasingly used it as a convenient forum for expounding their own ideas. Such newcomers believed that the United States could use its moral and material influence to develop a more stable, orderly, and nonrevolutionary world for the Western imperial powers, and they rather easily equated the cause of peace with the interests of their own nation. But they were not merely defenders of the imperial status quo, for they advocated international reform if it could be obtained through gradual, orderly processes. Not surprisingly, the Hague Peace Conferences' requirement for unanimity and their deliberative, formal features appealed to the newcomers. Part of the surge of interest in peace undoubtedly sprang from the hopeful prospects of the Second Hague Peace Conference, and the National Arbitration and Peace Congress was organized specifically to arouse public interest in that forthcoming gathering.

Another impetus to peace sentiment was the progressive reform movement, which permeated all aspects of American life. The idealistic overtones of the domestic reform impulse affected the outlook of both liberals and conservatives who thought about world politics during these years. Pacifistic liberals, believing in the essential goodness of man and the application of human reason to control or eliminate social evils, expressed confidence in the possibilities of the peace movement to achieve the supremacy of law and reason and the gradual elimination of war and militarism. While more conservative peace spokesmen were more restrained, in general they too basked in the sunny optimism of the decade and projected onto the world stage their cautious hopes for a more orderly domestic society.

While America's more important role in world politics as well as domestic reform helped to arouse the interest of all new peace recruits, many of them gravitated to the peace movement because it simultaneously served certain professional aspirations and psychological needs. Several international lawyers, for example, joined the peace movement because they found it a potentially useful vehicle for advancing the status of their professional careers. While the evidence motivating the participation of businessmen is not so clear, many of them discovered that the peace movement provided a readily available instrument for demonstrating their sense of social responsibility and enhancing their reputations as men of civic importance. For those men the movement served as a convenient outlet for satisfying their mildly reformist propensities. They were not disposed to support the domestic reform programs of advanced progressives intent on democratizing the American social and political order and found it easier to support vague hopes for reform on the remote world stage than to face change at home.

Much the same sentiments may have motivated the involvement of Americans with strongly religious backgrounds. We have seen how religion profoundly influenced many of the earlier peace advocates, but it operated in a more subtle way among later recruits. Just as the social gospel movement among Protestant churches aroused more clergymen's active involvement in domestic social problems after about 1900, so did many more of them begin to perceive the problem of war as a growing social issue. Not Christian pacifism but a more worldly, hopeful, and—one must add—superficial approach to the problems of war and peace influenced those churchmen's associatic n with the peace movement. Peace societies filled many of their official positions with Protestant clergymen, most of whom left their parishes in the process. There is some evidence that they found in the peace cause an accessible moral reform movement for widening their social role and influence beyond their congregations. Similarly, a few others who had initially considered the ministry or church service as a career but ultimately chose other professions (such as teaching) joined the peace movement. To all such newcomers participation in the peace cause may have helped to revitalize their fond memories of the morally simpler truths and gentlemanly standards of their Mugwump backgrounds while satisfying their desire to participate in a "progressive" cause.

Thus, many factors contributed to the rapid growth of the American peace movement after 1905. The motives prompting specific individuals to join the cause, however, were as diverse as the origins and programs of specific peace and internationalist groups in the 1905–1912 period.

Peace workers had always stressed the importance of educating the public on the goals, tactics, and achievements of the international peace movement, and in the first years of the twentieth century many educators increasingly shared this emphasis. Those educators not only joined old peace groups but formed new ones. The new organizations stressed the publication and distribution of literature on the peace movement to schools, colleges, and the general public.

In the foreground of that educational campaign was the Boston textbook publisher Edwin Ginn. Though not a professional educator, Ginn believed that school books profoundly contributed to the glorification of patriotism and the military, which in turn fostered the growth of armaments and "the war power."[5] His antidote to unhealthy militarism was a new emphasis in education on the basic idealism and nobility of all peoples. He particularly wanted schools to stress the peaceful aspirations of all peoples. Ginn's educational philosophy involved more than genteel uplift, however, for he emphasized that "children should be taught that military parades in holiday dress, the manoevres [*sic*] of armies and navies to the strains of martial music, do not paint war in its true light. Take them rather to the battlefield of Waterloo, as painted by Victor Hugo; to the retreat of the French army from Moscow. Put before them the horrors in the Russian-Japanese war." Such new amity would eventually enable nations to transfer a major portion of their armed might to an international peace-keeping agency that would enforce the peace against recalcitrant powers.[6]

Ginn's thoughts on the problem of world peace had in fact matured rapidly. The futility of his opposition to the Spanish-American War and imperialism hastened his loss of faith in what he considered negative tactics, and with the defeat of Hay's arbitration treaties in 1905 he began to reject arbitration treaties as inadequate. Thereafter he became an advocate of authoritative international institutions and the creation of an international police force. He proposed a permanent international legislature with sufficient power to employ the international police force in specified kinds of crises. His vision of peace increasingly looked toward world government. As Ginn's private secretary recalled much later, "He must be classified among those we now call world federalists, and among world federalists he would have belonged to what we might call the left wing. He would have been puzzled by the recurrent differences of opinion among avowed world federalists. To him the case for a strong and widely serviceable world government seemed clear and convincing."[7]

In 1902 Ginn established an International Library in Boston, which published and distributed at cost peace literature to interested individuals, schools, and private associations.[8] He continued to expound his educational philosophy at various peace congresses but increasingly criticized the peace societies. In his view they were reaching more people but had failed to enlist them as active participants in the peace crusade. The militarists were already organized, he asserted, as rapidly expanding appropriations for the navy demonstrated; what was now needed was a centralized, efficient, and heavily endowed organization that would coordinate peace efforts and conduct an intensive educational campaign on a national and even on an international scale.[9]

As a successful businessman Ginn believed that the peace movement had to be organized on business principles. "We must make a *business* of educating the people, beginning with the children in the home and in the school," he asserted. He placed special emphasis on the organizational talents and financial resources of successful entrepreneurs like himself. Accordingly, he appealed to Andrew Carnegie and other businessmen-reformers to create a peace endowment.[10] When he received no encouraging response, he took the initiative himself by formally establishing an International School of Peace in July 1910 with his gift of $50,000 yearly and the promise of a million dollar endowment upon his death. Even that, he believed, would be only "the nucleus and beginning of a great endowment contributed by others and perhaps by governments themselves to forward this great cause."[11] He often mused that an endowed fund of ten million dollars would be needed before the peace movement would achieve real success. Deliberately publicizing his bequest of a million dollars, he hoped to encourage affluent individuals to contribute their own money to an endowment, which upon his death would receive even greater financial support.[12]

In late December 1910, Ginn reincorporated his school as the World Peace Foundation. That decision reflected Ginn's uncertainty concerning the proper educational program for the creation of a peaceful world. Since he felt he could not yet offer a panacea for implementation of his ideas in world politics, he decided that the World Peace Foundation would study methods for selling the public the idea of an international police force as a substitute for national armaments and designing the arrangements for the protection of national sovereignty from potential abuses of the international army.[13] In some ways the foundation was modeled after the emerging American university. Although it enrolled no students, it had a board of trustees who served without pay and were responsible for general policy, and salaried directors who wrote the peace propaganda and delivered lectures to teachers, school gatherings, private associations, and peace societies. The composition of the board of trustees and the directors illustrated the pedagogical emphasis of the foundation. Five of the ten trustees and two of the seven directors were leading educators in American colleges and universities. The other trustees and directors were progressive businessmen, editors, and clergymen.[14] Almost all of these latter trustees and directors were first exposed to the peace movement and in some instances to each other at the Lake Mohonk Conferences.[15]

Ginn's main collaborators in the World Peace Foundation were two of its directors, David Starr Jordan and Edwin D. Mead. Mead's influence on Ginn was more direct both because of their longer friendship and their frequent personal contacts at the foundation's headquarters in Boston. The scholarly Mead believed that a sound education was the key to good citizenship. When Ginn established the International Library he made Mead its head. Mead's crusading zeal brought him closer to professional educators as well as to others who eventually became trustees or directors of the World Peace Foundation.[16]

The foundation immediately organized and financed the peace movement in schools and colleges. In addition to its own propaganda campaign, it furthered the activities of three quasi-pacifist organizations which were already active on the college and secondary levels: the Intercollegiate Peace Association, the Association of Cosmopolitan Clubs, and the American School Peace League. Its contacts with the Intercollegiate Peace Association, organized in a few Quaker and Mennonite colleges in Ohio and Indiana in 1906, were informal and amounted to little more than publication of the group's prize orations on peace themes. Though the group quickly expanded to some fifty colleges and universities throughout the Middle West and Pennsylvania and enrolled as an auxiliary of the American Peace Society, it failed to attract the close attention of the World Peace Foundation's leaders who remained primarily interested in the Cosmopolitan Clubs and the American School Peace League.[17]

The foundation's commitments to the Cosmopolitan Clubs developed rapidly. The Association of Cosmopolitan Clubs was organized in 1907 by federating international friendship societies in eight universities and colleges. In promoting closer contacts between the growing numbers of foreign students and their American counterparts, the group attempted to break down national prejudices and promote international understanding. Though not avowedly a pacifist organization, it expressed the same idealistic internationalism of the leading pacifists. The motto of the Cosmopolitan Clubs—"Above all Nations is Humanity"—proudly expressed its idealism.[18]

When the foundation began its support of the Cosmopolitan Clubs in 1910, the movement was a small but thriving venture. Although the group had only two thousand members in twenty-two American colleges and universities, many university presidents strongly endorsed its activities. David Starr Jordan of Stanford, Charles R. Van Hise of Wisconsin, Charles F. Thwing of Western Reserve, Jacob Gould Schurman of Cornell, and Schurman's predecessor, Andrew D. White, for instance, attended its annual conventions and praised its idealistic internationalism.[19]

More directly related to the peace movement was the encouragement Trueblood and Edwin and Lucia Mead gave to those clubs. They stimulated pacific-minded internationalism in them by giving lectures to their gatherings and publicizing their activities in the *Advocate of Peace*. They soon persuaded the Cosmopolitan Clubs to enroll as an auxiliary of the American Peace Society.[20] When Mead joined the World Peace Foundation he continued to endorse the activities of the clubs. The dedication and youthful idealism of its two student leaders, Louis Lochner of the University of Wisconsin and George W. Nasmyth of Cornell, particularly impressed him. He believed that with guidance from the foundations they could make the Association of Cosmopolitan Clubs a major force in the peace movement. With Mead's strong endorsement, the World Peace Foundation provided a yearly subvention to the association for publication of a monthly magazine and paid Lochner's salary as secretary.[21]

Thus encouraged, Lochner and Nasmyth expanded their horizons to Europe. Missionary in outlook, they believed that only American leadership could achieve the "world wide union of students in the cause of international peace and the human brotherhood of man."[22] Accordingly, they began a concerted campaign to establish similar clubs in European universities. Already loosely affiliated with Corda Fratres (Latin for "brothers in heart"), an organization of European students with similar goals, the Cosmopolitan Clubs cooperated with them in organizing peace clubs among European students.[23] The spearhead of those transatlantic endeavors was Nasmyth who went to Europe in 1910 for the dual purpose of graduate study in mathematics and physics and expanding the international student movement.[24]

Meanwhile, the National Arbitration and Peace Congress in 1907 had led directly to the founding of the American School Peace League. Encouraged by the enthusiastic reception of school teachers at a peace meeting for school children during the New York Congress, a Boston school teacher, Fannie Fern Andrews, along with the Meads organized a committee to work out a plan to interest teachers in the international peace movement. The committee soon established the American School Peace League with headquarters in Boston. The league's general goal, its constitution stated, was "to promote, through the schools and the educational public of America, the interests of international justice and fraternity."[25] Specifically, it distributed literature to teachers on the international peace movement, promoted peace days, sponsored essay contests, and prepared materials on international good will that the teacher could use in the classroom.[26] Its dominant motif was the training of school children in the ideals of good citizenship and international understanding. One of its most interesting proposals was "A Course of Study in Good Will" for elementary and junior high school children. According to the syllabus: "The time has come when we can advance on a new crusade. Let all the teachers of our land unite to spur their pupils on to drive back evil, disease, and sin. Let them form with one another the unbreakable bonds of a common loyalty embodied in service to the nation and good will to men." Suggested subjects for study in the curriculum attempted to implement a genteel philosophy. Little children were taught how they could help around the home, then in the school and neighborhood. By the eighth grade they were presumed mature enough to absorb a simplified presentation of William James' essay, "The Moral Equivalent of War," and then to design worthwhile projects into which man could safely channel his aggressive impulses.[27]

For executive secretary of the American School Peace League, the organization committee secured Fannie Fern Andrews. An extremely energetic worker, Mrs. Andrews quickly became the driving force in the new organization. Not only did she deliver lectures and disseminate the league's propaganda throughout the United States; she also carried her message to Europe. She especially worked to recruit many college presidents and school administrators to her program. By 1913 the American School Peace League gained the loyal financial backing of the World Peace Foundation and a few wealthy patrons, formed thirty-seven state branches, held annual conventions, and received the endorsements of the National Education Association and the National School of Superintendents.[28] Perhaps its most significant accomplishment was the strong support which the United States Commissioner of Education, Philander P. Claxton, gave to the group's peace days in the schools.[29]

Despite the expansion of the American School Peace League's administrative apparatus, it is debatable how many schools actually introduced her course suggestions into the curriculum. In any case, the emphasis of the curriculum on "responsibility," "faithfulness," "obedience," "fair play," "cheerfulness," "loyalty," "service," and "self-control" suggests that the teaching of genteel citizenship as much as genuine internationalism inspired its authors.[30] Moreover, even those guidelines were so general as to allow teachers a wide latitude in introducing those moral precepts. The American School Peace League in fact best represented the generalist position in the peace movement. In the hands of imaginative and peace-loving teachers, the league's program inspired sentiments of idealistic inter-nationalism in their pupils, but in less competent hands stifled students' potentially creative and spontaneous feelings about peace and reinforced the public schools' many subtle forms of social control.

Mrs. Andrews epitomized a blend of old and new values present in gen-eralists entering the peace movement after the turn of the century. Raised in Boston, Mrs. Andrews absorbed its patrician reformers' interest in reli-gious and ethical education, and she was much less interested in recent pedagogical trends like specialization and innovation of the curriculum than in revitalizing its traditionally ethical emphasis. Perhaps because of her comparative youth—she was only thirty-nine in 1906—she was little affected by the Christian pacifism and antislavery radicalism that had nur-tured the youthful years of many older Boston peace workers. Her infec-tious idealism lacked the sharp edge of her more radical predecessors. She apparently articulated no strong opinions on the debate over imperialism but welcomed the United States' participation in the twentieth century's "new internationalism" represented by arbitration treaties and the Hague Conferences. Because she never seriously doubted the good intentions of her government, she naturally steered the American School Peace League away from potentially controversial subjects such as the horrors of war, militarism, or federalists' growing emphasis on the development of authori-tative institutions in favor of a vaguely defined, cooperative international-ism. At the same time, she seemed at home with the growing tendency of professional educators to unite people with similar functions on a national and even international level.

Meanwhile, prominent educators in New York City were also express-ing interest in the educational aspects of the international peace move-ment. Many New Yorkers were first drawn into the peace movement through their attendance at the Lake Mohonk Conferences, which increas-ingly discussed the task of carrying the peace movement to the "people." Encouraged by the accomplishments of the First Hague Peace Conference and the growing enthusiasm for the Second Conference, a group of promi-nent New Yorkers founded the New York Peace Society in 1906.[31] As might be expected, professors and professional educators dominated its leadership. Faculty members from Columbia University were especially prominent. Other founders included eminent New York lawyers, clergy-men, editors, and philanthropists. Those most active in cooperating with the Columbia educators in the formation of the new society were Holt, Straus, Jefferson, and Lynch. The founders were the epitome of New York City business and professional establishments.[32]

The new group elected Straus as president. When he resigned a few months later to assume the position of secretary of commerce and labor in the Roosevelt administration, the executive committee replaced him with Andrew Carnegie. Dutton served as secretary, but as the society grew and embarked on ambitious programs, its leaders decided that it needed a full-time executive secretary. In October 1908, they appointed the Reverend William H. Short to the new position. Born and raised on an Iowa frontier farm, Short graduated from Beloit College in Wisconsin and had studied for the ministry at Yale Divinity School where he met Frederick Lynch, and it was Lynch who persuaded the executive committee to offer the job to Short.

Never restricted solely to the ministrations of his congregations, Short exemplified the emerging breed of social gospel clergymen who were increasingly devoting their attention to contemporary problems. In his first pastorates in Wisconsin and Minnesota, he had successfully exhorted his congregations in various movements for social betterment. The offer of the New York Peace Society provided him with a unique opportunity to serve a much larger and more influential constituency, and he readily accepted the position because he had already expressed interest in the problem of world peace. He had given sermons on peace and even earlier, in 1893 while still a college student, had written a prize-winning essay that expressed his benevolently paternalistic assumptions about liberal education and his faith in human rationality. In that essay he wrote that when "humane education" was emphasized in schools and colleges, "wars will cease, crime will decrease, property and life will have a new security, and the morning of peace and good will of which the angels sang will rise upon our race, and not upon it only, but also the dumb races that toil and die in our service, minister to our comfort and happiness and depend upon our protection and care." Like Hamilton Holt, who became his close friend in the New York Peace Society, Short extended his liberal faith in America to international relations. He shared Holt's growing interest in the machinery of international organization and during the First World War would work closely with him in promoting a league of nations. Until the outbreak of the war, however, Short supported almost any nonradical peace proposals.[33]

The wisdom of the New York Peace Society in appointing a permanent secretary soon became evident, for its growth was phenomenal. At the end of the society's first year, the membership had grown to 600 and six years later it was to soar to more than a thousand.[34] The expanded membership represented a diversity of occupations and viewpoints. Although a few pacifists—Oswald Garrison Villard, his mother Fanny Garrison Villard, George Foster Peabody, and the liberal Unitarian minister John Haynes Holmes—joined the society, the overwhelming majority of new members had little sympathy for absolute pacifism. Clergymen and lawyers flocked to the new group, but the growing numbers of businessmen in the society were particularly noticeable. By 1912 one-third of both the vice-presidents and directors were businessmen, and they may have exceeded that percentage for total membership.

Concern for international peace and stability as necessary for the protection of their overseas investments may have prompted the participation of business executives representing companies with extensive foreign connections, such as Wall Street investment banking houses and certain mining and shipping corporations. The international mining engineer John Hays Hammond frankly admitted that considerations of economic self-interest in part motivated his growing participation in the peace movement. But those were a minority of businessmen in the society. Many more probably viewed participation in the peace society in much the same way as they viewed their memberships in local philanthropic and civic organizations. Association with those activities enhanced their sense of social responsibility and offered a safe outlet for their tepid reform inclinations. If many initially joined the new peace group in response to Andrew Carnegie's personal appeals, they quickly perceived that the growing predominance of businessmen and other wealthy people involved little sacrifice of their prestige and respectability. On the contrary, their prominent appearance at the society's formal receptions and banquets for visiting diplomats and peace people suggests that they believed their participation in those functions enhanced their public image. Although the more active and on the whole more idealistic founders of the society continued to dominate the policy-making executive committee, the increasing membership of business and other more practical people in the society provided a potential check against the society's official sponsorship of potentially outlandish pacifist or internationalist programs.[35]

The influence of the New York Peace Society rapidly expanded in several directions. What began as an intensive effort to sponsor lectures and distribute literature to private associations in New York City grew to include active cooperation with the American Peace Society in promoting the 1907 National Arbitration and Peace Congress and the organization of a New York branch of the American School Peace League. It also took advantage of the ethnic diversity of New York City by cooperating informally with friendship societies like the local Cosmopolitan Club and the German-American Peace Society and played small roles in helping to organize the Japan Society, Mexican Society, and American Scandinavian Society.[36] Those multifarious activities attracted the attention of oldtimers in the peace movement, and as early as 1909 Trueblood gratefully acknowledged that the New York Peace Society was "the strongest and most important of the local peace societies of the country."[37] By then it had become the second largest peace group in the country, rivaling the larger and much older American Peace Society in financial backing and influence.[38]

The growth of the New York Peace Society encouraged some of its leaders to broaden its horizons. If New Yorkers received the society's activities so warmly, they reasoned, why not champion the peace movement on a national and international scale? Although the leaders believed the existing peace societies and national peace congresses were important gatherings in furthering the aims of the peace movement, they concluded, as Ginn had earlier, that without a large endowment the peace workers would only scratch the surface.

The most obvious source for financial backing of a munificent peace fund was Andrew Carnegie. A series of influences and events between 1901 and 1910 seemed to conspire in bringing about Carnegie's acceptance. First, the sale of his steel business in 1901 intensified his deepening involvement in the peace cause, for thereafter he could devote much more of his attention to progressive and humanitarian causes. Carnegie derived great satisfaction from acting out his philosophy of the "Gospel of Wealth" in these years. His generous gifts made him even more hopeful for the future. He put it quite humbly: "I do find with every successive year of my life . . . that I have brighter and brighter visions of the future."[39]

In light of such lofty idealism, it was logical for Carnegie to commit himself wholeheartedly to the peace movement. In 1903, for example, he gave $1,500,000 for the construction of a "Temple of Peace" at The Hague, which would house the sessions of the Permanent Court of Arbitration. He also donated $750,000 for the construction of the offices of the Pan American Union in 1906 and $200,000 for a Central American Court of Justice in 1908.[40] Furthermore, he contributed liberally to peace societies and peace congresses; in 1910 he claimed that he was contributing at least $50,000 yearly to sixteen peace groups.[41] The retired industrialist even believed that his gifts to the cause of simplified spelling would make the English language "the lingua franca of the whole world," thereby eliminating the babel of tongues that had hindered international understanding. In like fashion he thought his endowed Hero Funds in several nations would counteract the glorification of military valor by remunerating ordinary citizens who performed heroic acts in saving the lives of their fellow men.[42]

Moreover, the former steelmaster became directly involved in the daily

operations of the peace movement. He had reluctantly agreed to succeed
Oscar Straus as president of the New York Peace Society, but once involved, he became its most enthusiastic promoter.[43] In addition, Carnegie
found his experience as president of the National Arbitration and Peace
Congress exhilarating, and he supported later biennial peace congresses
in other American cities.

Although his increased financial and personal involvement led to greater
undertakings, he remained reluctant to underwrite a peace endowment.
Thus, when friends of peace began to deluge him with financial requests
for new undertakings, Carnegie was unimpressed. William T. Stead had
asked him to form a peace and arbitration society in 1900, but Carnegie
had replied curtly, "if it were dependent upon any millionaire's money it
would begin as an object of pity and end as one of derision. . . . There is
nothing that robs a righteous cause of its strength more than a millionaire's
money—especially during his life. It makes a serious, holy cause simply
a fad."[44]

Nevertheless, the pressures on Carnegie for creation of a large peace
fund continued to mount.[45] Realizing that he tended to discount individual
appeals, Hamilton Holt and others carefully developed a new strategem,
which ultimately won over the reluctant philanthropist. Late in 1908 Holt
asked Nicholas Murray Butler, president of Columbia University, whether
Carnegie, who had already established endowments of $10,000,000 for
other causes, might be persuaded to establish a peace endowment of like
amount.[46]

Butler had invaluable assets in his quest for Carnegie's funds. He had
cooperated with Carnegie in formulating plans for the Carnegie Institution
in 1902. Moreover, Butler's recent emergence as a powerful voice in the
"practical" peace movement could not help but enhance his stature in
Carnegie's eyes. Butler's interest in peace represented an extension of his
philosophical outlook to the world scene. As a conservative Republican
his ideal of the good society envisioned a high-minded intellectual elite
ruling a stable social order according to established principles of law. His
elitism was undisguised. He had a genuine aversion to democratic movements and a corresponding worship of successful people. The latter carried
over into a love of pomp and circumstance; he wore medals and decora-
tions to official functions and once criticized King Haakon of Norway for
not appearing regal enough. He assumed that the elite's ethical principles,
civilized standards, and respect for law would trickle down to other elements in society, help uplift them, and eventually tame their rebellious
impulses.[47]

With the emergence of the United States as an imperial power, he had
extended the elitist ideal to the world. He had expressed dismay at "the

shocking recklessness of speech" and "wicked sensationalism of a debauched and debauching press" that had brought on the Spanish-American War but, always cautiously optimistic, believed that the emergence of the United States onto the world stage would hasten the slow march of the world's peoples toward civilization and peace. Butler had thus advised McKinley to take the Philippines from Spain after the war as a potentially important bargaining lever for the United States in world politics. Specifically, the takeover would demonstrate America's commitment to "internationalism" and would enable the United States to use its moral influence to temper Germany's imperial appetite. The approaching Second Hague Peace Conference deepened his involvement in peace questions. He used his position as presiding officer of the Lake Mohonk Conferences to expound his bright hopes for the evolution of a more just international order. His faith in a truly international elite instructing public opinion prompted him to establish an American branch of the Association for International Conciliation in 1907, the main office of which Baron d'Estournelles de Constant had established in France two years earlier. Carnegie's decision to finance this undertaking signified his confidence in Butler's plans.[48]

Butler proceeded to supervise plans for enlisting the reluctant philanthropist. He urged Holt and Mead to draft the proposal that soon received the written endorsements of Andrew D. White, Edward Everett Hale (now chaplain of the United States Senate), and a former and incumbent secretary of state respectively, John W. Foster and Elihu Root. The proposal emphasized the need for a permanent fund for a world-wide educational campaign "that would in time reduce the martial and jingo elements of the several populations to comparative insignificance." However, Carnegie, correctly noting its vague features, believed the proposal "too much up in the air" and contained "nothing of a definite character." Yet, he did not flatly reject the proposal and urged its restatement in more explicit terms. Specifically, he wanted Butler to clarify the purposes for which the money would be spent.[49]

Although the revised proposal also failed to impress the philanthropist, proponents of the endowed organization believed that Carnegie's opposition was weakening.[50] What was now needed, they reasoned, was more solid evidence of a strong and united front of the leading peace spokesmen. Accordingly, they decided to intensify their efforts to draw the Boston and New York peace advocates closer together.[51] The peace leaders of the two cities had cooperated in sponsoring the National Arbitration and Peace Congress in 1907, and they had held an informal meeting early the next year to discuss further efforts in that direction. The prospect of obtaining Carnegie's millions for the peace movement provided an additional motive for cooperation among the peace groups.

The first formal proposal for coordination of the peace societies occurred at the Lake Mohonk Conference in 1909. That meeting adopted a
resolution authorizing Nicholas Murray Butler to appoint a committee of
ten to consider the advisability of establishing a national council for arbitration and peace.[52] In addition to leading peace advocates from Boston
and New York, Butler wisely included Carnegie as well as their esteemed
personal friend, Elihu Root, and James Brown Scott on the committee.[53]
Root frankly admitted the close relationship between the appointment of
that committee and peace leaders' continuing hopes for an endowed peace
agency when he told Carnegie that the purpose of the committee of ten was
"to provide for a Peace Trust."[54] The committee of ten was probably not
decisive in finally motivating Carnegie's gift, but it served as an additional
incentive for his action.[55]

Other simultaneous developments pushed Carnegie toward the establishment of a great peace foundation. One was Carnegie's unenthusiastic
response to Ginn's International School of Peace, for he felt that the
School of Peace largely duplicated the propaganda methods of the peace
societies. Yet Ginn's gift moved Carnegie one step closer toward acceptance of the Butler proposal. Carnegie reasoned that the International
School of Peace, far from fulfilling the financial requirements and the
specific programs of the American peace movement, only dramatized the
need for something larger, and he intimated that a more liberally financed
agency might prove more effective[56] Surely part of his reasoning for another endowed agency was a rationalization to conceal his wounded pride.
Having pioneered in so many other fields of philanthropy, he suddenly
discovered that his procrastination had allowed another philanthropist to
preempt what in recent years had become his major interest. Was he going
to allow a textbook publisher to become the great philanthropist for peace?
For Carnegie, the question was the answer.[57]

The founding of the International School of Peace provoked anxious
discussions in the American Peace Society. As early as December 1908,
the society's directors had contemplated the possibility of moving the
group's headquarters from Boston to Washington, D.C., where it would
be closer to political developments and could more easily aspire to a truly
national organization, and Ginn's school accelerated discussions on the
subject. The society's directors feared that the financial resources of the
International School of Peace might diminish the prestige and influence
of the American Peace Society in the Boston environs, but Ginn's decision
to locate the school's offices only two doors away from those of the Boston
peace group compounded their concern. While the directors earnestly debated the question of relocation, Trueblood asked Carnegie, the society's
leading "angel," for advice and simultaneously appealed for a guaranteed

annual subvention of $50,000 for five years if the peace group moved to Washington, D.C. The society needed the subvention, Trueblood argued, to finance the expansion of its programs and the coordination of the peace societies.

What was Carnegie to do? On the one hand, he found demands for his money escalating at an alarming rate; on the other, if he rejected Trueblood's request for additional funds, the American Peace Society might decide to move anyway and raise the additional funds from other sources. Both would thus further limit his influence in shaping the future direction of the organized peace movement. He obviously had to commit his money soon if he wished to have a hand in determining the actual form of the consolidation of the peace forces.[58]

Two foreign policy initiatives prompted Carnegie's final commitment to an endowed peace organization. Probably less decisive was Carnegie's reactions to the failure of his personal diplomacy. In the first years of the twentieth century he began to realize that the European nations were developing into two hostile camps. Appalled at the prospect of such a general European conflict, in 1905 he outlined his proposal for a "league of peace" composed of the United States, Great Britain, France, Russia, and Germany. If those five powers agreed to refer their international disputes to the Hague Court or other arbitral machinery, war could be averted. Because he was not a nonresistant, he proposed that the league use economic sanctions and, as a last resort, military force against recalcitrant powers. He cited the cooperative military action of the five powers in helping to restore order during the Boxer Rebellion in China as a precedent for military cooperation. He hoped, however, that other nations would eventually join the league and that military force would be unnecessary.[59]

Carnegie increasingly believed that Kaiser William II of Germany was the key figure for the future peace of Europe. Britain, France, and Russia had already drawn closer together by alliances, ententes, and arbitration treaties, and he now hoped the Kaiser would call for a league of peace. It was in his hands, Carnegie said, "alone of all men, that the power to abolish war seems to rest."[60]

Carnegie remained hopeful for the Kaiser's conversion to a peace league even after Germany's intransigent attitude at the Second Hague Peace Conference. Late in 1909 he began to urge former President Roosevelt, who was hunting big game in Africa, to visit the Kaiser in Germany. The former steel magnate insisted that Roosevelt, whom William II greatly admired, could freely discuss the international situation with the Kaiser and perhaps receive some expression of the latter's willingness to relieve the diplomatic tension.

Carnegie's proposal once more underscored his simplistic view of foreign relations. That a visit between Roosevelt and the German Emperor, both of whom had frequently glorified the virtues of war and the military, could be the panacea for world peace required an extraordinarily sanguine disposition, but Carnegie really believed in the two men. Perhaps thinking of Roosevelt's successful mediation of the Russo-Japanese War, he even dubbed him the "Great Peace Maker." His hero worship of both men blinded him to mundane realities. It apparently never occurred to him, for example, that Roosevelt carried little weight as a private citizen without official authority to act for his government.

If Carnegie was overenthusiastic, a more modest view of such a meeting offered grounds for cautious optimism. Informal summitry might serve as a positive first step in thawing the cold diplomatic atmosphere in Europe. If a full-scale international police force was improbable, improved diplomatic relations might lead to an agreement stopping the armament race. Even the normally cautious Elihu Root warmed to the potentially beneficial results from a meeting between Roosevelt and the Emperor. The failure of arms limitation at the Second Hague Peace Conference he attributed in part to the inordinate difficulties in reaching agreement on intricate formulas for disarmament among a large number of powers at a single conference. If Roosevelt could coax William to adopt a more moderate stance toward Germany's neighbors, then perhaps the way would be opened for an international disarmament agreement. "England is ready to quit the arms race if the other fellow will," Root wrote Carnegie. "I do not know of anybody who would be more likely to make a lodgement in the Emperor's mind with this idea than Theodore Roosevelt."[61]

Carnegie's arguments, seconded by Root, finally convinced Roosevelt to meet with the Kaiser in Berlin. Though making his usual reservations that the discussions would have to be "practical" and not influenced by "silly" proposals of pacifist "extremists" whom Carnegie associated with, the former President was sincere in hoping for progress toward a friendly climate among all the major powers. But even Roosevelt's cautious approach to these problems failed. The death of King Edward VII of England resulted in the cancellation of all official engagements throughout Europe. When Roosevelt finally managed to meet briefly with the Kaiser, he did not push the league idea. The German press, apparently alerted by a suspicious German Foreign Office, branded as inappropriate any such discussions, and Roosevelt quickly surmised that the Kaiser was unwilling to discuss such a sensitive subject.[62]

Had Roosevelt's German visit stimulated interest in a European detente, Carnegie might have further pursued his personal diplomacy. In fact, he never lost faith in the Kaiser's essential good will and hoped until 1914 that he would undertake a peace initiative.[63] With the failure of the Roosevelt mission, however, Carnegie became more receptive to other proposals to improve international understanding.

If the combination of those developments by early 1910 had not yet converted Carnegie to the endowment proposal, his resistance had virtually dissolved. Whatever doubts might have persisted rapidly disappeared after President Taft espoused his ardent faith in international arbitration treaties. First suggested in vague, almost casual terms on March 22, 1910, and more fully elaborated in later speeches, Taft's treaty plan contemplated that all "justiciable" issues, not excepting questions of "national honor," would be referred to the Hague Court or an ad hoc arbitral agency. Carnegie, who had already attacked the concept of national honor in foreign relations, was elated at Taft's initial proposal. He wrote him an enthusiastic letter and published an article lauding the President's suggestion.[64] The willingness of Great Britain to conclude a treaty similar to Taft's proposal, moreover, appealed to the philanthropist's long-standing belief that Anglo-American cooperation would precede other nations joining in the promotion of a general system of arbitration. More important, Taft's action gave the peace movement even greater momentum and convinced Carnegie that its "practical" cast had at last confirmed its respectability among governments. Carnegie proceeded to minimize the general goals of the Butler proposal and to perceive his endowment as a vigorous booster of a specific British-American arbitral accord. The psychological moment had arrived, he believed, for a permanent and influential peace organization that would push the arbitration movement along the road toward the ultimate abolition of war.[65]

Even after he was emotionally committed to the gift of a peace endowment, he desired assurances that Taft really intended to conclude treaties that his proposed agency could immediately promote. He thus conferred with the chief executive before announcing the gift in an attempt to make it contingent upon an explicit presidential promise to negotiate an Anglo-American arbitration agreement. Taft of course refused any bargain. "The trouble with old Carnegie," the chief executive remarked after their meeting, "is he might secure what he wants in my [annual] message, and then not give the money. I think I will go a little slow until old Andrew becomes more specific."[66] Despite that rebuff Carnegie completed the arrangements for his gift and on December 14, 1910, formally announced that he was entrusting $10,000,000 of United States Steel Corporation five percent first mortgage bonds to his twenty-seven newly appointed trustees of the Carnegie Endowment for International Peace.[67]

The Carnegie Endowment for International Peace shared certain characteristics of the World Peace Foundation. Both were founded by businessmen-philanthropists anxious to eliminate the scourge of war from the earth. Moreover, both were organized like colleges and emphasized efficiency and scholarly research. But the differences between the two were just as important. While the World Peace Foundation also distributed peace propaganda in an effort to uplift and convert their readers, the Carnegie Endowment subsidized almost exclusively value-free, passionless research. While the foundation made at least some attempts to popularize the peace movement through the diffusion of its peace propaganda to all levels of American society, the educational programs of the endowment were unashamedly elitist. The endowment in fact spent its money only on the safest and sanest of peace proposals.

The cautious policies of the endowment reflected the conservative viewpoint of the board of trustees. Unlike the missionary zeal of Ginn, Mead, and Jordan, the foundation's most forceful personalities, the twenty-seven trustees Carnegie appointed were unusually conservative, not only in domestic affairs, which, in view of Carnegie's fear of radicalism, peace activists might have expected, but in international affairs as well. Of the six peace spokesmen who most actively promoted the proposal—Holt, Mead, Dutton, Hale, Smiley, and Butler—only the two most conservative, Smiley and Butler, became trustees. In fact, no outspoken opponent of the Spanish-American War became a trustee nor except for James L. Slayden, Oscar S. Straus, Charles W. Eliot, and John Sharp Williams had any participated even marginally in the anti-imperialist movement.[68]

When Carnegie composed his list of trustees, he may have deliberately excluded peace advocates like Mead, Jordan, and Dutton because they were already serving as directors or trustees of the World Peace Foundation. He also may have decided to overlook prominent officers of peace societies like Trueblood and Short for similar reasons. But he carried this exclusive policy to an extreme, for of the eighty-four officers of the American Peace Society in 1910, only three—John W. Foster, James Brown Scott, and Albert K. Smiley—were appointed trustees, and none of those had been an officer of the peace group before 1908. Moreover, the only names of trustees that had appeared on the society's membership list published two years earlier were Foster and Straus.[69] Except for Straus and perhaps a few other marginally "progressive" appointees (such as the aged Andrew D. White, seventy-eight years old in 1910), Carnegie even bypassed more idealistic establishment liberals such as George Foster Peabody, Hamilton Holt, or the Reverends Charles E. Jefferson and Frederick Lynch. Indeed, not a single member of the clergy became a trustee.

Considering Carnegie's well-known support of peace societies, his omission of their spokesmen from the board of trustees seems inexplicable. Had he kept his own counsel or turned to the most active peace workers for suggestions, he might have appointed at least some of them. At one point he intimated to Dutton that he believed he should appoint some of the foremost peace leaders to the board. Carnegie, however, chose to rely on the advice of his conservative friends, especially Nicholas Murray Butler and Elihu Root. He particularly valued Root's experience in public affairs and prevailed upon him to accept the presidency of the endowment.[70] Despite his enthusiastic activity for peace, Carnegie showed the same caution with his money in creating his peace fund as he had with previous gifts like the Carnegie Institution and the Carnegie Fund for the Advancement of Teaching. He turned to Butler and Root in part because he believed that their successful management of his existing endowed institutions would also result in carefully developed policies that would guarantee the perpetuation of the peace fund. Not surprisingly, their recommendations of conservatives as trustees included at least eight who had no prior institutional affiliation with the peace movement and who were appointed mainly because of their prestigious names or past experience in managing large institutions.[71]

Root and Butler also told Carnegie that pacifists had already denounced the evils of war, and internationalists had elaborated several blueprints for international organization. What was now needed, they counseled, was a "scientific" investigation of the various causes of wars and the adoption of educational and judicial methods that would eventually eliminate them. Actually, Root and especially Butler had little sympathy for peace societies. They felt that they were too "emotional" and detracted attention from internationalist organizations they supported. When membership declined in the New York Peace Society a few years earlier, for example, Butler had emphasized that he preferred to work with "the best minds" in groups like the American Association for International Conciliation. He had also opposed the word "peace" in the societies' names because of its possible radical connotations, and for the endowment would have preferred the name "Carnegie International Institute."[72]

Carnegie vetoed that suggestion but generally deferred to their advice. They defused Carnegie's suspicions concerning their reservations on peace societies by assuring him that they would urge the trustees to provide a subvention to the peace societies and thereby relieve him entirely of the future financial burden. Root's and Butler's low opinion of the peace societies foreshadowed future difficulties between the leadership of the peace societies and the endowment, but at the time Carnegie foresaw no problems. He expressed no doubts about the choice of trustees and apparently accepted almost all the names Root and Butler suggested. If he worried at all about the lopsided, conservative orientation of their list, two statements in his formal announcement of the gift suggest how easily he repressed them. First, he emphasized that he was most interested in the endowment's immediate promotion of Taft's arbitration treaties, and he presumed that whatever their long-range policies they would follow his wishes in supporting his penchant for a quick "victory." Second, because he assumed inevitable progress toward a warless world, he could rationalize that his peace endowment affected the pace of that development. He even provided that when war had been abolished, the trustees would divert endowment funds to their choice of the next most degrading social evil.[73]

As representatives of the conservative establishment, the trustees were remarkably similar in outlook. They quickly agreed that the Carnegie Endowment was not a "glorified peace society" and would deliberately try to project a more dignified image to the public. There was no dissent when Elihu Root remarked at the first meeting of the trustees that the endowed organization should be thoroughly practical, devoting most of its energies to "scientific" research. The endowment, he stressed, should seek "that deeper insight . . . attained only by long and faithful and continuous study" of the causes of war.[74]

The trustees decided at the outset to divide the work into three divisions, each headed by a director. The division of intercourse and education had the most general title, and Butler, who became its acting director, quickly interpreted its scope most broadly. Within a year he had initiated projects requiring expenditures of $230,000 or nearly one-half the endowment's annual income, but the trustees consistently endorsed his wide-ranging plans. In the United States he initiated discussions with peace leaders on a possible reorganization of the American Peace Society, which soon led to the movement of its headquarters to Washington and the grant of a generous annual subvention of $31,000 to the society as the central clearing house for disbursements to affiliated peace groups. His division also helped to finance the conventions of the Intercollegiate Peace Association and the Corda Fratres.

Butler also extended the endowment's influence to Europe and beyond. He developed plans to "internationalize" his department by establishing a secretariat in Paris for the coordination of the endowment's European activities and an advisory council of eminent peace workers, international lawyers, scholars, and former diplomats to advise the trustees on present and possible future work in Europe. Because Butler wished to avoid possible criticisms of American domination of European activities, he allowed the advisory council to develop programs freely. Since the council had little independent authority, its influence was limited, and in any case its members proved to be safely moderate. When it began to function in 1912, some members reacted negatively to Butler's subvention of $24,000 to the International Peace Bureau in Berne (part of which had to be distributed to various national peace societies) because it accounted for over ninety percent of the Bureau's income. Butler had authorized the sum less from conviction than to quiet potential criticism of the endowment in its initial phases. The advisory council's criticisms served as a convenient excuse for Butler to express his hopes for a gradual reduction in this appropriation until it totaled only about twenty to twenty-five percent of the Berne Bureau's income. His allotments to the Association for International Conciliation increased to about $60,000 by 1914, the largest single expenditure in his budget. He used much of that to develop new affiliates of the group in Germany, Great Britain, Canada, and Argentina. Those actions clearly demonstrated Butler's preference for fostering ties with "intelligent people" of "sound" opinion over distinctly pacific-minded, more "radical" members of national peace groups in Europe, many of which were attempting rather pathetically to check the escalating armament expenditures of their governments.[75]

The title, division of intercourse and education, implied involvement in "propaganda" and political activity, but even Butler preferred detachment whenever possible. The division's reaction to the Balkan wars illustrates its academic approach. Instead of denouncing the reckless policies of the warring powers or promoting mediation efforts to end the fighting, Butler organized an international commission of leading scholars and public officials to study the causes, excesses, and consequences of the wars. Although the belligerents denounced the published report that documented the reckless and inhumane policies of the warring powers, it in truth adhered to the endowment's standard of scholarly objectivity.[76] Butler's division also appealed deliberately to the intellectual elite of the world by financing cultural exchange programs for professors with Latin America and Japan.[77]

The other two departments were more explicitly scientifically neutral. The division of economics and history, headed by Columbia economist John Bates Clark, gathered scholars for research related to the problem of war. The division authorized them to study approved topics and it subsidized publication of their findings. The subjects covered all phases of international relations but because of Clark's influence they emphasized such economic aspects as the effects of tariffs, investments, and labor groups on war causation. The studies assumed that impartial investigation of the facts would conclusively demonstrate that the benefits of peace outweighed the costs of war. The division did not trumpet its findings but instead allowed other intellectuals to draw upon them in accumulating more evidence for additional writings against war. Peace would come, so it was thought, step by step in the ongoing process of intellectual enlightenment.[78]

The division of international law was Elihu Root's major interest. The embodiment of the conservative's reverence for law, he became a vigorous advocate of the rule of law in international relations. He accepted the presidency of the Carnegie Endowment only after Carnegie agreed to the appointment of his confidant, legal authority James Brown Scott, as secretary. He also made sure that the Carnegie Endowment had a division of international law, also headed by Scott, that would disseminate information on the nations' rights and responsibilities under existing international law and promote periodic international conferences to amplify and codify that law. A man of inexhaustible energy, Scott used his allotment of funds to swell the treasuries of international law societies in the United States and Europe, promote the study of international law in American universities, and found a summer school in international law at The Hague.[79]

[8]

The Growth of Legalism

THE CARNEGIE ENDOWMENT's promotion of international law reflected the growing influence of international lawyers in the peace movement. Part of their increased participation in the cause stemmed from their dissatisfaction with peace workers' unquestioning acceptance of international arbitration as a panacea for world peace. Although the vast majority of peace workers before 1905 welcomed the rapid proliferation of arbitration treaties and hoped that the Permanent Court of Arbitration would gradually formalize and regularize the resort to arbitration, they conceded the existence of some defects in the arbitral process. They readily admitted, for example, that arbitration agreements remained overwhelmingly voluntary on the contracting parties, still required negotiation of a separate *compromis* defining the issues for the arbiters in each controversy, and included many broad reservations, all of which underscored the reluctance of nations to sacrifice any state sovereignty. They remained faithful, however, to the arbitration principle and were confident in the prospects of reducing its defects in the future. They thus proposed the steady expansion of obligatory clauses in arbitration treaties, international agreement on a general arbitration treaty to facilitate the development of a network of agreements fostering international friendship, and provisions in the treaties for the automatic referral of ever widening categories of disputes to the Hague Court.

Several lawyers, however, criticized the arbitration movement more directly. The New York State Bar Association, it will be remembered, had pointed out in 1896 that because the disputing nations in an arbitration appointed their arbiters, they were almost always partisans and thus lacked the detachment necessary for impartial judgment. As a remedy, the association had suggested the formation of a world court. The authors of the

153

proposal had argued that the professional ethics and multinational representation of the judges would make them more inclined to hear cases dispassionately and render decisions more faithful to international law than nonlegal arbiters selected from the litigating states. Three years later a judge of the New York State Supreme Court had summarized lawyers' growing reservations on arbitration on the eve of the First Hague Conference when he wrote that "the success of arbitration has served to emphasize its defects."[1]

Others arrived independently at much the same conclusion. Former President Harrison became thoroughly disillusioned with ordinary arbitration tribunals following his experience as a counsel for Venezuela in the arbitration of the boundary dispute with Great Britain. Though he had assumed that the tribunal was constituted on a judicial basis and had made a strong plea for determination of the outstanding questions "in a purely judicial spirit," he was shocked by the blatant nationalist biases of the British judges, who, he claimed in disgust, "were almost as distinctly partisans as the British Counsel." He predicted that because the newly created Hague Court still allowed litigating nations to select their own arbiters, it would not establish the "right" in its decisions but merely serve as a convenient expedient for compromising differences, and he believed only a new court drawn up along more purely judicial lines offered hope for genuine international reform. "If it were possible," he said, "to organize a court composed of permanent members under a salary paid by governments who are signatories of the general treaties and to attain general results[,] it would be a magnificent step in the way of peace and civilization."[2]

John W. Foster's son-in-law Robert Lansing, also expressed marked dissatisfaction with the shortcomings of international arbitration. His experiences as counsel in various arbitrations convinced him that many decisions "had been reached through compromise and concession, methods of adjustment inimicable to absolute justice and destructive of popular confidence in the settlement of disputes between nations through the medium of juridical procedure." He argued that the opposition to the extension of the arbitration principle beyond its very narrow limits stemmed not from inherent opposition to the peaceful settlement of disputes but "from the suspicion, the doubt, the feeling of uncertainty which exists in men's minds as to whether or not justice will be fearlessly and impartially administered by an international court." As long as nations insisted on partisan arbiters of their own choice rather than "disinterested" judges, the world could not hope to obtain a true system of international justice, a prerequisite for the development of public confidence in the peaceful settlement of disputes.[3]

Fundamentally cautious in his approach to international reform, Lansing never expressed much confidence in changing diplomatic practice except perhaps between the United States and Great Britain, but a few lawyers began to speak in favor of reform of arbitration procedure. As Solicitor William L. Penfield stated the principle, "That no one can be truly a judge in his own cause is the primordial test of judicial competence."[4]

When the Hague Court in the Venezuelan debt case rendered a decision more favorable to the powerful blockading creditors than to the nonblockading creditors who had agreed to submit the validity of their claims to judicial decision, it resulted in widespread criticism of the Court's supposed deference to considerations of force rather than to abstract justice. Although prominent international lawyers John Bassett Moore, Simeon Baldwin, and William L. Penfield, and the Committee on International Law of the American Bar Association defended the decision by asserting that the Hague Court merely recognized that forcible collection of debts had always been accepted by nations as "a legal mode of action," even they conceded that the decision did not approximate the high standard of justice they desired.[5]

One result of that decision was the Latin American nations' promotion of the Drago Doctrine, which prohibited creditor nations from using force to collect their debts and insisted upon inter-American cooperation in implementing that policy. Though grateful for Latin American support of the Monroe Doctrine against European interventions in the Western Hemisphere, Roosevelt and Root were unwilling to grant in advance blanket endorsement to any Latin American government that brazenly refused to meet its financial obligations. Accordingly, the American delegation at the Second Hague Peace Conference successfully persuaded the other nations to accept a compromise, the so-called Porter resolution, which outlawed the forcible collection of debts by claimant states except in cases where the debtor nation refused or callously delayed impartial arbitration or rejected the decision of the arbiters.[6]

Another result of the Venezuelan decision was the further crystallization of sentiment among legal-minded individuals for corrective action that would purge the defects of arbitration and enhance nations' respect for international law. In the decade before the outbreak of the World War, legalists advanced two remedies: creation of a judicial world court composed of renowned jurists, and renewed efforts to induce nations to agree on a code of international laws. The two complemented one another. A world court would presumably gain respect of governments if it had a set of definite juridical standards on which to base its decisions; in like fashion a code of laws would gain stature in world councils when the court applied the laws to specific cases.[7]

Lawyers' dissatisfaction with the limitations of international arbitration as well as self-interested professional aspirations crystallized sentiment for a separate group devoted to international law. At the Lake Mohonk Conference in 1905, James Brown Scott, Robert Lansing, and George W. Kirchwey, professor of international law at Columbia University, informally polled several members about establishing a new society and found sufficient interest to call an organizational meeting at which he expressed his dissatisfaction with the sentimental moralizing and pious resolutions of the Lake Mohonk Conferences and his longing "for some exhibition of a more definite purpose." He was confident that the creation of an international law society would help to exalt "international law to its proper position, giving it its high recognition and emphasis, and making the spread of it, the dissemination of its principles, more and more general."[8]

Kirchwey's appeal received a sympathetic hearing among the twenty-seven lawyers, judges, and professors of international law at the conference. Most of those people, together with other legally-oriented individuals at the Conference, elected a committee of twenty-one who served as the nucleus for organizing the American Society of International Law a year later. The members of this organizing committee were a miniature Who's Who of the diplomatic and legal establishments: Supreme Court Justice David J. Brewer; American judges on the Hague Court, George Gray, John W. Griggs, and Oscar S. Straus; educator-diplomats, James B. Angell and Andrew D. White; former Secretary of State John W. Foster; New York attorney Everett P. Wheeler; prominent lawyers with experiences on arbitral tribunals or mixed commissions, Robert Lansing, Jacob M. Dickinson, William W. Morrow, Charles Henry Butler, and Chandler P. Anderson; and law professors John Bassett Moore, James Brown Scott, George W. Kirchwey, Leo S. Rowe, George G. Wilson, Joseph H. Beale, Jr., Charles N. Gregory, and Theodore S. Woolsey. Other legalists who quickly emerged as prominent figures in the American Society of International Law were Elihu Root, who became its president, scholar-diplomat David Jayne Hill, chief justice of the Connecticut Supreme Court Simeon E. Baldwin, and Theodore Marburg.[9]

The similarities of their professional training and experience gave the society's members a sense of common purpose. Many of them had reacted negatively to the political corruption of the Gilded Age, had participated in civil service and other "good government" reforms, and in general were products of genteel mugwumpery. They revered self-control, gentlemanly decorum, and correct deportment in their personal relationships and applied those standards as their ideal for international relationships. They believed they had a mission to raise international law to the status of an honorable profession. Just as one impulse behind the creation of the American Bar Association had been the desire to raise the standards of the legal profession, so they believed the American Society of International

Law could enhance international law as a suitable discipline for study and practice.[10]

Although the lawyers were not united in legal outlook, they did not analyze their differences. Some like Elihu Root and David Jayne Hill venerated natural law and insisted that judges could make decisions based on considerations of abstract justice—what they often termed "the dictates of right reason" or "the interpretation of the Law of Nature"—[11] but they did not quarrel with those like John Bassett Moore who accepted legal positivism, which had increasingly influenced nineteenth-century jurisprudence. Those latter, considering themselves "realists," often asserted the positivist notion that international law, much like municipal law in a much earlier and less certain stage of development, had evolved over the generations and could be studied historically as the gradual growth of a fairly clear set of rules. Many even believed that the study of international law was a "science." Legalists viewed international law as a constantly evolving process of accumulated precedents derived from arbitration treaties, conventions, and diplomatic practice. They emphasized that it was the willingness of nation-states to bind themselves to various international agreements that gave international law its substance and force.[12]

Legalists conceded that the analogy between municipal and international law did not yet extend to the area of sanctions. While the municipal court in theory could call on the police to enforce some of its rulings, no such authority existed on the international level. Thus, John Austin, noted British jurist, asserted the positivist notion that only those rulings capable of enforcement could be considered international law. If Austin was correct, the creation of an international executive with positive sanctions against nations that violated their international agreements was a logical remedy.

American legalists, however, were unwilling to carry legal positivism that far. They rejected such a solution and directly criticized the Austinians.[13] Politically conservative, American legalists were pessimistic concerning the ability of men and nations to undertake major obligations in world politics. On the domestic level they distrusted the wisdom of majority rule in legislative bodies and condemned the growing popular clamor for legislative recall of judges. Similarly, they were skeptical of the collective will of international bodies and claimed that any authoritative institutions sooner or later would become oppressive and unjust. Even George W. Kirchwey, perhaps the most liberal of the lawyers, frankly expressed his professional prejudice against nonlegal authoritative bodies: "I trust you will not believe I exalt unduly the horn of my profession when I say that I have little use for federations and parliaments, provided I am permitted to supply the courts which shall create and administer the law of the world." Referring to the legalists' dream of a judicial world court, he added, "The court will, from the time it is accepted by the leading powers of the earth, become the law-giver, the law-maker, as well as the law-interpreter and peace-maker of the world."[14] As Kirchwey's statement suggested, legalists believed that only renowned judges were impartial and the only acceptable sanction for their decisions was the gradual development of "a world-wide public opinion" properly educated in the rights and duties of nations in the international community. Although the lawyers' use of the phrase "public opinion" was vague, their distrust of the masses implied restriction of that concept to the professional and diplomatic elite. Legalists believed that a long-range campaign could successfully enlighten the educated classes in the moral foundations of international law. In the meantime, they suggested that the jural consciousness of "public opinion" already acted as a sufficient sanction in almost every case.[15]

There was an element of realism in the legalists' distrust of collective security. Certainly they were well aware of the dilemmas and potential abuses of positive sanctions and political international institutions. In view of the anarchic condition of world politics, they were not unreasonable in tolerating the international status quo until international laws were codified and generally accepted among nation-states. Indeed, since they contemplated no sudden changes in power relationships, their short-range views on world politics were quite realistic. Their own long-range view of international reform, however, was hopelessly idealistic, for they tended to subsume most international conflicts, even economic disputes, political differences, or racial or religious antagonisms, under the rubric of international law. For the immediate future, some legalists modestly limited the scope of justiciable disputes to questions of international law such as the interpretation of treaties or the establishment of facts in alleged violations of international obligations. Others, however, assumed that the growing influence of legalism in diplomatic circles would dignify the search for international justice. Eventually, they envisioned all conflicts reduced to judicial cases and nations' voluntary promotion of justice over expediency and force in world politics. They believed that just as man was evolving from a political into a legal animal, so the trend of the so-called civilized states was moving from political to essentially juridicial entities. In the international realm jurists would increasingly absorb the functions of diplomats, and as the latter became aware of the unquestioned rightness of impartial justice, they would join the jurists in a common search for a juridical world order.[16]

Despite the legalists' untested assumptions, the founding of the American Society of International Law and other judicially-oriented groups in the decade before the First World War would actually increase their confidence in their approach to the problem of world peace. They argued with increasing frequency that most peace workers placed too much emphasis on arbitration in the international peace movement. While the idealistic advocates of peace talked in general terms of substituting law for war in international affairs and desired the growth and scope of arbitration treaties, in practice they willingly accepted almost any arbitration agreement as a step toward abolishing war. The lawyers agreed that arbitration was useful but no panacea. Also like pacifists and world federalists, they disliked the temporary service of the judges in arbitral tribunals like the Hague Court, but the lawyers placed greater emphasis on their failure to build a system of international law. As James Brown Scott flatly stated, "It is common knowledge that international law is not developed by the awards of temporary tribunals."[17] The lawyers further pointed out that because the tribunals were not often composed of eminent jurists but of politicians and diplomats, the inevitable result was negotiation and compromise. Compromise was also common in arbitration because of the need to harmonize different or fragmentary concepts of international law. In the end, they claimed, arbitration often achieved less than its proponents claimed, because a nation that sincerely thought it was in the right was reluctant to submit the case to a tribunal of fallible diplomats and politicians, who, unrestrained by a concrete and determined international law, were likely to render a haphazard decision.[18]

The legalists' solution to those defects was an international court that would either replace or increasingly take over much of the jurisdiction of the existing Permanent Court of Arbitration. They envisioned, in short, a world court of real judges, with life tenure and regular meetings, who ruled on the "rights" of countries according to the "facts" and the established law. They affirmed that the judges on this court, together with future international conferences at The Hague, would develop a set of definite interpretations and precedents that would serve as the international law. In their view only the correct application of accepted international law would bring true international justice, a prerequisite for stable world order.

Legalists' conservative arguments were shared by many outside the legal profession. Nicholas Murray Butler, for example, amply summarized them as early as the eve of the Second Hague Peace Conference. The American delegation at the forthcoming conference, he said, "should ask that the Permanent Hague Court be transformed from a semi-diplomatic into a truly judicial tribunal. We should ask that judges be substituted for arbitrators. We wish to see a permanent international court which, like our United States Supreme Court, will have a status, a procedure, traditions, and precedents of its own. We wish to see international law declared as individual differences composed."[19]

One self-appointed task of the American Society of International Law was the formation of codes of law for possible adoption of future international conferences. Although its members spent much time studying the matter, some began to fear that codification would interfere with the natural evolution of international law and might also adversely affect the profession by diminishing the amount of litigation. In any event, they finally concluded that the immensity of the task would require a lifetime or more of concerted work.[20] Nevertheless, they grew increasingly optimistic about substituting the rudiments of a genuinely international legal system for the defects of arbitration. The second Roosevelt administration provided evidence supporting their views. Root, aided by Scott, State Department solicitor from 1906 to 1911, guaranteed the lawyers' efforts for official sanction, and the legalists made the most of the opportunity. They viewed the Second Hague Peace Conference as an opportunity to reform the abuses in the arbitration movement. Elihu Root explained the defects of the diplomatic character of arbitration and the advantages of impartial judicial settlement to the American delegation to the conference and instructed them to transform the Hague Court into a truly permanent world court composed of renowned jurists selected from several nations so that the different systems of law and procedure and the principal languages would be represented on the tribunal.[21]

Following Root's instructions, the United States' delegation presented a detailed plan for the transformation of the Hague tribunal into a court of fifteen judges who would be representative of the different systems of law and language. The new court would convene annually, define its procedure, and be authorized to decide all questions involving disputes submitted to it under arbitration treaties or other agreements. Although the American delegates quickly perceived that their proposal was too radical for adoption, the conference unanimously approved a modified plan calling for the establishment of an entirely new institution, a court of arbitral justice. The Hague Conference approved a draft convention for such a court, but the larger powers and smaller nations could not agree on a formula for the selection of the comparatively small number of judges. The big powers insisted on numerical dominance of judges from their own nations, while the smaller nations demanded equal representation. The American delegation advanced numerous formulas for their appointment, at one point even suggesting that each nation should have an equal voice in the selection of the judges. The current of nationalism, however, was so pervasive that such alternatives had no chance of unanimous acceptance.[22]

Although the Second Hague Peace Conference failed to establish a judicial court, the legalists still claimed that they had made significant gains. They pointed out that the conference's approval of a draft convention for a court of arbitral justice gave official recognition to the principle of judicial settlement. They derived added satisfaction that the United States, Germany, and Great Britain had cooperated in writing the draft and along with France had fully endorsed it in their official reports on the Hague Conference. The proponents of the court argued that the conference's unanimous endorsement of the draft convention facilitated the task of diplomatic negotiations leading to the creation of the judicial body once the nations devised an acceptable formula for the selection of judges.[23] James Brown Scott, who as technical representative of the American delegation had helped to draft the convention, hailed the importance of the agreement. One could "search in vain," he wrote, "for any work of a more far-reaching nature accomplished within the past centuries."[24] While the report of the American delegation was not so extravagant, it minimized the obstacles and optimistically predicted, "A little time, a little patience, and the great work is accomplished."[25]

They also pointed to the creation of the Central American Court of Justice in December 1907 as a prototype world court. Following chronic border skirmishes among the Central American nations, Elihu Root convened a Central American Conference in Washington, D.C. Working informally with the five Central American delegations, State Department representatives persuaded them to consider the draft of the court of arbitral justice as the basis for discussions on a Central American tribunal. The resulting convention obligated the five Central American states, each of which would appoint one judge, to submit all private and intergovernmental disputes to a newly established Central American Court of Justice. Although the United States did not join the Central American Court, it gave moral support to that body until the Wilson administration helped engineer its collapse a decade later.[26]

Legalists pointed to other encouraging results of the Second Conference. Like other peace advocates, legalists lauded the agreement to hold a third conference and the recommendation for an international committee to prepare the mode of organization and procedure for the conference. They also assumed that periodic conferences were indispensible in the resulting conventions developing international law, and even more than the pacifists were pleased with the Second Conference's preoccupation with the rules of land and maritime law for belligerent and neutral nations.[27]

In the latter category legalists especially welcomed the provision for an international prize court composed of fifteen expert jurists on questions of international maritime law. The eight major maritime powers (Great Britain, France, Russia, Germany, Austria-Hungary, Italy, United States, and Japan) would each appoint one judge, and the remaining seven judges, chosen by the other signatories, would serve on a rotating basis. Influenced by Root's endorsement of the prize court, President Roosevelt announced that the proposed maritime court "can not fail to accustom the different countries to the submission of international questions to the decision of an international tribunal, and we may confidently expect the results of such submission to bring about a general agreement upon the enlargement of the practice."[28]

Both the second Roosevelt and the Taft administrations attempted to implement the international prize court as an opening wedge for the creation of a court of arbitral justice. Assuming the gradual, evolutionary development of international institutions, they asserted that it would be easier to expand the functions and jurisdiction of an existing institution than to attempt to create one.[29] Accordingly, when Great Britain called a conference of ten major naval powers in London to define more clearly the legal principles that the prize court would apply before it would accede to that convention, Root's interim successor as secretary of state, Robert Bacon, instructed the American delegates at the conference to promote extension of the jurisdiction of the prize court to include the functions and to follow the procedure of the court of arbitral justice approved at the Second Hague Conference. Nothing came of that ingenious American proposal at the London Conference because England properly objected that it had promised the smaller nations excluded from the conference that the delegates would limit their discussions to maritime issues. Rather, the British promised to cooperate with a separate American diplomatic initiative to invest the prize court with the functions of a permanent international tribunal and prodded the delegates into expressing their support for the American proposition outside the London Conference.[30]

A few months later, Taft's Secretary of State Philander C. Knox formally proposed that the London Conference should formulate an agreement in which the judges of the prize court would also be competent to sit as judges of a court of arbitral justice for all questions nations submitted to it.[31] Great Britain, France, and Germany supported the Knox proposal in principle but raised specific objections concerning its realization. The British in particular questioned the feasibility of the proposal. How, they asked, could the United States expect the smaller nations to accede to the prize court, which they had accepted very reluctantly at the Second Hague Peace Conference, when it was proposed to enlarge the scope of the court already dominated by the larger nations? And why should the smaller nations suddenly change their minds about the composition of an arbitral court, which they had rejected at the Second Hague Peace Conference? England correctly believed that the objections of minor states to an arbitral court were legitimate because its functions would be "essentially dissimilar" to those of the prize court. The scope of the latter was relatively narrow and would offer some hope of protection to the private property of smaller neutrals; in any event, because of their small merchant marine the prize court would not materially affect their fortunes in wartime. A court of arbitral justice, however, would involve "all those matters of a general character which may properly become the subject of international arbitration." The British queries indicated the real obstacles to a court of arbitral justice based on big power control.[32]

When all three European governments suggested a meeting of technical experts of the four powers to discuss these difficulties, Knox dispatched Scott to Paris, and there, in March 1910, the powers negotiated a protocol that with minor changes accepted the American proposal of using the prize court as the basis for a court of arbitral justice. If eighteen or more powers adhered to such an arrangement, an arbitral court of fifteen judges could be established; if the proposal failed, the nations could continue the search for an acceptable formula.[33]

There were many theoretical conditions attached to the implementation of this protocol. It required the large naval powers' ratifications of the Declaration of London (1909), formal implementation of the prize court, and agreement of at least eighteen nations to extend its jurisdiction beyond maritime issues. Nevertheless, the legalists became increasingly optimistic. Their confidence stemmed in part from the expansion of their influence in the State Department. The increased work load of the solicitor resulted in 1906 in the addition of three assistant solicitors in the State Department, two of whom—William C. Dennis and J. Reuben Clark, Jr.—became active participants in the American Society of International Law. When the office of counselor was established three years later as second in command in the department, the three successive holders of the position after 1910 were leading lawyers, Chandler P. Anderson, John Bassett Moore, and Robert Lansing. Moreover, in Elihu Root's last days as secretary of state he arranged for two arbitral tribunals whose members more closely approximated his preference for extranational arbiters with judicial experience over politicians or diplomats appointed from the disputants. Root hailed those arrangements as hopeful precedents for the gradual acceptance of the idea of a truly judicial world court.[34]

Their confidence also derived from Knox's and Scott's reports of progress toward a permanent court of justice to peace congresses and the latter's prolific writings on the subject. In 1910 Knox authorized Scott to tell the Lake Mohonk Conference that the nations' favorable responses to his earlier proposal convinced him that the court of arbitral justice would become a reality before the third peace conference at The Hague.[35] Continued friendly negotiations with European states reinforced that belief. Thus, Nicholas Murray Butler cheerfully announced at the following conference: "It is now possible to say, again with the knowledge and approval of the Secretary of State, that the progress made during the past year has been so marked that in all likelihood such a Court, created by general agreement, will be erected at The Hague even earlier than seemed probable a year ago."[36]

Meanwhile, legalists began to broaden their campaign for a world court. Early in 1910 Baldwin, Scott, and others organized American elitist opinion behind a new group, the American Society for the Judicial Settlement of International Disputes. Elihu Root, noting the word "judicial" in the title, reminded the founders of the legalists' true aims. "I assume," he wrote Marburg, "that you are going to urge that disputes between nations shall be settled by judges acting under the judicial sense of honorable obligation, with a judicial idea of impartiality, rather than by diplomats acting under the diplomatic ideas of honorable obligations and feeling bound to negotiate a settlement rather than to pass without fear or favor upon questions of fact and law."[37] Along with the creation of the Carnegie Endowment for International Peace the same year, the legalists had two new powerful agencies for the promotion of their court idea.

Not content with the predominance of the legalist viewpoint in the United States, Scott attempted to recruit European legal scholars to the movement for a court of arbitral justice. He corresponded and personally conferred with many European legalists, most notably with Walther Schücking (Germany), Hans Wehburg (Germany), Ernest Nys (Belgium), Heinrich Lammasch (Austria-Hungary), Louis Oppenheim (Germany), and Baron d'Estournelles de Constant (France). When some of those authorities expressed reservations about the Knox proposal for a court of arbitral justice, Scott strongly defended the proposed institution.[38] If his initial arguments failed to convince his European counterparts, he invoked his faith in inexorable progress as an important reason for supporting the institution. "We can help the movement [toward the court], we cannot block it," he wrote Wehburg.[39]

Scott's European friends responded positively to Scott's requests for articles for the *American Journal of International Law,* liberally praised his writings on a permanent court of justice, and helped him win the endorsement of the Institute of International Law for the proposed judicial body. They did not share his incurable optimism but sincerely hoped for the establishment of a world court.[40] Perhaps even more than his friend Elihu Root who had other concerns as a United States senator in those years, Scott was the leading proponent of a world court in the United States. His singular quest prompted Lansing to remark that Scott was "undoubtedly today the most prominent American advocate of a [world] judicial system."[41]

[9]

Peace Issues and
the Taft Administration

PRESIDENT TAFT'S WHOLEHEARTED SUPPORT of the legalists' approach to foreign policy further encouraged the international lawyers. Like other legalists, Taft was certainly no pacifist. Though ambivalent on American territorial expansion, he was loyal to the Republican party and as governor of the Philippines had willingly served America's imperial aims[1] If he had publicly credited the anti-imperialists' vigilance with preventing additional excesses of American officials in the Philippines, he had privately fumed at the "rhetorical mouthings" of "self-interested" anti-imperialists like Herbert Welsh and Moorfield Storey. Those men, he had written Roosevelt in 1903, were "drunk with the desire of elevating themselves to a pedestal of peculiar morality and debauching themselves with invective, denunciation and ungentlemanly language."[2] Moreover, as secretary of war in the second Roosevelt administration, Taft had approved Roosevelt's large navy programs and, despite paying lip service to the hopes for international disarmament, proved as President to be a firm preparedness advocate.

Still, Taft's lifelong passion was the pursuit of justice. His experience as a lawyer and judge had instilled in him a great faith in courts of law, which he believed rendered speedy and impartial justice. He saw no reason why nations, like individuals, would not agree to arbitrate their differences before a tribunal. He had long been a proponent of international arbitration agreements and while still a circuit court judge in Ohio had served on the executive committee that had promoted the Olney-Pauncefote treaty.[3]

On the eve of war with Spain he had written McKinley praising his resistance to "the thoughtless jingoism of some and the blatant demagoguery of others in and out of Congress," and urging him to avert the "horrors of war" until all peaceable methods had been tried. "If war comes," he had concluded, "it must be a just war and it cannot be just if all that war could accomplish can be wrought by peaceful methods."[4] As President, Taft affirmed that not only the Spanish War but the War of 1812 and the Mexican War as well had been unnecessary and that "in very few cases, if any, can the historian say that the good of war was worth the awful sacrifice."[5] It was those antiwar proclivities that made Taft willing to foster peace and arbitration in the international arena.

President Taft's best remembered contribution to the American peace movement was his arbitration treaties with Britain and France in 1911 and 1912; less well known is his administration's earlier response to a more ambitious internationalist project advanced by a group of world federalists. Their proposal grew out of their naive faith in Theodore Roosevelt's destiny as the world's peacemaker.[6] Hamilton Holt, William H. Short, engineer-explorer Oscar T. Crosby, mining-engineer Henry G. Granger, lawyer Walter John Bartnett, John Temple Graves, editor of the *New York American,* and a few other idealistic internationalists, most of whom were active members of the New York Peace Society, were fascinated by Roosevelt's dynamic personality, enormous energy, political sagacity, and deft handling of foreign affairs. Like Andrew Carnegie, who was promoting a meeting between Roosevelt and William II to advance a European detente and simultaneously supporting his New York cohorts, they hoped to harness the former President's diplomatic talents to their own grandiose plans. They formed the World-Federation League in early 1910 for the mobilization of public sentiment to support a centralized governing body empowered to keep the peace.[7]

The World-Federation League sponsored a congressional resolution calling on the President to appoint a commission of five Americans to draft a proposal for a federation of nations with authority "limited to the maintenance of peace, through the establishment of an international Court having power to determine by decree all controversies between nations and to enforce execution of its decrees by arms of the Federation, such arms to be provided to the Federation and controlled solely by it." It also was authorized to make other recommendations that might lead to limitation of armaments and "lessen the probabilities of war."[8]

In April 1910, Richard Bartholdt introduced the World-Federation League's resolution in the House, which was soon endorsed by the International School of Peace and the New England Peace and Arbitration

Congress. President Taft supported Bartholdt's proposal, and Theodore Roosevelt, urged on by Carnegie, Holt, and their New York coworkers, spoke favorably of disarmament and the creation of a league of the great powers to preserve the peace in his Christiania address in which he accepted the Nobel Peace Prize.[9]

Even with that support, however, the resolution was too boldly innovative for most members of Congress who still accepted unquestioningly America's unilateralist and isolationist traditions. The House Foreign Affairs Committee proceeded to dilute the Bartholdt resolution, and both houses then passed unanimously a more moderate version in late June authorizing the commission "to consider the expediency of utilizing existing international agencies for the purpose of limiting the armaments of the nations of the world by international agreement, and of constituting the combined navies of the world in an international force for the preservation of universal peace, and to consider and report upon any other means to diminish the expenditures of government for military purposes and to lessen the probabilities of war." Because the resolution deleted references to world federation and urged only consideration of international agreement on armaments and an international police force, it demonstrated Congress's aversion to imaginative proposals for alteration of the political and diplomatic status quo.[10]

Although world federalists were mildly disappointed, they still liked the sections on armaments and an international police force. Yet even their more modest hopes were not realized. The federalists, overlooking or discounting Roosevelt's emphatic emphasis on "righteousness and not peace" and his marked preference for American unilateralism and balance of power diplomacy, soon discovered that the former President's recent espousal of a league of peace represented only an ideal, not a policy. When President Taft urged Roosevelt to accept chairmanship of the commission, he declined, confidentially telling Hamilton Holt that his recent talks with European statesmen, particularly William II, convinced him that a peace commission would be unsuccessful. Since Taft considered Roosevelt's acceptance of the chairmanship indispensable to positive achievements by the commission, he deferred immediate action.[11]

Far from discouraging the internationalists, Taft's procrastination only intensified their promotional activities. But their additional writings in magazines and newspapers, their personal appeals to the President, and the endorsements by European pacifists, the Universal Peace Congress, the International Peace Bureau, the third American Peace Congress, and the Wisconsin legislature were futile.[12] Such efforts were counterbalanced by resistance from Taft's conservative friends whose arguments ultimately subverted the commission. Secretary Knox, for instance, solicited the views of foreign governments on the proposal but tended to discount favorable replies and to interpret equivocal ones negatively.[13]

Even more important was the influence of Root and Butler. When they began to consider the implications of the entire proposal, it jarred their ingrained conservative preference for traditional diplomatic procedures. Root raised a variety of questions concerning the functions and composition of the body but singled out the difficulty of instructing and guiding commissioners who were not responsible to the State Department, yet officially represented the United States. "We shall be at the mercy of their discretion," he warned Taft. "If they make an ass of themselves they make an ass of us. If they are ridiculous we are ridiculous. If they make a humiliating failure we lose the respect of the nations pro tanto." Despite those criticisms Root said he would reluctantly acquiesce in a commission if Taft found considerable support from other governments.[14]

Butler was more definite in arguing that the appointment of the commissioners would be "premature, and if it had any effect at all would do harm rather than good." He claimed that his recent discussions with European statesmen convinced him that the diplomatic situation was so delicate that the proposed peace commission would only aggravate matters. Before creating the commission, he counseled fulfillment of a long list of conditions, such as the return of the Liberal government to power in the 1911 Parliamentary elections in England, Germany's decision not to renew the existing naval bill in 1912, the absence of serious anarchistic outbreaks in Europe, and the forestalling of racial conflict in the Dual Monarchy.[15] Butler's prerequisites for a commission would have sounded comical if he had not been perfectly earnest in mentioning them, and if Taft had not taken him seriously. But the combined effect of those cautious voices apparently did influence the chief executive. Taft at any rate never made the appointments to the commission.

Taft's failure to promote the World-Federation League's proposal revealed the limits of his internationalism. His own cautious temperament— he had earlier conceded that "I cannot be more aggressive than my nature makes me"—and the influence of his cautious friends combined to steer him away from more imaginative internationalist proposals.[16] His indecision over the proposed peace commission as well as his later willingness to go beyond most Republicans in supporting Woodrow Wilson's League of Nations indicate that he was far from resolutely opposed to a politically authoritative federation of nations, but he preferred to work for a peaceful world order through traditionally accepted diplomatic processes. Since the two Hague Conferences had emphasized extension of the scope of arbitration treaties and establishment of a permanent world tribunal, Taft easily focused on those objectives. Indeed, it is probable that he more readily abandoned the federalists' goal of a peace commission when he foresaw possible major advances for arbitration and legalism.

Taft in fact had supported the legalists' organizational efforts. In 1907 he became a vice-president of the American Society of International Law, and three years later he directed the State Department to cooperate "in every way" with Marburg's plans for founding the American Society for the Judicial Settlement of International Disputes.[17] Taft viewed the establishment of a world court as a milestone in man's slow but steady progress toward a peaceful world. As he told Marburg, "There is no other single way in which the cause of peace and disarmament can be so effectively promoted as by the firm establishment of a permanent court of justice."[18] Taft addressed both judicialist groups' annual meetings on a regular basis during his presidency. When he told the American Society of International Law in 1911 that "International Law is really a wonderful creation," he perfectly expressed his true sentiments.[19]

Taft followed the State Department's negotiations with European nations concerning a prize court and an arbitral court. He recognized the legitimacy of British and small nations' objections to the creation of an international prize court as a prototype of a court of arbitral justice when he conceded that the functions of the two would have to be "somewhat different," but he remained steadfastly optimistic about devising some ingenious formula that would allow the several nations to establish both.[20]

Further, Taft's promotion of arbitration treaties with Britain and France was directly related to his intense hopes for an arbitral court. He first indicated interest in new arbitration accords in an address on March 22, 1910, to the American Peace and Arbitration League, a newly formed group combining advocacy of naval preparedness with international arbitration. He spoke of his willingness to negotiate arbitration agreements including questions of national honor and hoped a truly judicial court would soon be established.[21] He was sincere a year later when he remarked to his military aide, Archie Butt, that he first announced his arbitration proposal "merely to offset the antagonism to the four [*sic*] battleships for which I was then fighting, and I threw that suggestion out merely to draw the sting of Old Carnegie and other peace cranks." He realized that his offer of a new "peace" plan would help to defuse antipreparedness advocates' inevitable criticisms of his appearance before a big navy group. His motive was not only political however; he also told Butt, "I have always believed these things, and I suppose if I had not said them then I would have got [*sic*] them out of my system sometime later on."[22] Taft's first announcement of his arbitration plan, only four days after Scott had signed the protocol on the court of arbitral justice with the three major European powers, may have been less a coincidence than his acute recognition of the potentially intimate relationship between the two developments. In any event he thought that his proposed treaties represented a transitional step from the principle of international arbitration to the realm of international law and assumed that ratification of his treaties would increase interest in the arbitral court.

He hinted at that relationship in a speech even before the State Department began formal negotiations with Britain and France. "If now we can negotiate and put through a positive agreement with some great nation to abide the adjudication of an international arbitral court in every issue which cannot be settled by negotiation," he said, "no matter what it involves, whether honor, territory, or money, we shall have made a long step forward by demonstrating that it is possible for two nations at least to establish as between the same system of due process of law that exists between individuals under a government."[23] Taft emphasized the importance of this relationship on numerous occasions the following year while promoting his arbitration treaties with Britain and France.[24] Since he realized that the prospect of war between the United States and these nations was remote, he valued them less as a preventer of war than as a more general precedent "toward the settlement of all international controversies between all countries by peaceable means and by arbitration."[25] No less than dedicated peace advocates, Taft envisioned the eventual triumph of the universal rule of law among nations.

There were additional influences affecting Taft's decision. One was Britain's and France's eager responses to his suggestion. Taft also began to perceive potential political benefits beyond neutralization of his antipreparedness critics. If he could persuade the Senate to consent to the treaties, they might help to bolster his sagging political fortunes and even become, as he expressed it, "the great jewel of my administration."[26] The spontaneous surge of public enthusiasm for his accords greatly raised his hopes. While the groundswell at first surprised the President, it increasingly nurtured his confidence. "Never in my experience," he later admitted, "was there such a unanimous expression of earnest interest in carrying out the proposal, and such fervent hope expressed for a successful issue in the matter."[27]

Much of the public support for Taft's treaties was organized and promoted by peace societies. In negotiating arbitration treaties with Britain and France, Taft became the beneficiary of a rapid growth of peace societies in the previous half dozen years, which, on the surface at least, portended more public influence for the cause of peace and arbitration. His campaign for Senate consent to his arbitration treaties also stimulated this growth. Nine of the twenty-five peace agencies first organized in the 1904–

1912 period were founded between Taft's first suggestion of his arbitration scheme in March 1910 and the Senate vote on the treaties in 1912. Another aspect of this growth was its nationwide character. Six, or two-thirds, of the new groups founded in the same two year period were established outside the Northeast.[28] Although the eastern peace societies and endowed organizations still dominated the peace movement, the trend toward dispersal of peace sentiment throughout the United States seemed a hopeful augury to the peace leadership.

Comprehensive records of most of these groups do not exist, but frequent notices in the *Advocate of Peace* about their founding and activities are informative. Local educators, editors, lawyers, and businessmen, occasionally in cooperation with a few veteran peace spokesmen, organized and directed the new groups. Similar to the flourishing New York Peace Society, these groups emphasized the importance of respectability and prestige in their leadership. The eleven officers of the Maryland Peace Society consisted of the governor of the state, mayor of Baltimore, president of Johns Hopkins University, president-emeritus of The Woman's College, a professor, a judge, a Catholic cardinal, three business executives, and Theodore Marburg. The *Advocate of Peace* remarked appreciatively, "This is a strong body of men, all well known in Baltimore."[29] Similarly, the president of the Utah Peace Society was a former governor, and the incumbent governor addressed one of its annual meetings and became its honorary president. The organizational meeting of the Redlands Peace Society in California was attended by the leading ministers, businessmen (including Albert K. Smiley whose winter residence was located there), and professional men and women in the area.[30] The president of Redlands University, who became head of the new peace group, immediately predicted that "most of the prominent men in town are likely to join and heartily endorse the movement."[31]

The Chicago Peace Society typified the new societies' establishment status. An earlier Chicago peace group had failed in the 1890s and another organized in 1902 had led a desultory existence, but after the National Peace Congress in that city in 1909, prominent Chicagoans stepped in and thoroughly reorganized the society. Although the socialist John C. Kennedy and prominent liberals Jane Addams, Jenkin Lloyd Jones, Rabbi Emil G. Hirsch, Ellen M. Henrotin, Florence Holbrook, Graham Taylor, and Judge Edward O. Brown joined the Chicago Peace Society, businessmen and bankers formed an overwhelming majority of the executive committee. They included three businessmen who served as president of the city's commercial association between 1908 and 1912, two presidents of Chicago banks (one of whom, George E. Roberts, served as director of the United States Mint after 1911), and an independent businessman. The following comprised about half of the society's twenty-five honorary vice-presidents: two presidents and a vice-president of other Chicago banks, the Methodist and Episcopal bishops of Chicago, three presidents of manufacturing companies, the presidents of Northwestern University and Lake Forest College, Secretary of the Treasury Franklin MacVeagh, Secretary of War Jacob M. Dickinson, Walter L. Fisher, lawyer and secretary of the interior from 1911 to 1913, and Julius Rosenwald, philanthropic head of Sears, Roebuck & Co.[32] In reviewing the new leadership, the *Advocate of Peace* correctly recognized that "all of them are prominent and influential in the life of the city."[33]

The American Peace Society aided the new group by transferring its recently appointed field secretary, Charles E. Beals, to Chicago where he also served as secretary of the new peace organization. Beals was another of the socially concerned clergymen whose attraction for peace work increased in rough proportion to dissatisfaction with the constraints of church service. Beals later wrote:

> Before I reached manhood's years I determined to invest my life so as to make it contribute most to human welfare. . . . After fifteen years of conscientious work in the pastorate, I felt that too largely the activities of the churches were devoted to saving the churches instead of to serving society. . . . Hence I left the pastorate and never have regretted taking the step.[34]

Largely because of Beal's aggressive promotional efforts, the Chicago Peace Society quickly became the best known peace group outside the East. Although it never seriously rivaled its New York counterpart in influence, it had more than 600 members by 1911; that was a tiny figure perhaps for the nation's second largest city, but a respectable showing in a time of peace and in a geographical region where isolation from international developments aroused little interest in foreign policy.[35]

As the number of societies increased, discussions within the peace movement on the closer coordination of their activities intensified. The American Peace Society encouraged the enrollment of local and state peace groups as branches by sending the *Advocate of Peace* free to all members of branch societies in return for the latters' payment of one-half of their membership receipts. Under that arrangement the number of affiliated societies increased from three in 1904 to eighteen in 1911.[36] The relocation of the American Peace Society in Washington, D.C., in the latter year reemphasized the national aspirations and purposes of the organization and more easily justified its appeals for the affiliation of state and local peace organizations. President Taft gave such federative tendencies a psychological boost when, in a speech to the American Peace Congress in May 1911, he gently chided the peace societies for their uncoordinated work and stressed the need for organization.[37] Over the next several months the American Peace Society proceeded to divide peace work into five geographical departments—New England, Middle Atlantic, South Atlantic, Central-West, and Pacific Coast—which were headed respectively by James L. Tryon, Samuel Train Dutton, James J. Hall, Charles E. Beals, and Robert C. Root. Root was a liberal school teacher and administrator, while Tryon and Hall, both ordained Protestant clergymen, duplicated Beals' decision to leave their pastorates for professional peace work. The department heads were paid modest salaries by the American Peace Society to lecture on peace and to organize local peace groups in their sections.[38]

If one looked only at those externals—numbers of societies, membership lists, burgeoning financial resources, feverish activity, and coordinated action—the American peace movement appeared to be a thriving venture. Not only had two endowed peace agencies with annual expenditures totaling $550,000 been established, but the American Peace Society had for the first time in its history become a truly national organization. From those appearances the peace movement never had such an opportunity for spreading its message to the masses throughout the nation. One would also have received the impression of a healthy and prosperous undertaking from reading the *Advocate of Peace,* which chronicled the growth and expansion of the movement. Readers of its pages discovered, for example, that the number of branch and auxiliary societies had increased from eighteen to twenty-four in the twelve months ending in April 1912. They also found that during the previous seven years the *Advocate of Peace* had doubled its circulation to 9,000 issues monthly, while membership had increased from about 700 to 1,000. Membership in its branch groups throughout the country totaled another estimated 4,000.[39] By quantitative and visible standards the American peace movement by early 1912 surpassed any previous activity. If peace advocates had not persuaded President Taft to appoint a peace commission, they were in an enviable position to champion his arbitration treaties with Britain and France.

Yet even while the peace movement expanded, it suffered two additional setbacks that indicated the limits of its influence on foreign policy. The first was the rejection of the Declaration of London by the House of Lords in Britain in December 1911.[40] Since England's ratification of the Declaration was a precondition to any viable prize court and in turn to an arbitral court, the hope for realization of an international judiciary in the foreseeable future collapsed like a house of cards. That blow was followed shortly by another: Senate rejection of Taft's arbitration treaties in March 1912.

Those two reverses, to be sure, were partly or wholly beyond the immediate influence of the peace movement. American peace advocates, of course, had no influence on events in Britain leading to rejection of the Declaration of London. They cannot be faulted, moreover, for lack of effort in promoting Taft's arbitration treaties. Even before the British, French, and American negotiators had completed the final draft of the accords, Taft noted that "I have received a great many invitations from varied associations whose titles indicated that their purpose was the promotion of peace;"[41] and following the formal signings of the treaties peace societies continued to hold meetings, draw up petitions, and send out literature. When in late 1911 Taft launched a coast-to-coast speaking tour, on which he spent much time defending his treaties, peace groups joined other private associations in sponsoring some of the meetings.[42] The Carnegie Endowment underwrote publication of 100,000 copies of the December 1911 issue of *Advocate of Peace,* which was devoted entirely to the treaties. It also appropriated $50,000 to a National Citizens' Committee, composed of several hundred eminent men and headed by trustee Joseph H. Choate, which worked with local groups in organizing public meetings in support of the treaties and distributed a favorable pamphlet. The American Association for International Conciliation used much of its allotment of endowment funds to circulate a pamphlet containing the text of the treaties, the majority and minority reports of the Senate Foreign Relations Committee, and the endorsements of Taft and others to 250,000 "people of intelligence" as well as another pamphlet containing a reprinted magazine article by Taft elucidating the merits of the treaties.[43] As public debate on the accords intensified, the Senate received as many as forty petitions a day supporting them from the WCTU and peace, church, college, and business groups. Press opinion was clearly favorable, one estimate claiming that seventy percent of newspapers in the nation endorsed them without reservation. All measurable indices of public sentiment indicated overwhelming support for the unamended treaties.[44]

The treaties, however, encountered opposition from the day of their signing on August 3, 1911. Many senators began to complain about the administration's failure to consult with their membership during treaty negotiations with Britain and France. Although the *Advocate of Peace* claimed that during negotiations Taft and Knox were taking several senators into their confidence and Knox later made vague references to such consultations, there is little evidence to indicate that the administration made more than a few casual gestures in that direction.[45] Taft admitted he and Knox had not consulted with senators, offering the weak excuse, "It did not seem wise to submit the matter to the Senate until after we had found that the other countries were willing to join us in such treaties."[46] The main reason for their disregard of Senate opinion, however, was their accurate appraisal of that body's marked reluctance to conclude any far-reaching arbitral agreements. They surmised that consultations with prominent senators would lead to demands for severely restrictive amendments that would nullify hopes for progress in the arbitration movement. Neither Taft nor Britain and France would accept crippling amendments that would have rendered the treaties little different in content from the existing Root treaties. Rather than join the issue with the Senate during the negotiating stage, Taft chose to delay confrontation until after the signing of the treaties. Why he chose that course is not entirely clear, but it is probable that he perceived the growing public support for Anglo-American (and, less ardently, for Franco-American) understanding and calculated that presentation of the Senate with a popular *fait accompli* might overcome its obstinacy.[47] Whatever his reasons, Taft's neglect of the Senate did not agree with lawmakers' notions of their self-importance in the treaty-making process. Root pointed to the unhappy consequences of the administration's bungling when he wrote Carnegie early in the debate, "The trouble could have been averted easily if some of the Senate had been consulted before the treaty was signed."[48]

Root discovered during the ensuing debate, however, that the "trouble" over consultation formed only a small part of the deep divisions over prerogatives, which in turn became linked with differences over ideas. Taft's desire to broaden the scope of international arbitration clashed with an intransigent Senate that remained just as nationalistic and just as jealous of its authority as it had been during discussions over the Olney-Pauncefote, Hay, and Root treaties. Taft's agreements provided that all disputes that were "justiciable in their nature by reason of being susceptible of decision by the application of the principles of law or equity" would be referred to the Permanent Court of Arbitration or some other tribunal; when one government disputed the other's contention of a justiciable question, an additional article provided for a joint high commission of inquiry composed of six members, each nation appointing three. If all or all but one of the commissioners agreed that the dispute met the treaty's definition of justiciable, then it would be referred to arbitration. Since the treaties specified no other reservations, the commission could decide to arbitrate questions involving national honor or vital interests if it determined that they were justiciable.[49]

The majority report of the Senate Foreign Relations Committee written by Henry Cabot Lodge criticized the treaties. Among its many objections the report particularly attacked the joint high commission, arguing that once the commission deemed a dispute justiciable the Senate would be deprived of its constitutional right to review all questions submitted to arbitration. The treaties stated that the commission's decisions would be referred to arbitration "in accordance with the provisions of this treaty," and one article specifically provided for Senate consent to a special treaty outlining the terms on which arbitration would commence. The majority report, however, ignored those phrases, which could be interpreted as a restriction on the commission's authority, and urged elimination of the commission from the treaties. The report also argued that the phrase "application of the principles of law and equity" as the definition of justiciable was too vague. If the phrase would not cause difficulties with friendly Britain and France, it might serve as a dangerous precedent for future arbitral agreements with less friendly nations since it could lead to misunderstandings and even be "promotive of dissension, ill feeling, and perhaps war." The majority's reasoning of the remotest and most dire contingencies suggested that the authors, fearful of the smallest possible erosion of their treaty-making powers, were determined to sabotage any accords that sought to extend the scope of international arbitration.[50]

It was precisely the vague, ambiguous language of the treaties, however, that allowed Senate opponents to demand clarifying amendments. If the proponents of the unamended treaties had agreed on their proper interpretation, they might have convinced at least some wavering senators. But they did not present a united front. The minority report written by Senators Root and Cullom neither conceded nor refuted the majority's contention of the joint commission's restricted authority, but argued instead that their objections could be met by adding a clause to the ratification of the accords exempting "any question which depends upon or involves the maintenance of the traditional attitude of the United States concerning American questions, or other purely governmental policy."[51] Many senators found the resolution too general and an evasion of their questions concerning the upper house's constitutional right to challenge the commission's decisions before arbitration commenced. Burton demonstrated the disunity among the minority when he gave a supplemental opinion arguing that the decisions of the joint commission were merely advisory and still required the Senate's prior approval of the terms of arbitration. More cautious arbitrationists, including Secretary Knox and John Bassett Moore, were willing to give the Senate the right to exclude questions of national policy.

Other arbitration proponents added to the confusion by refusing at first to concede any restrictive authority to the Senate under the accords. Benjamin Trueblood, Richard Bartholdt, Hamilton Holt, William Hull, George Edmunds, Simeon Baldwin, and Thomas Raeburn White upheld the constitutionality of the joint commission, criticized the Senate's obsession with its prerogatives, and urged ratification of the agreements without substantive changes.[52]

The central figure in the unfolding debate, President Taft, shared their view. Indeed, he said he would have preferred the treaties to bind the contracting powers to submit all their future controversies to the Permanent Court of Arbitration or some other tribunal. Automatic referral of such disputes to the Hague Court, for instance, would have followed the growing practice among litigants of selecting judges from outside nations and thereby furthered progress toward his ultimate goal of a world court composed of disinterested jurists. Just as domestic courts of superior jurisdiction determined finally for the parties whether they could try specific cases, so did the President believe that the arbitral courts provided for in his treaties could decide whether controversies fell within the boundaries of the agreements. He personally inserted the provision for a joint commission of inquiry, however, as a concession to senators' nationalist prejudices. Taft accepted the joint commission as a satisfactory substitute because he optimistically assumed that the three American appointees would be men of good judgment, and at least two of them would vote against and thereby prevent arbitration of all disputes submitted to the commission except for those instances where it was "reasonably clear" that the issue was justiciable. But he could not accept "the limited and narrow view" of the Foreign Relations Committee majority report and intimated that he viewed the joint commission as an impartial judicial body possessing final authority to bind the parties to arbitration.[53]

Taft readily admitted that the potentially broad powers given to the commission of inquiry signified his willingness to assume moderate risks to national interests in order to advance the arbitration principle. "We cannot make omelet without breaking eggs. We cannot submit international questions to arbitration without the prospect of losing,"[54] he said at the start of the debate on the treaties. Two weeks later he expounded:

> I do not think we are going to get ahead with this arbitration business unless we are willing to assume an obligation to execute a judgment that may bite and may be bad for us to take; and, if we are going to take the position that we will wait until the question arises and then conclude, because we do not think we can win in the arbitration case, that it is not a justiciable question, then we have written our promise in water and we have made agreements that will dissolve under the test of experience.[55]

Taft's statements on the treaties were actually quite at variance with Knox's, and opponents of the accords delighted in the discrepancies.[56]

Their different interpretations stemmed not so much from misjudgments and tactical blunders as from fundamentally divergent views concerning their willingness to have their country assume major obligations in world politics. Taft was moving hesitantly toward an advanced internationalist position that would put him in the forefront of proponents of an authoritative league of nations during the World War, while Knox, much more conventional in his approach to foreign relations, more skeptical of the chances for international cooperation, and more politically partisan, would end his public career as a senator irreconcilably opposed to Woodrow Wilson's League of Nations.

When Taft and Knox perceived the Senate's marked reluctance to tolerate even potential concessions of national interests, they cooperated with the Republican leadership in the Senate in drafting two compromises. The first specified Senate confirmation of the presidential nominees to the commission, and the second effectively nullified the authority of the joint high commission by giving the Senate a veto over its decisions as well as the right to draft and consent to a special agreement in each case. Because the word "justiciable" still remained in the treaties and questions of national honor or vital interests were not specifically excepted, the scope of arbitration remained theoretically unlimited; but the effect of those compromises seriously emasculated the treaties and rendered them in essence little different from the Root treaties.[57]

Politics also contributed to the defeat of the treaties. Taft's arbitration accords were more victimized by partisan attacks than earlier proposals. Progressive senators loyal to Roosevelt or LaFollette, both of whom had presidential ambitions in the forthcoming election, revolted against Taft's lackluster and conservative leadership and thus more easily opposed the treaty in order to discredit his administration and advance the political fortunes of insurgent progressivism. Roosevelt began to criticize the proposed treaties even before the negotiations with Britain and France had been concluded. His frontal assaults throughout the Senate debate dispelled the illusions of those peace spokesmen who had counted on the Rough Rider as their champion for world peace and encouraged Roosevelt progressives to join the opposition. Democratic senators, frustrated by sixteen years of Republican presidents, would have inclined toward opposition to the treaties for partisan reasons alone, but the prospect of embarrassing Taft in a presidential election year increased their predisposition to criticize them.[58]

Senate opponents proved better judges than the President of the impact of the treaties on domestic politics. If Taft's advanced position on arbitration was personally courageous, it was politically untenable. On the one hand, he wanted to keep the treaty issue out of partisan politics; on the other, he simultaneously hoped it would prove a boon to his administration's political fortunes. He tried to minimize attacks on the treaties by remaining in the background during treaty negotiations, and he launched his speaking tour reluctantly and only after the Senate Foreign Relations Committee had recommended crippling amendments and deletions. When he finally began to champion the treaties in his speeches, however, he destroyed the last shred of hope that his opponents would try to view the agreements with any objectivity.

Thereafter Taft believed that public pressures would force the Senate to consent without serious amendments.[59] As he wrote William Jennings Bryan concerning his Senate opponents: "The more they abuse me for activity for the treaty, the less headway they will make against the popular desire for the treaties, because the 'prerogatives' of the Senate do not awaken profound interest in the popular mind." Although Taft hoped that Bryan's public support for his treaties would influence his Democratic friends in the Senate, the Great Commoner perceived their intractable partisanship and apparently made only perfunctory efforts to restrain their opposition.[60]

Moreover, senators, still elected indirectly by state legislatures for six-year terms, remained relatively immune to the presumed "popular desire" of their constituents. Senate opponents, calculating that the political impact of public support for the accords would prove ephemeral, proceeded to push through amendments by narrow margins that excluded issues relating to the admission of aliens to the United States and to American schools. In other close votes they eliminated entirely the joint high commission of inquiry and added a resolution of ratification stating that the treaties did not cover several categories of disputes, including territorial integrity of the several states, the United States debts, and the Monroe Doctrine, all of which were declared questions of national policy and therefore to be nonjusticiable. The fact that all Democrats voted for the resolution of ratification and all but three for elimination of the joint commission indicates the importance of political partisanship. Sorely disappointed, Taft refused to submit the emasculated treaties to the British and French governments for ratification.[61]

Although Taft incorporated his arbitration plan in the Republican party platform in 1912 and attempted to focus public attention on the issue during the presidential campaign, he found that support for arbitration was superficial. Interest in his treaties would have been difficult to sustain in times of peace and isolation; but domestic reform, which was approaching its zenith, was the overriding political reality of the times and further detracted attention from the treaty issue. Following his disappointing third-place finish in the election, Taft belatedly conceded that "peace" had not been a live, political issue.[62] Much later he accurately said: "I put them [the treaties] on the shelf and let the dust accumulate on them in the hope that the Senators might change their minds, or that the people might change the Senate; instead of which they changed me."[63]

The debate on Taft's arbitration treaties epitomized the difficulties facing peace spokesmen as their programs became enmeshed in the political process. Imposing obstacles would remain to plague Woodrow Wilson's quest for American membership in the League of Nations. The limitations of the peace movement during the Taft years also stemmed from its internal weaknesses. Indeed, even the more hopeful appearances of growth and activity were deceptive, for new discord in the peace movement simultaneously began to exacerbate existing tensions. If those tensions were less obvious to observers outside the peace leadership, they were nonetheless real. The peace cause suffered in part from normal growing pains, because the rising popularity of the movement inevitably added to the variety of temperaments and personalities. Those differences were more than temperamental or personal, however; they also involved fundamental differences in outlook that threatened to disrupt the peace movement. The growing involvement of functional elites—businessmen, educators, and lawyers— alongside more radical and liberal veterans of the peace cause suggested such divisions. So did legalists' criticisms of arbitration treaties and Root's and Butler's attacks on the World-Federation League's proposal for a peace commission. A closer look at the American peace movement as it coalesced in the last decade before the World War will reveal more precisely the nature and extent of those differences and their implications for peace activity during the Wilson administration.

[10]

The Peace Movement at High Tide

THE MOST DISTINCTIVE characteristic of the American peace movement in the decade before the outbreak of the World War was its heterogeneity. With so many individuals involved in the cause, it is not surprising that there were numerous approaches to peace. Indeed, their differences were in some respects fundamental. One crucial area of disagreement was the armament question. Most veterans in the peace movement, together with the few newcomers who inclined toward pacifism, continued to challenge reliance on large armaments. They wrote acidly about the "follies," "absurdities," "moral miasma," and "delusion" of large armaments, and compared the "contagion" of the armament "fever" to cholera.[1] While many pacifists desired to discredit the public's credulity of the military, Ernest Crosby, who charged that standing armies were "composed of puppets who smother thought and become brainless machines of blind obedience," was unsurpassed for his irreverent wit and withering satire.[2]

If pacific-minded Americans did not worry about a large standing army, they were concerned about naval preparedness, and they held President Roosevelt responsible for the large navy programs. They had never liked his boyish exuberance and bellicose rhetoric of the Spanish-American War. While the more pacifistic spokesmen paid grudging respect to his promotion of various domestic reforms as President and applauded his mediation of the Russo-Japanese War, his approval of Hay's and Root's arbitration treaties, and his restraint in trying to quiet anti–Japanese sentiment on the Pacific coast and in Congress, they did not excuse his navalism.[3] William

Hull best summarized pacifists' assessment of the militaristic proclivities behind Roosevelt's favorable public pose when he labeled him "the Dr. Jekyll and Mr. Hyde of the Peace Movement."[4] Peace advocates also claimed with some justice that his decision to send the American battleship fleet on an around the world cruise in 1907 and 1908 was a poorly disguised public relations gambit to cajole Congress into adopting his naval program and would foster Japanese suspicions concerning the sincerity of Roosevelt's professions of American-Japanese friendship.[5]

For his part, Roosevelt did not hesitate to censure his antipreparedness critics in his private correspondence. He wrote disparagingly of Robert Treat Paine's "wild vagaries," "crank mind," and "eccentric orbit," expressed a "contemptuous abhorrence" for Carnegie "who makes a god of mere money-making and at the same time is always yelling out that kind of utterly stupid condemnation of war," and censured Trueblood for belonging "to the type that makes a good cause ridiculous."[6] Moreover, he liberally sprinkled his annual messages to Congress with oblique references to peace workers' "shortsightedness," "folly," "sentimentality," "selfish indifference," "fanatical extremism," "demagoguery," and "hysterical pseudo-philanthropy."[7]

Naval preparedness assumed added importance following the failure of the Second Hague Peace Conference to discuss armaments. Much as pacifistic Americans had not liked Roosevelt's large navy programs during his first administration, they had grudgingly conceded that he was trying to set an example of national restraint by proposing the addition of only one new battleship annually to the American navy in the two years preceding the Second Hague Conference. The conference's failure, Europe's escalation of the armament race with the construction of dreadnoughts, and the crisis in Japanese-American relations prompted Roosevelt to ask Congress to appropriate an additional $60,000,000 for the construction of four battleships and several support ships. Rather than pretend that they were for defensive purposes, Roosevelt candidly explained that he wanted "an aggressive sea-going navy" that could perform "hard hitting of the offensive type."[8] That was going too far even for most moderate peace advocates, who proceeded to deluge Congress with antipreparedness protests.[9] When Roosevelt renewed his request for four battleships the following year, the American Peace Society, Boston businessmen, and 224 clergymen protested, and Lucia Mead composed a remonstrance which received the signatures of about three hundred national "opinion leaders."[10]

The antipreparedness forces believed they had cause for alarm. Although congressmen's growing uneasiness about military spending resulted in naval appropriations cutting Roosevelt's requests for four battleships in half in his last two years in office, this number still represented a two-fold increase of the battle fleet over the previous two years. Roosevelt succeeded in increasing the military budget by more than 600 percent during his two administrations. More menacing to antimilitarist peace workers was the development of a sophisticated armament lobby that portended a long-term struggle. Financed by the Navy League of the United States, founded in 1902, that lobby berated Congress for its supposed naval parsimony. Roosevelt openly boosted the Navy League's program, which had not yet exerted any appreciable influence on politicians, but was at least well-known and was a growing force with which peace workers would have to contend.[11] Charles Jefferson expressed pacifists' alarm when he charged that the naval lobby was "composed of the most dangerous set of men since the oligarchy of slaveholders in the fifties."[12]

Even some of Roosevelt's most loyal supporters in the peace movement could not approve of his preparedness program. Despite his unbounded confidence in Roosevelt's peacemaking abilities, Andrew Carnegie gently protested Roosevelt's obsession with national honor and his exaggerated fears of Japan, and played a prominent role in organizing New Yorkers' antipreparedness petitions to Congress.[13] Bartholdt went further. He had earlier criticized peace advocates' emphasis on armament limitation before the Second Hague Peace Conference. He had acted partly out of party loyalty to the President and partly because he genuinely believed that his own program of a general arbitration treaty would have to precede armament limitation. He had even believed that the United States should be prepared to "construct a navy of enormous size" as a veiled threat to the other major powers if they vetoed a general arbitration treaty at the forthcoming Hague gathering. However, the failure of the Second Hague Conference, the ensuing, escalating naval race, and his own maturing pacifism convinced him that the United States should rely entirely on its moral leadership to heal the deep cleavage between the two European power blocs. Roosevelt's refusal to participate in the peace commission, his criticisms of Taft's arbitration treaties, which Bartholdt vigorously supported, and his open break with Taft convinced Bartholdt that Roosevelt's obsession with national power was matched by his quest for personal power, and he blasted the Rough Rider's pretensions for a third presidential term as the acme of uncontrolled ambition.[14]

Pacifists became increasingly restive at the American public's acceptance of their nation's place in big-power rivalries. Unable to stop the drift, pacifists found comfort in their own ranks. As a symbolic gesture, they managed to purge Lyman Abbott's name from the list of honorary vice-presidents of the American Peace Society in 1913. Abbott's unabashed defense of America's imperial role, his undisguised racism, and his vigorous support of Roosevelt's navalism joined the issue. Even his cautious endorsement of Taft's arbitration treaties and his mild disagreement with his friend Roosevelt on the issue failed to deter pacifists' alienation from Abbott. His signature on a Navy League petition in early 1913 provided the catalyst for ending his honorary status.

But Abbott's removal was only temporary, for protests from the membership and the Carnegie trustees resulted in his reinstatement the following year.[15] In fact, the direction of the American Peace Society and even more the peace movement as a whole was toward acceptance of the need for more military preparedness. Earlier peace advocates did not compromise their antimilitarism, but deaths rapidly depleted their ranks. When Alfred Love died in 1913, the Universal Peace Union died with him.[16] Although a few of the post-1900 recruits showed deep concern over the escalating armament race, they were more hopeful for an international agreement on armaments and therefore did not make disarmament their first priority in the peace movement. Even more significant, because most of the newcomers more easily accepted existing power realities among nation-states, they were proportionately less discomfited by the problem of naval power.

The armament mania particularly infected Hayne Davis. Since he had earlier favored armament increases in the absence of an enforceable world order, he was consistent in advocating military preparedness following the Second Hague Peace Conference's tabling of the issue, but Davis' zeal for national armaments exceeded what most peace leaders considered "adequate." In late 1907 he organized the North Carolina Peace Society and cajoled it into drawing up a memorial to President Roosevelt endorsing his four battleships. Davis' efforts led to the founding of the American Arbitration and Peace League a year later. Davis may have been influenced by his cousin Richmond Pearson Hobson, a naval hero of the Spanish-American War, whom he had helped to elect to the House of Representatives in 1906. His close association with Hobson, a confirmed racist and military booster, increasingly alienated antipreparedness people, who began to label the Davis-Hobson program "suspicious" and "insane."[17] Butler became so dissatisfied with Davis' erratic behavior that he forced his resignation as secretary of the American Association for International Conciliation.[18]

The clearest indication of the dilution of antipreparedness sentiment in the peace movement occurred at the 1906 Lake Mohonk Conferences. Pacific-minded leaders protested increases to the United States Navy but their pleas received little support. Delegates agreed instead to a milder resolution urging the Roosevelt administration to prod the upcoming Hague Conference to adopt a "plan for the restriction of armaments and if possible for their reduction by concurrent international action."[19] On the eve of the Second Hague Conference the following year, Edwin Mead and his antipreparedness allies pressed the Mohonk meeting to adopt the same mild resolution. However, Abbott, joined by Smiley and others, spoke in opposition and it was defeated by a 69 to 83 vote.[20] Trueblood, noting that Mead's proposal was "supported by nearly every one of the experienced Mohonk workers,"[21] hinted at the lines of division between veteran peace advocates and military, business, and professional people whom Smiley had lured to his arbitration conferences in increasing numbers after 1900, but who otherwise had no connection with the peace cause. At the 1908 Conference, Smiley, tired of past wranglings on the preparedness issue, persuaded pacifists to withdraw their plank on limitation of armaments, which undoubtedly would have failed anyway. Succeeding Mohonk Conferences belatedly recognized the increasing military tensions in Europe, but their resolutions calling for leadership by the United States government on the armament question did not specifically demand unilateral limitations on American armaments as evidence of their nation's moral commitment to the principle.[22]

The newer peace organizations reflected that more moderate position on armaments. From its inception in 1906, the New York Peace Society officially avoided the question of military preparedness; its constitution insisted only that "the purpose of this Society is to foster the spirit of amity and concord among nations, and to create a public sentiment which will lead to the abandonment of war as a means of settling international differences and disputes."[23] When William H. Short declared in 1911, "For over three years no remonstrance of any kind has gone out from its office," he accurately summarized the group's apolitical orientation.[24] It is true that much of the society's leadership resisted Roosevelt's large navy programs and in fact drafted antipreparedness petitions in executive committee meetings, which they circulated in their capacity as private citizens to various professional elites, and consequently the New York Peace Society projected a public image of opposition to large armaments. A poll of the membership in 1910 showing that four-fifths of the respondents opposed as "excessive" the annual additions of two battleships reinforced its antipreparedness orientation.[25] However Carnegie, eager to expand membership in the peace group, believed that its unofficial small navy reputation inhibited its ability to attract as members those individuals favoring an enlarged naval force, and he urged the society to issue a public statement explicitly deemphasizing the armament question. Since he continued to oppose Taft's large navy programs, he had not changed his mind on the subject; rather, in typically optimistic fashion, he assumed that newer recruits initially attracted to the society's avoidance of controversial questions like military preparedness would gradually be won over to his and other pacific-minded members' views on these issues.[26] The leadership of the society finally accepted Carnegie's innocuous suggestion that "This Society should neither advocate nor oppose an increase of the American army or navy."[27]

Carnegie also revealed his avoidance of controversy when he rejected President Roosevelt's personal plea for the New York Peace Society's public support in his attempts to defuse anti-Japanese sentiment on the West Coast.[28] When Roosevelt subsequently complained about "the more foolish peace societies" that "blatantly or furtively oppose the navy and hamper its unbuilding while doing nothing to prevent insult against Japan," he was thinking mainly of Carnegie's New York peace group.[29] Not all peace associations failed to express good will toward Japan during this period of rising distrust between the two nations, and it is doubtful whether the New York Peace Society, either singly or in cooperation with other peace groups, could have helped Roosevelt quiet Californians' fears of the "Yellow Peril."[30] The inaction of the New York group, however, revealed that even its more modest, "positive" purpose of international friendship meant little in practice. The creation of a separate group, the World-Federation League, by the few federalists in the society was further evidence that the New York peace group went out of its way to avoid acrimonious debate within its ranks.

William Short attempted to justify the society's noncontroversial program as "the only one that can persuade the skeptical that international peace is obtainable."[31] While that policy enabled the society to obtain a larger membership and greater respect from the press and general public, it sacrificed the moral fervor and direct action tactics that a smaller society composed largely of the most dedicated peace spokesmen would have attained. The enlarged membership gave the society a mushy character. With such a diffuse focus, the society's prospects for becoming hamstrung during some future international crisis increased markedly.

A vocal pacifist minority in the New York Peace Society chafed under the group's public pose of neutrality on foreign policy issues, and they openly criticized its emphasis on respectability. Mrs. Spencer summarized their dissatisfaction with the society's timidity: "We have no reason for existence as a peace society if we are silent when there is talk all over the United States of the need of keeping up our navy."[32] Pacifists' arguments impressed some concerned nonpacifists on the executive committee, but their combined efforts to raise the armament issue failed to obtain decisive majorities and only intensified dissension and confusion within its ruling circles.[33]

The Chicago Peace Society and American Peace Congress in 1913 exhibited similar divisions. The geographic isolation of the Chicago Peace

Society from the less secure East Coast should have inclined them toward an unequivocal antipreparedness stand. When the peace group appointed a committee to report on whether membership in the Navy League should disqualify a person from membership in the Chicago Peace Society, however, disagreement within the committee prevented formulation of a statement, and the conservative executive committee, over the protests of antipreparedness advocates, voted to discharge the study group.[34]

The officers of the American Peace Congress allowed delegations from large navy groups, the American Peace and Arbitration League and the Navy League, to speak at the sessions. Recognizing the growing tolerance of the American public for the peace movement, the representatives of the large navy groups were particularly anxious to inform the delegates that they supported international arbitration and thus were also "peace" men but differed only on preparedness. The field secretary of the Navy League even had the audacity "to ask recognition of the Navy League as a Peace Society."[35] A few peace advocates questioned the ideas of the large navy spokesmen but most remained silent or were willing to agree with the preparedness advocates that the United States needed an "adquate" navy, although never quite specifying what they meant.[36] Arthur Deerin Call, recently appointed executive director of the American Peace Society, put it mildly: "Well, I don't know, but what we all believe in an adequate army and navy." In fact, the only gains from the mutual expressions of good will between the large navy boosters and the peace leadership went to the Navy League, which obtained membership pledges from several delegates attending the peace congress.[37]

Tensions also developed between the legalists and other peace spokesmen. As the lawyers' numbers and influence in peace circles increased, they became bolder in challenging pacifists' traditional reliance on arbitration treaties. Yet when they methodically criticized the practice of men trained in politics and diplomacy rather than noted jurists deciding arbitration cases, less legal-minded peace advocates came to the defense of arbitration. If their criticisms were temperate, their preference for the flexible give-and-take of arbitration over the precise legalism of international law was unmistakable.[38]

If legalists and pacifists disagreed on the value of arbitration treaties, both criticized the world federalists. Compared with the latter, lawyers and pacifists held a more pessimistic view of human nature that molded their views on authoritative international bodies. If pacific-minded individuals like Hull and Trueblood were more quick than the lawyers to criticize the ease with which larger powers were willing to embark on military adventures for the advancement of their national self-interest, they both emphasized the potential abuses of consolidated power. Not surprisingly, they defended the legal equality of sovereign states as practiced at the Hague Peace Conferences against the federalists' emphasis on great power primacy, and they began to brand federalists' schemes for world order as too radical and therefore impractical.[39]

Differences even existed within each group. Among the world federalists, Hamilton Holt backed away from his advocacy of an international police force in 1911 when Theodore Marburg warned him that his proposal was too advanced.[40] So, too, although most of those inclining toward pacifism feared the possible harmful consequences of an international police force, two of the strongest opponents of national armaments—Lucia Ames Mead and Edwin Ginn—endorsed the formation of a small international police force with limited powers to enforce the peace.[41] Furthermore, Jane Addams, influenced by the polyglot ethnic communities in Chicago, developed a peculiar brand of pacifism that had little in common with other pacifists. Much as she wrote about peace, she often seemed more interested in domestic than international reform. In the presidential election of 1912, for example, she supported Theodore Roosevelt, by then no friend of any peace faction.[42]

Although all legalists agreed on the need for a permanent world court, even they were not united. Some followed James Brown Scott and Elihu Root in criticizing ad hoc tribunals composed of arbitrators from the disputing nations as harmful to the cause of international justice; but others, including John Bassett Moore and William Howard Taft, argued that these tribunals could contribute positively to the advancement of international law. In addition, a few legalists stressed the impracticality of the legal equality of states in a world of great and small nations, and they contemplated other formulas for subordinating legalistic doctrines to power realities.[43] For all of Taft's reverence for the law, he thought in grander terms of world order before the First World War, and he perceived that an effective international organization might require an international police force to carry out the decisions of the prospective world court. Although Taft did not implement the World-Federation League's resolution calling for the creation of some such international policing body, his endorsement of the principle separated him from the antisanctionist views of many prominent legalists. He intimated that he might be receptive to collective security as another major task of the peace movement following the establishment of a court of arbitral justice.[44]

Theodore Marburg's commitment to the legalists remained tenuous. He was not a lawyer and thus had no inbred professional biases that might have narrowed his perception of the possibilities of world order. Further, though he had strongly endorsed America's war with Spain and its takeover of the Philippines and thought that almost all areas except the United States and Europe were "backward,"[45] he had more faith than international lawyers in the ability of industrialized states to cooperate in developing a stable international order.[46] When he said that "[i]t is the will of man, God-inspired, that determines what man shall be," he expressed his optimistic belief in the ability of "civilized" man to mold his international environment.[47]

Moreover, for all Marburg's disdain of "backward" nations, he wished to "exclude utterly the use of force" to collect debts from weaker states.[48] That, however, was an ideal that he believed could not be realized under present circumstances. He assumed that industrialized nations inevitably expanded and would use military force, if necessary, to protect their economic interests. At times he even thought that great power hegemony was desirable. He told John Bassett Moore shortly after the outbreak of civil war in Mexico, for example, that the American takeover of that country would mean "another advance of our race."[49] He rejected the ultranationalist position expounded by Roosevelt and others, however, as giving the great powers carte blanche in their dealings with weaker neighbors and began to grope toward some practical alternative.[50]

Marburg's confidence in great power cooperation suggested an alternative solution. He believed that once the major nations recognized their community of interest in controlling weaker and unstable areas, they could keep their own imperial rivalries within manageable limits and cooperate in establishing a new agency that would deliberate on alleged illegal and unjust actions of "backward" peoples and provide a multinational (if not fully international) sanction limited to interventions. He suggested that the proposed court of arbitral justice could be given power to authorize large nations' interventions in recalcitrant small states. If the major nations agreed, Marburg claimed, "not only will it disarm suspicion when called upon so to act, not only may it then suggest that the powers share the expense of such action, but, what is of far more importance, such agency will save the United States from the otherwise inevitable absorption of some of the backward countries."[51] His proposal foreshadowed the creation of a system of mandates under the League of Nations that sought both to legitimize temporarily and to soften the impact of great powers' imperialism. The outbreak of the World War finally convinced him that the lawyers' program for a world court would not suffice, and, far from shaking his faith in big power cooperation, strengthened his belief in authoritative international machinery as the best hope for preserving the peace.

Temperamental and tactical differences also threatened the fragile unity of the peace movement. Such differences were particularly evident in the

World Peace Foundation, which despite its generous financial resources made only modest inroads on American public opinion. It was not for want of zeal that the foundation failed to stimulate greater pacifist activity. The foundation, however, encountered more problems than Edwin Ginn anticipated. Although the trustees and directors agreed that the foundation should stress the educational side of the peace movement, they were far from one mind in developing practical policies. Their lack of tactical cohesion prevented coordinated and imaginative programs.

Ginn's fiscal and organizational theories were a thorn in the side of his endowed agency. Along with his sturdy moralism, Ginn's entrepreneurial career shaped his thinking on the foundation, which he viewed as another business enterprise.[52] Determined to avoid the inefficiencies of the peace societies, Ginn operated the foundation as if it were a business. Ginn, like many of his contemporaries, was obsessed with twentieth-century efficiency. Under Ginn's active direction, the foundation's success was measured not by the quality of its propaganda but by its quantity. Ginn promoted peace, as a fellow worker said, as though he were selling textbooks.[53]

Ginn's puritanical values of self-help and thrift were manifested in a financial conservatism that prevented him from fully exploiting the foundation's possibilities.[54] He was reluctant, for example, to spend the foundation's full income. If it had proven a sound practice in the first years of Ginn and Company to pursue cautious financial policies, he reasoned, similar policies were prudent for his newly established peace organization. Besides, he envisaged conservative fiscal practices only until other millionaires lavished their funds on the foundation. In order to conserve money while awaiting financial aid, Ginn continued the practice of the International Library of selling the foundation's peace books at cost; and he even raised the price of the books when he saw the opportunity for larger revenues.[55]

His bequest of one million dollars also signified his fiscal conservatism. Although he advertised his posthumous gift ostensibly to attract contributions from other wealthy individuals, it seemed to indicate his reluctance to invest a major portion of his fortune. Carnegie expressed their dismay at Ginn's parsimony: "Frankly, . . . I think you will find great difficulty in obtaining additional funds unless you transfer the $1,000,000 to your organization."[56] Ginn, refusing to heed that advice, convinced himself that Carnegie refused to contribute money to the foundation because he was jealous that Ginn had become the first great philanthropist for peace. In 1912 Ginn persuaded the trustees to hire Albert G. Bryant as business manager to approach potential donors, but Bryant's efforts also failed.[57]

Ginn's value of self-help was reflected in his curiously ambivalent premises on human psychology. According to Ginn, "People are interested in what they pay for, and they don't care much for anything that is given to them—books, lectures, of [*sic*] anything else."[58] He assumed that the individual's financial investment in the peace movement was the surest guarantee of his emotional involvement. It was partly for that reason that Ginn condemned the peace societies that largely overlooked his stake-in-society approach in favor of appeals to the hearts and minds of their audiences. He also had little use for the lecture tours of the foundation's directors that in his view momentarily entertained but did not convert their audiences.[59]

Ginn's opposition to appropriating funds to the American School Peace League pointedly illustrated the narrowness of his business approach. He argued that the World Peace Foundation's limited resources precluded financial assistance to outside organizations. Just as important, however, an outright annual gift to the league contradicted his own value of self-help. In his view such a donation really amounted to a dole and would "pauperize" the teachers in the nation by discouraging their own financial involvement. "There is not one of those teachers," he insisted, "but could give $1 or $5 for carrying on this work if they were sufficiently interested. If the School Peace League were established on such a plan, it would be self-supporting and a hundred times as much could be done as now."[60]

Ginn's colleagues, principally Mead and Jordan, in the foundation consistently resisted his attempts to implement his financial and organizational theories. They saw the peace movement as the most recent of the many moral reforms of modern history and were confident that the force of peace workers' arguments would eventually convert the masses to pacifist thinking and reform the bases of world politics.[61] They found little merit in Ginn's businesslike approach to the foundation and had more faith than Ginn in peace societies. One of Mead's closest associates in the peace movement was Trueblood, yet Ginn claimed that Trueblood was responsible for making the American Peace Society "feeble for so many years."[62] Mead and Jordan also firmly supported the peace workers' reliance on the content of their propaganda. Jordan believed that "the best efforts of a few great men who have shown their power to mould and to guide public opinion" rather than businessmen of Ginn's stripe should formulate the foundation's policies.[63] When Ginn criticized a lecture tour by Hamilton Holt under the foundation's auspices, Mead defended him as "one of our very best helper's" [*sic*].[64] Similarly, when Ginn first proposed a business manager, Mead sharply opposed it: "It is perfectly evident to me, as it has been from the beginning, and as I expect is now evident to you also, that whatever titles have been carelessly distributed, the real responsibility for the administration of the foundation must rest with me, just as the preliminary work of these years for bringing the foundation to its present position has been mine."[65]

Mead and Jordan also criticized Ginn's constrictive thrift. They recognized that money was a prerequisite for carrying on the foundation's propaganda, and Mead even tried to secure additional funds from Carnegie; but they were more anxious than Ginn to spend the full budget. When Ginn initially opposed any expenditure to the American School Peace League, they strongly defended the league as an important educational agency in the movement. They saw the issue, insignificant in itself, as a test in the future direction of the foundation. To support the American School Peace League, they argued, would broaden the foundation's activities. On the other hand, if the foundation refused to appropriate any funds to the league, it would demonstrate a cautious approach to the peace movement, discourage potential donors, and perhaps stagnate. But Ginn, imprisoned by his values, acquiesced reluctantly to the trustees' allotment of a paltry $2,500 to the league.[66]

Not too much should be made of those temperamental and tactical differences, for all the directors and Ginn himself inclined toward pacifism. Moreover, they were tolerant liberals who confidently believed that they could amicably settle their disagreements. Shortly after Ginn's death, for example, Mead admitted that he had often found many of Ginn's ideas impulsive, inconsistent, and extravagant; but he added emphatically that he had always worked closely with Ginn, even regularly criticizing his speeches upon Ginn's request, and had never doubted his profound and persistent devotion to the pacifist cause.[67] There is also no evidence before the World War that the other directors and trustees allowed their disagreements to develop into personal or factional feuds. On the contrary, they had such high regard for each other and their common endeavor that they freely and frankly expressed what they believed were only honest and healthy differences of opinion.

Nevertheless, it is obvious that the World Peace Foundation could not formulate coherent programs so long as the leadership frequently disagreed on basic policies. Ginn admitted that he was very discouraged with the disparity between the lofty purposes of his endowed organization and its meager accomplishments.[68] Although Ginn's sudden death on January 21, 1914, might have led eventually to a more congenial atmosphere in the foundation, the outbreak of the World War only six months later presented such serious problems to its personnel, as we shall see, that the disunity of the pre-war years was further exacerbated.

The peace leaders' diverse temperaments, tactics, and programs were real and substantial, and in combination they seriously weakened the potential effectiveness of the peace movement. Their differences, however, paled in comparison with the cleavage between active peace workers and the trustees of the Carnegie Endowment. Conservatively Brahmin almost without exception, the Carnegie trustees lacked the internal difficulties that faced the World Peace Foundation. But the trustees quickly aroused misgivings of several peace spokesmen outside the endowment. Of course, pacific-minded internationalists had initially hailed the founding of the endowed organization as a milestone, but many of these paeans of praise were directed at Carnegie's generosity rather than his choice of trustees. Mead, Villard, Jordan, and Holt early expressed misgivings about the conservatism of the trustees. Essentially optimistic, they initially suggested specific projects for the endowment in the hope that the trustees would be receptive to their suggestions. The endowment's emphasis on scholarly studies and international law soon confirmed their fears that it was a research institution more interested in writing tomes for some future library than in active, vital peace work in America.[69]

Thus, pacifists and federalists made the endowment their whipping boy. The leadership of the World Peace Foundation complained about the endowment's indifference to the armament race, European insecurity, and other immediate concerns of the peace movement. "So far I have not seen very much evidence of a practical live wire in their work," Ginn noted, "but mostly work among fossils and among the economists, which in the next millennium may be operative, but where are the live wires they are placing and influencing immediately the people?"[70] Holt remarked with evident sarcasm that "some of the trustees prefer peace but are not much averse to war," and Jordan lamented their failure to mobilize public opinion both at home and abroad against the growth of armaments.[71]

They could afford to criticize the Carnegie Endowment because their own endowed group was financially independent. The American Peace Society was not entirely self-sufficient, however, and its leaders found themselves in a dilemma. They realized that the Carnegie trustees were little interested in their activities but could not freely criticize their cautious policies if they were to continue to receive the endowment's subvention. Accordingly, they either remained silent or praised those actions of the Carnegie Endowment, such as the subvention and cultural exchange programs, which in their opinion genuinely merited approval. Their few public complaints cited the lopsided support the endowment gave to international law, friendship, and other nonpacifist organizations. Members of the peace group complained that the endowment's subvention to the American Peace Society, less than one-sixteenth of the endowment's annual budget, was a mere pittance.[72]

In private the pacifist leadership of the American Peace Society expressed increasing concern over the group's subordination to the Carnegie Endowment. Edwin Mead, Hull, Bartholdt, Holt, and Trueblood conducted a rather frenetic correspondence from 1911 to 1914 in which they variously criticized the new "timid and conservative folk" and "half-baked 'new' pacifism" infiltrating the peace movement, defended the "old pacifism" of those "not addicted to 'high finance,' " and discussed possible ways to recover some of the society's independence.[73]

The trustees of the Carnegie Endowment were in full control from the start, however, and initiated policies with scant regard for the concerns of outsiders. The reorganization of the society in 1911 and 1912, though outwardly a smooth and deliberate process, was in reality imposed on the American Peace Society as a precondition for receiving the subvention. The national composition of the reorganized board of directors came at the cost of reducing the membership of the more idealistic and pacifistic Boston directors from twenty-three to three, and thenceforth the more "practical" leadership of the group prepared no petitions protesting naval preparedness or any other foreign policy issue. The endowment also used its financial leverage to require the appointment of an executive director and to demand veto power over the society's selection. While the avowed purpose of the executive directorship was need for a full-time person to handle most of the expanded organizational and administrative work, the trustees also saw the new position as a convenient excuse to circumscribe Trueblood's role in the society, in effect limiting his authority to editing the *Advocate of Peace*. Butler told Trueblood that he did not wish to advise the American Peace Society "because it would easily be made to appear that . . . the support of the Carnegie Endowment was being used as a club," but his frequent recommendations of policy, combined with generous praise for those the society followed and disapproval of its more outlandish proposals, left no doubt about the Carnegie Endowment's carrot-and-stick policy. In 1912 the local peace societies were required to affiliate with the American Peace Society as a precondition for financial support, and the endowment even hired a statistician to determine the "weight," "standing," and "practicality" of the activities and publications of the various peace groups as the basis for annual revisions of financial rewards.[74]

Actually, Butler claimed with some justice that he was not using the subvention as a coercive tool but was merely conveying the dominant viewpoint of the trustees, several of whom were sharply critical of peace societies from the start. In 1913 the endowment began serious discussions on the possibility of curtailing all financial aid to peace societies. The prospect was all the more alarming because individual supporters of peace organizations, believing the endowment's subvention provided the peace movement with sufficient funds, no longer donated so generously to them. The private donations to the American Peace Society steadily declined from $17,160 in the 1909–1910 fiscal year to $8,632 in 1913–1914. Mead complained about the endowment, "It makes people think this movement has got all the money it needs, and that they need not exert themselves."[75] Decline in private donations similarly occurred in local peace groups. Charles Beals, for example, became so discouraged with the Chicago Peace Society's conservatism, declining memberships, and private donations that he resigned the secretaryship in January 1914.[76]

The many views and temperaments in the peace movement foreshadowed the divergent responses to the world crisis after 1914, but before then a tenuous consensus existed among the peace forces. Indeed, a major theme of the American peace movement before 1914 was the relative absence of overt controversy. Leaders of all viewpoints in the movement frequently appeared on the same platform at peace and arbitration congresses and rarely engaged in extensive debate over their different viewpoints. When they recognized their differences, they usually assumed that they were more complementary than conflicting. Especially absent was severe public criticism of their colleagues. Despite Edwin Mead's private fears of the Carnegie Endowment's financial dominance of the movement, he publicly lavished praise on Elihu Root and argued that it was "ridiculous" to believe that the Carnegie trustees did not advocate reduction of armaments, although he well knew that some of them, including its president Root, were prominent supporters of the Navy League.[77]

In addition to dependence on Carnegie's endowment, there were other explanations for the peace leaders' failure to emphasize their real differences. Most important, during these years of relative peace and isolation the pressures for defining and defending one's position on peace questions were minimal. Because the prospects for realization of their respective programs in the immediate future were remote, they could well afford to treat their colleagues' different peace theories as intellectual exercises. The mild disagreements within the pacifist, generalist, federalist, and legalist positions blurred the lines separating them, and the diversity of approaches gave the appearance of flatness to peace theories. The overlapping membership in peace societies and endowed organizations further muddied their differences. It increased the peace leaders' personal contacts and the chances for resolution of conflicting viewpoints. The generalists participating in more than one peace organization found very little difficulty in cooperating with their associates. Samuel Train Dutton, who served as trustee of the World Peace Foundation, section head of the American Peace Society, secretary of the New York Peace Society, and American representative on the Carnegie Endowment's Balkan Commission, worked as closely with Nicholas Murray Butler, his colleague at Columbia, as he did with more pacifistic spokesmen like Trueblood, Mead, and Jordan. An even-tempered bureaucrat, Dutton was a compromiser and harmonizer among the peace factions. In 1909, it will be recalled, he introduced the plan for federation of the peace societies around the American Peace Society. In late 1913 he urged Butler to consider an even more ambitious project: "a great international journal, which would, of course, absorb the American Peace Society's *Advocate of Peace* and be supported and directed largely by the Carnegie Endowment, the World Peace Foundation, and the American Peace Society."[78] In view of the marked differences in the peace movement, Dutton's proposal was overly sanguine and nothing more was heard of the matter. Nevertheless, Dutton's mention of the subject signified his confidence in the cooperative spirit of the peace leadership.

Moreover, the overwhelming majority of peace leaders were sufficiently moderate and practical to realize that compared with their differences with their super-patriotic opponents those between peace spokesmen were marginal; and in any case it did their cause little good to air their dirty linen in public. Jordan summarized the views of most peace participants when he said that the purpose of the peace movement was "to lead men to think, to undo the poisoned teachings of centuries as to history, morals, and patriotism," and any arguments that led people to think war was wicked were good propaganda. "Hence," Jordan concluded, "I think we should not belittle one form of peace activity in the interest of any other."[79]

Almost as important, there existed a few areas of general agreement that helped maintain an uneasy unity in the movement. First, all endorsed periodic international congresses for the discussion of questions of common interest. Second, they all assumed that the United States as a satiated and relatively secure power should take the lead in advancing specific proposals leading to a more harmonious international order. Their nationalist biases of course fostered that assumption, but European peace workers also repeatedly emphasized that their hopes for restoration of sanity among the major European powers rested ultimately with the moral leadership and friendly interposition of the United States in Old World affairs. When Baron d'Estournelles de Constant wrote that "Europe has need of America to be regenerated and saved," he expressed the sentiments of European peace workers; and both he and Baroness Bertha von Suttner tirelessly reiterated this theme in their lecture tours in the United States in 1912.[80] Third, although only the legalists were very precise in their definitions of international law, all conceded the importance of "law" in establishing nations' rights and duties in the world community. Faith in the law, shared by American liberals and conservatives alike, was not surprising in the existing American stable and progressive social order. Finally, no peace worker opposed the establishment of a court of arbitral justice as the next, most practical step toward instituting a new world order following the Second Hague Peace Conference's endorsement in principle of the institution.[81]

Yet there were other, often more fundamental reasons for their cooperative behavior. One was their similar backgrounds. With the increasing number of deaths among veteran peace advocates, the origins of almost all the surviving peace leaders after about 1909 were so remarkably alike that it was relatively easy for them to tolerate different approaches to world peace than if their backgrounds had been more diverse. Despite their wide age span and different lengths of service in the movement, from every other sociological perspective their social origins were virtually identical. All but a handful had received college degrees, and these exceptions were among the most articulate peace spokesmen.[82] Moreover, about two-thirds also had earned professional certification in their chosen fields of law, education, or religion. Since only relatively affluent families could usually afford to send their children to college, these figures, together with other information on their parents' social standing, indicate that almost all the leading peace spokesmen came from the middle or upper classes and, upon reaching maturity, formed an educated elite among the professional classes.

Those similarities went beyond their social class. Almost all were native Americans born east of the Mississippi and north of the Mason-Dixon line. Several were reared in small towns and, like many reformers of their generation, they retained nostalgic memories of their rural origins; but they early moved to large cities and by 1909 approximately three-fourths of the peace leadership lived in six metropolitan areas: Boston, New York, Philadelphia, Baltimore, Washington, D.C., and Chicago. In addition, all were Protestants, and about one-half came from strongly religious households, seriously considered the ministry as a career, or were ordained clergymen.

In sum, the social characteristics of the peace leadership were overwhelmingly urban, professional, Anglo-Saxon, and Protestant. In many instances, the sociological ties were more than casual. Among New York peace workers Frederick Lynch's contacts with Hamilton Holt and William Short extended beyond their common experiences as Yale classmates; Lynch also married one of Samuel Dutton's daughters in 1909 and earlier had introduced Short to his future wife. Kirchwey and Dutton had also received degrees from Yale and, along with James Brown Scott and Nicholas Murray Butler, became professors or administrators at Columbia University. They all were prominent in the formation and programs of the New York Peace Society or the Carnegie Endowment. Close ties also existed among Boston peace workers. Before moving to New York, Dutton was a school administrator in the Boston area and frequently discussed educational problems with Boston intelligentsia in the Twentieth Century

Club. His exposure to many Boston pacifists in the club first introduced him to the peace movement. Furthermore, Lynch's and Arthur Deerin Call's early contacts with Boston peace advocates helped foster their growing interest in the cause.

Their social origins per se did not separate them from ardent nationalists, many of whom (except perhaps for less pervasive religious influences) came from roughly similar backgrounds. A profile of the peace leadership suggests only that the individuals who gravitated toward the peace movement in these years tended to come from the Protestant establishment.

Of wider importance than their social backgrounds, though in some important respects derived from them, were the common values and attitudes the peace spokesmen expressed in the movement. The most direct link between their social origins and their approach to peace work (as well as domestic reforms) was their elitism. Political conservatives in the movement deliberately discouraged participation by the lower classes, but even more progressive elements gave little emphasis to them. With some exceptions among pacific-minded individuals, most notably Jane Addams and William Jennings Bryan, they assumed that literate gentlemen of the middle and upper classes could more easily understand the civilized quality of their movement than the unenlightened masses. Not surprisingly, they relied upon their contacts with friends in government circles for their influence and shunned involvement in politics and contacts with immigrant, moderate socialist, or labor groups. The high priced dinners and formal receptions of the New York Peace Society and the Carnegie Endowment, Albert Smiley's select conferences at Lake Mohonk, and the leadership of peace societies limited to educators, ministers, and philanthropists exemplified this same elitism.[83] A few pacifistic leaders occasionally criticized the peace societies' "undue striving after mere 'prominence' and 'influence' " and lamented the failure of the peace leaders to direct their appeals to the masses, but in the face of the pervasive elitism in the movement their appeals made little headway.[84]

In a few cases their exclusiveness was patently snobbish. Although Smiley invited a few Catholic and Jewish leaders to his arbitration conferences, he barred the latter from his hotel-resort during the rest of the summer season. When Rabbi Stephen Wise learned of this discrimination, he refused to accept Smiley's invitation to attend his arbitration conferences.[85] Most peace leaders, however, were not so deliberately undemocratic. Rather, reflecting the Mugwump traditions and teachings then common among reformers, they assumed that the man on the street was an important factor in public opinion only to the extent of his ability to absorb their own ideas. Until education could enlighten the general public, they assumed that they alone were the proper custodians of the peace movement.

Specifically, they believed that as soon as they had won over the schools, churches, and press, all essentially middle class institutions, they would have gained the only really important elements of American public opinion. Dutton hoped that universal education would eventually uplift the general public to acceptance of the peace movement, but for the present he was convinced that "even in the most intelligent nations there is so much apathy and so much ignorance that the masses can hardly be counted upon in civic affairs at home, much less in world politics."[86]

Even progressive reformers, while expressing greater faith in the populace, upheld the Mugwump emphasis on enlightened leadership and agreed that international reform would have to come from above rather than from below. Lynch assumed that "it is the prophets and leaders who make the changes of the world. The talk of *vox populi* is often more of a delusion than a reality."[87] While those reformers regularly expounded their views on peace questions to formal gatherings, they rarely engaged their audiences in public discussion or attempted to include them in the daily operations of the peace movement. Indeed, fascinated by great leaders of the past and present, they easily tolerated the growing involvement in the movement of influential conservatives whose participation seemed to confirm the dignity of their own peace work. In consequence, the peace movement increasingly acquired an aura of gentility and respectability but at the expense of widening the gap between the peace leaders and the masses.

Peace advocates managed to maintain an uneasy consensus on other values. Above all, they shared an unquestioning belief in the reality of moral values. The acceptance of moral values as the mainspring of human behavior was ingrained in the American character, as the Puritans, transcendentalists, and antislavery reformers had earlier demonstrated; and the most pacifistic internationalists continued to refer to the humanistic values of their forebears. They also continued to derive inspiration for their ethical values from Christian humanists and Enlightenment philosophers throughout the Western world. Those pacific-minded individuals' many frustrations over foreign policy issues going back to the turn of the century made them well aware of the virulent nationalism of large portions of American society. Unlike American ultranationalists who had little faith in the pervasiveness of ethical principles beyond the water's edge, these international reformers believed that these human values, though most obviously present in their own land, existed universally and already exerted an extensive influence on the foreign policies of other nations. More restrained international reformers, however, assumed that that was an ideal nations did not yet emulate.[88]

In the long run, the distinction between the pacifists' humanism and other peace leaders' more limited emphasis on civilized nations was crucial. The latter, more readily believing in the essential virtue of American conduct in foreign affairs, could more easily justify their nation's forceful intervention in other states' affairs for the sake of reforming their policies along American or "civilized" lines than those inclining toward pacifism, who were profoundly skeptical about the use of force in foreign affairs. Both the dwindling influence of pacifists and the continuation of world peace, however, meant that this distinction caused no real difficulties before 1914.

If the peace leaders had believed only in the reality of moral values in international life, they would have had difficulty in explaining why nations had resorted to wars throughout history. As the "practical" direction of the peace movement suggested, however, they were not Pollyannas. Admitting that man was not inherently good and might even be instinctively pugnacious, many peace leaders tempered their optimism with warnings about his combative instincts. Slayden lamented that "the spirit of the people is inclined towards war," and Holt agreed that "the great mass of men and women almost prefer war to peace."[89] Yet they stopped far short of the conclusion that mankind was therefore inevitably doomed to recurrent wars. Rather, they believed international cooperation was possible and worth the quest, and in the decade before the World War they advanced four explanations for resolving the apparent contradiction between their awareness of the persistence of international tensions and their continuing hopes for world peace.

First, the pacific-minded and a few other internationalists often blamed wars on a tiny minority of munitions makers and military men who, motivated by greed and glory, cleverly fabricated war scares and promoted wars. Even Butler occasionally criticized the self-interest of these groups in fostering the armament race, although usually he was inclined to blame the "gullible people" for believing them.[90] No sizable munitions industry or military establishment existed in the United States before the First World War, and peace leaders did not probe deeply for evidence of conspiratorial forces attempting to manipulate foreign policy. Although they occasionally pointed to specific corporations or military men, they did not develop a devil theory of war. Instead, their criticisms were usually directed broadly at the "powder trust" or "armament syndicates" or, more generally, at the "few selfish and reckless men [who] make all the trouble."[91] The tendency to single out the evil few was a natural inclination among peace leaders who wanted to maintain their belief in the great majority as basically rational and peace loving. Their remedy was gradual disarmament, which would enhance statesmen's opportunities for finding constructive solutions to existing world tensions.

Second, advocates of peace emphasized moral education. Assuming the individual had a moral sense and a capacity for reason, they stressed education as vitally important in developing those qualities. Proper education, they believed, could overcome man's selfish impulses and ignorance, the major reasons for this deviation from moral rectitude. They asserted the primacy of the educator's moral function. Bryan, Trueblood, Lynch, and the Meads stressed almost exclusively moral and religious education. They believed that the inculcation of moral principles would eliminate man's sinful thoughts and enhance his chances for goodness, perhaps even for moral perfection. Education was almost entirely a modern substitute for individual conversion to Christian principles. Although they often differed in temperament and in their faith in the masses to absorb genteel values, they all emphasized that education should develop what in those days was called "sound character."[92]

Third, they all believed that permanent international machinery would restrain man's passions and thereby reduce the chances for war. Once nations established arbitral tribunals, commissions of inquiry, and especially a world court, then international controversies could be removed from the potentially wrathful populace and placed in the hands of calm, impartial administrators who would combine the progressive generation's faith in "efficiency" and "uplift."[93] An imposing obstacle to the implementation of permanent international institutions, as we have seen, was the reluctance of governments to relinquish their freedom of action to international agencies. Many peace advocates, especially the legalists, seemed to understand the practical difficulties, but others minimized them. Reflecting their faith in enlightened leadership, these latter believed that politicians and diplomats already understood the advantage of such agencies and could establish them without waiting for the time consuming process of education and conversion of world public opinion. Lucia Mead maintained that mankind did not have to wait for the moral perfection of mankind in order to attain a peaceful world order. It could be achieved in the near future, she argued, through the development of arrangements and procedures for peace keeping among nations just as the framers of the United States Constitution had earlier developed them for the pacific resolution of disputes between the several states. What was needed was the firm commitment of the leaders of the major powers to establish these institutions. It was in short primarily a matter of statesmanship.[94]

Fourth and most common, peace leaders always linked morality to progress. Whatever doubts lingered in the peace leaders' minds concerning governments' commitment to the goal of world organization all but dissolved in the face of the assumption that progress was a natural force operating automatically in human affairs. While they differed on the desirability and direction of progressive currents, they all believed in moral progress.

Those inclining toward pacifism believed that moral progress was universal. Following a world tour, Jordan affirmed that "the influence [of peace workers] has been widespread, all the way from Korea to Hungary." Convinced that the world was exhibiting "growing reason and humanity," these optimists viewed history as a fairly smooth road on which the obstacles to human progress increasingly decreased in size and number.[95] True, they admitted, wars had regularly occurred in past ages, but with man's mental and spiritual advance they had become less frequent and could eventually be eliminated. As evidence of this advance, many cited the steady decline of major wars among Western nations.

Others, more restrained and less humanistic, stressed the slow, steady enlightenment of the sovereign nations. Butler, for instance, described the movement toward the organization of the world as "sure as that of an Alpine glacier." "Just as the individual has substituted faith in his fellow man for fear of him," he added, "so nations may well divest themselves of fear in favor of faith in the other nations of the world."[96]

In emphasizing the capacity of men and nations for moral improvement, peace advocates drew upon Social Darwinism. In one sense, the acceptance of "natural selection" and "survival of the fittest" implied ceaseless conflict and the ultimate triumph of might over right, and the imperialists of 1898, Theodore Roosevelt, and many of his followers used Darwinian language to justify the extension of national power and the use of force in international affairs.[97] Even some joining the peace movement after 1900 had occasionally defended American imperialism at the turn of the century in these terms. Actually, however, evolutionary theory was inherently neutral, and American support of the bellicose version of social Darwinism was neither widespread nor permanent.

Carnegie was only one of the first of the peace spokesmen who found in evolutionary theory additional intellectual support for their belief that the world was evolving away from primitive violence toward a more civilized order. Lynch accepted the Darwinian explanation of change in the natural world but denied that its laws relegated man to ceaseless struggle. On the contrary, he believed that evolution was a divinely inspired process in which man steadily progressed from the brute, physical world toward a spiritual realm where the ideal of human brotherhood would ultimately prevail. Many other friends of peace likewise domesticated Darwinism. If they did not interpret it teleologically, they still believed that evolution confirmed the idea of progress. Their writings and speeches included references to the "evolution" of human nature toward moral improvement and of political and judicial institutions toward world organization. Even William Jennings Bryan, who made anti-evolution a cause celebre in the 1920s, grudgingly conceded in 1907 that peace advocates' innumerable appeals to evolutionary thought had their place in the peace movement: "I had hoped we should be able to bring about peace by resting entirely upon the theory that Man is made in the image of his Creator, but I am glad to have peace brought to us even from the theory of man in the image of the ape."[98]

Peace leaders also explained progress in material terms. As the movement acquired a more practical outlook, the pacifists' attacks on war as murderous and therefore immoral declined, while they increasingly joined with their friends in the peace movement in opposing war because it was destructive of material comforts and generally wasteful. They also agreed with them in deploring the high costs of war preparations, which burdened the populace with taxes and restricted the funds available for programs of human betterment. Yet they refused to accept militarism as a growing evil of modern life. Rather, they regarded it as an anachronistic survival of an earlier, unenlightened era and as incompatible with modern industrialism. Whether drawing on free trade liberalism or more sophisticated notions of an interdependent world economy, they viewed as essentially beneficent the enormous productivity unleashed by the industrial revolution and the ensuing expansion of international trade. Commercial intercourse brought the business interests closer together, hastened the development of international amity, and facilitated the movement toward the federation of the world. "Commerce," Trueblood asserted, "has woven an economic web which binds all the nations closely to each other." Businessmen responded positively to the peace movement because they found that the peace leadership fully shared their elitism, acceptance of the values of liberal capitalism, fiscal conservatism, and faith in material progress. They warmly praised arbitration treaties as tangible manifestations of the rational, businesslike approach to international relations, and they characterized war as harmful to the material prosperity of all nations. Bartholdt stressed the enlightened self-interest of businessmen. "Business is with us," he said, "because it cannot prosper except in time of peace."[99]

Peace advocates' emphasis on material forces fostering the movement toward world peace found an extraordinary prolific spokesman in Norman Angell, a British pacifist. In 1910, Angell published *The Great Illusion,* which presented an economic argument against war. Angell contended that commerce and credit in the twentieth century had made the economies of mature capitalistic nations so interdependent that wars among them could never be waged successfully for profit. Likewise, he asserted that the expense of holding conquered territory would prove a political and economic liability to the "victor." Because war in the modern age could bring no tangible benefits to the conquering nation, Angell concluded that it was futile and ought to be an anachronism.[100]

The Great Illusion contained much facile reasoning. It underestimated nationalistic fears and ambitions, and consistently confused the "ought" with the "is" in international relations. Despite its defects the book was historically important for the peace movement. In an age when militarism was rampant in Europe, it bolstered peace leaders' sagging hopes that nationalism was declining and war was becoming outmoded. Peace workers popularized Angell's economic theory in lectures and articles, and the Carnegie Endowment and World Peace Foundation paid him to spread his message in lecture tours throughout the United States in 1913 and 1914.[101]

With such a sturdy faith in moral and material progress, it was virtually inevitable that the longer world peace prevailed the stronger the peace workers' convictions that the day of permanent peace was within their grasp. Even the setbacks of the Taft years did not appreciably dampen their confidence in the future. Events during the first year of the Wilson administration would seem to confirm the wisdom of their peace efforts.

[11]

The Onset of the
Wilson Administration

OPTIMISTIC ABOUT THE FUTURE, peace advocates needed only the hope of success to buoy their spirits and to inspire them once again to the heights of their previous campaign for Taft's arbitration treaties. The events of the first year of the Wilson administration more than satisfied their hopes. In the first months their high expectations derived not so much from the new President, whose relationship to the peace movement was not yet entirely clear, but from his Secretary of State William Jennings Bryan.

Bryan was not an absolute pacifist and showed little interest in conscientious objection, but he inclined toward pacifism. He abhorred war as a young man; and though he had strongly supported the war with Spain and even enlisted in the American army during the conflict, he emerged from the hostilities considerably sobered. He never apologized for his endorsement of the Spanish-American conflict, but he was repelled by a just war to liberate the Cubans from their Spanish oppressors becoming a war of conquest of innocent Filipinos and advancing imperialism and militarism. Thereafter he used his influence in the Democratic party in behalf of independence of the Philippines and against increases in the army and navy.[1]

Bryan's opposition to American imperialism exposed deeper reasons for his maturing pacifism. The mainsprings of his pacifistic sentiments lay in his early Christian training and his unbounded faith in man's moral progress. The two influences blended easily in his thought, for by progress and morality he meant the advancement of Christian morality. Bryan's Christianity was always social. His ideas on foreign affairs were similar to the social gospel clergymen who participated in the prewar peace movement. If Christianity emphasized that all men are brothers, the Great Commoner consistently argued, they were not just brothers in some future life but here and now in this world. In accepting the Democratic presidential nomination in 1900, he declared that the United States was "a republic gradually but surely becoming the supreme moral factor in the world's progress and the accepted arbiter of the world's disputes."[2]

In succeeding years he frequently asserted that the United States should champion the spirit of reason and moral suasion over physical force in international affairs. His foreign travels (including his visit to Russia in 1903 where Tolstoy reaffirmed Bryan's pacifistic inclinations) and the burgeoning reform sentiment within the United States seem to have strengthened his faith in man's progress toward the realization of the brotherhood of man, for he increasingly emphasized that the power of Christian love was growing throughout the world. A compulsive optimist, Bryan held fast to his belief that mankind soon would attain the desired goal of international peace.[3]

Not content with mere rhetoric, Bryan formulated a concrete plan that would advance the pacifist cause. Writing in his weekly newspaper *The Commoner* in 1905, he proposed conciliation treaties in which the signatory powers would automatically refer all their differences that diplomacy or arbitration could not settle to a permanent commission of inquiry. The commission would investigate and report on the dispute within a year. During the investigation Bryan's plan called for a "cooling off" period during which each nation agreed not to resort to the use of force, though reserving the right to fight after the report had been published if it was dissatisfied with the decision. He believed, however, that the period of delay and the restraining voice of public opinion would cool tempers and make wars very unlikely.[4] Bryan later wrote that his conciliation proposal "was the outgrowth of a plan which I had advocated for the settlement of labor disputes. I had for some time been favorable to investigation *in all cases,* the parties reserving the right of independent action, and it occurred to me that the same plan might be applied with advantage to international disputes . . . as a preventative of war."[5]

Actually, the notion of nations referring their disputes to third parties for friendly mediation was nothing new, and the principle of voluntary mediation had been embodied in the Treaty of Paris of 1856 and more recently in the Hague conventions of 1899 and 1907. Bryan's main contribution was his insistence that referral to the joint commission be obligatory on the contracting parties. Following his initial articles in *The Commoner,* he championed his peace plan in speeches on the Chautauqua circuit and at various peace congresses. Especially notable was the adoption of a similar plan presented by Richard Bartholdt at the meeting of the Interparliamentary Union in 1906. Bryan attended the meeting, and his speech persuaded the delegates to endorse Bartholdt's proposal, which the conference had earlier rejected.[6] Bryan also persuaded President Taft to insert an article in his arbitration treaties providing for a "cooling off" period of one year during which the joint high commission of inquiry was to investigate whether the dispute was justiciable. Taft did not share Bryan's Christian pacifism, but he credited Bryan with this contribution to his arbitration accords.[7]

Although President Wilson offered Bryan the position of secretary of state as a political reward for his past leadership of the Democratic party, Bryan accepted only after he received the President's full blessing of his treaty plan.[8] "I made up my mind before I accepted the offer of the Secretaryship of State," he said a few months after he undertook his new duties, "that I would not take the office if I thought there would be a war during my tenure."[9] Thereafter he began to negotiate conciliation agreements with foreign governments, and by 1915 he had concluded thirty, twenty of which were eventually ratified.[10]

Although Bryan's treaties obliged the parties to submit all unresolved disputes to the joint commission, they contained no enforcement machinery for punishing violators. Moreover, their provision allowing the parties to act independently after the commission submitted its report undercut internationalists' efforts to develop legal and moral principles restricting nations' freedom of action on war questions. It was, however, the laudable pacifist ideal behind Bryan's treaties that allowed friends of peace to give them their virtually unanimous support.

David Starr Jordon expressed most enthusiastically the reaction of peace advocates to Bryan's treaty plan. He met Bryan in late April 1913, in Sacramento, California, where the new secretary was attempting to persuade the California legislature to remove the harsh anti–Japanese provisions from the proposed alien land bill. Forgetting his criticisms of Bryan's endorsement of the peace treaty with Spain more than a decade earlier, Jordan, who meanwhile had warmed to the progressive reform movement, approved of Bryan's liberalism and was impressed by his personal magnetism. According to Jordan, Bryan's treaties were "an addition to arbitration, . . . I think most effective. He is devoting his whole strength for the rest of his days to international peace. He has the chance (and the will and the skill) to do more than any one yet has done. Success to him!"[11]

Almost all friends of peace—moderate and radical, Republican and Democratic, foreign and American—endorsed Bryan's treaties.[12] Samuel Dutton, for example, expressed his "joy" at learning of Bryan's treaty plan and accurately predicted, "All peace workers will sincerely wish that the nations may be brought into the proposed arrangement."[13] Some peace leaders were less sanguine concerning their ultimate benefit, but they all agreed that they would increase international understanding and help to prevent some wars.[14]

Pacifists and liberal internationalists warmed almost as quickly to Woodrow Wilson. They knew the new President was no pacifist and had shown very little interest in foreign affairs during the campaign. Nevertheless, he was well aware of the activities of the American peace movement and shared many of its aims. He had joined the American Peace Society in 1908 and had addressed the Universal Peace Union in February 1912.[15] And he had definite ideas about international politics in general and American foreign policy in particular. Although his historical writings had criticized American naval weakness before the War of 1812, all his other pronouncements on foreign affairs conveyed an idealistic outlook similar to most pacifistic advocates of peace. He had consistently applauded American efforts in the arbitration movement and believed that morality should be the proper guide in foreign policy, just as it should in domestic politics. Above all, he believed in the American mission: the United States should assume the leadership in promoting democracy, morality, and justice throughout the world. His internationalism was thus a projection of his fervent faith in American values and institutions. The application of American ideals in the international arena, he confidently believed, would advance the cause of world peace.[16]

Although Wilson's view of foreign relations contemplated the use of military force to impose his vision of a liberal world order on unyielding undemocratic states, friends of peace did not foresee his propensity for messianic interventionism. Even some pacific-minded partisans of Taft conceded that Wilson's credentials as a friend of peace were impressive, if yet untested. Consequently, peace leaders had high hopes that Wilson would confirm their most favorable first impressions and perhaps promote their cause even more aggressively than his predecessor in the White House.[17]

It should not be assumed, however, that the new President entered the White House with thoughts of catering to the peace leaders and obligingly promoting all their programs. Much as he shared their idealism, he was conscious of nationalist biases of public and congressional opinion and at least during his first term as President he was careful not to champion peace measures that might adversely affect his own political fortunes and perhaps those of his party. Furthermore, a streak of egotism and his own political theory of a strong, assertive, and independent chief executive combined to make him temperamentally unsuited to accept gratuitous advice from more than a narrow circle of his most trusted advisers.

Even before he became President he showed signs of a cautious approach to the peace movement. When he began to entertain presidential ambitions, he did not emphasize (and perhaps did not renew) his membership in the American Peace Society and politely but firmly declined to attend the American Peace Congress in Baltimore in 1911. Though he eventually endorsed Taft's treaties, he did not commit himself irrevocably to President Taft's unamended version of them during Senate debate.[18] Even his speech to the Universal Peace Union shortly before the Senate's final action on Taft's arbitration treaties was circumspect.

Between his inauguration and the outbreak of the World War, President Wilson was to remain on fairly friendly terms with the peace leadership. He occasionally cooperated with conservative Republican Senators Elihu Root and Theodore Burton on foreign policy, although their relationship remained for the most part formal and restrained. Nicholas Murray Butler had never particularly liked Wilson and remained cool toward him throughout his presidency, but even he kept his criticisms private. The new President sensed his differences with legalists, most of whom were Republican conservatives, in the peace cause and did not actively solicit their opinions. He even demonstrated that he did not want to encourage the peace leaders when he refused an interview with the more liberal Hamilton Holt, perhaps because Holt's journal, *The Independent,* had endorsed Taft.[19] His relationship to more liberal peace leaders was significant not so much because of any measurable influence they had but because he shared their idealistic internationalism and was sincerely interested in promoting the cause of world peace. His beliefs on foreign affairs and, just as important, what these peace workers thought he believed, were to stimulate them to advance a long list of idealistic proposals for a "new" American foreign policy.

Wilson had scarcely taken the oath of office when liberal peace spokesmen predicted that the President would support their programs. After praising the "fine moral tone" of the President's inaugural address, Edwin Mead concluded that Wilson would actively promote the international peace movement. Jordan was just as optimistic. He had known Wilson personally during their respective academic careers, had supported his presidential candidacy, and admired his high-mindedness and sincerity of purpose.[20] Confident that the new President would accept advice on international matters, Jordan wrote several letters to Wilson in the first months of his administration in which he urged a boldly imaginative and genuinely idealistic foreign policy: withdrawal of support from the Six Power Consortium in China, American leadership in recognizing the new Chinese Republic, noninterference in the ticklish Mexican situation, and the revision of the Monroe Doctrine as a joint American declaration against further colonization or intervention. Furthermore, he questioned the secretary of the navy's two battleship program and urged the administration to push the matter of a third Hague conference. In short, Jordan asked the President to promote all the major aims of the peace movement.[21]

The new President did not disappoint the peace leaders. They praised his speeches emphasizing America's moral obligation to encourage and support peace sentiment throughout the world.[22] Moreover, the President's actions spoke louder than his words, for in the months before the outbreak of the World War, his moral-minded administration, wholly dedicated to the implementation of a New Diplomacy in world affairs, not only endorsed Bryan's treaties but wrestled with all the international matters Jordan had mentioned and in most instances fulfilled peace advocates' highest hopes.

Wilson's China policy, his first major action in foreign affairs, expressed the aims of idealistic peace workers. On March 18, 1913, President Wilson, strongly supported by Bryan, withdrew the government's support from the Six Power Consortium which the Taft administration, in cooperation with a syndicate of New York bankers, had promoted. The New Freedom's repudiation of Dollar Diplomacy in the Far East was particularly gratifying to anti-imperialists and idealistic internationalists who had viewed their nation's participation in the Consortium as a striking example of the dominent influence of Wall Street interests in the government.[23] Less than two months later, the Wilson administration continued its moral diplomacy when it became the first major power formally to recognize the so-called Republic of China. The news of this action reached the American Peace Congress in St. Louis, which, to the sounds of enthusiastic applause, immediately dispatched a congratulatory message to the president of the Chinese Republic. No less than Wilson himself, more liberal advocates of peace naively concocted the image of "good" Chinese people patterning the future course of their nation along the lines of American democracy.[24]

The Wilson administration's Far Eastern policy foreshadowed other actions that were equally applauded by idealistic peace leaders. Another of their immediate concerns (the only one Jordan did not mention in his letters to the President) was repeal of the section of the Panama Canal Tolls Act of August, 1912, which exempted American coastal shipping from payment of tolls at the Canal.[25] The platforms of the three major political parties had endorsed this legislation, and Taft had refused British entreaties to submit the dispute to impartial arbitration. Because it involved the correct interpretation of the Hay-Pauncefote treaty of 1901, Taft could have agreed to refer the dispute to arbitration under the machinery of Root's arbitration treaty with Britain four years earlier. Given

Taft's firm commitment to broadening the scope of arbitration, his opposition seems inexplicable. Although most internationalists accepted the interpretation of treaties as a proper subject for arbitration, Taft argued somewhat inconsistently that this case involved a question of national policy and therefore was not subject to arbitration. Taft also claimed that the tribunal, lacking the safeguards of his abortive arbitration treaties, would be biased against the United States. His emotional involvement in overseeing the construction of the Panama Canal earlier, his interest in fostering American commercial expansion, and his desire to exploit the anti-British, nationalist sentiment among the public before the election probably molded Taft's stand on the issue.[26]

The political gains from his position were insignificant, however, and came at the expense of peace leaders' united opposition to the exemption clause of the Tolls Act. They pointed out that in their opinion the congressional action was in clear violation of the Hay-Pauncefote treaty that had guaranteed that the Panama Canal would be open to ships of "all nations . . . on terms of entire equality." The honor and moral example of the American Republic rather than any fear of war induced their campaign on this issue. True to their beliefs in the sanctity of international law, the peace leadership argued that the United States could never promote international understanding if it shamelessly violated its treaty obligations.

Particularly embarrassing to the administration were the criticisms of conservative Republicans associated with the peace movement. Butler privately labeled the Tolls Act "shocking," while Root and Burton, both of whom had discussed the issue with Hay during negotiations of the Hay-Pauncefote treaty, and Choate, who as ambassador to Great Britain had played an important part in drafting the treaty, claimed that Secretary Hay's understanding of the controversial portions of the treaty supported the British version. Carnegie seconded these arguments and shortly after the election urged Taft to reconsider his position on the tolls issue in light of the considered judgment of his anti-exemptionist friends.[27]

Though Taft did not acknowledge these pressures, he did begin to bend somewhat. He and Knox, probably hoping for one last success after a series of disappointments in foreign policy, attempted to revive the project of an arbitral court by linking it to the tolls question. They decided to send Scott to Paris to confer with British, French, and German representatives about the possibility of instituting a court of arbitral justice without awaiting the institution of the prize court. Because Britain's irritation over the exemption of American coastal shipping from the Panama Canal tolls and other issues would hinder its endorsement of the American proposal, Knox authorized Scott to suggest the submission of the coastal exemption under the Hay-Pauncefote treaty to the proposed court.[28]

Given the extremely tense diplomatic climate between the two rival alliance systems in Europe, the Taft administration's proposal was myopic. Indeed, Knox began to realize the hopelessness of the venture and only a few hours before Scott's scheduled departure for Europe suddenly cancelled his trip. Although the reasons for Knox's action are not entirely clear, it is probable that the arrival of a British note clarifying their strenuous objections to the tolls exemption, together with the news of the imminent convocation of the Conference of London for resolving the issues of the First Balkan War, convinced him that the European powers would not carefully consider the American proposal.[29]

The peace movement, however, did not let the matter rest. Butler, Carnegie, and Straus urged full mobilization of the Carnegie Endowment's resources behind a campaign for repeal or arbitration of the exemption clause, and Straus even wanted to summon all the Carnegie trustees to the nation's capitol to lobby for arbitration of the tolls dispute. The vast majority of the trustees, however, was more cautious, and the endowment's recent unsuccessful campaign for Taft's treaties reinforced their hesitation to draw their organization into political controversy. While they opposed formal sponsorship of any anti-exemption campaign, they were nearly unanimous for arbitration of the dispute and agreed to form a committee to draft a statement for their signatures as individuals. More than a million copies of this statement, signed by twenty-two trustees, were circulated throughout the nation. Elihu Root began to marshal support for repeal in the Senate, and his speech to that body in late January 1913 was an exhaustive brief for the anti-exemptionist position.[30]

President Wilson inherited that situation. He had accepted unquestioningly the Democratic platform endorsing the Tolls Act, but the reasoned protests by the British government and influential Americans caused him to study the issue more closely. He first indicated that he had changed his mind in January 1913, after listening to Choate and Root explain in detail that the British interpretation of the Hay-Pauncefote treaty was the correct one.[31]

Although Wilson deferred action on the matter until after he had completed much of his domestic program, he publicly repudiated that plank in the platform in January 1914.[32] Peace leaders were delighted but at first made no attempt to influence the outcome of the repeal bill in Congress. After a hard fought victory in the House, however, William Short decided that outside pressure might bolster the repeal forces in the Senate. He solicited letters urging repeal from prominent members of the New York Peace Society for consideration by the Senate Committee on Interoceanic Canals. Although Choate told him that he opposed outside influence and was entirely willing to trust the judgment of anti-exemptionist Republican

Senators to aid the President on this matter, Short enlisted Senator Burton's support in persuading Oscar Straus to interview Progressive Republican Senators on the matter and to appear before the Senate Committee.[33] Short also found that another member of the New York Peace Society, Professor Ernst Richard, was willing to testify.

At the same time, however, Short remained reluctant to involve the name of the New York peace group with political controversy. He pointed out to prospective witnesses that they should not appear as representatives of the New York Peace Society, which might arouse the antagonism of committee members who had little or no sympathy with the peace movement, but as interested private citizens or members of nonpacifist groups. Straus thus appeared before the committee solely as an experienced diplomat pointing out possible unpleasant consequences of the coastal exemption for American foreign policy, while Richard, a German-American claiming to represent 40,000 members of the North American Gymnastic Union, told the committee that this German-American group was not anti-British but, on the contrary, strongly favored repeal as a step toward better American understanding with all nations. Although their testimony was far less important than Wilson's personal influence on Democratic committee members, the views of New York peace advocates were received in a friendly spirit and helped to soften the opposition.[34]

The New York Peace Society managed to escape criticism, but the Carnegie Endowment, a more powerful and visible group, had to weather verbal abuse. Many derogatory comments followed the Carnegie Endowment's circulation of 741,000 copies of Root's speech to the Senate of May 1914, which was printed along with his earlier Senate speech on the tolls question. Root had consistently feared the potentially adverse effects of the endowment's participation in political controversy and had opposed circulation of his speeches, but in this instance he reluctantly deferred to Carnegie's personal appeal to use the endowment's funds to publicize his Senate pronouncements.[35]

Root readily deferred to Carnegie's request because he accurately perceived the disenchantment of the endowment's benefactor from his peace fund and did not wish to alienate entirely his friend's fatherly interest in his organization. Carnegie had indicated his disappointment with the conservatism of the trustees a few months earlier when he founded the Church Peace Union with an endowment of $2,000,000. He had assumed that his gift of $10,000,000 to the Carnegie Endowment for International Peace would be the capstone of his philanthropy, but the cautious leadership of the endowment only intensified his identification with more active, committed peace people. He became especially close to the Reverend Frederick Lynch who kept him informed of the peace work among Protestant churchmen and finally convinced him to underwrite peace work among the churches. Carnegie's gift was more remarkable when it is remembered that he had not expressed any strong interest in organized religion and had readily agreed to the exclusion of clergymen from the Carnegie Endowment. His appointment of five trustees from the officers of the World Peace Foundation and none from the Carnegie Endowment to the Church Peace Union further signified his dissatisfaction with the endowment's cautious leadership.[36]

Root's fears of identification of his personal position and the policy of the Carnegie Endowment were not imaginary. Several senators and other individuals unfairly accused him and the endowment of catering to British policy and of acting in behalf of American and Canadian transcontinental railroads, which feared the competition of coastal shipping interests exempted from payment of canal tolls. Fortunately for the repeal forces, these attacks did not undermine Root's influence among like-minded Republican senators on the issue, and he helped to solidify the bipartisan coalition that passed the repeal bill in June 1914.[37]

The President's decision to champion repeal had the desired effect in improving Anglo-American relations, for a few months after his espousal of repeal England agreed to renew the Root treaty as well as sign Bryan's conciliation treaty. Together, these developments indicated that the peace leaders' campaign, though certainly not as decisive as the common desire of both American and British statesmen for more friendly relations, had not been in vain. Indeed, Anglo-American understanding reached its zenith in 1914.[38]

Peace advocates expressed cautious hopes for Wilsonian leadership on two other issues. First, they wanted his administration to promote the movement for a third peace conference at The Hague. The Second Conference had endorsed a proposal for a third meeting after a time interval corresponding to the one between the first two conferences, or about 1915, and following the 1912 election Taft had appointed a committee to prepare the American program for the third meeting.[39]

Yet neither President Wilson nor Secretary Bryan at first expressed any interest in a third conference. In fact, for all his interest in the peace movement, Bryan did not share other peace leaders' optimism on the value of such conferences in promoting international understanding and world organization. He had earlier praised the Hague Conferences as an indication of nations' advance from reliance on physical prowess to promotion of international justice, but he considered justice "a cold, pulseless, negative virtue" and thus had never enthusiastically emphasized the Hague Conferences.[40] Aside from his skepticism about federalists' more radical notions of world order, Bryan had in fact nothing in common with the conservative lawyers who were leading boosters of those meetings. He also believed that the meager accomplishments of the Second Hague Peace Conference revealed how difficult it was "to secure peace by agreement when so many nations are to be consulted and so many conflicting interests are to be harmonized." Partly for that reason, he had placed even greater emphasis after the Second Conference on the moral example of America's independent leadership in promoting world peace as exemplified by his own treaty plan.[41]

It was not so much Wilson's or Bryan's disapproval or disinterest, however, that caused their inaction; more probably it resulted from other pressing domestic and diplomatic problems that needed their immediate attention. The peace leadership at first did not seem eager to impress on the administration the importance of initiating steps for the calling of the conference. Only a few worried from the outset about the administration's neglect of arrangements for the third Hague meeting. When Butler finally asked Dutton to inquire at the State Department about the matter, Dutton was told that the American preparatory committee had not made much progress.[42]

Yet in late 1913, new developments aroused the administration's interest in the conference. In September the preparatory committee submitted its final recommendations for the American program for the third conference. While the report was not well publicized in the press, the peace leadership knew that it fully explored the relative merits of several alternative proposals for the apportionment of judges to the proposed court of arbitral justice and generally laid the groundwork for later action.[43] Amply prepared for the conference, the United States could more easily be prodded into seizing the diplomatic initiative. More important, when press reports mentioned that the State Department seemed willing to cater to the European powers, especially Great Britain, which advocated delaying the conference to 1916 or 1917 at the earliest and hinted at postponing the conference altogether, numerous Americans—members of the Hague Court, delegates to previous Hague Conferences, international lawyers, and ardent peace workers—appealed directly to Secretary Bryan and President Wilson urging them to seize the initiative. The Carnegie Endowment, American Peace Society, and New York Peace Society even cooperated in developing plans for organizing a national citizens committee composed of surviving American delegates to the First and Second Hague Conferences, American appointees on the Hague Tribunal, and other prominent friends of the peace cause. The committee intended to raise the issue with the Wilson administration if it failed to act.[44]

All those participants in the peace movement believed that unless the

United States assumed the world's leadership in promoting the third conference, it would be delayed beyond 1915. The prospect of delay was especially discouraging because the Second Hague Conference had stipulated that an international commission consisting of one representative from each nation attending the conference would meet "some two years" before the third conference to collect the governments' proposals, select those most appropriate for possible agreement, and prepare the program for the upcoming conference. Since no nation had as yet appointed its international commissioner, by late 1913 it seemed that the conference could not meet before 1916. To delay their appointment any longer would mean an even later meeting date and perhaps indefinite postponement.

Elihu Root and the American minister in the Netherlands, Henry Van Dyke, clearly saw the obstacles preventing a third conference; and their concern ultimately influenced its promotion by the administration. In December 1913, Root, acting on behalf of the Carnegie Endowment's trustees, formally urged the Wilson administration to appoint the American representative to the international committee and to request information from the other powers on a meeting date. Root argued that this initiative might arouse enough interest in foreign governments to hasten the convocation of a third conference; in any case the American initiative would free the government "from any imputation of lack of interest in this subject."[45]

Wilson privately acknowledged that Root's suggestion was "a most timely one and that we ought to act on it;"[46] but a more elaborate proposal advanced by Van Dyke proved more important. Under Van Dyke's plan the United States would suggest to the other powers that the Permanent Administrative Council of the Hague Court, which consisted of the Netherlands Minister of Foreign Affairs and the diplomatic representatives of the contracting parties accredited to The Hague, should serve as the international preparatory committee and thus eliminate the inevitable delay if each government had to appoint a commissioner. Second, the United States should urge the Queen of the Netherlands to invite the nations to The Hague in 1915 or 1916, although Van Dyke personally believed it was already too late for a 1915 meeting. John Bassett Moore, now counselor in the State Department, endorsed Van Dyke's proposal in a memorandum,[47] and Secretary Bryan added that he favored the 1915 rather than the 1916 date "because we would have larger freedom of action in the selection of delegates, owing to the fact that there is no campaign on that year."[48] Wilson agreed with all these arguments and instructed the State Department to propose the 1915 date.[49]

When the State Department released the circular note to the press asking the powers to allow their representatives at The Hague to serve as the international preparatory commission for the third Hague conference, peace leaders were delighted. The national citizen's committee, originally planned as a dignified protest group, overnight became a cheerful chorus behind the Wilson administration's initiative. Although Great Britain objected to the American plan to save a year's time in preparing for the conference and the Dutch government ultimately ignored it in calling for the nations to appoint delegates to the international preparatory committee, the American proposal had stirred up interest in the third conference. Prospects for holding the third conference at The Hague in 1916 seemed fairly bright until the World War abruptly intervened.[50]

Related to the question of a third Hague conference was a second question: limitation of armaments. While most friends of peace realized that the recent popular enthusiasm for militarism in Europe precluded any real progress on armaments at The Hague, they hoped that the American delegation would at least broach the issue. So serious was the problem of militarism and so infrequent were the Hague Conferences, they argued, that the delegates should explore every proposal that might lead to some agreement on armament limitation. Leaving no stone unturned, they also wanted the President to act independently by sounding out the great powers on the chances for an arms agreement.[51]

While awaiting some auspicious international arms development, antimilitarist peace workers continued their opposition to military preparedness at home. Since they believed that only the United States, the one great power geographically removed from the European power struggle, could assume effective leadership on the limitation of armaments, they wanted America first to practice at home what it ultimately hoped to preach abroad. If the American nation could uphold its antimilitary tradition, they reasoned, then its example might induce other nations to seek a reduction of armaments.[52]

Antipreparedness advocates found good reason to believe that their long campaign against the large navy forces was at last on the verge of success, for in the last two years of the Taft administration the congressional opponents of preparedness became increasingly numerous and vocal. Although many Middle Western and a few Southern Congressmen frequently opposed military preparedness, they used most of the same arguments as Eastern antimilitarist peace advocates, a curious but significant pattern that was to be repeated in the heated preparedness debate of 1915 and 1916. They mainly differed in emphasis. Eastern peace advocates, considering themselves true internationalists, stressed America's moral responsibilities in promoting good will among nations as the sure path to world peace, while inland politicians were more concerned with the possible betrayal of America's traditional isolation by a coterie of warmongers.

Actually, only a few members of Congress, especially Walter Hensley, James Slayden, Theodore Burton, and Richard Bartholdt, took any real interest in the organized peace movement in the decade before 1914. Thus, the antiwar sentiments of antipreparedness congressmen derived less from any direct pacifist influence on them than from the deeply ingrained isolationism in the Middle West.[53] Yet if the Middle Western populist-progressive tradition was more isolationist than pacifist, it was certainly steeped in antimilitarism. Consequently, its spokesmen agreed with Eastern antimilitarists in opposing the military tendencies in the nation and to any war that might advance the power of the military establishment and the pecuniary interests of Eastern bankers, businessmen, and munitions makers. In sum, only a war fought for the most idealistic and humanitarian reasons (like the Spanish-American War) could win their support.

Moreover, William Jennings Bryan's Christian pacifist sentiments were native to the Middle West.[54] Some antipreparedness congressmen were even called Bryan Democrats, because Bryan expressed most eloquently their own sectional prejudices on both domestic and foreign affairs. They followed the Peerless Leader, in part, not in spite of his marked antimilitarist and pacifist leanings but because of them.

The antipreparedness forces displayed their real strength in the House where in 1912 and again in early 1913 the small navy men, successfully resisting Taft's large navy programs, forced the Senate to accept their naval bills, each of which provided for only one battleship. Believing that those two congressional actions signified the stemming of the militarists' tide, pacific-minded Americans were jubilant.[55] Their faith in Congress increased during the first months of the Wilson administration, for on December 8, 1913, the House by an impressive 317 to 11 vote adopted a resolution, proposed by Hensley, endorsing the appeal of Winston Churchill, First Lord of the Admiralty in Great Britain, for a one year "holiday" in the building of battleships. Although the Senate never considered a similar resolution, the *Advocate of Peace* hailed the decisive vote in the House as the best expression of public reaction to the armament craze and urged affiliated state societies to champion a moratorium on naval construction. Protestant and Catholic clergymen even cooperated in forming a preliminary committee to organize a peace convention scheduled for November 1914 to crystallize national sentiment behind a year's suspension of battleship construction.[56]

Meanwhile, administration officials mulled over the idea of a naval holiday. President Wilson transmitted the Hensley resolution to Secretary Bryan suggesting that "it might be well to consult with the representatives of the leading naval powers as to the feasibility of agreeing upon such a policy."[57] Four days before the House passed the Hensley resolution, Secretary of the Navy Josephus Daniels gave Churchill's suggestion sympathetic treatment in the Navy Department's annual report, even favoring as a more practical alternative an international congress in Washington within the coming year to discuss limitations on the building of battleships.[58] Daniels' proposal probably facilitated the passage of the Hensley resolution. Bryan, who had earlier declared that it was "the imperative duty of the United States . . . to set a shining example in disarmament," also gave his qualified endorsement to the Hensley resolution.[59] Other cabinet members were just as sympathetic to some kind of international naval agreement.[60]

Despite the flurry of interest in naval disarmament, neither Hensley's nor Daniels' proposal was officially promoted by the administration, for the cabinet, believing that their government's endorsement of the naval holiday proposal might detract the attention of the major naval powers from the already pending Bryan treaties, finally advised the President to table the Hensley resolution.[61] Though Bryan was presumably willing to contemplate unilateral American initiatives on disarmament, he reiterated his skepticism concerning multinational agreements when he wrote Wilson: "It would be difficult to agree on a year for a naval holiday because of the [building] contracts different nations have already made. The idea is good, but it would not seem to me practicable."[62] Wilson deferred to the cabinet and took no action on the matter, although he implied that he might propose some kind of arms agreement in the future. As he reminded Bryan, "I like Secretary Daniels' suggestion very much indeed." He even asked Bryan to see Hensley and use flattery to soften his disappointment at the administration's inaction on his resolution.[63]

It was easy for the President to postpone action on the Hensley-Daniels proposals, for he had begun to express interest in another scheme that might better lay the groundwork for a disarmament conference. While he was considering the possibility of making a formal proposal to the major European powers, he also realized the advantages of informal, preliminary discussions with various European leaders to sound out their interest in and receptivity to some later American initiative for an international disarmament conference. Even before passage of the Hensley resolution, Wilson discussed with Sir William Tyrrell, private secretary of the British Foreign Secretary Sir Edward Grey, the necessity for curbing European armaments if peace was to be maintained.[64] No specific proposal resulted, but Tyrrell also had a lengthy discussion with Wilson's confidant, Colonel Edward M. House, who had carefully nourished plans for a "great adventure" in European diplomacy on disarmament from the onset of the administration. House's plan envisioned a visit to Europe to discuss with British, German, and French political leaders a four-power understanding on armaments.

There was nothing visionary about House's approach to world order, for the starting point of his analysis was full acceptance of the great powers' predominance in the international system. A second part of his plan even contemplated a kind of international dollar diplomacy whereby the four governments would cooperate in encouraging private investors to loan money at reasonable rates and to develop the economies of "backward" or "waste" places of the earth, especially those of South and Central America. Tyrrell endorsed House's proposed European trip, and shortly after the passage of the Hensley resolution House repeated the details of his disarmament scheme to the President. House noted in his diary that Wilson gave "his warm approval and cooperation." Remembering the recent passage of the Hensley resolution, Wilson told House that he would favor the incorporation of a congressional resolution for a naval holiday in the administration's two battleship program when it came up for consideration if by that time the three European powers had accepted a freeze on construction of battleships for the following year.[65]

It is doubtful whether Wilson thought very deeply about the implications of House's grandiose ideas for America as an honest broker between the power blocs. Nevertheless, his receptivity to House's scheme indicated his willingness to use unofficial diplomacy as a first, tentative step toward larger American involvement in European problems and presaged his preoccupation with his mediation between European hatreds during the First World War. Whatever Wilson's long range aims in early 1914, House had actually visited the major European capitals for a first round of discussions and had just returned home when the European war erupted.

Had American peace workers known the real purpose of House's European visit, they would have deluged the President with resolutions and letters of praise. But because the real intent of House's mission was a carefully guarded secret and Wilson did not publicize his private support for international disarmament, they could have easily concluded that Wilson was wedded to the large navy forces. The administration's two battleship program that Congress passed and Wilson signed on June 30, 1914, seemed to confirm their pessimism.[66]

They must have realized, however, that the large navy men had fallen short of their goal of four battleships that the General Board, an advisory group of naval officers, had endorsed but Daniels had ignored when he first presented the administration's program. The bill was moderate enough and Daniels' influence on Southern Democrats strong enough to win the support of several congressmen who had previously opposed increases in naval expenditures. Although the Navy League ultimately supported the two battleship program, it had no appreciable influence on the outcome of the bill. Indeed, small navy congressmen so severely ridiculed the Navy League in House debate that it seemed more a liability than an effective pressure group to the large navy forces. Small wonder, therefore, that its members were more discouraged than ardent peace advocates on the attitude of Congress and the administration toward naval preparedness.[67]

Peace spokesmen must also have realized that Wilson never strongly supported the preparedness movement; he spoke about the naval program only in general terms and without any apparent enthusiasm. He shared in fact the complacent attitude of other members of his administration that preparedness was not a serious issue in the United States since the nation was already adequately armed and in any case secure from attack.[68] From what pacifistic Americans knew on the eve of the World War, therefore, they could still derive some comfort from the President's moderate position. If militarism was rampant on the European continent and at least temporarily no longer on the wane in the United States, they could still believe it was only a matter of time—unfortunately, too short a time— before Wilson would take some specific action on the issue.

Finally, several peace workers hoped that the Wilson administration would adopt a new hemispheric policy. Although most remained oriented primarily to Europe, some of the more pacific-minded expressed increasing interest in Latin America. Partly as a reaction to Taft's Dollar Diplomacy and even more to Roosevelt's "Big Stick" policies, Lucia and Edwin Mead, David Starr Jordan, William I. Hull, and James L. Slayden added their voices to the rising chorus of criticisms from members of the American academic community who after about 1912 began to advocate a revision of United States' Latin American policy. They desired to revise the Monroe Doctrine, which previous American Presidents had used and expanded to justify frequent armed interventions in Latin America. They believed that if the Wilson administration transformed the Monroe Doctrine from a unilateral American defense policy into a joint American doctrine against future foreign exploitation or colonization, it would mollify much of the Latin American distrust of the "Colossus of the North" and eventually promote greater good will and trade.[69] Slayden even proposed a treaty whereby the United States would guarantee the "territorial integrity" and "sovereignty" of all Latin and South American nations.[70] He had introduced such a resolution in the House of Representatives in 1911, which was buried in the Foreign Affairs Committee; but Bryan subsequently brought it to the attention of the President who called it "striking."[71]

The Wilson administration did not formulate a new Pan-American policy until after the World War began, however, mainly because it was involved in the revolution in Mexico, which came within a hairbreadth of a full American intervention and prolonged war. Peace advocates' deference to political authority and their faith in America's benevolent intentions inclined them toward easy acceptance of the President's professions of friendship toward Latin America. Almost all peace advocates thus refrained at first from any direct criticism of Wilson's refusal to extend diplomatic recognition to the Mexican government of Victoriano Huerta who ruthlessly seized power early in 1913. They either praised the President's restrained policy of "watchful waiting" toward the revolutionary turmoil or remained silent. Sharing Wilson's aversion to Huerta's unconstitutional takeover and to his undemocratic government, the peace leadership did not even protest Wilson's diplomatic offensive to isolate and eventually topple the "illegal" Huerta regime.[72] A few pacific-minded internationalists privately worried that Wilson's policy might lead to military intervention in Mexico, while more practical or conservative people expressed alarm at the idealistic features of his policy. Butler, for instance, claimed that the Mexicans were "no more ready for representative democratic institutions than a tribe of wild bushmen would be. What they really need is another fifty years of enlightened dictatorship like that of the older Diaz."[73]

During these months of heightened tension in American-Mexican relations, Carnegie and Bartholdt were the only peace spokesmen publicly opposing all American interference in Mexican affairs, but for the moment even Carnegie, always prone to hero worship of American political leaders, willingly gave the President's policy the benefit of the doubt. The revolution, Carnegie said, was "a family affair of the Mexicans and I don't see that we have any right to interfere," but he added that the President was "acting for the best in the way he is handling this very delicate question. We must remember that President Wilson knows a great many things about the situation that the public does not know."[74] Not surprisingly, the result of all these ambivalent and confused voices was paralysis of the peace movement. The *Advocate of Peace* frankly confessed that it had no answer to the question of American rights and duties in the Mexican situation,[75] while the directors of the Pennsylvania Arbitration and Peace Society reported that they "had under frequent and careful consideration the current Mexican problem, but have been unable to decide upon an effective method of endeavoring to assist in its solution."[76]

The Tampico incident, however, aroused the peace movement. Following the failure of Mexican authorities to apologize satisfactorily for their alleged insult to the American navy at Tampico, Mexico, in April 1914, Wilson used this incident (in which some American sailors were arrested by Huerta's men and momentarily detained in Tampico before being released with an apology) as a handy pretext for military intervention by which he hoped to overthrow the obnoxious Huerta. Wilson was determined to intervene in any event, but he appealed to Congress and received approval for military action "to enforce demands made on Victoriano Huerta," though not without some opposition.[77]

Meanwhile, the crisis in Mexican-American relations, which culminated in the landing of American troops at Vera Cruz on April 21, galvanized the peace movement into open opposition. Peace societies, individual peace advocates, women's clubs, and church groups hastily called special meetings at which they drew up petitions strongly opposing any action that might lead to hostilities with Mexico. Indicative of the moderation of the peace movement, the petitions criticized neither Wilson's missionary assumptions leading to the intervention nor the United States' blatant aggression on Mexican soil, but instead emphasized their fear of and the absurdity of war, especially over such a minor grievance.[78]

The Commission on Peace and Arbitration of the Federal Council of the Churches of Christ in America, for example, sent a resolution to the President, his cabinet, and every member of Congress, claiming that the "citizens of our Republic want no war with our southern neighbor, nor do they desire to dominate it, or to interfere with its internal affairs, but . . . desire cordial relations and friendly intercourse." It specifically warned congressmen that "the voices clamoring for war do not represent the sentiment of the sane and substantial people of our Republic, . . . but of mischiefmakers and of certain vested interests whose aggrandizement is furthered by war."[79] Carnegie also summarized ardent peace people's abhorrence of hostilities. "Such a war as seems pending," he chided the President, "will in after days be held akin to the fabled war of the two kings to decide which end of the egg should first be broken."[80]

Partly in response to those appeals and even more to the general aversion of the American public to military intervention, Wilson, who also began to dread the prospect of an extended war, refused to press hostilities further and quickly accepted the timely mediation offer of Argentina, Brazil, and Chile as a way out of the impasse.[81] The reactions of the peace leadership to Wilson's reversal were predictably diverse. Some realized that they exerted little influence on the President and could not help extricate him from the crisis. After consulting with New York clergymen and peace people at the height of the crisis, Short complained, "I find few who believe with me that anything we do will be of service."[82]

Yet others were greatly encouraged by the outcome for two reasons. First, despite the inevitable cries of super-patriotic Americans for full-scale military intervention, the nation showed little jingoistic emotion.[83] As Stephen Wise explained, "[T]hank God there is no war spirit in the land. The Peace movement has achieved something. It keeps us unready for war."[84]

Second, the Mexican crisis reassured their beliefs that Wilson was a man of peace at heart.[85] A few ecstatically praised the administration. Hamilton Holt hailed the mediation offer as "one of the most dramatic and glorious strokes in the history of international relations. . . . President Wilson and Secretary Bryan, in accepting it, have shown a political genius equalled only by their humanity."[86] Carnegie's reaction to Wilson's change of heart was even more laudatory. He was attending a concert in Carnegie Hall when he received a telegram from Washington informing him of President Wilson's acceptance of mediation. Flushed with excitement, Carnegie left his box and hurried to the stage where he announced the good news. "This is the happiest moment of my life!" he exclaimed. "Our whole attitude with regard to the Mexican situation has been wrong. The United States should expect Mexico and all other Latin American republics to take care of their own affairs, and should not meddle in them."[87]

By the summer of 1914 the Wilson-Bryan "New Diplomacy" had strengthened peace workers' confidence in the future of their movement. When the pervasive moralism of the administration's foreign policies is added to three other strong influences, a century of free security, the continued growth of the peace movement, and the idealistic overtones of the domestic reform impulse, it is understandable that they increasingly believed that they had arrived at the threshold of a new era. In fact, the closer the date of Armageddon, the more those factors converged to bolster their conviction that the day of permanent world peace was within their grasp.

The major question was no longer whether but when the millennium of world peace would arrive. The secretary of the Nebraska Peace Society had one answer. "There will not be any more great wars," he said. "We know it. It is absolutely settled. That is percolating through the great masses of the people. It is not a question or matter of argument."[88] And William Jennings Bryan said in 1912, "The era of the brotherhood of man is not coming. It is here now." Nearly two years later, perhaps sobered by the failure of Taft's treaties, the outbreak of warfare in Mexico and the Balkans, and his responsibilities as secretary of state, he was more restrained in his optimism. World peace would come "not in our time perhaps," but he implied that it would arrive in the near future.[89]

Bryan's latter statement expressed the thoughts of many peace workers. Even the conservative Taft, echoing the optimistic rhetoric of his former rival for the presidency, stated that "the whole world is aroused to a more brotherly spirit, the whole world is aroused to the advantage of peace as it never has been before;" and he prophesied that once the international court of arbitral justice, which he believed the third Hague conference would establish, became a reality, then all international disputes would be resolved without war within "a few decades or half a century."[90] Others set no time limit for the Utopia but agreed that it was inevitable. One spoke for idealistic peace advocates when he stated that "the world is nearer the millennium of peace than ever before, and the dreams and hopes which yesterday were so dimly seen are today certain of consummation." Even those who refrained from prophecy and admitted the likelihood of future wars believed they would occur only in the underdeveloped areas of the world. It was "highly improbable," however, that the United States or "the more advanced countries of Europe" would ever experience another war.[91]

That peace advocates could predict the millennium during or immediately following the two Balkan wars, both of which threatened to plunge Europe into a general war, pointedly illustrated their optimism. Although they were disturbed by the horrors of those wars, they did not attach much importance to them as barometers of a general European insecurity. Instead, they viewed the conflicts as only temporary setbacks to the inevitable progress toward world peace. After all, they thought, war scares and military clashes in the Balkans had been the warp and woof of the European experience, yet no major war had occurred in Europe in more than forty years. Was that not proof enough of Europe's progress toward peace? Similarly, they showed little awareness of the relationship of these two wars to the major European powers, especially their potential and actual effects on the two rival alliance systems. If they did relate these wars to the broader European scene, they emphasized that the major European powers had cooperated in ending them. True, they admitted the fear of a major European war might have partly motivated the European governments' peace efforts, but even more significant were their genuine and tangible efforts to relieve the diplomatic stalemate.[92]

When all this is said, one must reemphasize that the overwhelming majority of participants in the peace movement were aware of unpleasant realities in world politics. Even most of those indulging in Utopian rhetoric realized in their more sober moments that their idealistic hopes had at best marginal relevance to present conditions. The appreciation of international realities was not limited to conservative lawyers and other professional people; it also affected to a lesser degree peace workers who had fought in vain against the rising tide of jingoism and emotionalism at the turn of the century. If these unhappy memories had faded somewhat with the return of peace, prosperity, and reform after 1900, all peace leaders regardless of persuasion who studied European conditions in these years were reminded of human frailty and nationalistic rivalries as obstacles to a stable world order.

Many peace leaders had traveled widely throughout Europe, attended the annual international peace congresses in various European cities, and regularly corresponded with their transatlantic counterparts on the European situation. Some had perceived the deepening European suspicions at the Second Hague Peace Conference, and Butler had emphasized the volatility of the European scene in objecting to establishment of a peace commission in 1910. Italy's unprovoked attack on Turkey a year later reinforced peace leaders' growing impression of an unstable, imperialistic European system. Aware of the existence and workings of the Triple Alliance and Triple Entente, they well understood that the Balkan wars had increased the already existing tensions between Austria and Russia to the point where a future clash between them might quickly involve all the major European powers. Dutton and Jordan had even visited the Balkans during the first war and accurately reported the incredibly nationalistic, religious, and racial rivalries in the area. These peace leaders also realized that these wars had led to a resurgence of the military spirit and war propaganda throughout Europe. The growth of war expenditures in Europe confirmed their beliefs in the folly and burden of militarism which increased the chance for a general European war.[93] Trueblood in fact predicted that war was virtually inevitable. "If . . . the long-talked-of general war in Europe does not occur," he declared grimly, "it will be next to a miracle."[94]

Trueblood, however, was the only peace worker who publicly took a truly alarmist position on the European situation. The others repressed any deeper fears about the European situation and remained outwardly much more hopeful for the future peace of Europe. Although their rhetoric was usually restrained, they came to the same general conclusion that a European war was highly unlikely.

The most involved rationalization of the European situation came from David Starr Jordan. Obviously influenced by Angell's economic theories, Jordan mixed together untested and superficial assumptions on human nature, economic theory, and the influence of interest groups on governmental policies to "prove" the impossibility of a European war. The basis of his argument was that the "financial exploiters"—a coterie of businessmen, bankers, and the armament makers—held the real political power in Europe and pulled the strings of their governments behind the scenes. Since these capitalists had invested large sums of money in the Turkish area of the Balkans, he believed they had a direct interest in resisting the nationalistic uprising against Turkey's control of the area. He even charged that French capitalists had armed the Turkish troops to prevent Turkey's expulsion from the area.

After painting an unattractive picture of the greed and chicanery of these parasitic "interests," he recoiled from the conclusion that they increased the war potential in Europe. Indeed, he concluded just the opposite: that the ever impending, ever threatening European war would never come. True, he admitted prophetically, the tinder was so well dried and laid in such a way that some half crazed man, by the touch of a match, could start a conflagration that would quickly engulf all of Europe. He insisted, however, that barring and perhaps even after such an "accident," the businessmen and bankers (he was not clear about the armament makers) would never allow their governments to fight a major war. Although they might tolerate small wars such as had already occurred in the Balkans, in the interest of local exploitation, he believed that they were the strongest guardians of the general European peace. Considerations of their self-interest alone, especially their fears of general economic chaos resulting from an European conflict, would restrain them from the abyss of war. Realizing that his one dimensional, economic interpretation was fallible, he concluded that the peoples of Europe, who were increasingly demanding a voice in their governments, also wanted peace and would help to restrain their political leaders from war.[95]

More typical of peace workers' arguments, however, was the simpler assertion that none of the major European powers wanted war, and that therefore there would be no war. After giving a long description of the atrocities and horrors of the Balkan wars and their dangers to the future peace of Europe, Lynch concluded that the European powers were closer to peaceful solution of their differences than ever before. The outstanding fact of the Balkan wars, he asserted, was not their dangers to peace, but the cooperation of five major European powers during the wars "in a concert hitherto unknown."[96]

There were of course outward signs of a lessening of tensions among the European powers by 1914. The dangers of a French-German conflict over Alsace-Lorraine and colonial rivalries had declined, the continued Anglo-German naval and commercial rivalry was somewhat blunted by growing cooperation among their businessmen in the Balkans and elsewhere, the Austro-Italian friction had somewhat abated, and the major powers had cooperated in ending the Balkan wars.[97] That the peace leadership could remain optimistic, therefore, in the face of existing European tensions, especially the apparently insoluble question of nationalism which continued to inflame the peoples in southeastern Europe, is not too surprising; almost all Americans and many Europeans shared the belief that a general European war was improbable. It is also important to remember that peace advocates had no crystal ball to predict future events and that historians are often guilty of overlooking the role of chance factors, and instead perceiving the period before 1914 as a neat series of events leading inevitably to war.

What is significant about the participants in the peace cause, however, as we have already seen, is that in most cases their vision of the millennium went not only undimmed but shined at its brightest in these twilight years of world peace. It was as though the closer the date of Armageddon, the greater their tendency to absolve an uneasy conscience by reaffirming the certainty of their vision of a peaceful Utopia. Yet if forebodings of a European war partly inspired their glowing prophecies, another important motivation was their sincere belief in the ultimate attainment of their goal. All but a few of the most cautious peace workers expressed in varying degrees this enthusiasm for the future, but the student leader George Nasmyth, now thirty-one years old, expounded it most emphatically. He had watched with dismay the military spirit in Europe, which he said was "in the throes of an international reign of terror," but after talking with students at several universities in almost every nation of Europe, he became much more hopeful. However gloomy the present situation, he was sure the sun's rays would soon break through the darkness. Writing Edwin Mead from Germany toward the end of the first Balkan War, Nasmyth rapturously described his impressions of the world's future:

> It is a wonderful period in the world's history and the change which has taken place in China is a prelude of still greater changes for which the stage is being prepared in Russia and all the other countries of Europe. A new era in human history is dawning—the era of the unity of the world of which you have been one of the prophets—and the men and women who are now students will play the chief part in this drama of history. . . . I feel that I must travel the length and breadth of America preaching this great doctrine of humanity and pleading for the organization of a great missionary movement which will send peace workers out to all countries, and that I must go through all the world, rousing the students to the significance of the coming dawn, revealing to them a vision of the great task of international reconstruction of our century in which each of them can have a share.[98]

In one sense, Nasmyth's prophecy was correct. The stage was being prepared for great changes in Russia as well as in the rest of Europe; a new era in human history was indeed dawning. But the Golden Age of international peace and justice, of the unity of the world, which Nasmyth and the other idealistic peace workers envisaged in the near future, did not come. Sarajevo lay in the immediate future, and with it the onrush of events that were to plunge the world into four years of unparalleled war and revolutionary turmoil.

[12]

Aftermath

THE ASSASSINATION OF the Austrian Archduke Franz Ferdinand, heir apparent to the Austro-Hungarian throne, in Sarajevo on June 28, 1914, set in motion a series of momentous decisions in European chancelleries that soon plunged Europe into war. In late June American peace workers were preparing for their annual pilgrimage to Europe where they expected to participate in various peace meetings, and several had already made the journey. The summer months were supposed to be a particularly active time for American and European advocates of peace. Norman Angell arranged for a conference outside London from July 17 to 27 for young people, which was to be addressed by several notable public figures in English life as well as by Mead, Jordan, and Nasmyth. Three more conferences were scheduled for August and September. The Church Peace Union, in cooperation with British and German church peace councils, sponsored a church conference in Constance, Germany, from August 2 to 5, and the Interparliamentary Union and Universal Peace Congress planned to meet later in Stockholm and Vienna.

As the Austrian-Serbian crisis unfolded in the days following the Sarajevo assassinations, peace leaders showed no real alarm, and even those who did not leave the shores of the United States until July 24, only four days before the Hapsburg monarchy declared war on Serbia, saw no reason to cancel their steamship reservations. By July 31, only hours before the continental powers began to mobilize their armies, more than thirty-five American peace advocates, almost all of whom were bound for the Church Peace Conference, arrived in Europe and were beginning the last leg of their journey to Constance. A few handfuls of American peace leaders who planned to attend the Interparliamentary and Universal Peace Congresses failed to reach the Old World. Richard Bartholdt was in mid-ocean on a German liner when the European war erupted, and the captain of the ship, fearing an enemy attack, immediately returned to the United States; and James Brown Scott, American representative on the international preparatory committee for the proposed third Hague meeting, canceled his European trip at the last minute. Nor did other American peace workers who had not planned to leave the United States until August or early September depart from the American shores, for the Austro-Serbian war forced the cancellation of the Interparliamentary and Universal Peace Congresses.[1]

The responses of the American peace leaders to the mounting diplomatic tension in the last critical days of July make for intensely interesting reading. Those on their way to Constance experienced firsthand the growing international anxiety, the frantic mobilization efforts, the popular fears that gave way to excitement and finally to hysteria, and the personal tragedies of grief as families were separated and the civilian populations shoved aside by the autocratic imposition of military rule.

American peace workers first reacted in disbelief. Following Norman Angell's conference, Edwin and Lucia Mead left London on what they thought would be a leisurely journey to Constance. After spending a day at The Hague (where they admired the Peace Palace completed a year earlier), they arrived in Brussels on July 28, just as the Austrian government declared war on Serbia. It was only then that the Meads began to realize the imminent possibility of a general European war.[2]

Louis Lochner's first thoughts were even more innocent. His ship did not arrive in Cherbourg, France, until July 31. As soon as he disembarked, he found awaiting him a letter from an officer friend in the German army with political connections in Berlin. His friend had written in no uncertain terms that his government was determined to go to war and fight *pro gloria et patria,* yet Lochner believed that the thought of a European war "seemed too stupendous for earnest consideration."[3] James L. Tryon, a representative of the American Peace Society at the Church Peace Conference, expressed the same feeling. As late as August 1, he said, "Most of us Americans were light-hearted, and laughed at the idea of leaving Constance at all; we discounted the war scare."[4]

Needless to say, the eyes of the American travelers were quickly opened. A few peace workers did their best to prevent the war that was about to descend upon Europe. When the Meads arrived in Brussels, they were met by Senator Henry La Fontaine, a leading Belgian peace worker and president of the Berne Peace Bureau, who was greatly alarmed at the prospect of a general European war. Edwin D. Mead, who was also a member of the Berne Bureau, for the moment abandoned his plans to visit Constance and conferred with La Fontaine and other Belgian peace workers on the critical situation. They immediately agreed to telegraph the European members of the Berne Peace Bureau and other European peace workers asking them to come at once to Brussels.

Despite the lateness of the appeal, more than fifty peace workers managed to assemble in Brussels on the morning of July 31. Belgian delegates predominated, but four came from Britain, seven from France, two from Italy, three from Germany, and a large contingent from Holland. Determined to do whatever they could to preserve the last thread of peace, they drew up carefully worded appeals and cabled them to the ruling sovereigns and foreign ministers of Russia, Germany, and Austria. Upon Mead's urging, they also dispatched a cable to President Woodrow Wilson requesting him to mediate the critical situation. Although those appeals failed to prevent the outbreak of the World War, they could at least take heart that they had done what they could to prevent the war.[5]

With the major continental powers on the verge of mobilization, the peace workers managed to arrive in Constance after experiencing considerable difficulties. Lochner and the eleven American delegates traveling with him did not get to Paris until August 1 and gave up the attempt entirely, but a little luck and the cooperation of a few border officials allowed the rest of the American participants to reach Constance safely.[6] By the time the churchmen gathered for religious services on Sunday morning, August 2, the nations' announcements of mobilization for war were occurring at a breathless pace. Whatever hopes they had previously had for a peaceful solution to the crisis quickly gave way to dismay and anguish. Nevertheless, British, French, and German delegates at the conference prayed side by side hoping for some miracle that would spare Europe from imminent war. When it became clear that the German government was commandeering all trains for the military, the delegates adjourned the conference, the French returning home through Switzerland and the remaining eighty delegates taking the last train northward to Cologne where the German authorities finally permitted the non-German delegates to enter Holland. Once again on neutral soil, the American and British church representatives boarded a boat for England and arrived in London on August 5, only hours after Great Britain declared war on Germany.[7]

As the war expanded in intensity and scope, American peace advocates offered explanations for its underlying and immediate causes. Their task required more than dispassionate analysis, however, for they realized that their movement seemed discredited in the eyes of world opinion. Unwilling to admit failure, they usually coupled their analysis of war causation with a vigorous defense of the peace movement. They especially argued that the World War vindicated their predictions that the escalating armament race would inevitably lead to a major war. A few days after the outbreak of hostilities, Samuel Dutton said, "Every advocate of peace who has studied the grounds for his faith has known that this clash was coming. Dr. Jordan saw it, and expressed that one nation would 'load itself up' on the border of another nation when this condition made it practically certain that sooner or later the loading nation would 'go off.' "[8] The Reverend Charles E. Jefferson and Representative James Slayden echoed the same refrain. "[T]he peace movement," Slayden contended, "has not been in vain. It has made the people think. Millions now see and understand the danger of being overarmed where only thousands saw it before."[9]

Such statements represented the instinctive reactions of individuals who were emotionally committed to the cause of world peace, but they sounded rather hollow and even hypocritical when compared with their utterances before the war. However much they had feared the outbreak of a general European war—and inwardly many of them had certainly dreaded the possibility—they had not stated their fears publicly. Dutton's remarks about Jordan's fears of a general European war were undoubtedly sincere but constituted a distortion of Jordan's own elaborate theory of an "impossible war."

Peace spokesmen's claims that they had consistently attacked the armament makers and military cliques were more to the point, but they were far from unanimous on the armament question. Even the strongest opponents of the military had issued no dire warnings concerning the awesome developments in military science and technology, such as the submarine, airplane, and gigantic artillery pieces, and the passive material and human destruction they would inflict in a major war. It is of course unfair to blame them for their failure to foretell the massproduced slaughter of a European war, but as the most concerned Americans about military preparedness one might have expected at least a few ominous predictions of the impending horrors and carnage of modern warfare. Nor had they shown much interest in the armament firms and their potential and actual influence in government circles. If anything, certain congressmen had shown a stronger disposition than the peace workers to level verbal blasts at the armament makers.

An even deeper flaw in their reasoning was their repeated assertion that the World War was the inevitable result of the accelerating armament race. Those sympathetic to pacifism surely overemphasized armaments as the most important underlying cause of the war. Although large armaments did contribute to the growing importance of the military in political decision making, especially in periods of diplomatic crisis, they were more an obvious and tangible symptom, just as were the formation and tightening of the rival alliance systems, of a growing feeling of insecurity among the European powers. Fundamental economic and imperial rivalries directly contributed to that insecurity and in turn to the escalating armament race.

More specifically, the growing restiveness among European nations was an outgrowth of Germany's rising ambitions as a major naval and a colonial power, which the other Western nations generally recognized as legitimate aims, and that nation's blustering and erratic foreign policies in the post–Bismarck era, which they feared and on occasion condemned. On an even more specific and immediate level, a fundamental cause of the World War was the failure of European statesmen to solve the problem of nationalism, especially as it related to the Balkans, for it was those national passions that provided the spark that set the alliance system in motion.

If friends of peace oversimplified the underlying causes of the First World War, their oversimplifications conformed to their general assumptions on human nature. Uncomfortable with the notion of man's irrationality as an integral part of his existence, they occasionally labeled an impersonal factor, the armaments themselves, as the major cause of the war. Thus, David Starr Jordan sprinkled his talks on the war with statements that 350,000,000 people in Europe did not want war but, "When nations are armed, war is bound to come." He even believed that the armament race had come to its "predestined end."[10] Frederick Lynch provided the clearest evidence of this reasoning. Upon his return to the United States, he wrote: "I am trying to convey to everybody in the United States two pictures: one of the boundary line between the United States and Canada; the other of the boundary line between France and Germany—their differences are the results of each. One, no weapons—no war. The other, weapons everywhere—war everywhere."[11]

When peace advocates argued that large armaments predetermined Europe's cruel fate, they came dangerously close to saying that the individual was a prisoner of society, especially of its productive processes; but yet they did not intend to eliminate free will entirely from their ideology. Recognizing that armaments alone could not produce war but required their actual use by individuals, most of them censured the small minority of war profiteers and military leaders as the most obvious culprits. Even conservatives Butler and Scott, who had placed their hopes for world order in the hands of an international elite of intellectuals, lawyers, and statesmen, on occasion conceded that it was irresponsible government leaders that had brought on the maelstrom, while the supposedly warlike masses had remained quiet.[12]

Peace advocates never seemed to understand the deeper reasons for the European armament race, but they realized that the vast quantity of arms subtly affected the quality of a few military men whose interests were most directly involved. As Jordan remarked, "To prepare for war is to breed a host of men who have no other business and another host who find their profits in blood."[13] Yet they triumphed because they were organized, influential, and through their clever appeals to "patriotism" and "duty" successfully duped the masses into fighting their wars.[14] An autocratic elite had triumphed over the democratic instincts of the more humble citizenry. "In the great struggle against privilege," Jordan wrote, "which is at the bottom of the present war, we have deprived the aristocrats of one thing after another in the interests of the people, but we have left the control of instruments of destruction in their hands for them to play with as boys plays with fireworks, and they have turned them against us."[15]

Jordan and some other pacific-minded Americans occasionally went further in specifying Germany as morally culpable for both the underlying and immediate causes of the World War. Carnegie, for instance, never doubted the responsibility of the German military leaders who had cajoled the "pitiable" Kaiser into acceptance of their aggressive war plans.[16] A few other peace leaders sprinkled their writings with unflattering comments about Bernhardi, Krupp, and German militarism as fundamental causes of the conflict. The belief in German war guilt, along with their lingering notions of the possible regenerative effects of American democracy on autocratic Europe, would ultimately allow them to acquiesce in American belligerency against Germany in 1917. Because those assumptions permeated the peace movement from the onset of the European war, many pacifistic Americans failed to participate actively in uncompromising antiwar movements during American neutrality. Their pacifistic instincts nonetheless impelled many of them to look for more complex causes of the war and to emphasize that a total Allied victory over German militarism and autocracy might nourish only the growth of reactionary elements in the Allied nations to equally dangerous proportions.[17]

As the war continued and increased in intensity, it became more difficult for international reformers to believe in a quick peace and the beginnings of a new international reconstruction. A few of them became so grief stricken that they became physically ill. Carnegie, Trueblood, and Edwin Mead all suffered serious illnesses in the first months of 1915 and never fully recovered their full strength during the war, and Carnegie and Trueblood died in 1916 and 1919. In the absence of detailed medical diagnoses, one can plausibly ascribe the illnesses of these three solely to the infirmities of old age, for they were all over sixty-five years and obviously were no longer as robust as they had been earlier. Trueblood had suffered a stroke in 1913, which caused some speech impairment; and though he was soon able to resume his duties as editor of the *Advocate of Peace,* he suffered a relapse in late 1914 after which he reluctantly decided to give up his post.[18]

Yet all three found the World War a deeply disturbing and emotional experience, and their illnesses may have been hastened and aggravated by psychosomatic causes. When Mead perceived the indecision and confusion in the World Peace Foundation and, more generally, throughout the American peace movement in the first months of American neutrality, he redoubled his activities in support of anti-preparedness and mediation, became overworked, and suffered a nervous breakdown in March 1915.[19] Lucia Mead nobly bore the burden of caring for her ailing husband, but her letters to friends in the peace movement revealed her travail. In August 1915, she wrote that her husband, now confined to a sanitarium, was in "a very depressed and nervous condition" and suffered from "insomnia and bowel trouble." A few years later she described "his strange double personality," which fluctuated between sanity and "groans and wild clamor," and she admitted, "He is lonely and wretched beyond all words and can not be reconciled to his cruel fate."[20] Edwin Mead never recovered during the war and was forced to retire for nine years from all peace work.[21]

The World War also painfully affected Carnegie's optimistic outlook. At first he could not believe that the worst was at hand and he went through the motions of reiterating his optimistic credo. "The world grows better," he could say with amazing disrespect of the facts of international life in November 1915, "and we are soon to see blessed peace restored and a world court established."[22] Deep in his heart, however, he could no longer believe what he so desperately wanted to believe. His wife later described the psychological effects of the war on him. After the outbreak of the war, she explained, her husband broke off the writing of his autobiography:

Henceforth he was never able to interest himself in private affairs. . . . Optimist as he always was and tried to be, even in the face of the failure of his hopes, the world disaster was too much. His heart was broken. A severe attack of influenza followed by two serious attacks of pneumonia precipitated old age upon him.[23]

Not all American peace advocates had such traumatic experiences, although they all felt aggrieved in varying degrees. In general, they suffered in proportion to their emotional commitment to the cause of world peace. David Starr Jordan was perhaps most vulnerable to mental or physical stress, for he had increasingly channeled his energies into the peace movement and had attempted to convince himself that a major war could not occur. Yet Jordan's interests were extensive, and his scientific training as well as his receptivity to new ideas had made him more resilient and flexible than Trueblood, Mead, and Carnegie, all of whom had based their pacifist faith on a single ideology. It is significant perhaps that Jordan used Darwinian evolution (wars destroyed the fit and promoted the survival of the unfit), Angell's economic theories, educational reform, and even William James' essay, "The Moral Equivalent of War," as intellectual tools to attack war, while Edwin Mead derived his almost entirely from idealists like Kant or Emerson, Carnegie from Spencerian optimism, and Trueblood from Christian pacifism.

To Oswald Garrison Villard, who derived his pacifism from his non-resistant relatives, the war came as a rude shock. "I can hardly sleep," he wrote, "and in fact have had many broken nights when I have waked up with thoughts of this war, as one has the impression of a nightmare."[24] Perhaps because of his comparative youth and extensive editorial interests, he managed to maintain his mental and physical balance throughout the conflict. Still others like William Jennings Bryan had so many other interests that outwardly the war did not seem to affect them.

International lawyers reacted somewhat differently. Although James Brown Scott could write, "I have been dazed by the war,"[25] his "daze" resulted much less from personal agony over the mass killing on European battlefields than from his professional dismay at the belligerents' flagrant violations of the Hague Conventions in starting and ruthlessly prosecuting the war. As the warring powers continued to treat international laws as worthless scraps of paper, the lawyers became increasingly sensitive to the eclipse of their past efforts. John Bassett Moore noted that violations of legal rights had convinced the "opinion of people at large that international law has gone to pieces."[26] That widespread public disaffection forced even the lawyers to admit the demise of international law. "It is disheartening to note the talk," Simeon Baldwin complained, "not only of the street, but of the bar and too many of the scholars, about the disappearance of International Law as a rule of conduct."[27] The demoralization of the profession became so pronounced that the executive council of the American Society of International Law approved a statement asserting that "the very existence of international law is now at issue."[28] Elihu Root conceded that the belligerents had smashed international law to its foundations. "God knows what the law is!" he lamented at the end of the war. "None of us know [sic]."[29]

The lawyers of course refused to admit defeat. A lifetime of experience in the law profession suggested an emotional involvement with international law that they could not easily discard. If they lost faith in international law, they would be abandoning the cornerstone of their hopes for international reform. The lawyers quickly developed explanations for their predicament. They insisted that the repudiation of international law was temporary and had occurred so easily because nations had not had sufficient time to develop precise definitions of nations' rights and responsibilities in the world community. Moreover, they agreed that international law could be vindicated if the lawbreakers were punished. Because Germany had attacked first, freely admitted its violation of the treaty guaranteeing Belgium's neutrality, and upset the existing rules of international law governing naval warfare with the introduction of the submarine, nearly all legalists easily singled out Germany as the principal outlaw; and by 1916 some lawyers were agitating for war with that nation. When the United States finally entered the war against Germany, the American Society of International Law proclaimed that the conflict was "essentially one for the vindication of law."[30]

The European war also adversely affected the peace organizations. With Trueblood seriously ill in 1915, the American Peace Society lost its leading crusader for peace, and thereafter the more cautious officers of the society, executive secretary Arthur Deerin Call and president Theodore Burton, and the trustees of the Carnegie Endowment, which provided the society with an annual subvention, soon guided the peace group toward a more conservative course.

The American Peace Society failed to take strong positions on any of the thorny political and diplomatic questions facing American policy makers during the period of neutrality. While the society opposed the most vehement preparedness advocates, it did not make antipreparedness a crusade. Nor did it give more than perfunctory support to the growing American sentiment for mediation of the war. The peace group upheld neutral rights and international law but did not attempt to educate the public on what exactly were a neutral's rights in wartime. Indeed, the *Advocate of Peace* said nothing at all about the legality or wisdom of shipping munitions, allowing private and governmental loans to belligerent nations, and American citizens traveling on belligerent passenger liners, and seemed content to make bland remarks about its devotion to "rational" and "sane" pacifism, "true" patriotism, "duty," "right thinking," and "constructive" action.[31] Such statements underscored the American Peace Society's intellectual bankruptcy on the immediate problems of the war in Europe and their actual and potential effects on the United States in particular and neutral nations in general.

That is not to say that the society had no program, for it did advocate periodic international conferences at The Hague and an international judiciary as prerequisites for a stable and peaceful postwar world. Yet even those institutional proposals had a vague and old-fashioned sound. The *Advocate of Peace* consistently opposed any international organization that envisioned a system of collective security but did not elaborate the details of these programs that might have served as a guide for diplomats at the peace settlement.[32] It said nothing about procedures for conciliation, arbitration, and the size and powers of an international congress and judiciary and freely admitted, "Whether we believe in a 'League of Peace,' a 'United States of Europe,' a 'federation of the world,' or what not, is relatively unimportant. . . . Now is the time to think, confer, and think again. . . . When men and women think, really think, upon these matters, then the problem of war will be solved."[33]

When the leaders of the American Peace Society thought about possible formulas for world order, however, they could look only backward to the ancient principles of the society's early leaders, notably William Ladd, as their guide for postwar reconstruction. As Call noted in May 1915: "The aims of the American Peace Society, as presented by its various branches and sections, have not been materially changed because of the European war. The two main principles of this society are as pertinent as in the days of William Ladd. The substitute for all of the problems incident to the crime of war must take the direction of an International Congress and a High Court of Nations."[34]

Since Call had demonstrated little sympathy for any specific course of peace action before 1914, he was sincere in espousing this cautious program, but his long career as a bureaucrat reinforced his timidity. Before becoming executive secretary of the American Peace Society, he had served as a school administrator and was well used to assuming the role of conciliator. Though fundamentally conservative, he seemed willing to endorse any viewpoint receiving large majority support among the membership. Without any clear consensus, however, Call more readily allowed the society to fall under the domination of the Carnegie Endowment, which was supplying three-fourths of its total income. As early as June 1915, in the midst of the difficulties between the United States and Germany over the sinking of the *Lusitania,* Scott wrote Call urging the American Peace Society to "withdraw within itself, as it were, during the present war, to consider carefully what can best be done in the future, to limit its program consciously, and, having so limited it, endeavor to carry it into effect when the conclusion of peace will give the Society a hearing."[35] If Mead, Bartholdt, and especially Trueblood had still been leaders in the society, it is barely possible that the group would have taken more positive stands on neutral rights, mediation, and preparedness and still received the Carnegie subvention; but Call was so anxious to please Scott that the society's program became almost a carbon copy of the Carnegie Endowment's.[36]

Some members of the American Peace Society grumbled about the inertia of the national society, but after Scott's views were published in the

Advocate of Peace with Call's approving comments, they became more outspoken in their criticism. They now fully realized that the officers of the American Peace Society and Carnegie Endowment were working together against any active peace work for the duration of the World War.

Louis Lochner, secretary of the Chicago Peace Society and head of the American Peace Society's Central-West Department, assailed that position. Lochner had said little during his association with the Cosmopolitan Clubs to suggest strong pacifistic leanings; but when he assumed the secretaryship of the Chicago Peace Society in early 1914, he worked closely with pacifistic liberals like Jane Addams and Jenkin Lloyd Jones. He was determined to make the society a more activist, pacifistic organization, and a few weeks before the outbreak of the war he and his allies succeeded in placing the executive committee on record in favor of the principle of government ownership and control of the manufacture of munitions and weapons of war. After August 1914, the pacifistic members managed temporarily to use the organization to promote mediation and antipreparedness movements in the Middle West.[37]

Lochner hoped that those activities might sustain President Wilson's and Secretary Bryan's initial interest in mediation and perhaps eventually encourage them to undertake a more active diplomatic campaign for ending the war under terms that would be acceptable to both sets of belligerents. He also wanted to nourish peace sentiment among the remaining neutral nations in Europe, which might also initiate mediation moves, and to support the efforts of foreign groups, such as the Union of Democratic Control in Great Britain, to establish a minimum program for a more liberal and peaceful postwar order. The efforts of these Chicago activists to receive financial support from the Carnegie Endowment got nowhere, and Scott even refused to appoint delegates to their meetings, which were supposed to discuss such activities.[38]

Increasingly frustrated by the endowment's noninterference policy, Lochner publicly charged in late 1915 that the Carnegie Endowment was "one of the pitiable and deplorable facts of the peace movement in America." Obsessed by the "governmental mind," it had bogged down in red tape and been "inoculated with the virus of inertia for which the Endowment will some day be world-famous."[39]

Nicholas Murray Butler's assistant attempted to refute Lochner's contentions but admitted that the Carnegie Endowment had curtailed all its work in Europe and was concentrating on the relations of the Republics in the Western Hemisphere and certain educational projects in the United States, such as study clubs on international relations in American universities. When Call told Lochner that his attacks on the Carnegie Endowment amounted to an attack upon the American Peace Society as well, Lochner, interpreting this criticism as an open invitation for his resignation, abruptly quit both the national body and the Chicago Peace Society. Lochner had little regret, for he was already helping to make the final arrangements for Henry Ford's peace ship, which was to become the most sensational effort to promote neutral mediation of the war. Lochner's resignation permitted more conservative members to move the Chicago peace group toward a timid course, which only hastened the departure of other pacifistic members.[40]

Most pacifistic Americans shared Lochner's feelings but expressed their opinions discreetly to their pacific-minded friends and to the leaders of the Carnegie Endowment and American Peace Society. Jordan, who had already praised Lochner as "one of the best of all our bunch" for promoting a more active pacifism,[41] supported Lochner's position. In a long letter to one of the trustees of the Carnegie Endowment, he complained that the inertia of the endowment and the American Peace Society was a disgrace to the peace movement. "It is this sort of cowardice and incompetence by no means new in pacifism, which weakens and makes absurd the peace movement and which is bringing the Carnegie Endowment into sharp and deserved criticism in England and America." He even believed that the Carnegie Endowment was "an obstruction rather than a help in the cause, partly because its existence creates the impression that the cause has all the money it needs, when so far as present efforts are concerned it has no money at all."[42]

Bartholdt and Trueblood were just as critical of the Carnegie Endowment. The former had announced his retirement from Congress shortly before the outbreak of the European war but during the lame-duck session in early 1915 led an unsuccessful campaign to enact a law placing an embargo on munitions, almost all of which were going to the Allies in control of the sea lanes. While German-American elements lobbied vigorously for this measure and pro–German sympathies partly motivated Bartholdt's actions, he also believed that his position reaffirmed traditional pacifist arguments. When the peace forces remained aloof from neutrality issues, he blamed the Carnegie Endowment. Expressing his entire agreement with Lochner's attack on Carnegie's institution, he also pointed out its harmful effects on the autonomy of peace groups: "I do honestly believe that the cause of peace has been retarded rather than helped by Mr. Carnegie's millions. The leaders [of the peace societies] now wear a rope around their necks, while formerly they were free."[43]

Those criticisms failed to check the increasingly conservative course of the American Peace Society in the following months. Its president, Theodore Burton, showed very little interest in the Washington based peace organization. Even Call complained that the Ohio Republican "has not lifted an ounce for us."[44] Claiming other pressing duties (such as his ambition to become the Republican presidential nominee in 1916), Burton finally resigned in December 1915, and thereafter showed slight interest in the peace movement.[45]

Call perceived that Burton's resignation provided an opportunity for bringing in fresh leadership that might extricate the group from its passive policy. He found support in the society for Bryan, who had recently resigned as secretary of state, and Jordan as Burton's replacement. Call found, however, that Butler of the Carnegie Endowment, believing Bryan and Jordan were too pacifistic, preferred the recently retired Columbia law professor, George W. Kirchwey, for the presidency. Call indicated where the real power in the American Peace Society lay when he remarked, "Butler favors Kirchwey and Mammon may therefore have a controlling voice in the situation."[46] Indeed, Butler and Dutton, a member of the society's executive committee, soon persuaded Kirchwey to accept the position.[47]

Kirchwey took the helm with the understanding that he could review the society's policies and institute changes, but he was indecisive. Though he inclined toward nonintervention in the war, he was not sure what policies the society should pursue during American neutrality. Rather than risk a challenge to the Scott-Butler faction, Kirchwey quietly followed their cautious program. Call attempted to find some consensus in the peace movement by calling a conference of peace advocates representing many different peace and internationalist groups in October 1916. The meeting merely confirmed the confusion and disunity in the movement, and it adjourned without agreement on specific guidelines for the American Peace Society.[48]

When no change in policy occurred, William Hull criticized the society's inaction and refused to attend the executive committee meetings, which in his opinion never amounted to anything. Hull still hoped that Kirchwey would revitalize the peace group and mobilize its energies behind the program of periodic congresses and a world court. Kirchwey's procrastination, however, delayed the meeting of the executive committee until the eve of Germany's renewal of unrestricted submarine warfare when it was too late to respond to the new crisis. Prospects for renewed life of the American Peace Society would have been bleak in any case, because Kirchwey had long before lost interest in the peace group and finally resigned from the presidency shortly after American entrance into the war.[49]

The position of the American Peace Society toward Germany's policy of unrestricted submarine warfare in early 1917 indicated that peace advocates' complaints failed to impress the society's lackluster leadership. The peace group debated the alternatives open to the American government during the fateful crisis but proposed nothing beyond hoping that President Wilson would leave no stone unturned in seeking a peaceful settlement of the submarine issues. Editorials in the *Advocate of Peace,* presumably written by Call, offered no answer to the question of arming American merchant vessels. At first they weakly suggested that "neutral ships might well remain unarmed" and pleaded for any policy that was based on the nation's "immemorial faiths in reason rather than passion, in justice rather than might, in ordered processes rather than mobbed lawlessness."[50] Once Wilson had decided to arm the merchantmen on his own authority, however, the executive committee on March 9 voted to support the President in whatever action he felt necessary.

Call summarized that policy. On the immediate question, should the United States arm its merchant vessels, he answered: "We do not know. That is not the business of the American Peace Society; it is for the Government to decide. And the government's decision in any case will be the decision for us all." On the larger question of a declaration of war against Germany, he replied, "the American Peace Society leaves the question whether we shall or shall not enter this war to the Government of the United States."[51] What Lochner had said of the "governmental mind" of the Carnegie Endowment applied equally well to the American Peace Society. It wanted peace at the same time that it wanted to uphold international law and neutral rights, but in the final crisis could offer 'no clear answer and ended up forfeiting whatever influence it might have had in shaping the opinions of the President, Congress, and the public at large. Thereafter the executive committee fervently boosted the war effort and avoided discussion of controversial questions like conscription and conscientious objection in the *Advocate of Peace,* preferring instead a policy of "little expression of opinion in the magazine on matters of immediate political significance."[52]

The World War also brought confusion and disunity to the World Peace Foundation. Although Samuel Dutton, chairman of the endowed group's committee on organization, emphasized a few months after the onset of the war that "this is the beginning of a new epoch in the history of the Foundation" and urged the development of "a well-defined policy" on American neutrality and postwar world order, the trustees had a difficult time in deciding what changes in the foundation's programs were necessary. The old confidence in the future was no longer evident. With Edwin Ginn dead and Edwin Mead seriously ill, the foundation had lost two of its leaders, who, in spite of their differences, had agreed that the World Peace Foundation should actively serve the cause of peace. Without their presence the endowed agency drifted aimlessly. When it finally began to formulate a specific policy, it served only to divide its members.

In the months immediately following the outbreak of the war, the trustees demonstrated their indecision. They appointed Charles Levermore, ex-president of Adelphi College, as acting chief director during Mead's illness but could not agree on a positive program. Instead, they decided to curtail all the foundation's activities "not involving legal and moral obligation, so as to have an emergency fund for possible new activity." In pursuit of this policy, or nonpolicy, they discontinued the foundation's meager support of women's clubs, left vacant the position of business manager after Albert Bryant's unexpected death in February 1915, and cut off the salary allowance of many of its directors. Several trustees recommended termination of the subvention to the American School Peace League, but after long discussion the trustees reluctantly voted to continue the appropriation. Since they also decided to prohibit publication of books and pamphlets without the consent of a majority of the five-man committee of organization, in practice that meant that the printed matter of the foundation was also curtailed. As Dutton remarked, "in many cases there have not been even three members of the Committee ready to approve of a publication proposed by the Acting Chief Director."[53]

These restrictive actions did not mean that the World Peace Foundation abandoned all peace work, for Levermore wanted to promote educational programs in the schools and colleges. Before his appointment as acting director, he had served as head of the college department of the foundation, and he continued this educational work during the war. While Edwin Mead had looked upon the foundation's work among students as a process of moral exhortation and conversion of American youth to active service in the peace movement, Levermore wanted only to organize student study clubs on international relations and to encourage college administrators to add foreign policy courses to their curricula. George Nasmyth, his missionary zeal for peace thoroughly deflated by the European slaughter, assisted Levermore in promoting the establishment of study clubs in several colleges and universities in the East and Middle West. Since those activities conformed to Butler's insistence on avoidance of "purely contentious questions" and on concentrated emphasis on "purely educational, scientific, and nonpartisan" peace work for the duration of the war, the Carnegie Endowment cooperated with Levermore and Nasmyth in promoting the study of international relations in higher education. By the end of 1916 the combined efforts of those two foundations had succeeded in organizing foreign policy groups, usually called International Polity Clubs, in more than forty American universities and colleges.[54]

Despite that modest undertaking the World Peace Foundation was very reluctant to embark on more ambitious programs. Given its obsession with saving money for future peace work—one estimate called for saving $20,000 per year for the duration of the war—the trustees' caution was understandable. Yet because of financial difficulties over Ginn's will and other unforeseen expenditures (such as major repairs to the foundation's buildings), the endowed organization was unable to save any money. As the finance committee sadly reported: "In spite of the fact that the Foundation has had for more than a year no very well defined policy or great apparent activity, we have spent most of our income."[55]

Finally, after long debate the trustees, awakening from their lethargy, decided to endorse a new internationalist organization, the League to Enforce Peace. The idea of a league of the great powers to enforce the peace was primarily the brainchild of Hamilton Holt, William Short, and Theodore Marburg, who agreed that the World War necessitated the creation of an authoritative world organization if future wars were to be prevented. Officially founded in June 1915, the League to Enforce Peace also gained the support of William Howard Taft, Oscar Straus, John Hays Hammond, Frederick Lynch, Fannie Fern Andrews, Lucia Mead, and George W. Nasmyth among the prewar peace leadership as well as many newcomers who for the first time began to show sustained interest in the problem of international organization.

The platform of the new internationalist group pledged the use of economic or military forces of member nations against any one of their number refusing to submit its justiciable disputes to a world court or its nonjusticiable disputes to a council of conciliation for judgment before resorting to hostilities. The leadership of the League to Enforce Peace agreed that nations were not yet prepared to provide for an international police force but assumed that they might be willing collectively to guarantee use of their economic powers and military forces against violators of the cooling-off guarantee. Fully convinced of Germany's aggression in August 1914, they further assumed that the world's leaders could easily identify the outlaw at the onset of any given future war and thus could move rapidly to punish the violator. They were confident, however, that the threat of united force among the members would prove sufficient in deterring war in almost every instance.[56]

Among the early promoters of the League to Enforce Peace was one of the World Peace Foundation's trustees, A. Lawrence Lowell, president of Harvard University. Shortly after creation of the new organization, Lowell asked the foundation's trustees to endorse the league's program. Some trustees were unhappy with the potential dangers of using force to counteract force in international affairs, but Lowell had immense prestige and influence in the endowed group. Using the threat of resignation, he persuaded the trustees to endorse the league's "general principles and policy." Given the trustees' general dissatisfaction with the foundation's paralysis, their desire for some kind of constructive action, and the memory of their benefactor's federalist leanings, their deference to Lowell's assertive leadership was virtually inevitable. In January 1916, he convinced the trustees to appropriate $10,000 annually to the new organization. The trustees actually increased that appropriation in 1916 and 1917 and abandoned all interest in the immediate questions of American neutrality.[57]

David Starr Jordan, a director of the World Peace Foundation, watched those developments with increasing dismay. Before the foundation began appropriating funds to the League to Enforce Peace, he criticized the growing conservatism of the trustees and their refusal to embark on active peace work. As he reported to his wife in October 1915, the foundation was "stuck in the mud" and in a "very unsatisfactory state." He suspected that Lowell, whom he privately called "the tory president at Harvard," was responsible for the trustees' initial caution; but after the trustees had endorsed the league, he accurately discerned Lowell's domination of the board.[58] Recognition of the principle of force to maintain the peace troubled Jordan, although he conceded that the fledgling internationalist group might provide one answer to the problem of international anarchy after the war. He reluctantly joined the League to Enforce Peace, mainly because he had already endorsed the plank calling for coercive sanctions in the nine-point "minimum program" of the Central Organization for a Durable Peace, an internationalist group with representatives from many nations founded at The Hague in the spring of 1915. Jordan liked the Central Organization's emphasis on pacifistic and liberal principles for a "new diplomacy" in the postwar world and as part of the package was willing to accept military sanctions against countries starting hostilities without first resorting to peace machinery. He ultimately proved sufficiently resilient to support Woodrow Wilson's bolder notions of collective security embodied in the Covenant of the League of Nations.[59]

It was not so much the World Peace Foundation's endorsement of the principle of force per se that disturbed Jordan but his realization that the foundation's financial support of the League to Enforce Peace meant the virtual abandonment of all other peace work for the duration of the war. Jordan told his friends on the board of trustees that if they would promote him as chief director, he might agree to serve until he could reactivate the fund. Jordan was not very optimistic about his proposal, for he realized that a majority of the trustees was reluctant to embark on a more active policy. "The trouble is," he complained, "they are afraid to endow anybody as Mr. Ginn wished to endow me, and any live man might jar the London Clubs, or the Republican Standpat Organization."[60]

Jordan's allies on the board had urged a more active working head, but a majority of the trustees had ignored the proposal. Indeed, since the trustees had endorsed the League to Enforce Peace, they failed to consult any of the directors except Levermore and Nasmyth who continued their modest efforts among institutions of higher learning. Once committed to the league, the trustees rejected all other suggestions. At one meeting alone they tabled proposals to endorse the Union of Democratic Control, establish a newspaper, and create a press bureau for newspaper campaigns. By late 1916 the foundation became little more than an administrative agency that distributed the largest single portion of its annual income to the League to Enforce Peace.[61]

Some trustees and directors who had previously expressed deep reservations about the possible unpleasant consequences of forceful sanctions also lost interest in the foundation and directed their attention to other internationalist organizations more congenial to their own outlook. Samuel Dutton, who placed greater faith in a purely judicial rather than a world organization with political authority, increasingly devoted more of his time to another new group, the World's Court League, whose main purpose was to mobilize American public sentiment behind a permanent international court following the World War. In October 1916, Dutton agreed to serve as its secretary. Charles Levermore, moving in the same direction, realized that his services as a director of the World Peace Foundation were virtually worthless and joined Dutton in promoting the judicial court.[62]

The New York Peace Society drifted along a similar course. At first some of its members were interested in spreading pacifist propaganda to educate the citizenry against American participation in the conflict and in promoting American mediation of the war. As long as its president, Andrew Carnegie, was healthy, he opposed such activity. Forgetting his prewar criticisms of the Carnegie Endowment's caution, he now urged the same inaction on his own peace group. His deference to President Wilson's call for neutrality in thought and action prompted his statement, "that of all things, silence, upon the part of our country, is the best policy."[63] What Carnegie desired of the country he demanded of the society, and a majority of the leadership agreed with him.[64]

Even after Carnegie became ill and began to lose touch with the peace movement, the society's directors failed to pursue an active policy. Although they still favored mediation on the part of the American government, they exerted no pressure on the Wilson administration and admitted by the autumn of 1916 that "we have not learned, during the year, of any further project which seemed to us to have in it promise of accomplishing this desired end." Unwilling to divide the society on the question of military preparedness, they avoided the issue entirely, claiming that the entire question was not "of essence to the peace movement."[65]

When the New York Peace Society did take a position, it decided to uphold international law as defined before 1914. In standing on neutral rights, it came close to advocating war whenever a German submarine sank a neutral or belligerent ship resulting in the loss of American lives. Ultimately, Holt and Short managed to gain a forum in the society for their ideas on a league of nations to enforce the peace, and a special committee was organized to debate the entire problem. Their realization that the society was inert and at any rate had only a local influence led to their decision to form the League to Enforce Peace. As the league grew in size and stature, the New York Peace Society endorsed the new organization, which served to rescue the New York group from its inaction, though at a cost of losing its independent identity. William Short, secretary of both organizations, guaranteed cooperation between the two groups, but he, along with Holt, Straus, and other members of the New York Society, increasingly made the League to Enforce Peace their primary loyalty.[66]

Several disagreed with the society's endorsement. Those who were more concerned with keeping the United States out of the war at all costs and in promoting policies to end the carnage and destruction in Europe became discouraged with the New York Peace Society's inaction and finally dismayed at its endorsement of collective security, and by 1916 several members had resigned in disgust.[67] Oswald Villard well expressed their displeasure with the society's indifference to pacifism. Quoting a friend, he called the New York Peace Society a "somnolent and inactive reform association," which despite its "aroma of original benevolence," was really an organization that "attracts respectable, rich, lazy, and conservative people."[68] With defections of collective security advocates and pacifists, the society became a rump organization without an effective program. Lacking a clear *raison d'etre,* the group died out by 1920.

From the foregoing it would seem that the outbreak of the World War shattered the superficial unity among the peace workers. Yet the American peace movement from 1914 to 1917 was not entirely shattered; rather it was reorganized. Those dissatisfied with the timidity of the peace organizations in the months following the outbreak of the war not only dissociated themselves from existing peace groups but formed new ones. Thus, just as proponents of international organization founded new groups like the League to Enforce Peace and the World's Court League, so did pacifistic Americans start and recruit new blood for peace organizations of their own. The American Union Against Militarism, Woman's Peace Party, Neutral Conference for Continuous Mediation, American Neutral Conference Committee, Fellowship of Reconciliation, and Emergency Peace Federation were the most important of the peace groups founded during American neutrality.

Those and other pacifistic organizations attracted not only peace workers who were dissatisfied with the conservatism of the existing peace societies; but the World War also impelled many more pacific-minded liberals who had shown no interest in the peace cause before 1914 into active cooperation with those new groups. Pacifistic social workers, social gospel clergymen, socialists, feminists, publicists, and a smattering of eccentric or reform-minded businessmen who first joined the peace movement after 1914 helped to organize the new groups and gave their vigorous support to them. Julia Grace Wales, Lella Faye Secor, Rebecca Shelley, Emily Greene Balch, Lillian D. Wald, Crystal Eastman, Max Eastman, Amos Pinchot, Roger N. Baldwin, Henry Ford, and Paul U. Kellogg were among the newcomers who swelled the pacifist ranks during the neutrality years.

The story of the formation and the extensive activities of the new peace and internationalist groups during the two-and-a-half years of American neutrality goes far beyond this study. It is clear, however, that American advocates of peace could no longer accept uncritically the complacent assumptions that permeated the prewar peace movement. The World War threatened the very foundations of America's geographical isolation and the relaxed atmosphere in which Americans previously debated questions of foreign policy. With the limits of America's freedom of action narrowed, most friends of peace realized that they could not so easily afford the luxury of vague programs and imprecise thinking on world problems. Henceforth, they began to rethink their own programs, precisely define "peace," "justice," and "internationalism" and the priorities they gave to these words, and then work long and hard for whatever policies espoused.

Most important, they could no longer be so confident about their grand vision of an enlightened world order. The longer the human bloodbath continued in Europe, the more difficult it became for idealistic pacifists and internationalists to uphold the lofty values that had permeated the prewar American peace movement. Those who did not despair during American neutrality succumbed to disillusionment by the early 1920s. The massive human and material costs of the war, the rising tide of xenophobia during and following American belligerency, the defeat of the League of Nations, and the failure to make Europe safe for democracy could not sustain their superficial hopes for the regeneration of beneficent progress.[69]

In the short term, however, it was fortunate for them that Woodrow Wilson, who shared their ideological and historical assumptions on America's place in world affairs, lived in the White House in this trying period. When he finally decided that American intervention was necessary, his war message invoked the highest principles of democracy, freedom, and justice. During America's military effort in Europe, Wilson received full support from international lawyers, most of whom viewed American belligerency as a necessary price for vindication of international law from the onset of the European hostilities, as well as from other internationalists who wished to resist Germany's "aggression" and perceived American involvement in the war as a necessary requirement for realizing the establishment of an authoritative league of nations at the peace settlement. Wilson even won over almost all the more pacifistic people, who had participated in the peace cause before 1914. Most of them resisted full American belligerency but endorsed the conflict with varying degrees of enthusiasm after Congress voted overwhelmingly for war. They conceded that the President's motives were sincere and his purposes lofty, and they rationalized that war as a last resort to promote a liberal, anti-imperialistic postwar world order in place of "Prussianism," "militarism," and "autocracy" might be justified.[70] Only a few of those identified with the prewar peace movement, most notably Louis Lochner, Jane Addams, May Wright Sewall, John Haynes Holmes, Jenkin Lloyd Jones, Charles F. Dole, Anna Garlin Spencer, and Oswald and Fanny Garrison Villard, refused to support the war effort. Their principled opposition highlighted their alienation from their erstwhile cohorts.[71]

Disagreement over American belligerency constituted only a small part of the factionalism facing the peace forces. Deep fissures also persisted on questions of postwar order. Debate increasingly centered around the program of the League to Enforce Peace, the most influential private association devoted to international organization. The growth of the League to Enforce Peace was impressive. One reason for its popularity was the shock of war. The continuing violations of international law and the totality of the conflict convinced many nonpacifists that the pre-1914 emphasis on international law and nonenforceable sanctions had proven inadequate for the prevention of war and that new approaches to the problem of world order were necessary. That was the reasoning of Holt, Straus, Taft, and Marburg. All had leaned toward creation of more authoritative international institutions before the war but moved more decisively in that direction after the outbreak of the European conflict. The war even convinced a few international lawyers to endorse collective sanctions against aggressor states.[72]

The presence of many prominent names among the founders of the league gave the group establishment status and attracted the support of people who could see its potentially immense influence in the future. Moreover, the leaders' exclusive emphasis on compulsory hearing of disputes before hostilities could commence was easily understood and appealed at the outset to many pro–Allied Americans who firmly believed that Germany was the aggressor and that some such international enforcement agency would be needed to discipline future aggressive moves by that nation or other autocratic powers. When the League to Enforce Peace vigorously boosted the American war effort after 1917, it encouraged the view that the purpose of the organization was to discipline aggressors like Germany before they could succeed on the battlefield. American supporters of the league were mainly Anglophiles, who remained more nationalistic than internationalistic, and uncritically assumed that democracies like the United States and Great Britain were peace loving. They thus did not contemplate that their own nation's aggressions—in Latin America and Russia, for example—might result in the proposed international organization using its collective forces against such interventions. Far from a novel system of collective security, the leaders of the League to Enforce Peace really desired multinational machinery to sanction America's unilateral intervention to moderate and solve controversies among the European powers. The League to Enforce Peace's deliberate avoidance of details until governments had accepted the outlines of their program also initially attracted people who might have objected to specific features but could accept its general principles. The league's program, for example, said nothing about mutual guarantees and territorial integrity, disarmament, the composition of the judicial tribunal, and the definition of justiciable disputes.[73]

Another reason for the rapid growth of the League to Enforce Peace was the inactivity of the established prewar peace organizations. Fannie Andrews, Nasmyth, Lynch, Storey, and Lucia Mead (in roughly ascending order) were sympathetic to pacifism and joined or cooperated with new peace groups emphasizing neutral mediation, antipreparedness, and antiwar activities. Yet their pacifism was not absolute and they could not endorse the more radical and flamboyant peace activities during American neutrality such as the Ford peace ship. As hopes for mediation, antipreparedness, and avoidance of war faded during American neutrality, they came to view these goals as exercises in futility and began to look for a middle position between absolute pacifism and a militant world organization. They turned to the League to Enforce Peace, not because they particularly approved of the use of military force but because they were liberal activists by temperament who were looking for a peace program that was potentially realizable. Like Jordan, Mrs. Andrews had come to endorse the League to Enforce Peace through her close association with the Central Organization for a Durable Peace. When the peace societies offered little hope for success, these activists supported the prestigious League to Enforce Peace. Lynch and Andrews swung the Church Peace Union and American School Peace League behind the league. Other Eastern peace groups like the Massachusetts Peace Society and Pennsylvania Arbitration and Peace Society likewise endorsed the internationalist group after looking in vain for aggressive leadership from their parent body, the American Peace Society.[74]

The plank in the League to Enforce Peace's platform calling for automatic imposition of coercive sanctions against nations refusing to submit their disputes to conciliation also aroused prolonged controversy in peace circles. Although federalists assumed that the threat of force and an aroused public opinion would suffice to prevent the use of force in almost every case, some pacifistic Americans like Bryan and Villard continued to oppose any kind of compulsion as incompatible with their pacifist faith.[75] Legalists remained skeptical for somewhat different reasons. Fundamentally cautious in their approach to international reform, legalists worried about the possible abuses of collective power to maintain the peace. In consequence, they insisted upon adequate rules of law, a world court, and general agreement among the nations on the specific powers of the court as indispensable prerequisites to any forceful sanctions.

Legalists were of course well aware of the failure of nations to utilize the existing peace machinery in the days preceding the outbreak of the European war, and some attempted to grapple with the implications of this failure in developing their proposals for postwar world order. Of all the American lawyers, Elihu Root reflected perhaps most fully during the war years on possible new arrangements for preserving the peace. In many respects he emerged as a full-fledged internationalist. The war convinced him that a breach in the peace between two or more powers was not an isolated matter but concerned all nations. He believed that nations collectively should develop agreements on rules of moral responsibility for international conduct similar to those adopted in municipal law for individual conduct, and violations of international law should be treated both in theory and in practice as crimes affecting all nations. Fully accepting the interdependence of nations' rights and obligations, he favored the creation of a world court and an international council that would convene automatically during international crises. The object of those institutions would be to prevent the outbreak of war before discussion of the controversy. While the international council would discuss political disputes, the world court would assume jurisdiction over justiciable questions.[76]

Root corresponded during the war with Lord Bryce, who headed a British internationalist organization.[77] The Bryce group recognized the need to define justiciable questions and in 1915 thrashed out an article defining them as "disputes as to the interpretation of a treaty, as to any question of international law, as to the existence of any fact which, if established, would constitute a breach of any international obligation, or as to the nature and extent of the reparation to be made for any such breach."[78] Although that definition was not perfect, Root accepted it as a great improvement over descriptions of the word in his own and Taft's arbitration treaties. He even went one step further in favoring obligatory jurisdiction for the court in such cases.[79]

Root advocated firm guidelines to circumscribe the jurisdiction of the proposed world court, and even more did he oppose compulsory enforcement of court decisions and of recommendations of the international council. Always worried about the potential abuses of consolidated power, he also believed that the American people should not agree to commit its forces to conflicts in which the United States had only remote interests. Perhaps the United States might eventually undertake obligations to fight upon the occurrence of some specific event (such as a later German reinvasion of France), but for the immediate future he opposed automatic sanctions and preferred to allow the moral sense of each nation to decide upon the question of war after the failure of all peaceful methods.[80]

At first some moderate internationalists wanted to believe that the programs of the legalists and collective security advocates were not incompatible and attempted to unite the two. The similar upperclass social standing of the legalists and collective security advocates, their common support of the war, international institutions, and periodic conferences to codify international law, and their awareness of the political liabilities of open disunity in their ranks all stimulated efforts to reconcile their differences. The World's Court League specifically prohibited direct attacks upon the League to Enforce Peace and for a time even hoped to merge with the latter body.

Leaders of the two groups could not bridge their differences over sanctions, however, and those who had strong views on the subject of sanctions refused to remain silent. Between 1915 and 1918 conservative legalists were in the forefront of critics of the program of the League to Enforce Peace. They asserted that the ironclad enforcement of hearing of disputes unavoidably favored the status quo, which might be unjust and impractical in a changing world, claimed that automatic sanctions against violators of the League to Enforce Peace contradicted its avowed aim of avoiding war, and branded as unrealistic its belief that economic sanctions would suffice in checking transgressors. They also attacked the "unfounded supposition" that it was always possible to define the aggressor in a given war. Referring to the controversial origins of the Franco-Prussian War, John Bassett Moore remarked, "How Bismarck would have smiled at this naive assumption!"[81] And he added the American conflicts of 1812 and 1898 to his list of debatable war origins. Legalists also charged that in defining aggression as the failure to agree to conciliation before going to war, the League to Enforce Peace failed to consider the diverse geopolitical and military realities in disputes between small states and more powerful neighbors. They further argued that it was idealistic to believe that nations would suddenly abandon the pursuit of their national interests and feel bound to honor their treaty obligations. In their view, only several generations of education and experience would enable governments gradually to understand and respect their commitments with foreign states. Such criticisms were astute and collectively they probably influenced many Americans who were wrestling with the fundamental question of America's future involvement in a postwar international organization, but they also highlighted the legalists' marked resistance to approval of their nation's participation in any extensive attempts to make the world over.[82]

Even generalists like Tryon, Dutton, and Levermore criticized the possible limitations on national sovereignty contemplated by the League to Enforce Peace.[83] Dutton, so often a conciliator between factions in the prewar peace movement, publicly assailed the league, arguing that it would enmesh the United States "in the shifting, uncertain, explosive affairs of the Old World."[84] While he continued to hope that the League to Enforce Peace would deemphasize coercive sanctions and eventually merge with the World's Court League, his own criticisms of the league hindered the remote prospects for such cooperation. The war increasingly forced generalists to define their positions on peace questions. Just as more pacifistic liberals and generalists moved toward acceptance of collective security, so did their more conservative counterparts move step by step in the opposite direction. Dutton's criticism of the League to Enforce Peace merely confirmed his earlier abandonment of the World Peace Foundation for the World's Court League and his preference for the legally oriented Kirchwey for president of the American Peace Society.

The League to Enforce Peace also contributed to friction between the two groups. In order to prevent public confusion over their program, leaders of the League to Enforce Peace required their supporters to withdraw from the World's Court League and other peace and internationalist groups. Moreover, Theodore Marburg vigorously asserted that the judicialists' preoccupation with international law as the indispensable prerequisite for a peaceful world order was too idealistic. The development of international law was a very slow process, and many people were unwilling to wait. Further, he correctly pointed out that wars rarely developed over justiciable disputes so that their narrow emphasis on a world court really contributed little to the advancement of the cause of world peace. When Scott continued to attack the League to Enforce Peace, Marburg protested to President Wilson about his harmful influence on the movement for world organization.[85]

While the new internationalist organizations helped to encourage Woodrow Wilson's growing interest in the principles for a new world order after the war, none had sufficient influence to convert him to a specific formula. In view of the President's sympathy for the general objectives of the League to Enforce Peace, perhaps he should have consulted with its leaders in formulating his own ideas for the Paris Peace Conference. He might thus have gained the support of influential internationalists without sacrificing his freedom of action. He might have profited from discussions with these internationalists who had given considerable thought to the complexities of devising institutions that might be potentially workable for war prevention as well as acceptable to the Allies and American opinion.

His failure to do so at first is understandable, for he was preoccupied with immediate war issues and frequently intimated that he did not want to stir up acrimonious debate by endorsing prematurely any specific formula for international organization. There is also merit in his view that he had to remain somewhat flexible until he could consider the views of Allied statesmen at the Paris Peace Conference and work out the details of world organization with them.[86] However, his deliberate avoidance of its leaders, especially Taft who was the most prestigious spokesman of collective security in the Republican party, in the critical post–Armistice months was an early and important sign of his temperamental rigidity, egotism, and political partisanship, all of which unnecessarily exacerbated his difficulties in gaining Senate consent to the Treaty of Versailles, which embodied the Covenant of the League of Nations.

While conceding Wilson's personal failings, one can see in retrospect that the lack of harmony among American international reformers was not well calculated to impress on the President the wisdom of any peace program. This disunity among internationalists might have even helped to reinforce his enormous confidence in his own ability to galvanize liberals into support of his own vision of world order.

In any event, American internationalists did not have much influence on Wilson's ideas on world organization. Although he incorporated some features of the League to Enforce Peace program into his drafts of the Covenant, he ignored its distinction between justiciable and nonjusticiable disputes and its provisions for regular conferences to codify international law and for a judicial body. He did not give an explicit endorsement to any group promoting world organization and showed no interest in cultivating the support of American internationalists.[87] He disparagingly spoke in private of leaders of the League to Enforce Peace as "butters-in" and "woolgatherers"[88] and singled out the judicially oriented Nicholas Murray Butler for special censure. "What he has to say about him," House noted in his diary, "I will not repeat, for I am sure he does him an injustice."[89]

Wilson's prejudices against the law profession in general and conservative lawyers in particular resulted in his opposition to establishment of a world court, which all American internationalists accepted, and he only reluctantly deferred to British insistence on inclusion of an article in the Covenant calling for establishment of the Permanent Court of International Justice. Moreover, other articles in the Covenant, which embodied his ideas on international institutions, called for an authoritative world organization with such potentially extensive powers that almost all American internationalists, including a majority of the leadership of the League to Enforce Peace, refused to endorse them without serious qualifications.[90]

Wilson's program for international organization thus failed to receive the loyal support of a large majority of peace leaders once they began to consider the specific features of the proposed League of Nations. In light of mounting congressional frustration over executive leadership during the war and the absence of any tradition of bipartisan foreign policy, it is probable that senators' concern over prerogatives, politics, and personality conflicts would have sufficed to defeat the Treaty of Versailles, just as they had previously frustrated proponents of the Olney-Pauncefote and Taft arbitration treaties. Even more than the defeats of those earlier, more limited international accords, the fundamental reason for the defeat of the League of Nations was ideological. Wilson's quest for American membership in the League of Nations encountered the inevitable opposition of ultranationalists and inflexible pacifists and isolationists, but he failed to receive the endorsement of conservative international lawyers and many moderate internationalists as well. With the roots of President Wilson's support thus narrowed, the defeat of American membership in the League of Nations became a virtual certainty.[91]

Conclusion

DIVERSITY CHARACTERIZED the American peace movement in the generation before the First World War. "Peace" was "in the eye of the beholder,"[1] and the movement remained divided between imperialists and anti-imperialists, legalists and federalists, and interventionists and noninterventionists. Divisions in any social movement are inevitable, but the various factions of the American peace movement rarely coalesced for very long before 1914 on any peace issue. Even the consensus among peace workers on the desirability of arbitration treaties and a world court, the most modest objectives of the peace movement, was fragile. Agreement on arbitration treaties disintegrated when peace advocates were forced to interpret their scope and meaning to a suspicious Senate, and to an increasing number of international reformers the onset of the First World War dramatized the inadequacy of a world court.

Despite divergences, the American peace movement from 1887 to 1914 reveals a broad pattern of development. A consistent thread running through the movement was idealism, but there was a definite trend from noninstitutional pacifism to institutional internationalism. It was not that individual peace advocates changed in these years; indeed, despite some shifts in emphasis their ideas on and approaches to the problems of war and peace remained remarkably consistent throughout this period, but the growing number of newcomers to the movement markedly influenced its direction.

In retrospect, the shift becomes noticeable during the first decade of the twentieth century. Before about 1900 religious pacifists, Garrisonian and Tolstoyan nonresistants, free trade liberals, and women reformers brought a utopian and anti-establishment dimension to the peace movement. Emphasizing the autonomy of the individual above organizational restraints, they developed highly personal and relatively simple blueprints for a peaceful world. They also took a broad view of reform, with peace as one important ideal inextricably linked with the larger goal of a morally pure society. They participated in loosely organized peace and arbitration groups on the local and regional level like the Universal Peace Union, American Peace Society, and Lake Mohonk Conferences. Superficial agreement developed during the movement for an Anglo-American arbitration treaty that culminated in the abortive Olney-Pauncefote accord in 1897, but dissolved under the pressures of the Spanish-American War and

256

imperialism between 1898 and 1900. Several peace workers reached back to the Christian pacifist, antislavery, or British Liberal anti-imperialist heritages to champion freedom and self-determination of the Filipinos; but just as many participants in the movement responded with confused voices or readily accepted America's expanded interests as a colonial power.

Anti-imperialism and antimilitarism remained concerns of the peace movement after 1900, but old age and deaths made their impact increasingly subdued. Though arbitration and conciliation treaties also remained prime goals, they were supplemented after about 1900 by interest in the creation of permanent international institutions. International lawyers and other moderate internationalists especially championed periodic congresses as the indispensable prerequisite for discussions leading to creation of a world court. Legalists believed in the legal equality of sovereign states, though as extremely cautious reformers they tolerated the inequality of power among them until regular international conferences could formulate a code of laws that all nations would accept. A few world federalists in the same decade or so before the First World War began to develop more elaborate formulas for world organization.

Changes in both domestic and foreign politics directly influenced the course of the peace movement. Domestically, the urban-industrial transformation markedly increased the complexity of the American social order. American social thought underwent a shift in emphasis from moral absolutes to specialized, utilitarian knowledge, from direct democracy to intervening bureaucratic forms, and from ethical purity to efficiency. The change was very gradual, however, and the onset of the progressive reform movement after about 1900 witnessed a revival of idealistic values, which in turn were joined with bureaucratic ones.[2] Moreover, just as many progressive reformers turned to local, state, and federal governments to wrestle with the increasingly complex problems of a pluralistic, urban society, so did participants in the peace movement begin to contemplate the establishment of international institutions for prevention of war. With a few exceptions, however, those gravitating to the peace movement after 1900 were politically conservative or middle-of-the-road, and they opposed or remained skeptical about the potential benefits of going beyond the establishment of a permanent court without positive sanctions in the area of world organization. Many of those participants in fact valued the peace movement because it served as a socially respectable outlet for their mildly reformist inclinations. Generalists joining the peace movement after the turn of the century reflected that ambivalence. While receptive to new and larger organizational efforts, they simultaneously attempted to reassert traditional morality in an increasingly utilitarian society.

America's emergence as a world power reinforced the tendency toward sophisticated and eclectic analyses of America's changing role in a more interdependent world. Many peace advocates in the decade before the outbreak of the First World War perceived the complexity of world politics and attempted to reconcile their idealistic hopes with international realities. Garrisonian, Tolstoyan, and Christian notions of the universal relevance of nonresistant pacifism gradually gave way to acceptance of great powers' primacy in world affairs and the search for permanent institutional arrangements to resolve future disputes among the "civilized" powers. Almost all peace advocates eschewed world government but attempted to balance their acceptance of national sovereignty with the need for some multilateral framework for the peaceful settlement of international disputes. In the same way, notions of moral men overseeing a peace loving commonwealth were increasingly supplemented by more detached, "scientific" experts who could administer international institutions in an objective, impartial manner.

The elitism of peace advocates constituted a salient characteristic of the peace movement. The elitism of active and dedicated peace workers before about 1900 was assumed and compatible with human values, but allowed them to tolerate and in some cases even welcome to the movement those whose elitist predelictions were more often conscious and arrogant. The rich and powerful increasingly penetrated the hierarchies of the established peace groups and foundations. In consequence, despite its growth the peace movement never developed meaningful contacts with movements for social and political change. Indeed, once conservatives succeeded in organizing the Carnegie Endowment, they used its enormous financial resources to control the peace societies and effectively stifle the last shreds of their independence.

The rhetoric of the peace movement reflected that elitism. While it had always been lofty in tone, it became less warmly humanistic and more coldly intellectual.[3] Reliance on the scientific administrator—whether the dispassionate research scholars in the great peace foundations, the impartial judges of a world court, the informed experts of an international legislature, or a morally perfect international executive—subtly deemphasized the earlier humanitarian thrust and introduced a mechanistic note into the movement for world organization. But because there were no compelling pressures for peace workers to specify in detail the actual workings of the international machinery for war prevention before 1914, their thinking remained fuzzy. They assumed that a rational public shared their views and would easily accept, if not openly endorse, their quest for establishment of a new international order.[4]

When peace advocates were forced to define the powers and procedures of their proposed international institutions during the World War, however, the differences between legalists and other conservative internationalists, on the one hand, and federalists and other more reform-minded peace workers, on the other, quickly became apparent. A peace movement divided over the authority of international institutions could hardly expect to convince large numbers of Americans to support any one blueprint for world order. Peace workers' elitism would have restricted their impact on the American people in any case, but their divisions served to intensify public confusion and make citizens outside the movement more susceptible to partisan and emotional appeals in the ensuing debate over Woodrow Wilson's League of Nations.

The pressures of the World War brought to the surface other internal weaknesses. The failure of peace workers was not their inability to prevent the European bloodbath that was beyond their control. Neither can they be faulted for their idealistic faith in man's ability to overcome national prejudices. One failing, however, was their uncritical assumption of the ease and speed of that triumph in international life. Their assumptions about world politics were too shallow and optimistic. Surely they placed too much faith in the rationality of man, were too confident in their reliance on religious and moral education, overestimated the applicability of American values and institutions, and underestimated the importance of national self-interest and power in international relations. Even anti-imperialists in the American peace movement at the turn of the century were not consistently skeptical of the menace of their nation's messianic interventionism in the affairs of weaker foreign states. Legalists on the whole were aware of that danger but were too fundamentally conservative and nationalistic to urge immediate institutional or behavioral changes that might have helped overcome this reality.

Further, the thought of peace workers was too optimistically deterministic. Specifically, in emphasizing inevitable progress, peace leaders tolerated the status quo in international life while still holding out hope for gradual evolution toward a peaceful world order. Such talk tended to gloss over the real and menacing international problems of their day. In particular, while disliking excessive nationalism, they did not submit it to trenchant critiques. The few who criticized the military and armament makers failed to probe deeply into the national and imperial rivalries that fostered the arms race. They were in fact too much a part of the established social order to advance any well-developed theoretical criticisms of it. Moreover, if all peace advocates disagreed with the ultranationalists' emphasis on national power and prestige as legitimate ends of foreign policy, many expressed a sense of mission that they could invoke to justify the forceful application of American ideals of peace, freedom, and justice on an aberrant Europe. As the pressures for American involvement in the European conflict increased, only the few most principled pacifists consistently resisted the temptation to approve military intervention as a prerequisite for obtaining an American version of international order.

Judgments on the peace movement, however, should be placed in proper historical perspective. Imperialism and nationalism predominated as respectable ideologies throughout the Western world, and it would have required extraordinary personal courage on the part of peace leaders and their unswerving devotion to their own visions of world order to escape entirely the infection of these pervasive values. Nor can they be blamed for the streak of messianic interventionism in the American psyche that consistently inhibited the spread of genuinely pacifist or internationalist sentiments and quickly suffocated them during wartime. It is also charitable to recall that they lived in an age removed from the intense ideological conflicts and cataclysmic wars of post-1914 generations. Theirs was a confident era when all kinds of reform really seemed possible. In view of that hopeful mood in American domestic life and Americans' inexperience in world affairs, it is understandable why peace workers often made strained analogies between their nation's values and institutions and international reform. Since there was no large munitions industry before the First World War, it is also understandable why the "merchants of death" theme received only sporadic attention. Even as late as the 1930s the revelations of the Nye Committee would fail to develop a comprehensive exposé of the lineaments of military and business cooperation that would provide much of the foundation for the military-industrial complex in our own day.[5]

Furthermore, only a few pacifists were radical enough to be dismissed as eccentrics by the American public; the overwhelming majority of peace advocates represented part of a larger, cultural elite that assumed moral progress and thought in abstract, if not idealistic terms. If one insists upon moral judgments in history, then it is better to view the peace movement within the broader context of the inadequacies of that entire culture. In light of their assumption of inevitable progress, there seemed to be no pressing need to complete their rather abstract theories on world organization with the intricate administrative and bureaucratic mechanisms for peacekeeping until the First World War dramatized both the inadequacy of the old diplomacy and the opportunities for American leadership in forging new international institutions for war prevention. Finally, it is charitable to remember that neither governments nor peace workers in later generations have succeeded in exalting humane values and perfecting workable peace machinery in the elusive quest for a warless world.[6]

Abbreviations

Listed below are the abbreviations used in the notes:

ACIA 1896 The American Conference on International Arbitration, Held in Washington, D.C., April 22 and 23, 1896 (New York: Baker & Taylor Co., n.d.)

ACIA 1904 The Second American Conference on International Arbitration, Held in Washington, D.C., January 12, 1904 (Washington, D.C.: Gibson Bros., 1904)

AFPC The American Friends' Peace Conference, Held at Philadelphia, Twelfth Month 12th, 13th, and 14th, 1901 (Philadelphia: Ferris & Leach, 1902)

AJIL American Journal of International Law

AJP American Journal of Politics

AMC American Magazine of Civics

AP Advocate of Peace

APC 1911 Proceedings of the Third American Peace Congress, Held in Baltimore, Maryland, May 3 to 6, 1911, ed. Eugene A. Noble (Baltimore: The Waverly Press, 1911)

APC 1913 Book of the Fourth American Peace Congress, St. Louis, May 1, 2, 3, 1913, ed. Walter B. Stevens (St. Louis: n.p., 1913)

APS American Peace Society

APS (year) *... Annual Report of the Directors of the American Peace Society, 1910–1917* (n.p.: American Peace Society 1910–1917)

ASIL (year) *Proceedings of the American Society of International Law, at Its ... Annual Meeting, Held at Washington, D.C., 1907–1920* (New York: American Society of International Law, 1908–1920)

ASJSID (year) *Proceedings of the American Society for Judicial Settlement of International Disputes, 1910–1916* (various cities: n.p., 1911–1917)

ASPL (year) *... Annual Report of the American School Peace League* (Boston: n.p., 1909–1917)

CEIP Carnegie Endowment for International Peace

CEIP (year) *Carnegie Endowment for International Peace, Year Book for 1911–1918* (Washington, D.C.: Carnegie Endowment for International Peace, 1912–1919)

CPS Chicago Peace Society

CPS (year) *Chicago Peace Society, Report, 1910–1917* (Chicago: Chicago Peace Society, 1911–1917)

CR   Congressional Record

FR (year)   *Papers Relating to the Foreign Relations of the United States, 1887–1914* (Washington, D.C., 1888–1915)

HI   Hoover Institution on War, Revolution, and Peace

IPB   International Peace Bureau

JPC   David Starr Jordan Peace Correspondence

JPSC   David Starr Jordan Papers, Supplementary Correspondence

LC   Library of Congress

LMC (year)   *Report of the . . . Annual Meeting of the Lake Mohonk Conference on International Arbitration, 1895–1916* (n.p.: Lake Mohonk Conference on International Arbitration, 1895–1916)

MHS   Massachusetts Historical Society

NA   National Archives

NAPC 1907   Proceedings of the National Arbitration and Peace Congress, New York, April 14th to 17th, 1907, ed. Robert Erskine Ely (New York: n.p., 1907)

NAR   North American Review

NEAIL (year)   *Report of the . . . Annual New England Anti-Imperialist League, 1899–1914* (n.p.: n.p., 1899–1914)

NEAPC 1910   Report of the Proceedings of the New England Arbitration and Peace Congress, Hartford and New Britain, May 8 to 11, 1910, ed. James L. Tryon (Boston: American Peace Society, 1910)

NEM   New England Magazine

NPC 1909   Proceedings of the Second National Peace Congress, Chicago, May 2 to 5, 1909, ed. Charles E. Beals (Chicago: Peterson Linotype Company, 1909)

NYPS   New York Peace Society

NYPS (year)   *Yearbook of the New York Peace Society, 1907–1919* (New York: n.p., 1907–1919)

NYSBA (year)   *Proceedings of the New York State Bar Association . . . Annual Meeting. Held at . . .* (various cities: n.p., 1878–   )

PAPC 1908   Official Report of the Proceedings of the Pennsylvania Arbitration and Peace Conference, Held in Philadelphia, May 16, 17, 18, and 19, 1908 (Philadelphia: Ferris & Leach, 1908)

SCPC   Swarthmore College Peace Collection

Sen. Doc. No. (number)   *Senate Document No.*

Sen. Misc. Doc. (number)   *Senate Miscellaneous Document*

UNL   United Nations Library, Geneva

UPC (year)   *Official Report of the . . . Universal Peace Congress, Held at . . ., 1889–1913* (various cities: various publishers, 1889–1913)

WPF   World Peace Foundation

Notes

Preface

1. See the analysis by Manfred Jonas in "Internationalism as a Current in the Peace Movement: A Symposium," *Peace Movements in America,* ed. Charles Chatfield (New York: Schocken Books, 1973), pp. 176-177.

2. *Ibid.* Two standard works on American peace movements after 1914 are Charles Chatfield, *For Peace and Justice: Pacifism in America, 1914–1941* (Knoxville: University of Tennessee Press, 1971); and Lawrence Wittner, *Rebels Against War: The American Peace Movement, 1941–1960* (New York: Columbia University Press, 1969).

3. Warren F. Kuehl, *Seeking World Order: The United States and International Organization to 1920* (Nashville: Vanderbilt University Press, 1968).

4. On the problem of defining "internationalist" (and indirectly the other words as well), see the discussion by Sondra Herman, Manfred Jonas, Robert A. Divine, Walter LaFeber, Richard D. McKinzie and Theodore A. Wilson in "Internationalism as a Current in the Peace Movement," pp. 171-191.

5. Michael Arnold Lutzker, "The 'Practical' Peace Advocates: An Interpretation of the American Peace Movement, 1898–1917" (Ph.D. Dissertation, Rutgers University, 1969); and C. Roland Marchand, *The American Peace Movement and Social Reform, 1898–1918* (Princeton, N.J.: Princeton University Press, 1972).

Chapter 1

1. Richard Hofstadter, "Manifest Destiny and the Philippines," in *America in Crisis: Fourteen Crucial Episodes in American History,* ed. Daniel Aaron (New York: Alfred A. Knopf, 1952), pp. 173-200.

2. *AP,* LXV (June, 1905), p. 120.

3. Merle Curti, *The American Peace Crusade, 1815–1860* (Durham, N.C.: Duke University Press, 1929), pp. 88-95, 122-123, 166-188, 194-200; Merle Curti, *Peace or War: The American Struggle, 1636–1936* (New York: W. W. Norton & Co., 1936), pp. 75-76, 143; Edson L. Whitney, *The American Peace Society: A Centennial History* (Washington, D.C.: The American Peace Society, 1928), pp. 123-124, 129, 148-153, 317-318. *AP,* LV (June, 1893), p. 125.

4. Robert Wesley Doherty, "Alfred H. Love and the Universal Peace Union" (Ph.D. Dissertation, University of Pennsylvania, 1962), pp. 39-43, 59, 66-69, 96-98, 102-105; Curti, *Peace or War,* pp. 76-80; Peter Brock, *Pacifism*

in the United States: From the Colonial Era to the First World War (Princeton, N.J.: Princeton University Press, 1968), pp. 924-929; Jessie Ackermann, "The Universal Peace Union," *Madame,* I (March, 1904), pp. 175, 201. For Love's antimilitarism, see his articles, "Military Instruction in Schools, Colleges, and Churches," *AJP,* V (August, 1894), pp. 205-211; and "The Modern Peace Movement," *ibid.,* I (December, 1892), pp. 607-621.

5. The journal began with the title *Bond of Peace* in 1868, changed its name to *Voice of Peace* in 1874, and finally to *Peacemaker* in 1882. To avoid possible confusion, only the last title appears in the text.

6. Doherty, "Love," pp. 66-67, 78-87.

7. *Peacemaker,* XI (May, 1893), pp. 201-202; Ackermann, "Universal Peace Union," pp. 175, 201; Curti, *Peace or War,* pp. 79-80.

8. In the latter year Love was nominated for the vice-presidency of the same party, and though declining the nomination because of its conflict with his no-government principles, his name was not removed from all the ballots by election day. Doherty, "Love," pp. 92-93, 139-141. For Mott's pacifist activities, see Otelia Cromwell, *Lucretia Mott* (Cambridge, Mass.: Harvard University Press, 1958), pp. 1, 174, 179-183, 189-191, 196, 202-206.

9. Curti, *Peace or War,* p. 116. For Mrs. Lockwood's antimilitarism and pacifism, see her essays, "How Shall the Columbian Exposition be Opened?" *AJP,* I (July, 1892), pp. 44-47; and "The Growth of Peace Principles, and the Methods of Propagating Them," *AMC,* VI (May, 1895), pp. 504-515. Lobbying of the National Arbitration League appears in *Sen. Doc. No. 140,* 54th Cong., 1st sess., pp. 1-2; and Love to Emily Howland, May 23, 1882, with printed enclosure, Emily Howland Papers (Cornell University Libraries), Box 3.

10. Lockwood to Cleveland, September 28, 1885, Grover Cleveland Papers (LC, on microfilm), Reel 20.

11. Hubbard in *UPC 1893,* pp. 67-68; Whitney, *American Peace Society,* p. 117; Amos Arnold Hovey, "A History of the Religious Phase of the American Movement for International Peace to the Year 1914" (Ph.D. Dissertation, University of Chicago, 1930), pp. 178-183.

12. Irwin Abrams, "The Emergence of the International Law Societies," *Review of Politics,* XIX (July, 1957), pp. 361-380; Curti, *Peace or War,* pp. 97-101.

13. *Ibid.;* Abrams, "International Law Societies," pp. 377-380; Whitney, pp. 126-135.

14. *Voice of Peace,* I (August, 1874), pp. 73-74.

15. *CR,* 43rd Cong., 1st sess., II, pp. 5114, 5124, 5407. The quotation appears in *Parliamentary Debates,* 3rd ser., CCXVII, cols. 52-90.

16. Curti, *Peace or War,* pp. 102-103, 174, 176.

17. Benjamin F. Trueblood to Robert Treat Paine, January 16, 1894, Robert Treat Paine Papers (MHS), Box 2.

18. Curti, *Peace or War,* p. 81.

19. Doherty, "Love," pp. 155, 156; *AP,* LVIII (December, 1896), p. 266. The year of birth of six of the twenty-three directors could not be determined

and were not included in computing the average age. The median age of the seventeen was fifty-eight.

20. Doherty, "Love," p. 156; Whitney, *American Peace Society,* pp. 141-142; Hovey, "History of the Religious Phase," pp. 185-186.

21. Curti, *American Peace Crusade,* pp. 218-223; George M. Fredrickson, *The Inner Civil War: Northern Intellectuals and the Crisis of the Union* (New York: Harper & Row, 1966), pp. 41-44, 56-58, 61-64; Brock, *Pacifism in the United States,* pp. 667-712.

22. Curti, *Peace or War,* pp. 51-53, 91-93, 111, 115-116; Edward Everett Hale, "The United States of Europe," *Old and New,* III (March, 1871), pp. 260-267; A.C.F. Beales, *The History of Peace: A Short Account of the Organised Movements for International Peace* (New York: The Dial Press, 1931), pp. 136, 174, 186, 195-196; Tobey to Harrison, January 24, 1889, Benjamin Harrison Papers (LC, on microfilm), Reel 62.

23. Many peace participants, for example, were simultaneously involved with Quakers, women, and other moral reformers in a broad-based crusade against prostitution and, more generally, for the purification of domestic society. See David J. Pivar, *Purity Crusade: Sexual Morality and Social Control, 1868–1900* (Westport, Conn.: Greenwood Press, 1973); and especially compare Pivar's lists of the members of the executive board of the American Purity Alliance in 1895 and the organizations represented on the executive board of the American Purity Alliance (pp. 281-285) with the individuals and groups allied with the American peace movement in the following chapters of the present study.

24. Thomas A. Bailey, *A Diplomatic History of the American People,* 4th ed. (New York: Appleton-Century-Crofts, 1955), ch. 26; David M. Pletcher, *The Awkward Years: American Foreign Relations under Garfield and Arthur* (Columbia: University of Missouri Press, 1963). Bailey omitted the word "nadir" from the chapter titles of later editions of his textbook, but if public interest is a measure of a nation's diplomatic history, particularly in comparison with earlier and later periods, the word is still an accurate one.

25. Brock, *Pacifism in the United States,* pp. 879-883.

26. Information on the free trade associations of pacifistic Bostonians is derived from a close perusal of the *Boston Globe* for the years 1895 to 1900 and various biographical directories and secondary works.

27. Curti, *Peace or War,* p. 130.

28. For peace workers' reservations on sanctions, see *AP,* LIV (November, 1892), p. 186; LV (March, 1893), p. 58; LVIII (April, 1896), p. 78; Beales, *History of Peace,* pp. 122, 136, 138, 142, 150, 171, 222-223, 225.

Chapter 2

1. Charles S. Campbell, *Anglo-American Understanding, 1898–1903* (Baltimore: The Johns Hopkins Press, 1957), pp. 1-3; R. G. Neale, *Great Britain and United States Expansion, 1898–1900* (Lansing: Michigan State University Press, 1966), pp. 157-161, 214.

2. A. M. Stuyt, *Survey of International Arbitrations, 1794–1938* (The

Hague: Martinus Nijhoff, 1939), pp. 3-160. Slightly different totals are given in John Bassett Moore, *ACIA 1896*, pp. 195-199.

3. Bright to Augustine Jones (Boston area Quaker), March 10, 1884, *The Public Letters of the Right Hon. John Bright*, ed. H. J. Leech (London: Sampson Low, Marston & Company, 1895), p. 172.

4. *AP*, LV (November, 1893), pp. 252-253; (December, 1893), pp. 276-277; Campbell, *Anglo-American Understanding*, pp. 8-9.

5. With the possible exception of the Universal Peace Union, which valued its contacts with pacifists on the European continent, almost all American peace advocates worked primarily for British-American friendship. The French Chamber of Deputies passed resolutions endorsing a Franco-American arbitration treaty in 1888 and 1895, but these actions did not detract attention from the movement for an Anglo-American accord. J. B. Wood (Philadelphia Quaker) to Cleveland, May 12, 1887, Grover Cleveland Papers (LC, on microfilm), Reel 48; Love to Cleveland, November 22, 1895, and Lockwood to Cleveland, November 25, 1895, *ibid.*, Reel 91; *Sen. Doc. No. 140*, 54th Cong., 1st sess., p. 2.

6. *Arbitrator*, No. 183 (May, 1887), p. 1; No. 184 (June, 1887), p. 2. *Arbitrator* was the journal of the British International Arbitration League; Cremer, the league's secretary, was the main leader.

7. The quotations appear in *Autobiography of Andrew Carnegie* (Boston: Houghton Mifflin Co., 1920), pp. 282-283, 339; also see Burton J. Hendrick, *The Life of Andrew Carnegie*, 2 vols. (New York: Doubleday, Doran & Co., 1932), I, pp. 24, 238-239. Carnegie's early involvement in peace activity is derived from my article, "Andrew Carnegie's Quest for World Peace," *Proceedings of the American Philosophical Society*, CXIV (October 20, 1970), pp. 371-373.

8. Andrew Carnegie, *Triumphant Democracy, or Fifty Years' March of the Republic* (New York: Charles Scribner's Sons, 1886), p. 23; Andrew Carnegie, "Americanism Versus Imperialism," *NAR*, CLXVII (January, 1899), p. 6. Joseph Frazier Wall, *Andrew Carnegie* (New York: Oxford University Press, 1970), pp. 96-100, 130-132, 423ff. For Carnegie's confidence in Gladstone's support for an Anglo-American treaty, see Carnegie to Gladstone, June 29, September 16, 1887, Andrew Carnegie Papers (LC), Vol. 10.

9. Carnegie to W. C. Whitney, August 31, 1887, enclosing Joseph Chamberlain to Carnegie, August 22, 1887, Cleveland Papers, Reel 115; Andrew Carnegie, "The Venezuelan Question," *NAR*, CLXII (February, 1896), p. 144.

10. William Jones to George W. Childs, September 20, 1887, Cleveland Papers, Reel 53; *Peacemaker*, VI (December, 1887), pp. 101-102.

11. Alfred H. Love Diary, October 31, 1887, Universal Peace Union Papers (SCPC). William Jones, Andrew Carnegie, Rowland B. Howard, Philip C. Garrett, and perhaps one or two others joined the British delegation for this interview.

12. *Arbitrator*, Nos. 189-192 (November, December 1887, January, February, 1888), pp. 8-11; Garrett in *LMC 1895*, p. 37. Cleveland apparently

failed to acknowledge the arbitrationists' letters to him. J. B. Wood to Daniel S. Lamont, November 17, 24, 1887, Cleveland Papers, Reel 54. For the impact of politics on foreign policy questions, see Allen Lawrence Burnette, Jr., "The Senate Foreign Relations Committee and the Diplomacy of Garfield, Arthur, and Cleveland" (Ph.D. Dissertation, University of Virginia, 1952), especially pp. 388ff.

13. *Arbitrator,* Nos. 189-192, pp. 11-30; quotations are in *ibid.,* pp. 27, 28, 29, 30. Love Diary, November 4, 5, December 9, 1887.

14. *Arbitrator,* Nos. 189-192, pp. 12-13; *CR,* 50th Cong., 1st sess., XIX, pp. 17, 25, 2796.

15. Gompers, "Let Us Have Peace," *American Federationist,* III (February, 1897), pp. 259-260; Tobey and Howard to Cleveland, October 17, 1887, Cleveland Papers, Reel 53; Edwin Mead to Lamont, January 22, 1888, *ibid.,* Reel 119; David Dudley Field, Andrew Carnegie, Morris K. Jesup, Charles A. Peabody, Dorman B. Eaton, and Abram S. Hewitt, *Memorial to Congress in Favor of Arbitration for the Settlement of International Disputes,* printed copy in IPB Papers (UNL); *Arbitrator,* Nos. 189-192, p. 2; No. 193, pp. 1-2. *Sen. Misc. Doc. 141,* 50th Cong., 1st sess., pp. 18-19, 26-36; *CR,* 50th Cong., 1st sess., XIX, p. 6958.

16. David Dudley Field, *et al., Memorial to Congress,* p. 3.

17. *CR,* 50th Cong., 1st sess., XIX, pp. 5196, 5239.

18. *Ibid.,* 51st Cong., 1st sess., XXI, pp. 581, 1325, 2986.

19. For background to the Pan American Conference, see A. Curtis Wilgus, "James G. Blaine and the Pan American Movement," *Hispanic American Historical Review,* V (November, 1922), pp. 687-691; and Edson L. Whitney, *The American Peace Society: A Centennial History* (Washington, D.C.: The American Peace Society, 1928), pp. 154-156.

20. James G. Blaine, *Political Discussions: Legislative, Diplomatic, and Popular, 1856–1886* (Norwich, Conn.: The Henry Bill Publishing Co., 1887), pp. 403-406, 411; *International American Conference, Reports of Committees and Discussions Thereon,* 4 vols. (Washington, D.C.: Government Printing Office, 1890), II, p. 1167.

21. *Ibid.,* II, pp. 1110-1111, 1145-1146.

22. *CR,* 51st Cong., 1st sess., XXI, pp. 9852, 9635. Harrison's remark is reproduced in British Parliamentary Papers, *United States of America,* 60 vols. (Shannon: Irish University Press, 1971), LX, pp. 888-889.

23. Fredrick B. Pike, *Chile and the United States, 1880–1962: The Emergence of Chile's Social Crisis and the Challenge to United States Diplomacy* (Notre Dame, Ind.: University of Notre Dame Press, 1963), pp. 62-85; Thomas F. McGann, *Argentina, the United States and the Inter-American System, 1880–1914* (Cambridge, Mass.: Harvard University Press, 1957), pp. 145-158; *The International Conference of American States, 1889–1928,* ed. James Brown Scott (New York: Oxford University Press, 1931), pp. 40n4-41; *AP,* LV (April, 1893), pp. 87-88; British Parliamentary Papers, *United States of America,* LX, pp. 882-888.

24. Carnegie to Harrison, telegram, October 26, 1891, Carnegie Papers, Vol. 13; Pike, *Chile and the United States,* pp. 76-80.

25. "Editor's Table," *NEM,* VI (March, 1892), pp. 134-136.

26. As late as 1892 there were only eleven state and regional peace societies, excluding branches, in the United States. *AP,* LV (January, 1893), p. 23. *Peacemaker,* XII (October, 1893), facing p. 61, lists thirty-five local, state, and regional societies, excluding branches.

27. Quoted by Hannah W. Blackburn in *AP,* LX (June, 1898), p. 142.

28. Typescript copy of *Union Signal,* June 1, 1893, Hannah J. Bailey Papers (SCPC), Box 1; Bailey Diary, November 4, 1889, *ibid.,* Box 5; Mary Earhart, *Frances Willard: From Prayers to Politics* (Chicago: University of Chicago Press, 1944), pp. 260-262.

29. A good biographical sketch of Mrs. Bailey appears in *Peacemaker,* XVI (May, 1898), pp. 205-206.

30. Quoted in *AP,* LVII (April, 1895), p. 80.

31. Earhart, *Willard,* pp. 263-265; *Peacemaker,* VII (December, 1888), pp. 108-109.

32. *AP,* LIV (September, 1892), p. 132; *Christian Arbitrator and Messenger of Peace,* XXIII (November, 1893), p. 175; Bailey in *LMC 1895,* p. 67; Amos Arnold Hovey, "A History of the Religious Phase of the American Movement for International Peace to 1914" (Ph.D. Dissertation: University of Chicago, 1930), pp. 187-191.

33. Quoted in Earhart, *Willard,* p. 263.

34. *Ibid.,* pp. 265-268; Sewall in *AP,* LXXII (March, 1910), p. 65; *Peacemaker,* VIII (August, 1889), p. 38; XIII (January, 1895), pp. 122-123; (March, 1895), p. 176; (April, 1895), pp. 189-193; XV (February, 1897), pp. 158-159; "National Council of Women," *Woman's Journal,* XXVI (February 2, 1895), p. 36; "The National Council of Women," *ibid.,* XXVIII (October 16, 1897), p. 333. *Genesis of the International Council of Women and the Story of its Growth, 1889–1893,* ed. May Wright Sewall (Indianapolis: n.p., 1914), *passim.*

35. A.C.F. Beales, *The History of Peace: A Short Account of the Organised Movement for International Peace* (New York: The Dial Press, 1931), pp. 66-67, 154-158, 191; *UPC 1889,* pp. 4, 5, 15, 16, 18, 21, 22. Merze Tate, *The Disarmament Illusion: The Movement for a Limitation of Armaments to 1907* (New York: The Macmillan Company, 1942), ch. 3, summarizes the early Universal Peace Congresses. *Peacemaker,* XXIII (September, 1904), pp. 205-207.

36. *AP,* LIX (April, 1897), p. 84.

37. Trueblood to his wife, October 19, 29, 1890, May 19, 1891, APS Papers, Box 17; Charles E. Beals, *Benjamin F. Trueblood—Prophet of Peace* (New York: Religious Society of Friends, n.d.), pp. 1-9.

38. *AP,* LIV (June, 1892), pp. 66-67; (November, 1892), pp. 188-189; (December, 1892), pp. 210-211; LV (February, 1893), pp. 31-32; (April, 1893), p. 87.

39. Edwin Mead, introduction to Benjamin F. Trueblood, *The Development of the Peace Idea, and Other Essays* (Boston: Plimpton Press, 1932), p. xxii.

40. *Parliamentary Debates,* 4th ser., XIII (June 16, 1893), cols. 1240-1273.

41. *FR 1893,* p. 346. Paine and Trueblood had at least one more "brief, but satisfactory interview" with Gresham shortly after the President's annual message of December 1893. Paine in *LMC 1895,* pp. 35-36.

42. *FR 1893,* p. 352; *A Compilation of the Messages and Papers of the Presidents,* ed. James D. Richardson, 20 vols. (New York: Bureau of National Literature, 1897–1917), XII, p. 5874. Josiah W. Leeds (Pennsylvania Quaker) to Cleveland, December 6, 1893, and Paine to Cleveland, December 9, 1893, Cleveland Papers, Reel 81.

43. *CR,* 53rd Cong., 2nd sess., XXVI, pp. 5693, 6551.

44. Paine in *LMC 1895,* pp. 35-36; *AP,* LVII (April, 1895), p. 84.

45. *Arbitrator,* Nos. 276-277 (February and March, 1895), pp. 16-20.

46. *Ibid.,* pp. 16-17. Also see Gresham, letter dated December 31, 1894, cited in *The Nation,* LXVII (February 13, 1896), p. 133.

47. *CR,* 53rd Cong., 3rd sess., XXVII, pp. 1154-1155.

48. *Arbitrator,* Nos. 276-277, p. 17; also see Philip Stanhope to Bertha von Suttner, March 10, 1895, Alfred Fried—Bertha von Suttner Correspondence (UNL), Stanhope File. *CR,* 53rd Cong., 3rd sess., XXVII, p. 104, conveniently indexes resolutions on international arbitration introduced in Congress in early 1895.

49. The following summary of the Venezuelan crisis is based largely on Dexter Perkins, *The Monroe Doctrine, 1867–1907* (Baltimore: The Johns Hopkins Press, 1937), pp. 152-205, 217-224; A. E. Campbell, *Great Britain and the United States, 1895–1903* (London: Longmans, Green & Co., 1960), ch. 2; and Ernest R. May, *Imperial Democracy: The Emergence of America as a Great Power* (New York: Harcourt, Brace & World, 1961), pp. 39-59.

50. One American citizen in particular, William Lindsay Scruggs, who served as lobbyist for the Venezuelan government in the United States, conducted a one-man propaganda campaign to focus the attention of Cleveland, Gresham, Congress, and the newspaper press on the Anglo-Venezuelan dispute. Scruggs, who was aware of Cremer's lobbying in Washington, hastened to see the President before Cremer's interview, and it is safe to say that he helped to dampen temporarily the President's enthusiasm for an Anglo-American arbitration treaty. John A. S. Grenville and George Berkeley Young, *Politics, Strategy, and American Diplomacy: Studies in Foreign Policy, 1873–1917* (New Haven, Conn.: Yale University Press, 1966), pp. 133-148.

51. Matilda Gresham, *The Life of Walter Quintin Gresham, 1832–1895,* 2 vols. (Chicago: Rand McNally & Co., 1919), II, p. 795; John Bassett Moore, Memorandum of his two conversations with Gresham on the Venezuelan dispute in March 1895, John Bassett Moore Papers (LC), Box 1.

52. Frederick E. Partington, *The Story of Mohonk* (Fulton, N.Y.: The Morrill Press, 1911), *passim.* Smiley had earlier testified before the Senate

Foreign Relations Committee in support of an Anglo-American arbitration accord. *Sen. Misc. Doc. 141*, 50th Cong., 1st sess., pp. 18, 20.

53. Smiley best stated his position in *LMC 1896*, pp. 50-51.

54. *LMC 1895*, pp. 81-82, *passim*.

55. Edward Atkinson, "Jingoes and Silverites," *NAR*, CLXI (November, 1895), pp. 554-560; Atkinson to Lord Farrer, letter and cable, December 20, 1895, Atkinson to William L. Wilson and John G. Carlisle, December 20, 1895, Atkinson to J. Sterling Morton, December 20, 1895, Atkinson to Cleveland, telegram, December 20, 1895, Atkinson to Colonel Charles R. Codman, December 20, 1895, and Reuen Thomas to Atkinson, December 21, 1895, Edward Atkinson Papers (MHS), Box 16. See also Harold Francis Williamson, *Edward Atkinson: The Biography of an American Liberal, 1827–1905* (Boston: Old Corner Book Store, 1934), pp. 212-216.

56. William Lloyd Garrison, Jr., *The Things That Make for Peace* (New York: n.p., 1895); Garrison to Editors, *Woman's Journal*, XXIX (April 30, 1898), p. 137; *Boston Globe*, December 19, 21, 23, 1895.

57. *New York Times*, December 23, 1895.

58. *Ibid.*, December 24, 1895; cf. Lyman Abbott, *Reminiscences* (Boston: Houghton Mifflin Co., 1915), pp. 435-436.

59. *New York Times*, December 23, 1895; also see Ira V. Brown, *Lyman Abbott, Christian Evolutionist: A Study in Religious Liberalism* (Cambridge, Mass.: Harvard University Press, 1953), pp. 162-164.

60. Love to Cleveland, November 22, 1895, Cleveland Papers, Reel 91.

61. *CR*, 54th Cong., 1st sess., XXVIII, pp. 482, 2517; *Peacemaker*, XV (April, 1897), pp. 217-218.

62. Edwin D. Mead, "Boston Memories of Fifty Years," in *Fifty Years of Boston: A Memorial Volume*, ed. Elisabeth M. Herlihy (Boston: Goodspeed's Bookstore, 1932), pp. 37-38; Charles F. Dole, *My Eighty Years* (New York: E. P. Dutton & Co., 1927), pp. 391-392, 400; Mead is quoted in "Editor's Table," *NEM*, XIII (February, 1896), p. 801.

63. *AP*, LVIII (January, 1896), pp. 5-11; (February, 1896), pp. 34-36.

64. "The Venezuelan Question," especially pp. 139, 143-144.

65. See Carnegie's books, *An American Four-in-Hand in Britain* (New York: Charles Scribner's Sons, 1883), pp. 14-16; *Round the World* (New York: Charles Scribner's Sons, 1884), pp. 14-15, 109-110, 114-115; and *Triumphant Democracy*, pp. 6-9, *passim*. The quotation is from Carnegie's testimony in *Sen. Misc. Doc. 141*, 50th Cong., 1st sess., p. 16.

66. *New York Times*, January 8, 1911; Wall, *Carnegie*, pp. 645-654; *AP*, LVIII (March, 1896), p. 58.

67. Benjamin F. Trueblood, "The United States, Great Britain and International Arbitration," *NEM*, XIV (March, 1896), p. 22. Also see his biting comments on Carnegie's *NAR* article in *AP*, LVIII (March, 1896), p. 58.

68. Quoted in *Arbitrator*, Nos. 288-289 (February and March, 1896), pp. 21, 22. The same sentiments appear in Trueblood in *LMC 1896*, p. 28; Belva A. Lockwood, "International Arbitration, Venezuela, Cuba, and the National

Conference at Washington," *AMC,* IX (July, 1896), p. 15; and *Arbitrator,* No. 287 (January, 1896), p. 3.

69. For a full account, see Nelson M. Blake, "The Olney-Pauncefote Treaty of 1897," *American Historical Review,* L (January, 1945), pp. 228-243. The quotations and other relevant background appear in *ACIA 1896,* pp. 1-7, 226-233. Also see Stanley Waterloo to Atkinson, January 9, 1896, Atkinson Papers, Box 17; Lockwood, "International Arbitration," pp. 17-20; *New York Times,* February 19, 1896; and *AP,* LVIII (March, 1896), pp. 55-57.

70. *ACIA 1896,* pp. v, ix-xiv, 24, 88-110, *passim.*

71. *Ibid.,* pp. 58-59, 72-73, 82, 83, 85-87, 100; Chamberlain is quoted in *ibid.,* p. 29.

72. *Ibid.,* pp. 28, 96. Lockwood, "International Arbitration," pp. 22, 25, 28, noted that the only members of Congress in attendance were Representative William F. Aldrich, member of the Universal Peace Union, for the first day's sessions and Senator John Sherman for the final session.

73. *Ibid.,* pp. 22, 23, 25.

74. *ACIA 1896,* pp. 109, 110, 149.

75. The treaty stated that the contracting parties agreed to arbitrate: first, pecuniary claims; second, matters in which either party "shall have rights against the other, under treaty or otherwise;" and third, territorial claims. For the first two classes of claims, it provided for ordinary arbitral tribunals of three or five persons, each government appointing one or two and those appointed naming the third or fifth; if they could not agree, the joint action of the United States Supreme Court and the Judicial Committee of the British Privy Council would appoint the final arbitrator; and if these bodies could not agree within three months, the king of Sweden and Norway would appoint him. But territorial claims (including navigation rights and fisheries) and any claim in the second class involving "the decision of a disputed question of principle of grave general importance" affecting national rights as distinguished from private rights (to be decided by majority vote of the ordinary tribunal after the motion by one of the governments) were to be dealt with by a special tribunal of three American and three British jurists from specifically enumerated judicial bodies appointed by the president of the United States and queen of England respectively. This tribunal could render an award only by the concurrence of at least five out of the six judges. With a lesser majority, the award would still be final if neither government protested the proposed settlement within three months. If disagreement persisted, there could be no recourse to any kind of hostilities until one or both of the contracting parties had invited the mediation of one or more friendly powers. The treaty was to remain in force for five years but would be renewed automatically until one of the parties gave a one-year advance notice of its termination. *FR 1896,* pp. 238-240.

76. For exuberant praise of the agreement, see Edmunds to Olney, January 12, 1897, Richard Olney Papers (LC), Vol. 70; Trueblood, Eliot, and others in *Boston Globe,* January 12, 1897; Reverend Reuen Thomas in *AP,* LIX

(February, 1897), pp. 43-45; Carnegie to John Morley, February 9, 1897, Carnegie Papers, Vol. 41.

77. *CR,* 54th Cong., 2nd sess., XXIX, pp. 1045-1047; *Boston Globe,* January 12, February 11, 15, 19, 1897.

78. Richard E. Welch, Jr., *George Frisbie Hoar and the Half-Breed Republicans* (Cambridge, Mass.: Harvard University Press, 1971), pp. 206-207; Hoar to Atkinson, March 3, 1897, Atkinson Papers, Box 18. With the exception of the Reverend A. A. Berle, who throughout the Senate debate accused Hoar of calculated delay in frustrating the public will in favor of the treaty, the pleas of its supporters were far from "angry or impassioned."

79. *CR,* 54th Cong., 2nd sess., XXIX, pp. 1046-1047.

80. Senators' arguments can be followed in *New York Times* from January to May 1897, but are well summarized in *Sen. Doc. No. 231,* 56th Cong., 2nd sess., VIII, pp. 388-427; *Sen. Doc. No. 161,* 58th Cong., 3rd sess., pp. 8-33; *Arbitration and the United States: A Summary of the Development of Pacific Settlement of International Disputes with Special Reference to American Policy,* in *World Peace Foundation Pamphlets,* IX (1926), Nos. 6-7, pp. 504-508; and W. Stull Holt, *Treaties Defeated by the Senate: A Study of the Struggle between President and Senate over the Conduct of Foreign Relations* (Baltimore: The Johns Hopkins Press, 1933), pp. 154-162.

81. *CR,* 54th Cong., 2nd sess., XXIX, p. 1044; *ibid.,* 55th Cong., 1st sess., XXX, pp. 34, 347, 654, 702, 758, 774, 848, 902; *New York Times,* March 19, 1897; Blake, "Olney-Pauncefote Treaty," pp. 234-235; "Irish, French, Spanish, and German American Papers on the Arbitration Treaty," *Literary Digest,* XIV (February 20, 1897), pp. 482-483.

82. Whitney, *American Peace Society,* pp. 129, 140, 141. Dodge's father had earlier served as president of the Evangelical Alliance.

83. Dodge to Dear Sir, January 16, 1897, and Chamberlain to Atkinson, January 19, 1897, Atkinson Papers, Box 18.

84. McCook to Olney, January 15, telegram, 16, 18, 20, 1897, Olney Papers, Vol. 71; Frederic R. Coudert to Olney, January 14, 1897, *ibid.,* Vol. 70; Sigourney Butler to Olney, February 7, 1897, *ibid.,* Vol. 73.

85. Dodge to Olney, January 18, 21, 1897, *ibid.,* Vol. 71; Dodge to Olney, January 29, 1897; Olney to Dodge, January 30, 1897, and Dodge to Olney, February 1, 1897, *ibid.,* Vol. 72.

86. Dodge, Suggestions as to the Proposed Amendments to the Arbitration Treaty, January, 1897, typescript in Cleveland Papers, Reel 96. Quotations appear in *New York Times,* January 30, 1897.

87. Dodge and Chamberlain to Reverend and Dear Sir, January 28, 1897, and Dodge to Cleveland, February 10, 1897, Cleveland Papers, Reel 96; *ACIA 1904,* pp. 7-8. *Sen. Doc. No. 63,* 55th Cong., 1st sess., gives the figures of the *New York World.* Random samplings of individuals and English-language newspapers early in the debate showed broad support for the accord. "Arbitration Treaty between England and the United States," *Literary Digest,* XIV (January 23, 1897), pp. 357-358; "Arbitration Treaty and the Monroe Doctrine," *ibid.* (January 30, 1897), pp. 385-386.

88. *CR,* 54th Cong., 2nd sess., XXIX, pp. 872, 1003, 1044, 1045, 1088, 1148, 1238, 1239, 1289, 1376, 1377, 1419, 1509, 1556, 1639, 1670, 1690, 1758, 1788, 1824, 1963, 2022, 2225, 2397, 2398, 2323; *ibid.,* 55th Cong., 1st sess., XXX, pp. 34, 35-36, 45, 64, 116, 154, 212, 262, 559, 571, 572, 679, 680, 681, 749, 758, 845. Several of these resolutions are deposited in the Olney Papers, Vols. 71-74. Giles B. Stebbins, "Women Should Favor International Arbitration," *Woman's Journal,* XXVIII (January 30, 1897), p. 33.

89. *Boston Globe,* January 29, February 3, 1897; Butler to Olney, February 7, 1897, Olney Papers, Vol. 73; Dodge to Cleveland, February 10, 1897, Cleveland Papers, Reel 96.

90. Trueblood to Hoar, January 25, 1897, and Hoar to Trueblood, January 29, 1897, George F. Hoar Papers (MHS), General Letters 1896–1897; *AP,* LIX (February, 1897), pp. 32-33; (March, 1897), pp. 53-54, 64-65; (May, 1897), pp. 101-102; and reprints of statements favoring early ratification by Frances Willard, John Fiske, the National Arbitration Committee, and others in these issues.

91. Moxom to Hoar, January 18, 1897, Hoar Papers, General Letters 1896–1897; *Boston Globe,* January 19, 23, 28, February 11, 19, 1897.

92. *New York Times,* March 11, 12, 1897; Josiah Strong (Arbitration Committee, New York and Brooklyn) to Hoar, January 20, 1897, Hoar Papers, General Letters 1896–1897; Love to Olney, February 11, 1897, Olney Papers, Vol. 73. Edmunds' defense of the treaty, written in cooperation with Olney, was widely reprinted.

93. Olney to H. L. Nelson, February 11, 1897, Olney Papers, Vol. 73; Butler to Olney, February 16, 1897, *ibid.,* Vol. 74; Dodge to Cleveland, February 10, 1897, Cleveland Papers, Reel 96; Blake, "Olney-Pauncefote Treaty," p. 237.

94. Samuel Gompers, *Seventy Years of Life and Labor: An Autobiography,* 2 vols. (New York: E. P. Dutton & Co., 1925), II, p. 324.

95. H. L. Nelson to Olney, February 10, 1897, Olney Papers, Vol. 73.

96. An overwhelming majority of senators from the Northeast and Middle West voted for the amended version; the two outstanding exceptions were Boies Penrose and Matthew Quay, both of Pennsylvania.

97. Simeon E. Baldwin to Moore, March 23, 1897, Moore Papers, Box 147; James B. Angell to Moore, April 21, 1897, *ibid.,* Box 5. Cf. May, *Imperial Democracy,* pp. 63-65; Bradford Perkins, *The Great Rapprochement: England and the United States, 1895–1914* (New York: Atheneum, 1968), pp. 28-29.

98. Richardson, *Messages and Papers,* XIII, p. 6242; *Arbitration and the United States,* pp. 509-513.

99. The debates in closed executive session as well as the crossing of party lines on the final vote indicate that partisanship and personal vindictiveness were not of decisive importance in the defeat of the treaty.

100. *New York Times,* May 7, 1897.

101. For additional peace advocates' complaints and hopes, see *ibid.,* May 7, 26, 1897; *AP,* LIX (June, 1897), pp. 126, 130-131, 132; Bailey, cited in *ibid.* (November, 1897), p. 242; *Peacemaker,* XV (May, 1897), pp. 236-237;

"Editorial Notes," *Woman's Journal,* XXVIII (May 8, 1897), p. 145; John Addison Porter (McKinley's secretary) to Lockwood, November 9, 1897, William McKinley Papers (LC, on microfilm), Reel 23. For particularly strong criticisms of the Senate, see Mead and Moxom in *LMC 1897,* pp. 19-26, 62-63.

102. *Ibid.,* p. 14.

103. Platform in *ibid.,* p. 130; Trueblood, Love, and Paine in *ibid.,* pp. 14-16, 18, 69, 94-95; *New York Times,* June 20, 1897; *AP,* LIX (July, 1897), pp. 149-150; Sherman to Dodge, May 28, 1897, Moore Papers, Box 147.

104. *Washington Post,* November 19, 1897; Garrett in *LMC 1900,* p. 50; Dodge to Moore, November 26, 1897, Moore Papers, Box 147. Trueblood is quoted in *AP,* LIX (December, 1897), pp. 254-255.

105. Porter to Hodgson Pratt, April 6, 1897, McKinley Papers, Reel 17; W. Evans Darby to McKinley, January 5, 1898, *ibid.,* Reel 59; *New York Times,* November 14, 1897; *Arbitrator,* No. 310 (July, 1898), pp. 48-50.

106. Richardson, *Messages and Papers,* XIII, p. 6267; *AP,* LX (January, 1898), p. 8; *Arbitrator,* No. 310 (July, 1898), p. 49.

107. *Ibid.* Also see Margaret Leech, *In the Days of McKinley* (New York: Harper & Brothers, 1959), pp. 100-102, 151-155.

Chapter 3

1. Love to Cleveland, November 22, 1895, Grover Cleveland Papers (LC, on microfilm), Reel 91; J. B. Wood to Cleveland, November 15, 1896, *ibid.,* Reel 95; *AP,* LVIII (April, 1896), pp. 79-80; LIX (June, 1897), pp. 126-127; (December, 1897), pp. 256-258; *Peacemaker,* XV (February, 1897), pp. 158, 163-164, 168-169; Belva A. Lockwood, "International Arbitration, Venezuela, Cuba, and the National Conference at Washington," *AMC,* IX (July, 1896), pp. 15-16. For early petitions by peace groups and the National WCTU, see *CR,* 54th Cong., 1st sess., XXVIII, pp. 188, 723, 812, 813, 955, 1023.

2. For background I have relied mainly on Margaret Leech, *In the Days of McKinley,* (New York: Harper & Brothers, 1959), ch. 7; Ernest R. May, *Imperial Democracy: The Emergence of America as a Great Power* (New York: Harcourt, Brace & World, 1961), chs. 11, 12; and Julius W. Pratt, "The Coming War With Spain," in *Threshold to American Internationalism: Essays on the Foreign Policies of William McKinley,* ed. Paolo E. Coletta (New York: Exposition Press, 1970), ch. 2.

3. Straus to McKinley, March 12, 1898, Oscar S. Straus Papers (LC), Box 2; Straus Diary, March 19, 1898, *ibid.,* Box 22. Also see Naomi W. Cohen, *A Dual Heritage: The Public Career of Oscar S. Straus* (Philadelphia: Jewish Publication Society of America, 1969), pp. 49-53.

4. Straus answered the Cuban objections and continued without success to promote his suzerainty plan. Straus to McKinley, March 23, 24, April 8, 1898, Straus Papers, Box 2.

5. Memorial of The Representatives of the Religious Society of Friends for Pennsylvania, New Jersey, and Delaware, March 25, 1898, William McKinley Papers (LC, on microfilm), Reel 4; *CR,* 55th Cong., 2nd sess., XXXI, pp. 3408-

3409, 3447, 3451-3452, 3648; "Women and Cuba," *Woman's Journal*, XXIX (April 16, 1898), p. 124; "Anna Garlin Spencer on the War," *ibid.* (May 7, 1898), p. 145. "Women's Council on War," *ibid.*, p. 149; John Addison Porter to Sewall, March 31, 1898, McKinley Papers, Reel 27; *Boston Globe*, April 2, 1898; *New York Times*, April 6, 1898.

6. *Boston Globe*, April 4, 1898; Atkinson is quoted in his letter to McKinley, March 25, 1898, McKinley Papers, Reel 60.

7. *Boston Globe*, April 9, 1898. Atkinson had made the same proposal for jingoes during the Venezuelan dispute. Harold Francis Williamson, *Edward Atkinson: The Biography of an American Liberal* (Boston: Old Corner Book Store, 1934), pp. 215n-216.

8. *CR*, 55th Cong., 2nd sess., XXXI, pp. 3276, 3447-3448, 3648; *Boston Globe*, April 4, 1898.

9. The quotations appear in Ginn to Long, March 15, 1898, and Capen to Long, March 28, 1898, John D. Long Papers (MHS), Box 38. Also see Mead to Long, March 31, 1898, and Capen to Long, February 21, 1898, *ibid.*, Box 37; Porter to Capen, March 29, April 2, 1898, and Porter to Mead, April 5, 1898, McKinley Papers, Reel 27.

10. Daniel B. Schirmer, *Republic or Empire: American Resistance to the Philippine War* (Cambridge, Mass.: Schenkman Publishing Co., 1972), p. 53.

11. *Boston Globe* (evening), March 25, 1898. I found no evidence that Capen protested the inclusion of these amendments.

12. Atkinson to McKinley, March 24, 1898, McKinley Papers, Reel 60; William Lloyd Garrison, Jr. to Long, March 4, 1898, and Ginn to Long, March 15, 1898, Long Papers, Box 38.

13. *Boston Globe*, April 8, 1898.

14. *Ibid.*, April 2, 3, 1898.

15. *AP*, LX (April, 1898), p. 81; Isabel Barrows, *A Sunny Life: The Biography of Samuel June Barrows* (Boston: Little, Brown and Co., 1913), pp. 151-155.

16. Paine and Trueblood to McKinley, March 28, 1898, McKinley Papers, Reel 60.

17. Porter to Paine, March 31, 1898, *ibid.*, Reel 27.

18. Atkinson to Dodge, February 15, 1898, Atkinson to Charles W. Eliot, February 23, 1898, Eliot to Atkinson, February 24, 1898, Charles F. Adams to Atkinson, March 2, 1898, Chamberlain to Atkinson, March 4, 1898, Moore to Dodge, March 4, 1898, Dodge to Atkinson, March 10, 1898, and Horace Kenney to Atkinson, March 19, 31, 1898, Edward Atkinson Papers (MHS), Box 19.

19. Atkinson did not allow the pessimistic responses to his neutralization scheme to discourage his enthusiasm for it. For his opposition to imperialism, see below, ch. 4.

20. Porter to Capen, March 29, April 2, 1898, Porter to May Wright Sewall, March 31, 1898, Porter to Love, April 2, 1898, Porter to Mead, April 5, 1898, McKinley Papers, Reel 27.

21. Quoted in *FR 1898,* pp. 759-760.

22. General Officers of the National WCTU to McKinley, telegram, April 11, 1898, McKinley Papers, Reel 3; *Boston Globe* (evening), April 12, 1898.

23. Ginn to Atkinson, March 9, 1898, Atkinson Papers, Box 19.

24. *AP,* LX (March, 1898), p. 54.

25. *Ibid.* (April, 1898), pp. 77-78; also see *ibid.* (June, 1898), p. 134.

26. Straus to McKinley, telegram, April 11, 1898, McKinley Papers, Reel 3.

27. *CR,* 55th Cong., 2nd sess., XXXI, pp. 4375-4376.

28. *Boston Globe,* March 18, 1897; May, *Imperial Democracy,* pp. 27, 29; Hodgson Pratt to Paine, August 17, 1895, Robert Treat Paine Papers (MHS), Box 2; Dole in *LMC 1897,* pp. 64-65, 109-110. Frances Willard died in mid-February 1898, but much like the five men described in the text she had openly advocated joint military intervention of the powers against Turkey in 1896 and apparently never expressed sympathy for American intervention in Cuba.

29. Dodge, Chamberlain, and Strong to Cleveland, undated (1896), Cleveland Papers, Reel 142; and James B. Angell to Cleveland, October 17, 1896, *ibid.,* Reel 95.

30. Porter to Dodge, December 28, 1897, McKinley Papers, Reel 24; and Stephan B. L. Penrose, Jr., *That They May Have Life: The Story of the American University of Beirut 1866–1941* (New York: The Trustees of the American University of Beirut, 1941), p. 874.

31. Roosevelt to William Wingate Sewall, May 4, 1898, *The Letters of Theodore Roosevelt,* ed. Elting E. Morison, 8 vols. (Cambridge, Mass.: Harvard University Press, 1951–1954), II, p. 823.

32. Ira V. Brown, *Lyman Abbott, Christian Evolutionist: A Study in Religious Liberalism* (Cambridge, Mass.: Harvard University Press, 1953), pp. 132-136, 181. Abbott's remarks appear in his editorial, "What We Can Do," *Outlook,* LVI (May 1, 1897), p. 11.

33. "The President's Message," *ibid.,* LVIII (April 16, 1898), p. 953.

34. Edward Everett Hale, Introduction to "The Man Without a Country," *ibid.,* LIX (May 14, 1898), p. 116.

35. Brown, *Abbott,* pp. 170ff.; Porter to Dodge, February 7, 1899, McKinley Papers, Reel 37; Josiah Strong, *Expansion under New World Conditions* (New York: The Baker and Taylor Co., 1900). On Moxom, see William A. Webster to Atkinson, December 12, 1898, Atkinson Papers, Box 20. Hale initially cooperated with Boston anti-imperialists but almost as quickly backed away from involvement in the anti-imperialist cause. Hale to Long, July 29, 1898, Long Papers, Box 41; Edwin D. Mead, "Edward Everett Hale," *NEM,* XL (July, 1909), p. 525.

36. Carnegie to H. C. Frick, December 15, 1897, Andrew Carnegie Papers (LC), Vol. 47; Carnegie to McKinley, telegram, no date but before war was declared, *ibid.,* Vol. 50; *Autobiography of Andrew Carnegie* (Boston: Houghton Mifflin Co., 1920), pp. 361-362; Joseph Frazier Wall, *Andrew Carnegie* (New York: Oxford University Press, 1970), p. 691.

37. Carnegie to H. C. Frick, April 23, 1898, Carnegie Papers, Vol. 51;

Carnegie to Dr. Adolf Gurlt, June 1, 1898, misfiled under June 1, 1896, *ibid.,* Vol. 38.

38. Carnegie to McKinley, April 27, 1898, McKinley Papers, Reel 3.

39. Quoted in "Reception to Mrs. Howe," *Woman's Journal,* XXIX (July 2, 1898), p. 212; also see "Mrs. Howe's Appeal," *ibid.,* XXVIII (August 28, 1897), p. 273.

40. See Henry B. Blackwell's articles, all entitled "Woman Suffrage Means Peace," *ibid.,* XXVII (January 25, 1896), p. 28; (March 14, 1896), p. 84; and (May 16, 1896), p. 156.

41. Henry B. Blackwell, "Woman Suffrage Means Peace," *ibid.,* XXVII (January 25, 1896), p. 28; "Editorial Notes," *ibid.,* XXVIII (May 8, 1897), p. 145.

42. "The Abolition of War," XXVII (August 15, 1896), p. 260.

43. Henry B. Blackwell, "Things That Make for Peace," *ibid.,* XXVI (August 31, 1895), p. 276.

44. "Woman Suffrage Means Peace," *ibid.,* XXVII (January 25, 1896), p. 28.

45. Henry B. Blackwell, "The War with Spain," *Woman's Journal,* XXIX (April 16, 1898), p. 124.

46. Garrison to Editors, *ibid.* (April 30, 1898), p. 137; Henry B. Blackwell, "The War with Spain," *ibid.,* p. 140.

47. The quotations in the preceding two paragraphs come from *ibid.,* and Alice Stone Blackwell, "Mr. Garrison on Women and War," *ibid.*

48. Garrison to Editors, *ibid.* (May 14, 1898), p. 156.

49. Love to Cleveland, November 22, 1895, Cleveland Papers, Reel 91; Love to Cleveland, March 12, 1896, *ibid.,* Reel 93; Lockwood to Cleveland, December 8, 1896, *ibid.,* Reel 96; *Peacemaker,* XV (February, 1897), pp. 167-169; (May, 1897), p. 233.

50. *Ibid.,* XVI (February, 1898), pp. 156-157; (March, 1898), p. 174.

51. *Ibid.* (March, 1898), pp. 165-169, 170-172; (April, 1898), pp. 190-192; Alfred H. Love Diary, March 1, 1898, Universal Peace Union Papers (SCPC). Love's Diary is cited in the following notes only when it significantly clarifies information in *Peacemaker.*

52. Merle Curti, *Peace or War: The American Struggle, 1636–1936* (New York: W. W. Norton & Co., 1936), pp. 169-170; Elie Ducommun to E. T. Moneta, April 5, 1898, IPB Papers (UNL); *Peacemaker,* XVI (April, 1898), pp. 188-189. For additional information on the finances of the Berne Bureau, see *AP,* LX (December, 1898), p. 262.

53. Love Diary, March 28, 29, 30, 31, April 1, 2, 3, 4, 1898; *Peacemaker,* XVI (April, 1898) p. 193. I could find no record of the Union delegation calling on the President.

54. *Ibid.* (March, 1898), pp. 170, 172. Woodford had also endorsed a petition of several Christian churches for arbitration accords at a public meeting in December 1891. *AP,* LV (January, 1893), p. 5.

55. Woodford is quoted in *Peacemaker,* XVI (April, 1898), p. 192.

56. The quotations appear in *ibid.*, p. 194; and (May, 1898), p. 206.

57. *Ibid.* (April, 1898), p. 190; (May, 1898), p. 207; Love Diary, April 11, 18, 1898.

58. Polo is quoted in *Peacemaker*, XVI (May, 1898), pp. 207-208; cf. *FR 1898*, pp. 757-759.

59. *Peacemaker*, XVI (May, 1898), pp. 208-209; XVII (August, 1898), pp. 34-35; *AP*, LX (May, 1898), pp. 107-108. The rumors prompting Love's letter to Pauncefote involved a second joint note drawn up by the ambassadors in Washington. That note was more strongly worded than the first and was never presented to the United States because of opposition from the home governments.

60. *Peacemaker*, XVI (May, 1898), p. 209; (June, 1898), p. 244; Love Diary, May 20, 1898.

Chapter 4

1. Lockwood in *Peacemaker*, XVII (July, 1898), p. 9; Ames in *AP*, LX (June, 1898), pp. 138-142.

2. Dole to Long, December 5, 1898, John D. Long Papers (MHS), Box 44.

3. Quoted in *LMC 1898*, p. 5; also see his remarks in *LMC 1899*, p. 5.

4. The Reverends R. R. Meredith, R. S. MacArthur, and Theodore L. Cuyler in *LMC 1898*, pp. 31, 68, 106.

5. *LMC 1899*, p. 106.

6. Among the prominent peace people bypassing Mohonk Conferences after 1899 were Edmunds, Mercer, Love, Welsh, Boardman, Richard Henry Thomas, and Reuen Thomas.

7. Garrison to Editors, *Woman's Journal*, XXIX (May 28, 1898), p. 172; Garrison in *AP*, LX (October, 1898), pp. 208-209; also see above, ch. 3, notes 48, 60; *AP*, LX (June, 1898), pp. 137-138; (May, 1898), pp. 101-102; (June, 1898), pp. 125-126, 127-129; (July, 1898), pp. 151-152; (August and September, 1898), pp. 174-176.

8. *Philadelphia Evening Bulletin*, May 26, 1898; Alfred H. Love Diary, May 26, 27, 1898, Universal Peace Union Papers (SCPC); *Peacemaker*, XVII (July, 1898), pp. 1-2.

9. *Philadelphia Evening Bulletin*, May 27, 28, 1898.

10. Love Diary, May 28, 29, 30, 31, 1898; *Peacemaker*, XVII (July, 1898), pp. 8-9.

11. "Editor's Table," *NEM*, XVIII (May, 1898), pp. 385-387; "Editor's Table," *ibid.*, XIX (September, 1898), p. 134.

12. See Edwin D. Mead, "The Message of Puritanism for This Time," *ibid.*, IV (June, 1891), pp. 462-469; also his books, *The Philosophy of Carlyle* (Boston: Houghton Mifflin and Co., 1881); *Martin Luther: A Study of Reformation* (Boston: George H. Ellis, 1883); and *The Influence of Emerson* (Boston: American Unitarian Association, 1903).

13. Lucia Mead, "Apostles of World Unity: X—Edwin D. Mead," *World Unity*, II (August, 1928), p. 337; Edwin D. Mead, "Boston Memories of Fifty

Years," in *Fifty Years of Boston: A Memorial Volume,* ed. Elisabeth M. Herlihy (Boston: Goodspeed Bookstore, 1932), pp. 8-10, 31, 32, 38; "Editor's Table," *NEM,* XIII (February, 1896), p. 801; "Editor's Table," *ibid.,* XV (November, 1896), pp. 380-384.

14. *AP,* LXI (May, 1899), p. 103; for Mead's involvement in reform causes, see his "Boston Memories of Fifty Years," pp. 8, 10, 31-32, 35-37; Edwin D. Mead, *The Old South Work* (Boston: Old South Meeting House, 1899); "Editor's Table," *NEM,* IX (January, 1894), pp. 666-669; Mead to Paine, November 21, 1896, Robert Treat Paine Papers (MHS), Box 3; Chauncy J. Hawkins, *Samuel Billings Capen: His Life and Work* (Boston: The Pilgrim Press, 1914), pp. 159-163; *The Twentieth Century Club of Boston, 1894–1904* (Boston: The Davis Press, n.d.), pp. 3, 9, 22; Edward Everett Hale to Helen Kimball, December 31, 1895, Edward Everett Hale Papers (New York State Library), Box 11; *Lend a Hand: A Record of Progress,* XVIII (January, 1897), p. 71.

15. Lucia Mead, "Apostles of World Unity: X—Edwin D. Mead," p. 343.

16. Charles S. MacFarland, *Pioneers for Peace Through Religion: Based on the Records of The Church Peace Union (Founded by Andrew Carnegie), 1914–1945* (New York: Fleming H. Revell Co., 1946), p. 19.

17. See Lucia Ames' writings: *Memoirs of a Millionaire* (Boston: Houghton Mifflin and Co., 1889); "The Home in the Tenement-House," *NEM,* VII (January, 1893), pp. 394-399; "Saints and Sinners," *Lend a Hand: A Record of Progress,* XI (September, 1893), pp. 213-216; "City Homes for the Poor," *ibid.,* XII (March, 1894), pp. 163-170.

18. Lucia Ames in *LMC 1897,* p. 99.

19. *Ibid.,* p. 96.

20. Lucia Mead in *LMC 1902,* p. 63.

21. David Starr Jordan, *The Days of a Man, Being Memories of a Naturalist, Teacher and a Minor Prophet of Democracy,* 2 vols. (New York: World Book Company, 1922), I, p. 130. Sewall House Visitors' Register, 1885–1908, May Wright Sewall Papers (Indianapolis Public Library), discloses that Jordan and his wife were house guests of Mrs. Sewall on March 26, 1891.

22. Jordan, letter in *ACIA 1896,* p. 160; *New York World,* March 30, 1897.

23. Jordan, *Days of a Man,* I, pp. 605-606.

24. *Ibid.,* pp. 2-4, 9, 30-34, 74; also see Jordan's essay on Thoreau, "The Last of the Puritans" (1892), in his *Imperial Democracy: A Study of the Relation of Government by the People, Equality before the Law, and Other Tenets of Democracy, to the Demands of a Vigorous Foreign Policy and Other Demands of Imperial Dominion* (New York: D. Appleton and Company, 1899), pp. 277-293.

25. *Ibid.,* p. 9.

26. *Ibid.,* pp. 14, 91; Jordan, *Days of a Man,* I, pp. 613-616.

27. *Ibid.* It is debatable whether Woodford really felt he had been so deeply wronged as Jordan stated. For contradictory evidence (including Woodford's reticence), see Jordan's and others' letters in *New York Times,* April 1, 13, 15,

17, 1915; *The Critic,* XXXIII (October, 1898), p. 287; Love Diary, September 8, 1898; *Peacemaker,* XVII (December, 1898), p. 111.

28. *Ibid.* (August, 1898), p. 22.

29. Jordan, *Days of a Man,* I, pp. 616, 695-699.

30. For their cooperation with the Anti-Imperialist League or its branches, see *NEAIL 1900,* pp. 14-45; *NEAIL 1901,* p. 16; *NEAIL 1905,* pp. 19-21; *AP,* LXI (February, 1899), p. 31; (May, 1899), pp. 106-108; (June, 1899), p. 131; (September, 1899), p. 181; (November, 1899), p. 235; (December, 1899), pp. 256-257. Perry E. Gianakos, "Ernest Howard Crosby: A Forgotten Tolstoyan Anti-Militarist and Anti-Imperialist," *American Studies,* XIII (Spring, 1972), pp. 13-17, 27n14, believes that Crosby's *Captain Jinks, Hero* (1902) and Raymond L. Bridgman's *Loyal Traitors* (1903) were the only two explicitly anti-imperialist novels written by Americans in reaction to the expansionist mania. Oscar S. Straus Diary, August 11, 1898, Oscar S. Straus Papers (LC), Box 22; Belva Lockwood in *Peacemaker,* XVII (December, 1898), p. 113; and petitions to Congress: *CR,* 55th Cong., 3rd sess., XXXII, pp. 90, 205, 322, 400, 401, 1414, 1442, 1477-1478; *ibid.,* 56th Cong., 1st sess., XXXIII, p. 175. *Boston Globe,* April 4, 1899, October 4, 29, 1900. Also, Allen F. Davis, *American Heroine: The Life and Legend of Jane Addams* (New York: Oxford University Press, 1973), pp. 141-143; Richard Harlan Thomas, "Jenkin Lloyd Jones: Lincoln's Soldier of Civic Righteousness" (Ph.D. Dissertation, Rutgers University, 1967), pp. 101-102; "Editorial," *Unity,* XLII (December 15, 1898), pp. 283-284. The most recent historian of the American peace movement found that at least thirty-two officers (out of about eighty) of the American Peace Society "gave active support to anti-imperialist organizations or spoke at anti-imperialist meetings during the late 1890s, some arguing that the two movements were inseparable." C. Roland Marchand, *The American Peace Movement and Social Reform, 1898–1918* (Princeton, N.J., Princeton University Press, 1972), p. 12.

31. *CR,* 55th Cong., 3rd sess., XXXII, pp. 90, 205.

32. Ginn to Atkinson, March 1, 1899, Edward Atkinson Papers (MHS), Box 20. For another view of Ginn's indecision, see Ernest R. May, *American Imperialism: A Speculative Essay* (New York: Atheneum, 1968), pp. 53-54, 202.

33. *Boston Globe,* October 12, 1900.

34. Jordan, *Imperial Democracy,* p. 19; *AP,* LX (July, 1898), p. 150; *Peacemaker,* XVII (May, 1900), pp. 219-220. For parallel arguments of other anti-imperialists, see E. Berkeley Tompkins, *Anti-Imperialism in the United States: The Great Debate, 1890–1920* (Philadelphia: University of Pennsylvania Press, 1970), pp. 6, 18-19, 25, 132, 146, 182, 203.

35. Andrew Carnegie, "Americanism Versus Imperialism," *NAR,* CLXVIII (January, 1899), p. 2; Belva A. Lockwood, *Peace and the Outlook* (Washington, D.C.: Thos. W. Cadick, 1899), pp. 9-10.

36. The writings of Atkinson, Jordan, Carnegie, Mead, Garrison, and Trueblood in particular made numerous favorable references to these British Liberals and, less frequently, to two others, Goldwin Smith and James Bryce.

Edwin D. Mead, "The Expansion of England," *National Geographic Magazine*, XI (July, 1900), pp. 253-257; Jordan, *Days of a Man*, I, pp. 83, 91; Jordan, *Imperial Democracy*, pp. 34, 50, 106, 114, 163-166; Goldwin Smith to Atkinson, January 25, 1897, Atkinson Papers, Box 18; Smith to Atkinson, December 10, 1898, *ibid.,* Box 20. Tompkins, *Anti-Imperialism*, pp. 66, 99-100, 148, mentions the influence of Bright, Cobden, and Bryce on American anti-imperialists. Most of the pacific-minded individuals' writings on imperialism cited in the following notes (see especially note 61) contain favorable references to British anti-imperialist Liberals.

37. "Editor's Table," *NEM*, XVIII (July, 1898), pp. 631-636; "Editor's Table," *ibid.,* XIX (December, 1898), p. 519; "Editor's Table," *ibid.,* XXI (December, 1899), pp. 250-256; *AP*, LX (June, 1898), pp. 128-129; LXII (January, 1900), pp. 7-8; Carnegie, "Americanism Versus Imperialism," pp. 1-10; Carnegie, letter in *New York Times*, December 12, 1898; Jordan, *Imperial Democracy*, pp. 17-19, 26-27, 29-30, 32-36. For more general aversion to alliances, see Ames in *AP*, LXI (April, 1899), pp. 87-88; Paine in *LMC 1900*, p. 58; and aversion to England, May, *American Imperialism*, pp. 204-205.

38. See especially Atkinson's speeches and writings featured in *AP*, LX (June, 1898), p. 133; (November, 1898), p. 227; LXI (May, 1899), p. 107; and LXII (February, 1900), pp. 38-40.

39. George F. Edmunds in *AP*, LX (December, 1898), p. 258. For Edmunds' knowledge of English political writing, see May, *American Imperialism*, p. 107.

40. Jordan, *Imperial Democracy*, pp. 23, 53; also see Carnegie to Editor, *New York World*, November 27, 1898, Andrew Carnegie Papers (LC), Vol. 57.

41. "Editor's Table," *NEM*, XX (July, 1899), p. 636.

42. *Ibid.;* Jordan, *Imperial Democracy*, pp. 52, 142-143; Carnegie, letter in *New York Times*, October 24, 1898.

43. Andrew Carnegie, "Distant Possessions—The Parting of the Ways," *NAR*, CLXVII (August, 1898), pp. 242-243, specifically repudiated the label "little Americans" as applied to himself.

44. "Editor's Table," *NEM*, XIX (September, 1898), p. 132.

45. Raymond L. Bridgman, "Brute or Man—The Annexation Problem," *ibid.,* p. 83; Garrison to Editors, *Woman's Journal*, XXIX (May 14, 1898), p. 156; Love in *New York Times*, August 26, 1898.

46. *AP*, LXI (September, 1899), p. 183; LXII (January, 1900), p. 9; (September, 1900), pp. 171-172.

47. Carnegie, "Distant Possessions—The Parting of the Ways," pp. 242-243; Carnegie, "Americanism Versus Imperialism," p. 12; Lockwood, *Peace and the Outlook*, p. 8; Carnegie, letter in *New York Times*, October 24, 1898. Carnegie initially favored American sovereignty over a coaling base in Puerto Rico but had fully acquiesced in the complete takeover by 1900. Straus Diary, August 11, 1898, Box 22.

48. Jordan, *Imperial Democracy*, pp. 52, 57-58, 107-108, 175; David Starr

Jordan, "The Control of the Tropics," *Gunston's Magazine,* XVIII (May, 1900), pp. 408-410.

49. *Boston Globe,* March 27, 1898.

50. Atkinson to McKinley, January 26, 1899, William McKinley Papers, (LC, on microfilm), Reel 5; also see Robert L. Beisner, *Twelve Against Empire: The Anti-Imperialists, 1898–1900* (New York: McGraw-Hill Book Co., 1968), pp. 94-96.

51. Walter LaFeber, *The New Empire: An Interpretation of American Expansion, 1860–1898,* (Ithaca, N.Y.: Cornell University Press, 1963), pp. 412-416; commentary by Thomas J. McCormick, in *Studies on the Left,* III, No. 1 (1962), pp. 28-33; William Appleman Williams, *The Roots of the Modern American Empire: A Study of the Growth and Shaping of Social Consciousness in a Marketplace Economy* (New York: Random House, 1969), pp. 440-442, *passim.*

52. Beisner, *Twelve Against Empire,* pp. 96, 220. That judgment on the post-1901 years must be applied cautiously, however, because all those interventions resulted from executive initiatives which severely curtailed the opportunities for debate, and most of the leading anti-imperialists had died by 1905. For an outstanding example of outspoken protest against American Caribbean meddling, see William B. Hixson, Jr., *Moorfield Storey and the Abolitionist Tradition* (New York: Oxford University Press, 1972), pp. 68-80. For later reactions of the peace movement to United States' policies in Latin America, see below, chs. 7, 10, 11.

53. See especially Jordan, *Imperial Democracy,* pp. 12-13, 93-97; Andrew Carnegie, "Americanism Versus Imperialism—II," *NAR,* CLXVIII (March, 1899), pp. 363, 366-367; Atkinson to McKinley, November 14, 1898, McKinley Papers, Reel 5. For an extreme interpretation, see Christopher Lasch, "The Anti-Imperialists, the Philippines, and the Inequality of Man," *Journal of Southern History,* XXIV (August, 1958), pp. 319-331.

54. See comments by Quakers—Trueblood, Garrett, Richard Henry Thomas, James Wood, and Augustine Jones—in *American Friend,* V (July 7, 1898), pp. 629-635. Augustine Jones was also an officer of the American Peace Society. Also see the names of other Quakers on the petitions to Congress cited in note 30; *AFPC 1901, passim;* and *AP,* LXIV (January, 1902), p. 5.

55. Beisner, *Twelve Against Empire,* pp. 94-95, 98; Atkinson to Editor, *New York World,* December 14, 1898, Atkinson Papers, Box 20; Atkinson to Hoar, August 13, 1900, *ibid.,* Box 21.

56. Atkinson to McKinley, November 14, 1898, McKinley Papers, Reel 5.

57. Edward Atkinson, "Anglophobia," *Harper's Weekly,* XLII (December 24, 1898), pp. 1259-1260; Beisner, *Twelve Against Empire,* pp. 101-102.

58. Dole to Atkinson, February 10, 1900, Atkinson Papers, Box 21. Concerning Atkinson's rigid economic liberalism, see Atkinson in *LMC 1899,* p. 68; and John G. Sproat, *"The Best Men": Liberal Reformers in the Gilded Age* (New York: Oxford University Press, 1968), p. 147.

59. Carnegie, "Distant Possessions—The Parting of the Ways," pp. 242-

243. Carnegie, however, let slip his predominant concern with geopolitical rather than moral considerations. "Americanism Versus Imperialism," p. 12. Lockwood, *Peace and the Outlook,* p. 8.

60. The quoted remarks appear in Jordan, *Imperial Democracy,* pp. 33, 36, 53, 54; Carnegie, letter in *New York Times,* October 24, 1898; "Editor's Table," *NEM,* XX (July, 1899), p. 643; "Editor's Table," *ibid.,* XIX (September, 1898), pp. 131, 133; Dole to Long, December 5, 1898, Long Papers, Box 44; Bridgman, "Brute or Man—The Annexation Problem," pp. 90, 92-93; Jenkin Lloyd Jones, "Eighteen Hundred and Ninety-eight," *Unity,* XLII (January 12, 1899), p. 362; Slayden in *CR,* 56th Cong., 1st sess., XXXIII, p. 5551. Early in the debate Carnegie, typically inconsistent, showed little regard for the Filipinos' aspirations, just as he had earlier perceived no imperialism in British colonization of North America—the presence of the Indian natives apparently never occurred to him. But he stressed the merit of Filipinos' opinions when he began to perceive McKinley's capitulation to the annexationists. "Distant Possessions—The Parting of the Ways," pp. 241-242; Joseph Frazier Wall, *Andrew Carnegie* (New York: Oxford University Press, 1970), pp. 674, 695.

61. Berle in *NEAIL 1901,* pp. 20-25; "Platform," *The Chicago Liberty Meeting Held at Central Music Hall, April 30, 1899. Liberty Tract, No. 1* (Chicago: n.p., 1899), p. 4; "Editor's Table," *NEM,* XXI (October, 1899), p. 256; "Editor's Table," *ibid.,* XVIII (July, 1898), pp. 632-636; Jordan, *Imperial Democracy,* pp. 50-58, 77-78; *AP,* LXI (February, 1899), p. 32.

62. Carnegie, "Americanism Versus Imperialism," p. 13; Jordan, *Imperial Democracy,* pp. 65-66; *Ex-Senator Edmunds on Imperialism* (n. p.: n.p., n.d.), pp. 1-4; Bridgman, "Brute or Man—The Annexation Problem," pp. 91-93; Jones, "Eighteen Hundred and Ninety-eight," p. 363; Anna Garlin Spencer to Editors, *Woman's Journal,* XXX (January 14, 1899), p. 13; Hixson, *Storey,* pp. 59-60. Even Slayden, a self-styled Bourbon Democrat, occasionally made favorable references to the Declaration. Slayden to Atkinson, April 5, 24, 1899, Atkinson Papers, Box 20; *CR,* 56th Cong., 1st sess., XXXIII, pp. 5550-5551.

63. Garrison's letter of January 1899, quoted in *Peacemaker,* XVII (April, 1899), p. 204.

64. Carnegie, "Americanism Versus Imperialism—II," pp. 371-372; "Editor's Table," *NEM,* XX (July, 1899), pp. 645-646; Jordan, *Imperial Democracy,* pp. 31, 46, 101-102, 162; Love to Atkinson, July 27, 1899, Atkinson Papers, Box 20; *Boston Globe,* October 4, 1900. For parallel arguments of anti-imperialists both within and outside the peace movement, see Beisner, *Twelve Against Empire,* pp. 29, 160; Tompkins, *Anti-Imperialism,* pp. 151-152, 156.

65. Jordan, *Imperial Democracy,* pp. 65-68.

66. Carnegie, "Americanism Versus Imperialism," p. 13; Carnegie, "Americanism Versus Imperialism—II," pp. 367-371. Carnegie also opposed the presence of American and British missionaries in China. Wall, *Carnegie,* pp. 367-368, 1070n12.

67. Jordan, *Imperial Democracy,* p. 50; Dole to Long, December 5, 1898,

Long Papers, Box 44. Carnegie had an interview with McKinley on the matter in late November 1898, which is recounted in Carnegie to McKinley, February (?) 1899, but before the first outbreak of fighting in the Philippines, McKinley Papers, Reel 6; and Carnegie to John Hay, November 20, 1898, William Jennings Bryan Papers (LC), Box 22.

68. Tompkins, *Anti-Imperialism*, pp. 191-192.

69. Carnegie, "Americanism Versus Imperialism—II," pp. 367ff; Dole to Long, February 22, 1899, Long Papers, Box 45; Dole to Long, March 21, 1899, *ibid.*, Box 46; Jane Addams, "Democracy or Militarism," in Central Anti-Imperialist League, *Chicago Liberty Meeting*, pp. 35-39; Mercer in *LMC 1899*, pp. 104-106.

70. Jordan, *Imperial Democracy*, pp. 268, 274. Both Jordan and Mercer sharply criticized Lyman Abbott for his resolute support of the McKinley administration's policy in the Philippines. Also see *AP*, LXI (May, 1899), p. 105; (November, 1899), pp. 228-230; Mead to Editor, *Outlook*, LXVI (September 15, 1900), pp. 184-186.

71. See Trueblood's critiques in *AP*, LXI (September, 1899), pp. 179-180; (November, 1899), pp. 232-233; Leeds in *ibid.*, LXII (January, 1900), pp. 19-20; Atkinson to Charles J. O'Malley, January 20, 1900, Atkinson Papers, Box 21; Jenkin Lloyd Jones, "World Politics Versus Party Issues," *Unity*, XLVI (October 18, 1900), p. 105; Crosby to Roosevelt, September 29, 1901, Theodore Roosevelt Papers (LC, on microfilm), Reel 19; speeches in *AFPC 1901*, pp. 32, 42-43, 81, 110, 114, 118, 203-204, 209; "Editor's Table," *NEM*, XXII (May, 1900), pp. 369-380; "Editor's Table," *ibid.* (August, 1900), pp. 748-756; Mead to Atkinson, June 2, 1900, Atkinson Papers, Box 21.

72. Carnegie, letter in *New York Times*, November 10, 1899.

73. For continued interest of peace advocates in the fate of the Philippines, see Daniel B. Schirmer, *Republic or Empire: American Resistance to the Philippine War* (Cambridge, Mass.: Schenkman Publishing Co., 1972), pp. 244, 247; Mead to McKinley, April 10, 1901, McKinley Papers, Reel 15; Paine and Trueblood to McKinley, March 25, 1901, *ibid.*, Reel 77; and *AP*, LXIV (April, 1902), p. 48.

74. Tompkins, *Anti-Imperialism*, pp. 258ff. Storey did serve, however, as honorary counsel and gave speeches to the peace group after 1897. See *AP*, LXV (June, 1903), p. 111; and Hixson, *Storey*, pp. 80ff. Also, Haskins in *LMC 1901*, pp. 80-81. Another possible exception was Herbert Welsh, who continued to support the campaigns for peace and arbitration but devoted most of his time publicizing American atrocities in the Philippines in the columns of his magazine, *City and State*. Welsh to Paine, April 27, 1902, Paine Papers, Box 3.

75. Beisner, *Twelve Against Empire*, pp. 10-12, 69, 82, 290, *passim;* Geoffrey Blodgett, *The Gentle Reformers: Massachusetts Democrats in the Cleveland Era* (Cambridge, Mass.: Harvard University Press, 1966), pp. 265-268; Frederic Cople Jaher, *Doubters and Dissenters: Cataclysmic Thought in America, 1885–1918* (New York: The Free Press of Glencoe, 1964), especially pp. 75-78; Tompkins, *Anti-Imperialism*, pp. 140-160, 295.

76. *Ibid.*, pp. 258-260; Beisner, *Twelve Against Empire,* pp. 9-10, 186, 196, 228.

77. Blodgett, *Gentle Reformers,* pp. 266-267.

78. Beisner, *Twelve Against Empire,* pp. 13-17, 154, 229-230, 233.

79. Barbara Miller Solomon, *Ancestors and Immigrants: A Changing New England Tradition* (Cambridge, Mass.: Harvard University Press, 1956), p. 104; Capen to Cleveland, telegram, February 20, 1897, Grover Cleveland Papers (LC, on microfilm), Reel 96. The quotation by (and other information on) Capen can be found in Valentin Hanno Rabe, "The American Protestant Foreign Mission Movement, 1880–1920" (Ph.D. Dissertation, Harvard University, 1964), pp. 155-156, *passim.*

80. The quotations can be found in *Boston Globe,* March 2, 1897; and Thomas to Atkinson, December 6, 1898, Atkinson Papers, Box 20.

81. Charles E. Jefferson, "The New Navy," *Independent,* LVII (October 27, 1904), pp. 972-973.

82. This average is computed from the fourteen out of twenty directors whose ages could be ascertained. Marchand, *American Peace Movement,* p. 8, gives the average of all officers of the American Peace Society between 1900 and 1905 (using 1903 as the year of his computation) as sixty-three. Trueblood noted very early "that the older statesmen of the nation are almost without exception opposed to the colonial imperialistic policy now so much talked of." *AP,* LX (November, 1898), p. 225.

83. Robert Wesley Doherty, "Alfred H. Love and the Universal Peace Union" (Ph.D. Dissertation, University of Pennsylvania, 1962), p. 155.

84. Beisner, *Twelve Against Empire,* pp. 230-232, 237-239, the latter pages giving perfunctory recognition of the anti-imperialists' contributions. For more positive summaries, see Tompkins, *Anti-Imperialism,* pp. 295-296; Richard E. Welch, Jr., "Motives and Objectives of Anti-Imperialists, 1898," *Mid-America,* LI (April, 1969), pp. 119-129; and Richard E. Welch, Jr., *George Frisbie Hoar and the Half-Breed Republicans* (Cambridge, Mass.: Harvard University Press, 1971), pp. 286-289.

85. As one indication of their sturdy liberalism, Solomon, *Ancestors and Immigrants,* pp. 176-179, cites Atkinson, Garrison, Mead, Dole, as well as tepid anti-imperialists and hopeful international reformers Samuel Barrows and Edward Everett Hale as "the minority with faith" in the immigrant in late-nineteenth century Boston.

86. "Editor's Table," *NEM,* XX (July, 1899), p. 641.

87. Dole to Long, December 5, 1898, Long Papers, Box 44. For Dole's more jaundiced, retrospective view, see his autobiography, *My Eighty Years* (New York: E. P. Dutton & Co., 1927), pp. 319-320, 408-409, 416-417, 443.

88. Jordan, *Imperial Democracy,* p. 81; the latter statement is quoted in Edward McNall Burns, *David Starr Jordan: Prophet of Freedom* (Stanford: Stanford University Press, 1953), p. 35.

89. "Address to Voters by Representative Clergymen," *Unity,* XLVI (November 1, 1900), p. 130.

90. Jefferson in *LMC 1900,* pp. 101-102; Charles E. Jefferson, "The Delu-

sion of Militarism," *Atlantic Monthly*, CIII (March, 1909), pp. 379-388.

91. Tompkins, *Anti-Imperialism*, pp. 150, 153-154, 197, 214-235; Beisner, *Twelve Against Empire*, pp. 122-132, 190-192, 196, 203.

92. Edwin D. Mead, "Our Silver Experiment," *AJP*, V (October, 1894), pp. 399-407; "Editor's Table," *NEM*, XIII (February, 1896), p. 801; and *New York Times*, January 10, 1898. As an early indication of his emerging political sympathies, in the election of 1884 Mead supported the Republican presidential candidate, James G. Blaine, whom the Mugwumps deserted *en masse* because of his public indiscretions. Edwin D. Mead, *The Case of Mr. Blaine: An Open Letter to the Boston Advertiser. By an Independent* (Boston: J. S. Cushing & Co., 1884).

93. Mead, "Boston Memories of Fifty Years," p. 34; *Boston Globe*, October 18, 1900. Mead even perceptively depicted the conservative element ("individualism") in Bryan's progressivism ("for a very high measure of State control"). Mead to Editor, *Outlook*, LXVI (September 15, 1900), p. 185.

94. *Boston Globe*, October 4, 9 (evening), 14 (evening), 1900.

95. Winslow to Carnegie, November 7, 1900, Carnegie Papers, Vol. 79.

96. *Peacemaker*, XIX (November, 1900), pp. 105-106; Trueblood to Atkinson, March 21, 1899, Atkinson Papers, Box 20; *AP*, LXII (September, 1900), p. 169; (November, 1900), p. 205; (December, 1900), pp. 228-229. An extreme example was Love's close pacifist friend, David Ferris, an eighty year old radical Republican, who had never voted a Democratic ticket; but he decided to vote for Bryan in 1900 because of the McKinley administration's "crushing out the aspirations for Liberty of a weak people asking our friendship." Ferris to Bryan, October 24, 1900, Bryan Papers, Box 25.

97. "Address to Voters by Representative Clergymen," p. 130, and Jenkin Lloyd Jones, "World Politics Versus Party Issues," pp. 102-106, urged an anti-McKinley vote, and both articles were friendly to Bryan. Mercer to Bryan, July 26, 1900, Bryan Papers, Box 25; on Welsh, see Beisner, *Twelve Against Empire*, p. 130.

98. Carnegie to Bryan, December 15, 26, 27, 1898, January 10, 1899 (misdated 1898), Bryan Papers, Box 22; *Autobiography of Andrew Carnegie* (Boston: Houghton Mifflin Co., 1920), p. 364; Jordan to Bryan, February 7, March 7, April 13, 1900, Bryan Papers, Box 24. Atkinson's remark is found in his letter to Carnegie, November 19, 1900, Carnegie Papers, Vol. 79.

99. Atkinson to Carnegie, June 22, 1899, *ibid.*, Vol. 66.

100. Beisner, *Twelve Against Empire*, pp. 89, 93-94, 103, 221.

101. Carnegie to Editor, *New York World*, December 30, 1900, Carnegie Papers, Vol. 80.

Chapter 5

1. Crosby quoted in *AP*, LX (November, 1898), p. 227.

2. *Ibid.* (August and September, 1898), pp. 176, 191; *Peacemaker*, XVII (October, 1898), pp. 74-76; "Czar Nicholas for Peace," *Woman's Journal*, XXIX (September 3, 1898), p. 284; "International Disarmament," *ibid.*; Jen-

kin Lloyd Jones, *A Search for an Infidel: Bits of Wayside Gospel* (New York: The Macmillan Company, 1901), pp. 61-62.

3. *AP,* LX (October, 1898), pp. 197-198.

4. *Ibid.,* p. 202; Paine and Trueblood to McKinley, September 26, 1898, William McKinley Papers (LC, on microfilm), Reel 62.

5. *New York Times,* October 21, 1898.

6. Charles L. Hutchins to Paine, November 24, 1898, Robert Treat Paine Papers (MHS), Box 2; *AP,* LX (November, 1898), p. 225; Belva A. Lockwood, *Peace and the Outlook,* (Washington, D.C.: Thos. W. Cadick, 1899), p. 18; *Peacemaker,* XVII (January, 1899), pp. 139-140.

7. *New York Times,* October 30, 1898; Lucia Mead, "How to Cooperate with the Czar," *Woman's Journal,* XXIX (December 3, 1898), p. 386.

8. Paine in *LMC 1900,* p. 59.

9. Merze Tate, *The Disarmament Illusion: The Movement for a Limitation of Armaments to 1907* (New York: The Macmillan Company, 1942), ch. 12, summarizes nonpacifist opinion on the Czar's rescript. *AP,* LX (August and September, 1898), p. 176; (October, 1898), pp. 197-198; "Peace Notes," *Woman's Journal,* XXX (April 1, 1899), p. 101; Mary A. Livermore, cited in "Woman's Peace Meeting," *ibid.,* XXX (April 8, 1899), p. 112.

10. Calvin DeArmond Davis, *The United States and the First Hague Peace Conference* (Ithaca, N.Y.: Cornell University Press, 1962), p. 50.

11. *Ibid.,* pp. 43-48, is a careful analysis of these factors. Also see Ernest R. May, *Imperial Democracy: The Emergence of America as a Great Power* (New York: Harcourt, Brace & World, 1961), p. 236.

12. *AP,* LX (November, 1898), pp. 226-227; (December, 1898), pp. 254, 255, 257.

13. *Ibid.,* p. 251.

14. *Ibid.,* LXI (February, 1899), p. 34. Tolstoy was misquoted, for he shortly attacked the conference and reasserted his belief that universal peace would come only from mass "disobedience to the Government that exacts military service from individuals for violence and organized murder." *New York Times,* February 12, 1899. He also is quoted in "Peace Notes," *Woman's Journal,* XXX (April 1, 1899), p. 101.

15. *Arbitrator,* No. 311 (December, 1898), pp. 64-67, 73-74.

16. *AP,* LX (December, 1898), pp. 259-261; LXI (January, 1899), p. 10.

17. Frederic Whyte, *The Life of W. T. Stead,* 2 vols. (Boston: Houghton Mifflin Company, 1925), II, pp. 10, 27, 35-53, 78-87.

18. W. T. Stead, *The United States of Europe on the Eve of the Parliament of Peace* (New York: Doubleday & McClure Co., 1899), pp. 115-144, 351-355; Whyte, *Stead,* II, pp. 129-134.

19. Stead's report, quoted in *Arbitrator,* No. 311 (December, 1898), p. 70; Stead, *United States of Europe,* pp. 369-394, 443-447.

20. *AP,* LXI (January, 1899), p. 6.

21. Stead, *United States of Europe,* pp. 461-468.

22. *New York Times,* January 6, 1899.

23. *AP,* LXI (January, 1899), pp. 6-7.

24. *Ibid.* Even before Stead began his crusade, Trueblood suspected him. *Ibid.*, LX (March, 1898), pp. 61-62.

25. Davis, *First Hague Peace Conference,* pp. 59-60.

26. *AP,* LXI (February, 1899), p. 33.

27. Davis, *First Hague Peace Conference,* pp. 51-53.

28. *AP,* LXI (March, 1899), p. 51.

29. See *Peacemaker,* XVII (February, 1899), p. 154, and other examples cited in many of the following notes.

30. Sylvester John Hemleben, *Plans for World Peace through Six Centuries* (Chicago: The University of Chicago Press, 1943), pp. 1-3, 16-17, 86-87, 105-106, 109-114, 122.

31. *Ibid.,* pp. 105-111; Merle Curti, *The American Peace Crusade, 1815–1860* (Durham, N.C.: Duke University Press, 1929), pp. 10, 55, 58-60.

32. W. Evans Darby, *International Arbitration. International Tribunals. A Collection of the Various Schemes Which Have Been Propounded, and of Instances Since 1815* (London: J. M. Dent and Co., 1900), pp. 122-123.

33. Lockwood, *Peace and the Outlook,* p. 19; American Arbitration League, *Annual Report, 1884–1885* (n.p.: n.p., n.d.), pp. 14-15; *CR,* 49th Cong., 1st sess., XVII, pp. 154, 475, 732, 806, 1142, 1808, 2204, 2286, 2321, 2381, 2519, 2608, 2734, 2982; *ibid.,* 49th Cong., 2nd sess., XVIII, pp. 1175, 1601, 1801; *ibid.,* 50th Cong., 1st sess., XIX, pp. 25, 2409, 2796, 5828; *ibid.,* 52nd Cong., 2nd sess., XXIV, p. 44.

34. *AP,* LV (October, 1893), pp. 237-238. The plan of the American Peace Society borrowed freely from the Pan-American Congress' treaty of arbitration, Field's draft code, and essays by and suggestions from interested friends. Also, *UPC 1893,* pp. 159-185, 292, 295.

35. Hans Wehburg, "The Interparliamentary Union and the Development of International Organization," in *The Interparliamentary Union from 1889 to 1939* (Lausanne, Switz.: n.p., 1939), pp. 39, 41-43, 45-46; and Christian L. Lange, "The Interparliamentary Union," *International Conciliation,* No. 65 (April, 1913), pp. 6-7; Darby, *International Arbitration,* pp. 290-295.

36. *AP,* LVIII (March, 1896), pp. 54-55; (April, 1896), pp. 77-78; and some of the following notes.

37. Walter S. Logan in *LMC 1896,* pp. 60-65; *NYSBA 1896,* pp. 275-295. For a similar plan, see David Jayne Hill, "International Justice," *Yale Law Journal,* VI (October, 1896), especially pp. 14-18.

38. Quoted by W. Martin Jones in *LMC 1897,* p. 69.

39. W. Martin Jones in *LMC 1899,* pp. 44-45; W. Martin Jones to White, May 16, 1899, Andrew D. White Papers (Cornell University Libraries, on microfilm), Reel 78; Aubrey Lawrence Parkman, "David Jayne Hill" (Ph.D. Dissertation, University of Rochester, 1961), pp. 236-240.

40. Edward Everett Hale, *Memories of a Hundred Years,* 2 vols. in 1 (New York: The Macmillan Company, 1904), II, p. 282; *The Works of Edward Everett Hale,* 10 vols. (Boston: Little, Brown, and Company, 1898–1901), VI, pp. 399-400.

41. Edward Everett Hale, "The High Court of America," *Lend a Hand: A*

Record of Progress, IV (December, 1889), pp. 845-848; Hale in *LMC 1896,* pp. 22-23.

42. *UPC 1893,* pp. 166-168; *AP,* LXI (March, 1894), p. 59.

43. Hale in *LMC 1896,* p. 19; platform in *ibid.,* p. 130; Hale in *LMC 1897,* pp. 12, 44, 65; platform in *ibid.,* pp. 130-131.

44. Hale in *LMC 1895,* p. 22; and *LMC 1896,* pp. 19-20.

45. *Ibid.,* p. 19; Edward Everett Hale, "The United States of Europe," *Old and New,* III (March, 1871), pp. 260-267.

46. Hale to Emily P. Hale (his wife), April 24, 1896, and Hale to Mr. Clayden, May 6, 1897, Edward Everett Hale Papers (New York State Library), Box 11; Hale in *LMC 1897,* pp. 11-12.

47. Edward Everett Hale, "Out of the Mouth of Czars," *NEM,* XIX (January, 1899), p. 583.

48. Hale in *LMC 1899,* p. 8; Mercer in *ibid.,* pp. 39-40; "Editor's Table," *NEM,* XX (April, 1899), pp. 254-255. Undated petition to Nicholas II signed by twenty-nine Philadelphians in the White Papers, Reel 78.

49. Hale to My Dear One (his wife?), March 20, 1899, Hale Family Papers (LC), Box 21; Hale to Jack Hale (his son), March 23, 1899, Hale Papers, Box 12.

50. "Women's Peace Meeting," *Woman's Journal,* XXX (April 8, 1899), p. 112.

51. May Wright Sewall, "Universal Peace Meetings," *ibid.,* XXX (April 29, 1899), p. 129; "Women's Appeal for Peace," *ibid.,* p. 136; "American Women for Peace," *ibid.* (May 27, 1899), p. 168; Sewall to Editors, *ibid.* (June 3, 1899), p. 170; "Women's Appeal for Peace," *ibid.,* p. 175; also, C.C.H., "Peace Meeting in Orange," *ibid.* (January 14, 1899), p. 15; "A Woman for Peace Commissioner," *ibid.* (May 13, 1899), p. 148.

52. G. Vogelsang, unidentified newspaper clipping, attached to Vogelsang's letter to White, August 29, 1898, White Papers, Reel 78.

53. *AP,* LXI (March, 1899), p. 51.

54. No figures on the circulation of *Peace Crusade* are available, but the number of extant issues is very limited.

55. *Peacemaker,* XVII (June, 1899), p. 228; also see Hale to My Dear One (his wife?), March 23, 1899, Hale Family Papers, Box 21.

56. Hale to Edward Hale (his son), June 1, 1899, Hale Papers, Box 12.

57. According to Holls' minutes of the conference, the American delegation received letters and cablegrams endorsing the conference from six Society of Friends' monthly meetings, one Mennonite conference, three Christian Endeavor conventions, one Evangelical Alliance group, six other church organizations, four suffragist and women's groups, Universal Peace Union, Lake Mohonk Conference, five "mass meetings," and four miscellaneous groups or individuals. This total apparently excepts those petitions sent directly to individual American delegates. Minutes, May 19-June 10, 1899. U.S. Delegation to the First International Peace Conference, 1899, RG 59 (NA), Box 1.

58. See Trueblood's many letters to his wife, especially those dated May

21, 23, 29, and June 9, 1899, APS Papers, Box 17; Benjamin F. Trueblood, "The International Peace Conference at The Hague," *NEM,* XX (August, 1899), pp. 667-668.

59. White to George L. Burr, May 26, 1899, White Papers, Reel 78.

60. The quotations (and biographical information) appear in White to George Park Fisher, May 29, 1899, White to Juliet Lewis Hill, June 5, 1899, White to Goldwin Smith, June 23, 1899, and White to George L. Burr, July 11, 1899, *ibid.*

61. Davis, *First Hague Peace Conference,* pp. 149-167, 170-171, 188-189, 195, 212-213, *passim.*

62. *Ibid.,* pp. 197-202. Also, Dodge to Harrison, December 4, 1899, January 12, 1900, Benjamin Harrison Papers (LC, on microfilm), Reel 42; Porter to Dodge, December 30, 1899, McKinley Papers, Reel 44; Hale to McKinley, November 16, 1899, *ibid.,* Reel 70; Hale to My own child (?), March 25, 1900, Hale Papers, Box 12.

63. *AP,* LXI (September, 1899), p. 176; LXVI (December, 1904), p. 225; Straus in *UPC 1904,* pp. 62, 63; Lockwood in *ibid.,* p. 198; Paine in *LMC 1900,* p. 59; *AFPC 1901,* pp. 208-209.

64. Paine in *LMC 1901,* p. 57; Trueblood in *ibid.,* pp. 13, 24; *AP,* LXIII (January, 1901), p. 11; (March, 1901), p. 49; (July, 1901), p. 138; LXIV (December, 1902), p. 219.

65. Platform in *LMC 1900,* p. 105; platform in *LMC 1901,* p. 91; *AP,* LXIII (January, 1901), p. 9; Hale to Theodore Roosevelt, November 14, 1901, *The Life and Letters of Edward Everett Hale,* ed. Edward Everett Hale, Jr. (Boston: Little, Brown and Company, 1917), pp. 385-386.

66. *Theodore Roosevelt: An Autobiography* (New York: The Macmillan Company, 1913), p. 581; Paul H. B. D'Estournelles de Constant, *America and Her Problems* (New York: The Macmillan Company, 1915), pp. 307-308; *AP,* LXIV (August, 1902), p. 152; W. L. Penfield in *LMC 1903,* pp. 83-90. Francis J. Weber, "The Pious Fund of the Californias," *Hispanic American Historical Review,* XLIII (February, 1963), pp. 78-94, discusses the arbitration.

67. *AP,* LXIV (December, 1902), pp. 213-214; LXV (November, 1903), p. 192; LXVI (March, 1904), pp. 41-42; (August, 1904), p. 141.

68. *Ibid.,* LXV (February, 1903), p. 26; LXVI (January, 1904), pp. 1-2; *Peacemaker,* XXIII (March, 1904), pp. 58-59; John W. Foster, *Arbitration and the Hague Court* (Boston: Houghton Mifflin and Co., 1904), pp. 70-72. D'Estournelles in *New York Times,* September 18, 1904.

Chapter 6

1. Raymond L. Bridgman, *World Organization* (Boston: Ginn and Company, 1906), *passim.*

2. Benjamin F. Trueblood, *The Federation of the World* (Boston: Houghton Mifflin and Co., 1899), *passim.*

3. Paine in *UPU 1904,* p. 36.

4. *AP,* LXV (February, 1903), pp. 21-22.

5. *Ibid.,* pp. 23-25; (March, 1903), pp. 37-38; (April, 1903), p. 57; (May, 1903), p. 81; LXVI (May, 1904), pp. 91-93; (June, 1904), p. 108. Also see Warren F. Kuehl, *Seeking World Order: The United States and International Organization to 1920* (Nashville, Tenn.: Vanderbilt University Press, 1969), pp. 62-66.

6. *CR,* 55th Cong., 2nd sess., XXXI, p. 3225; *ibid.,* 56th Cong., 1st sess., XXXIII, Appendix, p. 44.

7. *Address of Hon. Richard Bartholdt, President of the American Group, at the XIII Conference of the Interparliamentary Union at Brussels, August 29, 1905,* printed speech, p. 4, Richard Bartholdt Papers (Missouri Historical Society).

8. Richard Bartholdt, *From Steerage to Congress: Reminiscences and Reflections* (Philadelphia: Dorrance & Co., 1930), pp. 159-160; the quoted phrase is in *New York Times,* November 8, 1913.

9. Bartholdt to White, August 12, 19, 1899, Andrew D. White Papers (Cornell University Libraries, on microfilm), Reel 78.

10. Bartholdt, *Address . . . August 29, 1905,* p. 2, Bartholdt Papers; also see Bartholdt, *From Steerage to Congress,* pp. 172-173, 178-183.

11. Bartholdt, *Address . . . August 29, 1905,* Bartholdt Papers; Bartholdt in *LMC 1906,* pp. 50-51; and Bartholdt, *From Steerage to Congress,* pp. 216-223.

12. For earlier, ephemeral interest in the Interparliamentary Union among congressmen, see *AP,* LVI (March, 1894), pp. 62-63; *Among the World's Peacemakers: An Epitome of the Interparliamentary Union,* ed. Hayne Davis (New York: The Progressive Publishing Co., 1907), p. 16; and Samuel J. Barrows in *LMC 1900,* pp. 17-20.

13. Bartholdt, *From Steerage to Congress,* pp. 171-178.

14. *Ibid.,* pp. 213-216; *New York Times,* January 14, 1904; *Peacemaker,* XXIII (February, 1904), pp. 42-43.

15. Forrest Crissey, *Theodore E. Burton: American Statesman* (Cleveland: The World Publishing Co., 1956), pp. 238-239. Ellen M. Slayden, *Washington Wife: Journal of Ellen Maury Slayden from 1897–1919* (New York: Harper & Row, 1963), pp. 55, 62, 71-79, 86, 89, 95, 124, 153, 160, 216, 351, 365, documents her husband's participation in the Interparliamentary Union and American Peace Society.

16. Davis to Mary Baker Eddy, October 8, 1906, reproduced in *Christian Science Sentinel,* October 20, 1906, detailed the origins of his interest in international institutions.

17. Davis' ideas are most fully presented in five of his articles: "The Promoters of the Union of Nations," *Independent,* LV (February 12, 1903), pp. 384-386; "The Final Outcome of the Declaration of Independence," *ibid.* (July 2, 1903), pp. 1543-1547; "The Development of the Union," *ibid.,* LVI (May 12, 1904), pp. 1072-1076; "A World's Congress," *ibid.,* LVII (July 7, 1904),

pp. 11-19; and "President and the Interparliamentary Union," *Harper's Weekly,* XLVIII (October 22, 1904), pp. 1611-1612, 1627-1628.

18. *LMC 1904,* pp. 119-122.

19. Davis, *Among the World's Peacemakers,* pp. 22-23, 25, 27-30.

20. *Union Interparliamentaire pour L'Arbitrage International, Session de 1904, Compte Rendu de la XIIe Conference Tenue à Saint Louis, Missouri du 12 au 14 Septembre 1904,* (Washington, D.C.: Government Printing Office, 1905), p. 60.

21. *Ibid.,* p. 61; *New York Times,* September 25, 1904; and Ellen Slayden, *Washington Wife,* pp. 56-61.

22. Roosevelt to Trueblood, October 20, 1904, *The Letters of Theodore Roosevelt,* ed. Elting E. Morison, 8 vols. (Cambridge, Mass.: Harvard University Press, 1951–1954), IV, p. 987; *FR 1904,* pp. 10-13.

23. Theodore Marburg, "Apostles of World Unity, VI—Hamilton Holt," *World Unity,* I (March, 1928), p. 412.

24. Warren F. Kuehl, *Hamilton Holt: Journalist, Internationalist, Educator* (Gainesville: University of Florida Press, 1960), pp. 66-74, 269n20, summarizes Holt's conversion to the peace movement and *The Independent's* clear supremacy among general-interest periodicals on the subjects of peace and internationalism. Also see the editorial comment introducing Hayne Davis' article, "The Old Order Changeth," *Independent,* CV (April 2, 1921), p. 336.

25. "A World Congress," *ibid.,* LVII (July 7, 1904), pp. 46-47.

26. "A Constitution of the World," *ibid.,* LXII (April 11, 1907), p. 826.

27. Bartholdt, *Address . . . August 29, 1905,* Bartholdt Papers; Bartholdt, typescript of supporting speech to the Interparliamentary Union at Brussels in 1905, *ibid.; New York Times,* May 1, 1905. Bartholdt, *From Steerage to Congress,* pp. 267-275.

28. *CR,* 59th Cong., 2nd sess., XLI, Appendix, pp. 49-51; Bartholdt, *From Steerage to Congress,* pp. 277-281; Bartholdt in *ASIL 1907,* pp. 246-251.

29. CEIP, Division of International Law, *The Final Acts of the First and Second Hague Peace Conference, Together with the Draft Convention on a Judicial Arbitration Court,* Pamphlet No. 10 (Washington, D.C.: CEIP, 1915), pp. 25-40.

30. See the absence of any strikingly new proposals in Union Interparlementaire, *Compte Rendu de la XVIIe Conference, Tenue à Génève, du 18 au 20 Septembre 1912* (Bruxelles: n.p., 1913), especially pp. 348-355; and Union Interparlementaire, *Compte Rendu de la XVIIIe Conference, Tenue à La Haye, du 3 au 5 Septembre 1913* (Bruxelles: n.p., 1914), especially pp. 355-358. Also, Bartholdt, *From Steerage to Congress,* pp. 282-284, 352-353.

31. *AP,* LXIX (August and September, 1907), pp. 278-279.

32. Belva A. Lockwood, *The Central American Peace Congress and an International Arbitration Court for the Five Central American Republics* (Washington, D.C.: n.p., 1908), pp. 3, 12-13; *Peacemaker,* XXVI (July, 1907), pp. 154-155; (September, 1907), pp. 196-197.

33. *AP,* LXIX (November, 1907), pp. 229-230; (December, 1907), p.

249; LXX (February, 1908), pp. 32-34; *Peacemaker,* XXVI (November, 1907), pp. 241-242.

34. Mead in *NPC 1909,* p. 38; and *AP,* LXX (February, 1908), p. 32. Also see *ibid.,* LXIX (October, 1907), p. 211; William P. Rogers in *NPC 1909,* p. 112; Frederick Lynch in *LMC 1908,* p. 34; and *Peacemaker,* XXVI (December, 1907), p. 267.

35. Foster in *LMC 1908,* p. 12.

36. Holt, "The Federation of the World," undated Ms. [1907–1914], pp. 20-24, Hamilton Holt Papers (Mills Memorial Library, Rollins College), Box 91; Smiley in *LMC 1908,* pp. 9-10; Trueblood in *NEAPC 1910,* p. 24; Hull in *NPC 1909,* pp. 217-220; Davis in *Peacemaker,* XXVI (December, 1907), pp. 276-278; Raymond L. Bridgman, "The World's Legislature Is Here," *NEM,* XXXVIII (May, 1908), pp. 355-361.

37. Frederick Lynch, "The Leaders of the New Peace Movement in America," *Independent,* LXIX (September 22, 1910), p. 629. Also see William I. Hull, *The New Peace Movement* (Boston: The World Peace Foundation, 1912), pp. v-ix, 1, *passim.*

38. Frederick Lynch, *Personal Recollections of Andrew Carnegie* (New York: Fleming H. Revell Co., 1920), p. 24.

39. Henry F. May, *The End of American Innocence: A Study of the First Years of Our Own Time, 1912–1917* (New York: Alfred A. Knopf, 1959), Part I, ch. 2.

40. For juxtaposition of the words "practical" and "idealistic," see Robert Erskine Ely in *NAPC 1907,* pp. 7-8; Short in *NPC 1909,* p. 362.

41. For rising acceptance of sanctions, see below, pp. 166-167; and Kuehl, *Seeking World Order,* pp. 88-94, 111, 117-122.

42. "Federation of the World," pp. 27-28. *NPC 1909,* pp. 333-335, gives a printed summary of Holt's lecture.

43. Hull in *ibid.,* p. 204. The origins of Hull's involvement in the peace movement are somewhat obscure. There is a reference to a Dr. William I. Hill [sic] of Swarthmore College writing a pacifist speech for a peace meeting. *AP,* LVII (April, 1895), p. 92. Despite the surname Hill, the reference is almost certainly to Hull, but I could find no references to Hull's opposition to the Spanish-American War or imperialism.

44. Mead, "The Results of the Two Hague Conferences and the Demands upon the Third Conference," *World Peace Foundation, Pamphlet Series,* No. 1, Part I (April, 1911), p. 6; Bridgman, "World's Legislature Is Here," pp. 357-360.

45. Denys B. Myers, ed., "Arbitration Engagements Now Existing in Treaties, Treaty Provisions and National Constitutions," *World Peace Foundation, Pamphlet Series,* V, No. 5, Part III (October, 1915), pp. 9-27, 30. Slightly higher totals are given in Denys B. Myers, ed., "List of Arbitration Treaties: Pacts to Which Pairs of Nations are Parties with Statistics and Notes," *World Peace Foundation, Pamphlet Series,* No. 2, Part I (July, 1911), pp. 3-16; and Lucia Mead, *Swords and Ploughshares, or the Supplanting of the Sys-*

tem of War by the System of Law (New York: G. P. Putnam's Sons, 1912), facing p. 246.

46. A. M. Stuyt, *Survey of International Arbitrations, 1794–1938* (The Hague: Martinus Nijhoff, 1939), pp. 153-317, lists ninety-one arbitration cases between 1887 and 1900 and only seventy-nine from 1901 to 1914.

47. Pax Pace (pseudonym) in *AP*, LXVI (January, 1904), pp. 11-16.

48. Storey's speech is summarized in *ibid.* (June, 1904), p. 104. Also see the critique by international law professor, Charles Cheney Hyde, in *NPC 1909*, pp. 23-31.

49. *NEAIL 1905*, pp. 50-53; *NEAIL 1912*, p. 8.

50. *AP*, LXV (December, 1903), pp. 214-215; and LXVI (June, 1904), pp. 97-98.

51. Roosevelt to John Hay, with Straus' attached memorandum, November 6, 1903, *Letters of Theodore Roosevelt*, III, pp. 648-649.

52. Quoted in Naomi W. Cohen, *A Dual Heritage: The Public Career of Oscar Straus* (Philadelphia: Jewish Publication Society of America, 1969), pp. 112-113.

53. *Ibid.*

54. Marburg in *LMC 1910*, p. 86.

55. Foster in *LMC 1903*, p. 9; A. Maurice Low in *ibid.*, p. 44; platform in *ibid.*, p. 119.

56. Resolutions in *ACIA 1904*, p. 12. Also see Mead's discussion in *PAPC 1908*, pp. 89-91.

57. *Ibid.;* Holt to Scott, September 23, 1909, Holt Papers, Box 1; *AP*, LXVII (January, 1905), pp. 1-2; (February, 1905), p. 25; Cohen, *Dual Heritage*, p. 112.

58. Moore to Foster, February 8, 1904, and Moore to L. T. Chamberlain, November 12, 1904, Moore Papers, Box 10. Moore agreed that the treaties should except questions that either nation decided affected its "vital interests," but he also wanted them to say that the parties would not resort to hostilities until effort had been made to settle all questions either by submitting them to a commission of jurists composed of an equal number of members from each side, or by invoking mediation of one or more friendly powers. See his draft of resolutions for the Washington Arbitration Conference, enclosed in Moore to Simeon E. Baldwin, January 10, 1904, Baldwin Family Papers (Yale University Library), Box 107.

59. For an account of one municipal meeting, see *Record of the Proceedings at a Mass Meeting of the Citizens of New York Held Under the Auspices of the New York Executive Committee of the American Conference on International Arbitration at Carnegie Hall, On Friday Evening, December 16, 1904* (n.p.; n.p., n.d.).

60. For Roosevelt's position, see especially Roosevelt to Shelby Moore Cullom, February 10, 1905, *Letters of Theodore Roosevelt*, IV, pp. 1118-1119.

61. *AP*, LXVII (February, 1905), p. 26; Cohen, *Dual Heritage*, p. 112.

62. Bartholdt in *AP*, LXVII (April, 1905), p. 87; Kuehl, *Seeking World Order*, p. 62.

63. Platform in *LMC 1908*, pp. 7-8; Foster in *ibid.*, p. 13; *AP*, LXX (March, 1908), p. 50; Lockwood, *Central American Peace Congress*, p. 14.

Chapter 7

1. See Albert Smiley's remarks and membership lists in *LMC 1904*, pp. 5, 162-165; *LMC 1905*, pp. 9-10, 171-175; *LMC 1906*, pp. 167-171; *LMC 1907*, pp. 192-197.

2. Quoted in *NAPC 1907*, pp. 7-10; also see the membership list in *ibid.*, pp. 447-478.

3. *AP*, LXIX (December, 1907), pp. 250-251; LXX (June, 1908), pp. 126-128; LXXII (June, 1910), pp. 125-131.

4. Arthur Deerin Call in *APS 1915*, p. 23, listed twenty-three state and local peace societies founded between November 1904 and March 1912. This total included only those groups having the words "peace society" in their titles as well as having formal affiliation with the American Peace Society in 1915.

5. Edwin Ginn, *Are Our Schools in Danger?* (n.p.: n.p., 1895), pp. 1-3; Ginn in *LMC 1901*, p. 21; Ginn in *NAPC 1907*, p. 155.

6. Ginn is quoted in *UPC 1904*, pp. 217-218. Also see his speeches in *LMC 1901*, pp. 20-21; and *NAPC 1907*, pp. 152-156.

7. Arthur N. Holcombe, *A Strategy of Peace in a Changing World* (Cambridge, Mass.: Harvard University Press, 1967), pp. 175, 176, 181-182, 206.

8. Mead in *LMC 1910*, pp. 188-192.

9. Ginn's addresses in *NAPC 1907*, pp. 153-155; and *UPC 1904*, pp. 217-218; Ginn to Samuel T. Dutton, January 22, 1908, NYPS Papers (SCPC), Box 4. Ginn to Atkinson, July 20, 1904, Edward Atkinson Papers (MHS), Box 25.

10. Edwin Ginn, "The International School of Peace," *Nation*, LXXXIX (September 23, 1909), pp. 275-276. Also, Ginn to Carnegie, January 19, 1907, Andrew Carnegie Papers (LC), Vol. 139.

11. Ginn to Jordan, March 1, 25, 1910, JPSC.

12. Ginn in *NPC 1909*, p. 322; and *NAPC 1907*, p. 156.

13. Holcombe, *Strategy of Peace*, p. 176.

14. The trustees were its president, Edwin Ginn; Samuel Train Dutton, head of Teachers College, Columbia University; W.H.P. Faunce, president of Brown University; Sarah L. Arnold, dean of Simmons College; Joseph Swain, president of Swarthmore College; A. Lawrence Lowell, president of Harvard University; Samuel W. McCall, former governor and congressman from Massachusetts; Edward Cummings, a Unitarian minister in Boston; George A. Plimpton, an executive in Ginn and Co.; and George W. Anderson, a Boston lawyer. The directors were Charles R. Brown, dean of the Yale Divinity School; David Starr Jordan; Edwin D. Mead; Hamilton Holt; James A. MacDonald, editor of the *Toronto Globe;* James Brown Scott, international lawyer and State Department Solicitor; and John R. Mott, secretary-general of the Christian Students Federation. Others had served as trustees in 1910 but had resigned by the end of the year. Those listed here were the trustees and directors elected at the third meeting of the trustees on December 22, 1910. Albert E. Pillsbury, Boston lawyer and former anti-imperialist, and Samuel B. Capen were added to the board

of trustees in 1911. Two directors, Mott and Scott, were soon replaced by George W. Nasmyth and William I. Hull, since the former two could not devote much time to the foundation. Meetings of July 12, November 29, December 22, 1910, November 28, 1911, November 26, 1912, pp. 12-13, 15-16, 17, 28, 31-34, 40-42, Minutes of the Meetings of the Board of Trustees, 1910–1926, WPF Files (WPF, Boston).

15. Ginn in *ASJSID 1910*, pp. 313-315. I am indebted, here and elsewhere, to Peter Filene, "The World Peace Foundation and Progressivism, 1910-1918," *New England Quarterly*, XXXVI (December, 1963), pp. 478-501.

16. See Edwin D. Mead's articles: "Adjustment of Education to Contemporary Needs," *Educational Review*, XIX (May, 1900), pp. 472-480; and "Peace Teaching in American Schools and Colleges," *Outlook*, LXXXIII (June 16, 1906), pp. 376-382.

17. *AP*, LXVII (July, 1905), pp. 145-146; LXVIII (May, 1906), pp. 97-98; (August, 1906), p. 173; George Fulk, "The Intercollegiate Peace Association," *Independent*, LXIV (June 19, 1908), pp. 1396-1398; *Prize Orations of the Intercollegiate Peace Association*, ed. Stephen F. Weston (Boston: The World Peace Foundation, 1914).

18. Louis P. Lochner, *Always the Unexpected: A Book of Reminiscences* (New York: The Macmillan Co., 1956), pp. 33-35; Bjarne H. Graff, "A Resume of the Cosmopolitan Movement in the United States," *The Cosmopolitan Annual: Official Organ of the Association of Cosmopolitan Clubs*, II (Ithaca, N.Y.: Andrus S. Church, 1908), pp. 59-61; Louis P. Lochner, "The Cosmopolitan Club Movement," *International Conciliation*, Pamphlet No. 61 (December, 1912), p. 14.

19. Lochner, *Always the Unexpected*, pp. 35-36; *The Diaries of Andrew D. White*, ed. Robert Morris Ogden (Ithaca, N.Y.: Cornell University Press, 1959), p. 441; Andrew D. White, "Some Hints as to the Future Work of the Hague Conference," *The Cornell Cosmopolitan Annual*, I (1906–1907) (Ithaca, N.Y.: Andrus & Church, 1907), pp. 47-49.

20. Lochner in *AP*, LXXI (February, 1909), p. 43; and LXXII (January, 1910), p. 15. Edwin D. Mead in Benjamin F. Trueblood, *The Development of the Peace Idea, and Other Essays* (Boston: Plimpton Press, 1932), p. xxi. Trueblood's addresses are reproduced in *The Cosmopolitan Annual: Official Organ of the Association of Cosmopolitan Clubs* (Madison, Wisc.: The Post, 1909), pp. 74-80; and Benjamin F. Trueblood, "War, a Thing of the Past," *Cosmopolitan Student, I* (April, 1910), pp. 49-50.

21. Lochner in *AP*, LXXII (April, 1910), p. 88; Charles E. Beals in *ibid.*, LXXIV (May, 1912), p. 119; and (December, 1912), pp. 269-270; Mead to Carnegie, January 13, 1910, Edwin and Lucia Mead Papers (SCPC), Box 1.

22. George W. Nasmyth, "The Peace Movement in the Colleges," *Independent*, LXVIII (February 17, 1910), p. 363.

23. Lochner in *AP*, LXXII (January, 1910), p. 15; and LXXIII (June, 1911), pp. 139-140.

24. Biographical Sketch of George William Nasmyth, typescript in George

W. Nasmyth Papers (SCPC), Box 1; *AP,* LXXIV (September and October, 1912), p. 209; Lochner, *Always the Unexpected,* pp. 34-38.

25. *ASPL 1909,* p. 26.

26. Andrews in *APC 1913,* pp. 211-213.

27. Fannie Fern Andrews, "A Course of Study in Good Will," *Religious Education,* VI (January, 1912), pp. 570-573. Also see *ASPL 1911,* pp. 44-46.

28. Mead to Finance Committee, Board of Trustees, World Peace Foundation, February 9, 1911, Mead to Ginn, February 15, 1911, and Mead to Andrews, March 15, 1911, WPF Papers (SCPC), Box 2; Edwin D. Mead, "The World Peace Foundation: Work in 1913," *World Peace Foundation, Pamphlet Series,* III, No. 12 (December, 1913), p. 14. Andrew Carnegie gave $1,000 annually to the League until 1911 when the Carnegie Endowment for International Peace continued the same contribution. A wealthy Bostonian, Mrs. J. Malcolm Forbes, gave at least $5,000 annually to the League. The World Peace Foundation contributed $1,250 in 1911 and $2,500 in the succeeding prewar years. See the treasurer's reports in *ASPL,* for the years 1909 to 1915.

29. *New York Times,* May 12, 1912; Andrews in *APC 1913,* pp. 78-80. Also see the peace literature Mrs. Andrews compiled and Claxton's office distributed: United States Bureau of Education, "The Promotion of Peace," *Bulletin* (1913: No. 12); and "Peace Day (May 18)," *Bulletin* (1912: No. 8).

30. *A Course in Citizenship,* comp. Ella Lyman Cabot, Fannie Fern Andrews, Fanny E. Coe, Mabel Hill, and Mary McSkimmon (Boston: Houghton Mifflin Company, 1914), pp. v-ix, *passim.*

31. The original name, Peace Society of the City of New York, was changed to New York Peace Society in 1910. For convenience, I have used the latter title throughout.

32. Charles Herbert Levermore, *Samuel Train Dutton: A Biography* (New York: The Macmillan Company, 1922), pp. 80-83; *AP,* LXVIII (February, 1906), p. 33; (March, 1906), p. 65.

33. Author's interview with Short's son, Frederick W. Short, in Geneseo, New York, February 13, 1969. The quotation comes from Frederick W. Short's typescript compilation, "Life Sketch & Selected Peace Papers of William Harrison Short" (courtesy of Frederick W. Short). Also see Warren F. Kuehl, *Hamilton Holt: Journalist, Internationalist, Educator* (Gainesville: University of Florida Press, 1960), pp. 90, 119, 125ff.

34. *NYPS 1906-1907,* p. 9; *NYPS 1912,* p. 21.

35. John Hays Hammond in *APC 1911,* p. 425; C. Roland Marchand, *The American Peace Movement and Social Reform, 1898-1918* (Princeton, N.J.: Princeton University Press, 1972), pp. 86-97.

36. *NYPS 1912,* pp. 13, 17-21; NYPS Minutes, January 21, 1910, NYPS Papers, Box 1; Levermore, *Dutton,* pp. 89-91; Short in *APC 1911,* p. 221.

37. Trueblood in *APS 1909,* p. 5.

38. Compare private incomes in *APS 1912,* pp. 13, 24; and *NYPS 1912,* pp. 21-23.

39. Carnegie in *NAPC 1907,* p. 381. The following pages in the text on

Carnegie's growing involvement in the peace movement are adapted from my article, "Andrew Carnegie's Quest for World Peace," *Proceedings of the American Philosophical Society,* CXIV (October 20, 1970), pp. 375-378.

40. *New York Times,* November 21, 1915, summarized these larger gifts.

41. Carnegie to Trueblood, December 21, 1906, and February 5, 1908, APS Papers (SCPC), Box 6; *Peacemaker,* XXIII (September, 1904), p. 198; *AP,* LXVIII (June, 1906), p. 124; Marchand, *American Peace Movement,* p. 115. See also above, note 28.

42. Joseph Frazier Wall, *Andrew Carnegie* (New York: Oxford University Press, 1970), pp. 880, 890-897.

43. Frederick Lynch, *Personal Recollections of Andrew Carnegie* (New York: Fleming H. Revell Co., 1920), pp. 26-28.

44. Quoted in Wall, *Carnegie,* p. 885.

45. Carnegie to Mead, April 9, 1902, Mead to Carnegie, March 27, 1905, Carnegie to Mead, April 2, 6, 1905, and Mead to Carnegie, April 7, 1905, Mead Papers, Box 1. Almost every peace leader urged Carnegie to finance various peace schemes. See Alfred H. Love's proposal, for example, in *New York Times,* June 20, 1905.

46. Butler to Holt, enclosing memorandum, December 6, 1908, Nicholas Murray Butler Papers (Butler Library, Columbia University), Holt File. Carnegie's initial gifts to the Carnegie Institution of Washington and the Carnegie Foundation for the Advancement of Teaching had both totaled $10,000,000.

47. See the stimulating analysis in Sondra R. Herman, *Eleven Against War: Studies in American Internationalist Thought, 1898–1921* (Stanford, Calif.: HI, 1969), pp. 22ff.

48. Nicholas Murray Butler, "The Scope and Function of Secondary Education," *Educational Review,* XV (May, 1898), p. 515; Nicholas Murray Butler, "The Outlook in Education," in National Education Association, *Journal of Proceedings and Addresses of the Thirty-eighth Annual Meeting, Held at Los Angeles, California, July 11-14, 1899* (Chicago: n.p., 1899), p. 175; Butler to McKinley, September 14, 1898, William McKinley Papers (LC, on microfilm), Reel 62; Butler to McKinley, March 16, 1899, *ibid.,* Reel 66.

49. Butler to Holt, enclosing memorandum, December 6, 1908, and Smiley, Hale, Mead, Dutton and Holt to Butler, December 21, 1908, Butler Papers, Holt File; Butler to Carnegie, January 8, 1909, and Carnegie to Butler, January 11, 1909, Carnegie Papers, Vol. 161.

50. Butler to Carnegie, April 6, 1909, with enclosure, *ibid.,* Vol. 165; Levermore, *Dutton,* pp. 94-96.

51. Mead to Butler, December 21, 1909, and Butler to Mead, December 22, 1909, Butler Papers, Mead File; Mead to Carnegie, January 13, 1910, Carnegie to Ginn, January 19, 1910, and Mead to Dutton, February 14, 1910, Mead Papers, Box 1.

52. NYPS Minutes, November 20, 1906, December 21, 1907, February 1, 1908, NYPS Papers, Box 1; Samuel Train Dutton, "Missing Factor in the Peace Movement," *Independent,* LXIV (April 9, 1908), pp. 786-788; Dutton in *LMC 1909,* pp. 26-30; resolution in *ibid.,* pp. 185-186.

53. The committee of ten (eleven including Dutton as secretary) consisted of Abbott, Butler, Carnegie, George W. Kirchwey (professor of law at Columbia University), Mead, Root, Scott, Smiley, Trueblood, and E. D. Warfield (president of Lafayette College). *LMC 1910,* pp. 196-197.

54. Root to Carnegie, February 11, 1910, Carnegie Papers, Vol. 174. For other evidence of this relationship, see Butler to Carnegie, February 4, March 7, 1910, Butler Papers, Carnegie File; Mead to Butler, December 21, 1909, and Butler to Mead, December 22, 1909, *ibid.,* Mead File; Mead to Carnegie, January 13, 1910, Carnegie to Ginn, January 19, 1910, and Mead to Dutton, February 14, 1910, Mead Papers, Box 1.

55. It may not have been a coincidence that Carnegie began outlining his plans for an endowment only a few days after he learned that the committee of ten had begun its deliberations. Dutton and Kirchwey to Carnegie, October 21, 1910, Carnegie Papers, Vol. 181. Carnegie's first typed draft of the plan for the Carnegie Endowment is dated November 3, 1910, *ibid.* Once Carnegie established his peace fund, its managers acquired the financial leverage to define the nature and extent of its relationships with less affluent peace groups, and the need for a national council for arbitration and peace became superfluous.

56. Carnegie to Trueblood, December 20, 1909, APS Papers, Box 6; Carnegie to Ginn, December 8, 1909, Butler Papers, Carnegie File.

57. For expressions of personal jealousy between the two, see below, pp. 190-193.

58. Trueblood to Carnegie, December 15, 1909, Carnegie Papers, Vol. 172; Trueblood to Carnegie, October 29, 1910, *ibid.,* Vol. 181; Marchand, *American Peace Movement,* pp. 118-119.

59. *A League of Peace: A Rectorial Address Delivered to the Students in the University of St. Andrews, 17th October, 1905* (Boston: Ginn and Company, 1906), pp. 32-34.

60. Carnegie in *NAPC 1907,* p. 54; also see Carnegie to Roosevelt, February 14, 1907, Theodore Roosevelt Papers (LC, on microfilm), Reel 72.

61. The entire story is in Wall, *Carnegie,* pp. 929-939; Root's remarks are quoted on p. 933.

62. See *The Letters of Theodore Roosevelt,* ed. Elting E. Morison, 8 vols. (Cambridge, Mass.: Harvard University Press, 1951–1954), VII, pp. 36-37, 42, 47-49, 55, 75-76, 377-379, 398.

63. *New York Times,* August 30, 1913; Wall, *Carnegie,* pp. 926, 1005.

64. *New York Times,* March 23, 1910; Bradford Perkins, *The Great Rapprochement: Great Britain and the United States, 1895–1914* (New York: Atheneum, 1968), pp. 252-253. Carnegie's remarks in *NAPC 1907,* p. 55, which he repeated in *CEIP 1911,* pp. 1, 6. Carnegie to Taft, March 26, 1910, Carnegie Papers, Vol. 175; Andrew Carnegie, "Peace *Versus* War: The President's Solution," *Century Magazine,* LXXX (June, 1910), pp. 307-310.

65. Carnegie's reasoning appears most clearly in *CEIP 1911,* pp. 3, 5-6.

66. Quoted in Archibald W. Butt, *Taft and Roosevelt: The Intimate Letters of Archie Butt, Military Aide,* 2 vols. (New York: Doubleday, Doran & Co., 1930), II, p. 559.

67. Taft to Carnegie, October 28, 1910, and Carnegie to Taft, October 29, 1910, Carnegie Papers, Vol. 181. Carnegie's later claim that the form of his gift came to him "like a revelation" while playing a round of golf the previous summer in Skibo oversimplified the pressures on him. Lynch, *Personal Recollections*, p. 155.

68. Michael A. Lutzker, "The Formation of the Carnegie Endowment for International Peace: A Study of the Establishment-Centered Peace Movement, 1910–1914," *Building the Organizational Society: Essays on Associational Activities in Modern America,* ed. Jerry Israel (New York: The Free Press, 1972), pp. 150-151, 285n42, categorized the twenty-seven trustees as follows: eight elder statesmen of diplomacy (Elihu Root, Oscar S. Straus, Joseph H. Choate, John W. Foster, Charlemagne Tower, Andrew D. White, John L. Cadwalader, Luke E. Wright); six businessmen (Thomas Burke, Robert S. Brookings, Jacob G. Schmidlapp, George W. Perkins, Samuel Mather, Cleveland H. Dodge); four former or active educators (Nicholas Murray Butler, Charles W. Eliot, Albert K. Smiley, Arthur William Foster); four Southern Democratic politicians (William M. Howard, James L. Slayden, and John Sharp Williams, all in Congress, and former governor of Virginia, Andrew J. Montague); four members of Carnegie's official family already responsible for managing some of his endowed funds (Robert W. Woodward, Charles L. Taylor, Robert A. Franks, Henry S. Pritchett); and one personal appointee (James Brown Scott selected at Root's request). Marchand, *American Peace Movement,* p. 121n44, differed slightly in categorizing the trustees. Irrespective of categories, the important point is that the trustees overwhelmingly represented the conservative establishment.

69. *AP,* LXVIII (September, 1906), pp. 199-205.

70. Dutton to Ginn, February 15, 1911, WPF Papers, Box 2. Also see Butler's later comments in *Andrew Carnegie Centenary, 1835–1935* (New York: n.p., 1935), p. 55; Root to Carnegie, November 1, 3, 1910, and Carnegie to Morley, November 4, 1910, Carnegie Papers, Vol. 181; Carnegie to Butler, November 14, 1910, *ibid.,* Vol. 182; Taft to Carnegie, November 11, 1910, William Howard Taft Papers (LC, on microfilm), Reel 504.

71. Lutzker, "Formation of the Carnegie Endowment for International Peace," p. 284n31.

72. Butler to Dutton, January 21, 1908, NYPS Papers, Box 2; Root to Taft, August 20, 1910, Taft Papers, Reel 455; and Root's remarks in Minutes, Executive Committee, March 9, 1911, CEIP Papers (Butler Library, Columbia University).

73. *CEIP 1911,* pp. 3, 5-6.

74. Stenographic Report of Proceedings, First Meeting of the Board of Trustees, December 14, 1910, CEIP Papers.

75. *CEIP 1912,* pp. 56, 62-66, 77-80; *CEIP 1913–1914,* pp. 52, 59-63, 72-76, 82.

76. CEIP, Division of Intercourse and Education, *Report of the International Commission to Inquire into the Causes and Conduct of the Balkan Wars,*

Publication No. 4 (Washington, D.C.: CEIP, 1914). For attacks on this report, see *New York Times,* June 1, 7, 8, 1914.

77. *CEIP 1912,* pp. 58-59, 69-75; *CEIP 1913–1914,* pp. 69-75.

78. *CEIP 1912,* pp. 85-95; *CEIP 1913–1914,* pp. 89-95.

79. *CEIP 1912,* pp. 24-26, 46-54, 99-158; CEIP, *Report on the Teaching of International Law in Educational Institutions of the United States* (Washington, D.C.: CEIP, 1913), p. 29, *passim; New York Times,* August 24, 1913.

Chapter 8

1. Alden Chester in *LMC 1899,* p. 47. For the 1896 report of the New York State Bar Association, see above, pp. 102-103.

2. Harrison to Dodge, December 12, 1899, January 15, 1900, Benjamin Harrison Papers (LC, on microfilm), Reel 42. Also see Harrison's influence on John W. Foster's criticisms of the defects of ordinary arbitration. *ASIL 1909,* pp. 26-28.

3. Lansing in *LMC 1904,* pp. 142-144.

4. William L. Penfield in *NYSBA 1904,* especially pp. 256-257.

5. Penfield in *LMC 1904,* pp. 35-40; Moore in *ibid.,* pp. 61-66; Baldwin in *ibid.,* pp. 71-73. The quoted phrase is Moore's, *ibid.,* p. 64. The American Bar Association's Committee on International Law, chaired by New York lawyer Everett P. Wheeler, issued a statement which epitomized the tension between the legalists' ideal of abstract justice and their acceptance of existing power relationships among nation-states. The committee also complained about nationals from both sides sitting on the Hague tribunal deciding the case. "Report of the Committee on International Law," *Report of the Twenty-Seventh Annual Meeting of the American Bar Association, Held at St. Louis, Missouri, September 26, 27 and 28, 1904* (Philadelphia: n.p., 1904), pp. 416-417.

6. James Brown Scott, *The Hague Peace Conferences of 1899 and 1907,* 2 vols. (Baltimore: The Johns Hopkins Press, 1909), I, pp. 399-422; II, pp. 357-361.

7. Charles Henry Butler in *LMC 1904,* p. 133; William J. Coombs in *ibid.,* pp. 149-150; George W. Taylor in *LMC 1905,* p. 51. Throughout this work I apply the word "legalist" to individuals who placed primary emphasis on the development of legal principles in international relations. Legalists were overwhelmingly lawyers but included a few prominent non-lawyers like David Jayne Hill, Nicholas Murray Butler, and (to 1914) Theodore Marburg.

8. Kirchwey in *ibid.,* pp. 128-130. Also see *ASIL 1907,* pp. 23-38.

9. The twenty-one are listed in *LMC 1905,* p. 142. C. Roland Marchand, *The American Peace Movement and Social Reform, 1898–1918* (Princeton, N.J.: Princeton University Press, 1972), p. 40n4, listed a "core group" of forty-five individuals who were most active in founding and participating in the American Society of International Law. Since all active members of the society revered international law and favored creation of a world court, I have been less concerned with developing precise criteria defining membership in the American Society of International Law than with the major policies and

actions of this group and a later organization, American Society for Judicial Settlement of International Disputes, discussed in the following pages.

10. *Ibid.,* especially pp. 47-51, 56-57.

11. David Jayne Hill, *World Organization As Affected by the Nature of the Modern State* (New York: Columbia University Press, 1911), pp. 104ff., *passim.*

12. John Bassett Moore, *A Digest of International Law,* 8 vols. (Washington, D.C.: Government Printing Office, 1906); and *Cases on International Law, Selected from Decisions of English and American Courts,* ed. James Brown Scott (Boston: The Boston Book Company, 1902), exemplified the case law approach. Scott also served as general editor of a series of books on case law. Also see Baldwin in *LMC 1904,* pp. 71-72; James Brown Scott, "The Legal Nature of International Law," *Columbia Law Review,* V (February, 1905), pp. 124-152; and the addresses by Olney, Foster, Theodore S. Woolsey, Bartholdt, and Moore on the subject of international law as a "science" in *ASIL 1907,* pp. 218-259.

13. Scott in *LMC 1904,* p. 134; George Gray in *ibid.,* p. 25; Hill, *World Organization,* pp. 120-121. On Root's views, see Sondra R. Herman, *Eleven Against War: Studies in American Internationalist Thought, 1898–1921* (Stanford, Calif.: HI, 1969), pp. 40-41.

14. Kirchwey in *LMC 1910,* p. 95. Also see Hill, *World Organization,* pp. 138-139.

15. Elihu Root, *Addresses on International Subjects,* eds. Robert Bacon and James Brown Scott (Cambridge, Mass.: Harvard University Press, 1916), pp. 25-32; Kirchwey in *LMC 1908,* p. 75; Scott in *LMC 1910,* pp. 67-69.

16. Herman, *Eleven Against War,* pp. 23-24; Hill, *World Organization,* pp. 125-137, 188-196.

17. Scott in *ASJSID 1912,* p. xxi.

18. Foster in *ASIL 1909,* pp. 25-34; Root, *Addresses on International Subjects,* pp. 140-142, 148-150; William Cullen Dennis, "Compromise — The Great Defect of Arbitration," *Columbia Law Review,* XI (June, 1911), pp. 490-494; Thomas Raeburn White in *ASJSID 1912,* p. 187; Simeon Baldwin in *ibid.,* pp. 188-189.

19. Butler in *LMC 1907,* pp. 16-17.

20. Marchand, *American Peace Movement,* pp. 67-68; also see Hill, *World Organization,* pp. 123-125.

21. *Instructions to the American Delegates to the Hague Peace Conferences and Their Official Reports,* ed. James Brown Scott (New York: Oxford University Press, 1916), pp. 79-80.

22. Scott, *Hague Peace Conferences,* I, p. 459; Scott to Hans Wehburg, June 28, 1911, James Brown Scott Papers (Georgetown University Library). Also, Thomas Raeburn White in *LMC 1911,* pp. 103-107.

23. Robert Bacon to Root, July 21, 1908, and Scott to Root, July 22, 1908, Elihu Root Papers (LC), Box 57; S. Pichon to M. Bompard, August 16, 1907, *Documents Diplomatiques Francais (1871–1914),* 12 vols. (second series [1901–1911], Paris: National Imprimerie, 1950), XI, pp. 226-227.

24. James Brown Scott, "The Work of the Second Hague Peace Conference," *AJIL,* II (January, 1908), p. 27.

25. Quoted in Scott, *Hague Peace Conferences,* II, p. 248.

26. James Brown Scott, "The Central American Peace Conference of 1907," *AJIL,* II (January, 1908), especially pp. 140-143; Foster in *LMC 1908,* pp. 12-13; Trueblood in *ibid.,* p. 18; John Barrett in *ibid.,* p. 49; William I. Buchanan in *LMC 1909,* pp. 51-54; Baldwin in *LMC 1910,* pp. 81, 84-85. Also, Robert Ewing Hosack, "The Central American Court of Justice" (M.A. Thesis, University of Chicago, 1934), pp. 41-46, *passim.*

27. Scott in *LMC 1908,* pp. 20-23; Hill, *World Organization,* pp. 162-163.

28. *FR 1907,* I, p. lxiii. Philip Jessup, *Elihu Root,* 2 vols. (New York: Dodd, Mead & Co., 1938), II, p. 82, indicates Root's influence on Roosevelt.

29. Knox in *FR 1910,* p. 604. See Roosevelt's similar reasoning in *FR 1907,* p. lxiii.

30. *British Documents on the Origins of the World War, 1898–1914,* eds. G. P. Gooch and Harold Temperley, 11 vols. (London, 1926–1938), VIII, pp. 306-307, 347-349; James Brown Scott, *The Status of the International Court of Justice, with an Appendix of Addresses and Official Documents* (New York: Oxford University Press, 1916), pp. 41-42.

31. *FR 1910,* pp. 597-605.

32. *Ibid.,* pp. 606-613; Scott, *Status of the International Court,* pp. 45-47.

33. Scott to Knox, telegram, March 21-22, 1910, 12655/423-425, Scott to Knox, July 29, 1910, 500.A2/A2b, Memorandum, September 2, 1910, 500.A2/701, David Jayne Hill to Knox, September 14, 1910, 500.A2/617, and Scott to Knox, telegram, September 20, 1910, 500.A2a/522, United States Department of State Papers, Record Group 59 (NA). Texts of the two agreements appear in James Brown Scott, *An International Court of Justice* (New York: Oxford University Press, 1916), pp. 91-97.

34. *ASIL 1909,* pp. 14-15.

35. Scott in *LMC 1910,* p. 75.

36. Butler in *LMC 1911,* p. 30.

37. Root, *Addresses on International Subjects,* p. 151.

38. Scott to Wehburg, June 28, July 20, August 3, November 6, 1911, Wehburg to Scott, May 25, July 22, August 20, 1911, Scott to Nys, July 21, 1911, Scott to Lammasch, June 28, 1908, Scott Papers. "Editorial Comment," *AJIL,* III (October, 1909), pp. 1046-1048; and "Editorial Comment," *ibid.,* V (April, 1911), pp. 472-474.

39. Scott to Wehburg, November 6, 1911, Scott Papers.

40. Many European legalists contributed to the *American Journal of International Law* between 1907 and 1914, and Scott later arranged for the translation of their books on international justice into English. About a decade later Wehburg complained bitterly that American peace workers so severely criticized his work against German militarism as impractical that he foolishly deemphasized its importance. Though not naming the Americans, Wehburg obviously thought Scott was one of the foremost among them. Hans Wehburg, *Als Pazifist im Weltkrieg* (Leipzig: n.p., n.d.), pp. 27-29.

41. Lansing's remark, made in 1912, is quoted in Arthur Deerin Call, "James Brown Scott: A Sketch of His Services to the Cause of Justice Between Nations," *World Court,* IV (June, 1918), p. 357.

Chapter 9

1. Daniel B. Schirmer, *Republic or Empire: American Resistance to the Philippine War* (Cambridge, Mass.: Schenkman Publishing Co., 1972), p. 249. A recent interpretation of Taft's prepresidential years is Ralph Eldin Minger, *William Howard Taft and United States Foreign Policy, 1900–1908* (Urbana: University of Illinois Press, 1975).

2. Taft is cited in Roosevelt to Root, July 17, 1903, *The Letters of Theodore Roosevelt,* ed. Elting E. Morison, 8 vols. (Cambridge, Mass.: Harvard University Press, 1951–1954), III, p. 519.

3. *ACIA 1896,* pp. 89, 155.

4. Taft to McKinley, March 30, 1898, William McKinley Papers (LC, on microfilm), Reel 3.

5. Taft in *AP,* LXXIII (August, 1911), p. 178. Also see Donald F. Anderson, *William Howard Taft: A Conservative's Conception of the Presidency* (Ithaca, N.Y.: Cornell University Press, 1973), pp. 280-281.

6. My analysis of the entire abortive episode draws heavily on Warren F. Kuehl's books, *Hamilton Holt: Journalist, Internationalist, Educator* (Gainesville: University of Florida Press, 1960), pp. 75-88, and *Seeking World Order: The United States and International Organization to 1920* (Nashville, Tenn.: Vanderbilt University Press, 1969), pp. 124-137.

7. *The Peace Movement: The Federation of the World* (New York: The World Federation League, 1910), pp. 1, 20-21, 24, 46, 48-49, 63-67, 69, 91-92.

8. *Ibid.,* pp. 2-3.

9. Kuehl, *Seeking World Order,* pp. 125-127; Theodore Roosevelt, "International Peace," *The Works of Theodore Roosevelt,* 20 vols. (New York: Charles Scribner's Sons, 1920–1925), XVI, pp. 308-309. Hamilton Holt, "The United States Peace Commission," *NAR,* CXCII (September, 1910), pp. 301-302.

10. *CR,* 61st Cong., 2nd sess., XLV, pp. 7432, 8542, 8545-8547, 8713, 8874.

11. Short to Taft, July 11, 1910, and Holt to Taft, July 26, 1910, Hamilton Holt Papers (Mills Memorial Library, Rollins College), Box 1. For an earlier statement by Roosevelt on the impracticability "of establishing any kind of international power, of whatever sort, which can effectively check wrong doing," see *FR 1906,* I, pp. liv-lv.

12. *NYPS 1911,* p. 14; *APC 1911,* p. 387; *New York Times,* March 11, 1911; *CR,* 62nd Cong., 1st sess., XLVII, pp. 2735, 2751.

13. Kuehl, *Seeking World Order,* pp. 134-137.

14. Root to Taft, August 20, 1910, William Howard Taft Papers (LC, on microfilm), Reel 455.

15. Butler to Taft, November 5, 1910, *ibid.,* Reel 363; also see Butler to Holt, November 3, 1910, Nicholas Murray Butler Papers (Butler Library, Columbia University), Holt File.

16. Taft to E. N. Huggins, August 11, 1908, Taft Papers, Reel 91.

17. Henry F. Pringle, *The Life and Times of William Howard Taft,* 2 vols. (New York: Farrar & Rinehart, 1939), II, pp. 736-738; *ASIL 1907,* p. 260; Taft to Knox, October 26, 1910, Taft Papers, Reel 504.

18. Taft to Marburg, January 31, 1910, Theodore Marburg Scrapbooks (LC), No. 2.

19. Taft in *ASIL 1911,* p. 341.

20. Taft in *ASJSID 1910,* pp. 352-353.

21. *New York Times,* March 23, 1910.

22. Quoted in Archibald W. Butt, *Taft and Roosevelt: The Intimate Papers of Archie Butt, Military Aide,* 2 vols. (New York: Doubleday, Doran & Co., 1930), II, pp. 635-636. Actually, Taft was fighting for only two new battleships in 1910, but even this number was excessive to many peace advocates. See below, chs. 10, 11.

23. Taft in *ASJSID 1910,* pp. 352-353.

24. See his speeches reproduced in *AP,* LXXIII (December, 1911), p. 276; LXXIV (January, 1912), p. 11; and his letter to Scott, December 17, 1912, quoted in *ASJSID 1912,* pp. ix-x.

25. Taft, quoted in *AP,* LXXIII (December, 1911), p. 275.

26. Quoted in Butt, *Taft and Roosevelt,* II, p. 635.

27. Quoted in Anderson, *Taft,* p. 277.

28. For a few of the many references to new peace societies, see *AP,* LXX (April, 1908), p. 77; (November, 1908), p. 236; LXXI (October, 1909), p. 201; LXXIII (June, 1911), p. 123; LXXIV (February, 1912), p. 33. Also see the references in the following eight notes.

29. *AP,* LXXII (March, 1910), p. 55.

30. *Ibid.,* LXXII (July and August, 1910), pp. 157-158; LXXIII (January, 1911), p. 6.

31. Quoted in *ibid.* (February, 1911), p. 29.

32. *CPS 1912,* pp. 5-8; *CPS 1913,* pp. 28-30; *AP,* LXXII (February, 1910), pp. 30-32; Charles E. Beals in *AP,* LXXIII (February, 1911), p. 30.

33. *Ibid.,* LXXII (February, 1910), p. 31.

34. Beals in *CPS 1914,* p. 30.

35. Beals in *AP,* LXXIII (April, 1911), p. 88.

36. Trueblood in *ibid.,* LXX (June, 1908), p. 142; and LXXIII (May, 1911), pp. 101-103.

37. Taft in *APC 1911,* p. 15; Holt to Marburg, June 20, 1911, Holt Papers, Box 1.

38. *AP,* LXXIV (June, 1912), pp. 138-140.

39. *Ibid.,* pp. 139-141.

40. *New York Times,* December 13, 1911.

41. *APC 1911,* p. 15.

42. *CPS 1912,* pp. 23-24; *CPS 1913,* p. 8; *AP,* LXXIII (November, 1911), p. 244.

43. *CEIP 1912,* p. 78; *Citizens' National Committee on the Ratification of the General Arbitration Treaties, 1911* (New York: n.p., 1911), *passim; AP,* LXXIV (January, 1912), p. 19.

44. For resolutions endorsing the treaties, see *New York Times,* April 7, 10, 13, May 7, 20, June 7, November 22, 27, 28, December 4, 14, 1911; *AP,* LXXIV (January, 1912), pp. 1-2, 4, 20-22; (February, 1912), pp. 33-35, 47-48; (March, 1912), pp. 58, 59, 61; (April, 1912), p. 88; Tryon in *ibid.,* p. 90; "A Triple Alliance Against War," *Literary Digest,* XLIII (August 12, 1911), pp. 225-226; "War Over the Peace Treaties," *ibid.* (August 26, 1911), pp. 302-303; "The Denatured Treaties," *ibid.,* LXIV (March 16, 1912), pp. 521-522; "A Review of the World," *Current Literature,* LI (October, 1911), pp. 349-355.

45. *AP,* LXXIII (February, 1911), p. 25; (June, 1911), p. 122; Joseph Frazier Wall, *Andrew Carnegie* (New York: Oxford University Press, 1970), pp. 994-996.

46. Quoted in Anderson, *Taft,* p. 278.

47. *Ibid.*

48. Root to Carnegie, August 29, 1911, Andrew Carnegie Papers (LC), Vol. 197.

49. *Sen. Doc. No. 98,* 62nd Cong., 1st sess., pp. 47-50.

50. *Ibid.,* pp. 1-8.

51. *Ibid.,* pp. 9-15, 27.

52. Bartholdt to Trueblood, August 12, 1911, APS Papers (SCPC), Box 6; John Bassett Moore, "The Peace Treaties," *Independent,* LXXI (August 17, 1911), pp. 344-346; Moore to W. R. Raymond, September 10, 1911, John Bassett Moore Papers (LC), Box 17; Knox in *AP,* LXXIII (December, 1911), pp. 280-281; also see *ibid.* (September, 1911), pp. 193-194; (October, 1911), pp. 217-218; Thomas Raeburn White in *ibid.,* LXXIV (January, 1912), pp. 14-16; Bartholdt in *CR,* 62nd Cong., 1st sess., LXVII, pp. 3923-3926; Edmunds in *AP,* LXXIII (December, 1911), pp. 270-271; Simeon E. Baldwin, "The Constitutional Objection to the New Arbitration Treaties," *Independent,* LXXI (August 31, 1911), pp. 456-457. [Hamilton Holt] "To the Senate," *ibid.* (August 17, 1911), pp. 379-380; and William I. Hull, "The International Grand Jury," *ibid.,* LXXII (January 4, 1912), pp. 12-14.

53. See excerpts from President Taft's speeches reproduced in *AP,* LXXIII (December, 1911), pp. 275-277; also his articles: "The Dawn of World Peace," *Woman's Home Companion,* XXXVIII (November, 1911), pp. 4-5; "World-Peace and the General Arbitration Treaties," *World's Work,* XXIII (December, 1911), pp. 143-149; "The Arbitration Treaties," *National Geographic Magazine,* XXII (December, 1911), pp. 1165-1172; and "The Pending Arbitration Treaties: An Appeal for Their Ratification," *Century Magazine,* LXXXIII (January, 1912), pp. 459-466.

54. "The Dawn of World Peace," p. 4.

55. Quoted in *AP* (December, 1911), p. 276. Taft often repeated this theme in subsequent speeches.

56. Anderson, *Taft,* p. 282.

57. *Ibid.;* also see John P. Campbell, "Taft, Roosevelt, and the Arbitration Treaties of 1911," *Journal of American History,* LIII (September, 1966), pp. 283-284.

58. Theodore Roosevelt, "The Arbitration Treaty with Great Britain," *Outlook,* XC (May 20, 1911), pp. 97-98; Theodore Roosevelt, "The Peace of Righteousness," *ibid.,* XCI (September 9, 1911), pp. 66-70; Campbell, "Taft, Roosevelt, and the Arbitration Treaties of 1911," pp. 284-288.

59. Butt, *Taft and Roosevelt,* II, p. 635.

60. Taft to Bryan, January 16, 1912, Taft Papers, Reel 432. Also see Bryan to Taft, January 14, 1912, *ibid.*

61. *AP,* LXXIV (April, 1912), pp. 81-82; Pringle, *Taft,* pp. 753-755.

62. William Howard Taft, "The Time to Test Our Faith in Arbitration," *International Conciliation,* Pamphlet No. 63 (February, 1913), pp. 7-8.

63. *Taft Papers on the League of Nations,* eds. Theodore Marburg and H. E. Flack (New York: The Macmillan Company, 1920), pp. 178-179.

Chapter 10

1. Quoted remarks are by Garrison in *AP,* LXIII (February, 1901), p. 34; Mead in *ibid.,* LXIV (June, 1902), pp. 101-102; Lucia Mead in *ibid.,* LXV (August, 1903), pp. 142-143; Dole in *ibid.,* pp. 145-146; Crosby in *ibid.,* LXVII (February, 1905), pp. 37-39; Leeds in *ibid.* (December, 1905), pp. 256-257. Also see Trueblood to Burton, March 2, 1904, Theodore Burton Papers (Western Reserve Historical Society), Box 5; and many of the following fourteen notes.

2. Crosby in *AP,* LXIII (February, 1901), pp. 40-42.

3. Edwin D. Mead, *Gov. Roosevelt's "Exact Parallels"* (n.p.: n.p., n.d.); Dole in *AP,* LXVII (December, 1905), p. 255.

4. William I. Hull, *The New Peace Movement* (Boston: The World Peace Foundation, 1912), p. 96. Hull first made these remarks in a speech in August 1908.

5. *Peacemaker,* XXVI (July, 1907), pp. 153-154; Dole to Editor, *Outlook,* LXXXVII (December 7, 1907), pp. 791-792; *AP,* LXX (January, 1908), pp. 2-3; Edwin Ginn, "All Honor to Japan," *Journal of Education,* LXVIII (November 19, 1908), pp. 538-539; David J. Brewer in *PAPC 1908,* pp. 115-116.

6. Quotations are found in Roosevelt to Henry Cabot Lodge, September 20, 1904, *The Letters of Theodore Roosevelt,* ed. Elting E. Morison, 8 vols. (Cambridge, Mass.: Harvard University Press, 1951–1954), IV, p. 949; Roosevelt quoted in Joseph Frazier Wall, *Andrew Carnegie* (New York: Oxford University Press, 1970), p. 928; and Roosevelt to Carnegie, February 18, 1910, *Letters of Theodore Roosevelt,* VII, p. 49.

7. *FR 1906,* pp. liv-lv; *FR 1907,* pp. lii, lvi.

8. *Ibid.,* pp. lvi-lvii.

9. *Sen. Doc. No. 378,* 60th Cong., 1st sess., *passim; CR,* 60th Cong., 1st sess., XLII, pp. 1265-1266, 2360-2362, 2717-2719, 2952-2953, 3421, 3822-3823, 4743; Dole to Editor, *Outlook,* LXXXVII (December 7, 1907), pp. 791-792; Dole to Editor, *ibid.* (December 21, 1907), p. 881; *AP,* LXX (February, 1908), p. 27; (March, 1908), pp. 50-51; (April, 1908), pp. 88-89.

10. *Ibid.,* LXXI (March, 1909), pp. 63-64; (February, 1909), pp. 32-35. Also see Lucia Mead's articles: "How to Further National Defense," *Outlook,* LXXXVIII (January 4, 1908), pp. 49-50; "The Demand for More Battleships," *Independent,* LXIV (February 13, 1908), pp. 350-351; "Some Fallacies of Captain Mahan," *Arena,* XL (August-September, 1908), pp. 163-170; "Better Understanding of the Navy," *Outlook,* LXXXVI (April 17, 1907), p. 868; and "What Our Navy Costs Us," *World To-Day,* XVI (April, 1909), pp. 389-393.

11. Armin Rappaport, *The Navy League of the United States* (Detroit: Wayne State University Press, 1962), pp. 3-15, 17-23.

12. Quoted in *AP,* LXXI (March, 1909), p. 67. Also see Charles E. Jefferson's three articles: "Some Fallacies of Militarism," *Independent,* LXIV (February 27, 1908), pp. 457-460; " 'Peace at Any Price' Men," *ibid.,* LXVI (February 4, 1909), pp. 224-227; and "The Delusion of Militarism," *Atlantic Monthly,* CIII (March, 1909), pp. 379-388; Oswald Garrison Villard in *Peacemaker,* XXVI (January, 1907), pp. 7-14; *AP,* LXIV (September, 1902), pp. 169-170.

13. Carnegie to Roosevelt, April 10, 1907, Theodore Roosevelt Papers (LC, on microfilm), Reel 73; Carnegie to Roosevelt, November 18, 1907, *ibid.,* Reel 78; NYPS Minutes, February 1, 1908, NYPS Papers (SCPC), Box 1; Carnegie in *APC 1913,* p. 91; Wall, *Carnegie,* pp. 923-924.

14. Bartholdt to Roosevelt, July 30, 1905, Roosevelt Papers, Reel 57; Bartholdt to Roosevelt, September 7, 1905, *ibid.,* Reel 59; Bartholdt to R.M. Powers, June 14, 1912, *ibid.,* Reel 146.

15. Unidentified newspaper clipping, May 18, 1904, APS Papers (SCPC), Box 6; Mead to Trueblood, May 28, 1913, *ibid.; AP,* LXXV (June, 1913), p. 122; Andrew Carnegie, "The Latest Panacea," *Journal of Education,* LXXVIII (July 10, 1913), pp. 32-33. Abbott perhaps best expressed his basic views on foreign policy in *ASIL 1909,* pp. 255-257.

16. Richard H. Thomas, Atkinson, Garrett, Mercer, Reuen Thomas, Crosby, Leeds, Garrison, Hale, Howe, Paine, Ames, Smiley, Love, Ginn, and Capen died in the decade before 1914.

17. Martin David Dubin, "The Development of the Concept of Collective Security in the American Peace Movement, 1899–1917" (Ph.D. Dissertation, Indiana University, 1960), pp. 39, 43-49.

18. Mead to Bartholdt, March 10, 1908, Mead to Butler, March 12, 1908, and Butler to Mead, April 8, 1908, Nicholas Murray Butler Papers (Butler Library, Columbia University), Mead File; Hayne Davis, "The Foundations of International Justice," *Independent,* LXVIII (March 10, 1910), pp. 504-513.

19. *LMC 1906*, pp. 21-38, 135-139.

20. *LMC 1907*, pp. 128-142.

21. *AP*, LXIX (June, 1907), p. 127.

22. *LMC 1908*, p. 150; and platforms of 1909–1914 Mohonk Conferences.

23. *NYPS 1906–1907*, p. 22.

24. Short in *APC 1911*, p. 219.

25. NYPS Minutes, January 31, February 1, 12, 1908, January 29, April 12, 29, 1909, NYPS Papers, Box 1; *NYPS 1910–1911*, pp. 21-22. Slightly less than half the membership replied to the poll.

26. NYPS Minutes, October 8, 1909, January 8, 1913, NYPS Papers, Box 1.

27. *NYPS 1912*, p. 8.

28. Carnegie to Roosevelt, January 21, 1909, Roosevelt Papers, Reel 87.

29. Roosevelt to Knox, February 8, 1909, *Letters of Theodore Roosevelt*, VI, pp. 1512-1513.

30. *AP*, LXIX (March, 1907), p. 58, and Trueblood's numerous editorials in 1907–1908 indicate the American Peace Society's efforts at quieting anti-Japanese hysteria; also see *PAPC 1908*, pp. 135-136, 138, 157.

31. *APC 1911*, p. 219.

32. Michael Wreszin, *Oswald Garrison Villard: Pacifist at War* (Bloomington, Indiana University Press, 1965), p. 46; *New York Times*, May 2, 1907; Holmes to Short, January 27, 1914, NYPS Papers, Box 4. Spencer is quoted in *PAPC 1908*, p. 153.

33. NYPS Minutes, November 6, 1912, NYPS Papers, Box 1.

34. Minutes of the Executive Committee, October 2, 1913, February 5, 1914, CPS Papers (Chicago Historical Society), Vol. II.

35. Arthur Henry Dadmun in *APC 1913*, p. 234. Also see Jonathan Daniels, *The End of Innocence* (Philadelphia: J. P. Lippincott Co., 1954), p. 115.

36. See the discussion in *APC 1913*, pp. 141-158.

37. Rappaport, *Navy League*, p. 36. Call is quoted in *APC 1913*, p. 158.

38. Lockwood in *ASJSID 1910*, pp. 99-100; *AP*, LXXIII (January, 1911), pp. 3-4; Call in *ibid.*, LXXVI (March, 1914), pp. 61-62.

39. *Ibid.*, LXXII (June, 1910), p. 122; Trueblood in *ASIL 1912*, pp. 170-171; Hull, *New Peace Movement*, pp. 34-49; Hull in *ASIL 1911*, pp. 284-287; James Brown Scott, "The Constructive Peace Movement," *World To-Day*, XXI (February, 1912), pp. 1789-1790.

40. Warren F. Kuehl, *Hamilton Holt: Journalist, Internationalist, Educator* (Gainesville: University of Florida Press, 1960), pp. 93-94.

41. Warren F. Kuehl, *Seeking World Order: The United States and International Organization to 1920* (Nashville, Tenn.: Vanderbilt University Press, 1969), pp. 118, 152, 166; for very conditional endorsements of a police force, see Hull, *New Peace Movement*, pp. 93, 201-202; and Richard Megargee, "The Diplomacy of John Bassett Moore: Realism in American Foreign Policy" (Ph.D. Dissertation, Northwestern University, 1963), pp. 114-116.

42. On Jane Addams, see especially Sondra R. Herman, *Eleven Against*

War: Studies in American Internationalist Thought, 1898–1921 (Stanford, Calif.: HI, 1969), ch. 5; Jane Addams, *The Newer Ideals of Peace* (New York: The Macmillan Co., 1907); and Allen F. Davis, *American Heroine: The Life and Legend of Jane Addams* (New York: Oxford University Press, 1973), pp. 135-149, 194.

43. See the warm discussion in *ASIL 1909,* pp. 238-257.

44. Taft in *AP,* LXXIV (January, 1912), p. 11; William Howard Taft, *The United States and Peace* (New York: Charles Scribner's Sons, 1914), pp. 131-132, 179-180.

45. See his two essays: *Political Papers: The War with Spain* (Baltimore: John Murphy Company, 1898); and *Political Papers: Expansion* (Baltimore: John Murphy Company,1900).

46. Marburg in *LMC 1910,* pp. 86-88.

47. *Ibid.,* p. 86; also see Theodore Marburg, "A Few Considerations on the Settlement of International Disputes by Means Other Than War," *Proceedings of the American Political Science Association at Its Seventh Annual Meeting,* VII (1910), especially p. 201.

48. Marburg is quoted in *ASIL 1910,* pp. 187-189; also see Theodore Marburg, "A Modified Monroe Doctrine," *South Atlantic Quarterly,* X (July, 1911), pp. 228-230.

49. Moore's notes, December 5, 1913, are quoted by Michael Lutzker, introduction to Theodore Marburg, *Expansion* (New York: Garland Publishing Co., 1971 edition), p. 11.

50. Marburg to Taft, August 13, 1911, William Howard Taft Papers (LC, on microfilm), Reel 449.

51. Marburg, "Modified Monroe Doctrine," p. 230; also see Theodore Marburg, "The Backward Nation," *Independent,* LXXII (June 20, 1912), pp. 1365-1370.

52. Ginn in *LMC 1913,* pp. 24-25.

53. Ginn to Mead, March 7, 8, 1911, WPF Papers (SCPC), Box 2; George W. Anderson to Ginn, November 21, 1912, *ibid.,* Box 3.

54. Edwin Ginn, *Outline of the Life of Edwin Ginn, Including his Preparation for the Publishing Business and the Establishment of Ginn and Company* (Boston: Athenaeum Press, 1908), pp. 3-4 (emphasis Ginn's).

55. Ginn to Jordan, November 23, 1909, JPSC (HI); Ginn to Bridgman, April 26, 1913, WPF Papers, Box 4.

56. Carnegie to Ginn, March 22, 1911, *ibid.,* Box 3.

57. Ginn to Mead, November 12, 1912, *ibid.;* Ginn to Dutton, July 30, 1913, *ibid.,* Box 4; "The World Peace Foundation: Work in 1913," *World Peace Foundation, Pamphlet Series,* III, No. 12 (December, 1913), pp. 44-47; Jordan to Editor, *Milwaukee Sentinel,* September 5, 1915, JPC (HI), Box 4.

58. Ginn to Jordan, January 29, 1912, JPSC.

59. Ginn to Mead, May 16, 1912, and Ginn to Dutton, May 16, 1912, WPF Papers, Box 3.

60. Ginn to Mead, January [?], 1911, *ibid.,* Box 2; also see Ginn to Jordan, May 15, 1911, January 29, 1912, March 18, 1911, JPSC.

61. Edwin D. Mead, "The Literature of the Peace Movement," *World Peace Foundation, Pamphlet Series,* No. 7, Part IV (October, 1912), pp. 1-14.

62. Ginn to Jordan, March 18, 1911, JPSC.

63. Jordan to Ginn, February 3, 1912, JPSC.

64. Mead, marginal comment on Ginn to Mead, May 29, 1912, WPF Papers, Box 3.

65. Mead to Ginn, October 14, 1911, *ibid.,* Box 2.

66. Mead to Carnegie, May 13, 18, June 15, 1914, Hamilton Holt Papers (Mills Memorial Library, Rollins College), Box 1; Mead to Finance Committee of the Board of Trustees of the World Peace Foundation, February 9, 1911, and Mead to Ginn, February 15, 1911, WPF Papers, Box 2. Jordan to Ginn, February 3, 1912, JPSC; Jordan to Ginn, October 21, 1912, WPF Papers, Box 3; Ginn in *LMC 1913,* pp. 26-27.

67. Mead to Albert E. Pillsbury, December 12, 1914, Edwin and Lucia Mead Papers (SCPC), Box 1; Edwin D. Mead, "Edwin Ginn, Citizen of the World," *Journal of Education,* LXXIX (February 12, 1914), p. 173.

68. Ginn to Jordan, June 8, 1911, January 29, 1912, JPSC.

69. *New York Evening Post,* December 17, 1910; Oswald Garrison Villard, "Mr. Carnegie's Greatest Gift," *Nation,* XCI (December 22, 1910), pp. 597-598; cf. Holt to Carnegie, November 17, 1910, Andrew Carnegie Papers (LC), Vol. 182; "Mr. Carnegie's Greatest Gift," *Independent,* LXIX (December 15, 1910), pp. 1339-1341; and *New York Tribune,* December 25, 1910. *AP,* LXXIII (January, 1911), pp. 1-2; *Peacemaker,* XXX (February-March, 1911), pp. 36-37, 46.

70. Ginn to Mead and Jordan, March 29, 1912, WPF Papers, Box 3.

71. "Another Peace Endowment," *Independent,* LXXVII (February 16, 1914), p. 219; Jordan to Mead, February 12, 1913, Mead Papers, Box 1.

72. *AP,* LXXV (May, 1913), p. 99; (August and September, 1913), pp. 172-173; (November, 1913), pp. 228-229.

73. Quotations are in C. Roland Marchand, *The American Peace Movement and Social Reform, 1898–1918* (Princeton, N.J.: Princeton University Press, 1972), pp. 131-132.

74. *Ibid.,* pp. 132-133.

75. Cf. *AP,* LXXII (May, 1910), p. 101; LXXIII (June, 1911), p. 123; LXXIV (June, 1912), p. 140; LXXV (May, 1913), p. 113; LXXVI (June, 1914), pp. 134-135. Mead in *APC 1913,* p. 148. Many of the points in the preceding two paragraphs first appeared in my article, "Andrew Carnegie's Quest for World Peace," *Proceedings of the American Philosophical Society,* CXIV (October 20, 1970), pp. 380-381.

76. Cf. *NYPS 1909/1910,* p. 16; and *NYPS 1914,* p. 29. Also, *CPS 1911,* p. 31; *CPS 1912,* p. 31; *CPS 1913,* p. 38; *CPS 1914,* pp. 29-33, 35.

77. Edwin D. Mead, "Peace Trustees and the Armament Craze," *Unity,* LXX (October 3, 1913), pp. 72-74; Mead in *LMC 1913,* pp. 105-109. This material has previously appeared in my essay, "An Interpretation of the American Peace Movement, 1898–1914," *Peace Movements in America,* ed. Charles Chatfield (New York: Schocken Books, 1973), pp. 25-26.

78. Dutton to Jordan, January 3, 1914, JPC, Box 1. Also see Patterson, "Interpretation of the American Peace Movement," p. 26.

79. Jordan to Editor, *War and Peace,* I (December, 1913), pp. 63-64.

80. D'Estournelles to Roosevelt, August 5, 1906, Roosevelt Papers, Reel 66. Also see D'Estournelles to Roosevelt, March 7, 1907, *ibid.,* Reel 72; and Kuehl, *Seeking World Order,* pp. 82, 85, 99, 170.

81. *Ibid.,* pp. 104-106, 112, 114-116, 171.

82. The preceding three paragraphs and sociological conclusions in the rest of this chapter are developed more fully and documented more extensively in places in my essay, "Interpretation of the American Peace Movement," pp. 25-31, 36n16-37n37. The generalizations in that essay and reiterated in this chapter are based on the thirty-six most active participants in the movement for most if not all of the 1898–1914 period. See *ibid.,* p. 34n2. If a later base period like 1909–1914 is used after several oldtimers had died and latecomers who participated more marginally—Carnegie Endowment trustees and a larger sample of international lawyers, for example—had entered the peace ranks, then the generalizations would be even more conclusive.

83. For full documentation on peace advocates' roughly similar values, see *ibid.,* pp. 28-31, 36n24-27, 37n28-37. In the following eighteen notes I have cited only direct quotations in the text and additional references not mentioned in the relevant notes 24-37 of my article.

84. Bartholdt in *NPC 1909,* p. 327; Trueblood in *APC 1913,* p. 108; Hull in *ibid.,* p. 129; Edward Cummings in *LMC 1912,* p. 90.

85. *New York Times,* May 22, 1911.

86. *APC 1911,* p. 335.

87. Frederick Lynch, *The Peace Problem: The Task of the Twentieth Century* (New York: Fleming H. Revell Co., 1911), p. 111.

88. Root, *Addresses on International Subjects,* pp. 31, 151.

89. Slayden in *LMC 1906,* p. 60; Holt, "The Federation of the World," Holt Papers, p. 1, Box 91.

90. Butler in *LMC 1910,* p. 19.

91. Ginn, "All Honor to Japan," p. 539.

92. E.g., Jordan to Mead, October 12, 1912, JPSC.

93. For this theme, see Samuel Haber, *Efficiency and Uplift: Scientific Management in the Progressive Era, 1890–1920* (Chicago: University of Chicago Press, 1964).

94. Lucia Mead in *AP,* LXX (July, 1908), p. 169; also see Hull, *New Peace Movement,* pp. 47-49.

95. Jordan to Ginn, February 3, 1912, JPSC; and Mead in *NPC 1909,* p. 306; also see Raymond L. Bridgman, *The First Book of World Law: A Compilation of the International Conventions to Which the Principal Nations Are Signatory, With a Survey of Their Significance* (Boston: Ginn and Company, 1911), pp. iv, 304-05.

96. Butler in *LMC 1909,* p. 19; and *LMC 1910,* p. 23.

97. For a pioneer study noting this theme, see William E. Leuchtenburg,

"Progressivism and Imperialism: The Progressive Movement and American Foreign Policy, 1898–1916," *Mississippi Valley Historical Review,* XXXIX (December, 1952), pp. 483-504. A summary of more recent literature severely qualifying Leuchtenburg's paradigm of progressive reformers' imperialistic and militaristic proclivities appears in Joseph M. Siracusa, "Progressivism, Imperialism, and the Leuchtenburg Thesis, 1952–1974: An Historical Appraisal," *Australian Journal of Politics and History,* XX (December, 1974), pp. 312-325.

98. Lynch, *Peace Problem,* pp. 97-99; Mead in *LMC 1903,* pp. 35-36; Raymond L. Bridgman, *World Organization* (Boston: Ginn and Company, 1906), pp. 61, 90-108, 149-150; Lucia Mead in *AP,* LXVIII (April, 1906), pp. 80-82: Butler in *LMC 1909,* p. 21; Bartholdt in *ibid.,* pp. 171-172; Hull, *New Peace Movement,* pp. 50-64; Charles E. Beals, *The Higher Soldiership* (Chicago: CPS, 1912), pp. 7-14, 50-54; Jenkin Lloyd Jones, "Moral Evolution: From Hate to Love," *Unity,* LXX (February 6, 1913), pp. 359-363; David Starr Jordan, *The Human Harvest: A Study of the Decay of Races Through the Survival of the Unfit* (Boston: American Unitarian Association, 1907); George W. Nasmyth, *Social Progress and the Darwinian Theory: A Study of Force as a Factor in Human Relations* (New York: G. P. Putman's Sons, 1916).

99. Bryan's remark appears in *NAPC 1907,* p. 85. [Hamilton Holt] "Naval Madness," *Independent,* LXVIII (March 3, 1910), p. 489; Benjamin F. Trueblood, "War a Thing of the Past," *Cosmopolitan Student,* I (April, 1910), pp. 49-50; Bartholdt in *LMC 1909,* p. 170.

100. Norman Angell, *The Great Illusion: A Study of the Relation of Military Power in Nations to Their Economic and Social Advantage* (London: William Heinemann, 1911). Also, Norman Angell, *Peace Theories and the Balkan War* (London: Horace Marshall & Son, 1912); and Norman Angell, *War and the Essential Realities* (London: Watts & Co., 1913).

101. Norman Angell, *After All: The Autobiography of Norman Angell* (London: H. Hamilton, 1951), pp. 147-158; Angell to Lucia Mead, March 21, 1910, Mead Papers, Box 1; Jordan, *The Days of a Man: Being Memories of a Naturalist, Teacher and a Minor Prophet of Democracy,* 2 vols. (New York: World Book Company, 1922), II, pp. 318-319; Lusia Mead, *Swords and Ploughshares, or The Supplanting of the System of War by the System of Law* (New York: G. P. Putnam's Sons, 1912), pp. 139-152; Jane Addams, "Peace on Earth," *Ladies Home Journal,* XXX (December, 1913), p. 27; Paul David Hines, "Norman Angell: Peace Movement, 1911–1915" (Ed.D. Dissertation, Ball State Teachers College, 1964), pp. 65-74.

Chapter 11

1. Merle Eugene Curti, *Bryan and World Peace,* in *Smith College Studies in History,* XVI (April-July, 1931), pp. 117-118, 130-131, 134-140. In this section on Bryan, I have drawn particularly on Curti's study; Lawrence W.

Levine, *Defender of the Faith, William Jennings Bryan: The Last Decade, 1915–1925* (New York: Oxford University Press, 1965); and Willard H. Smith, "William Jennings Bryan and the Social Gospel," *Journal of American History,* LIII (June, 1966), pp. 41 ff.

2. William Jennings Bryan, *Speeches of William Jennings Bryan,* 2 vols. (New York: Funk & Wagnalls, 1909), II, p. 49. When Bryan became Secretary of State, he repeated his enduring faith in these principles. *New York Times,* March 7, 1913.

3. Bryan to Warren Worth Bailey, December 30, 1901, Warren Worth Bailey Papers (Princeton University Library); Bryan's addresses in *NAPC 1907,* pp. 353-360; *LMC 1910,* pp. 164-173; and *LMC 1911,* pp. 44-49.

4. *Commoner,* V (February 17, 1905), p. 1; (February 24, 1905), p. 1.

5. Bryan to Holt, August 28, 1914, Hamilton Holt Papers (Mills Memorial Library, Rollins College), Box 1.

6. *Ibid.;* Richard Bartholdt, *From Steerage to Congress: Reminiscences and Reflections* (Philadelphia: Dorrance & Co., 1930), p. 279.

7. William Jennings Bryan and Mary Baird Bryan, *Memoirs of William Jennings Bryan* (Philadelphia: John C. Winston Co., 1925), p. 385; William Howard Taft, "Why Not Arbitrate Everything?" *Independent,* LXXVII (March 16, 1914), p. 380.

8. Bryan to Harry Walker, January 20, 1915, William Jennings Bryan Papers (LC), Box 30.

9. *New York Times,* May 13, 1913.

10. Curti, *Bryan and World Peace,* pp. 157-161.

11. Jordan to Jessie Jordan, April 29, 30, 1913, JPC (HI), Box 1.

12. For peace workers' endorsements, see *AP,* LXXV (May, 1913), pp. 97-98; (July, 1913), pp. 146-147; (October, 1913), p. 200; Bartholdt in *APC 1913,* p. 359; Burton in *ibid.,* pp. 528-530; Mead in *LMC 1913,* p. 106; resolution in *ibid.,* p. 10; William Howard Taft, *The United States and Peace* (New York: Charles Scribner's Sons, 1914), pp. 130-131; "Mr. Bryan's Peace Plan," *Independent,* LXXIV (May 1, 1913), pp. 949-950; *New York Times,* August 24, 1913.

13. Dutton to Bryan, July 24, 1913, 500.A3/15 (NA).

14. The few critics were mostly foreign pacifists. Norman Angell thought that Bryan's work was too "declamatory and unscientific." Angell to Jordan, May 23, 1914, JPC, Box 2. See also Curti, *Bryan and World Peace,* pp. 152-153.

15. Trueblood to Wilson, September 19, 1908, Woodrow Wilson Papers (LC, on microfilm), Reel 17; *Peacemaker,* XXXI (March, 1912), pp. 56-59.

16. Wilson, letter in *ACIA 1904,* p. 129; Harley Notter, *The Origins of the Foreign Policy of Woodrow Wilson* (New York: Russell & Russell, 1965 edition), pp. 69-70, 82-84, 105, 116-119, 129-130, 156, 173, 178, 186-187, 228, 240, 277. Arthur S. Link, *Wilson the Diplomatist: A Look at His Major Foreign Policies* (Baltimore: The Johns Hopkins Press, 1957), ch. 1, is a provocative analysis.

17. *Peacemaker,* XXXII (January-February, 1913), pp. 6-7; Mead to Wilson, January 1, 2, 1913, and Carnegie to Wilson, January 1, 1913, Wilson Papers, Reel 37.

18. Wilson to Marburg, May 1, 1911, *ibid.,* Reel 533.

19. See Wilson's negative notes attached to Holt to Wilson, October 9, 1913, and Holt to Joseph P. Tumulty, October 14, 1913, Wilson Papers, Reel 255.

20. Mead to Nasmyth, March 18, 1913, George W. Nasmyth Papers, (SCPC), Box 1.

21. Jordan to Wilson, March 8 (two letters), May 14, December 28, 1913, Wilson Papers, Reel 237.

22. *AP,* LXXV (August-September, 1913), p. 177; (October, 1913), pp. 207-208; and LXXVI (January, 1914), p. 4. Wilson also endorsed the Fourth American Peace Congress. Wilson to Manley O. Hudson, May 19, 1913, reproduced in *APC 1913,* p. 6.

23. Jordan to Wilson, March 19, 1913, Wilson Papers, Reel 242; "President Wilson's Chinese Proclamation," *Independent,* LXXIV (March 27, 1913), pp. 671-672; Arthur S. Link, *Wilson: The New Freedom* (Princeton, N.J.: Princeton University Press, 1956), pp. 284-286.

24. Discussion in *APC 1913,* pp. 348-349.

25. Jordan's failure to mention the tolls issue was an apparent oversight because he attacked the exemption clause in his book, *War and Waste: A Series of Discussions of War and War Accessories* (New York: Doubleday, Page and Co., 1913), pp. 180-181.

26. Donald F. Anderson, *William Howard Taft: A Conservative's Conception of the Presidency* (Ithaca, N.Y.: Cornell University Press, 1973), pp. 240-241.

27. Butler to John Morley, August 31, 1912, Nicholas Murray Butler Papers (Butler Library, Columbia University), Morley File; Philip Jessup, *Elihu Root,* 2 vols. (New York: Dodd, Mead & Co., 1938), II, pp. 264-265; Burton to Harry E. Bruey, March 16, 1914, and Burton to C. A. Ricks, May 15, 1914, Theodore E. Burton Papers, (Western Reserve Historical Society), Box 19; Carnegie to Taft, November 14, 1912, William Howard Taft Papers (LC, on microfilm), Reel 361.

28. Scott to Bacon, November 29, 1912, Knox to Scott, December 13, 1912, and Knox to American Embassy, Paris (marked "not sent"), November 25, 1912, James Brown Scott Papers (Georgetown University Library).

29. Scott to Chandler P. Anderson, December 12, 1912, and Knox to Anderson, December 14, 1912, *ibid.* Scott continued to hope for successful implementation of this scheme. James Brown Scott, *An International Court of Justice,* (New York: Oxford University Press, 1916), pp. 1-5, 25-90.

30. NYPS Minutes, January 30, 1913, NYPS Papers (SCPC), Box 1; Straus to Carnegie, December 17, 1912, Carnegie to Straus, December 18, 1912, Root to Carnegie, December 20, 1912, and Butler to Carnegie, December 20, 1912, Andrew Carnegie Papers (LC), Vol. 211; Scott to Baldwin, De-

cember 27, 1912, Baldwin Family Papers (Yale University Library), Box 113; *CEIP 1913–1914*, pp. 27-38, 79-82.

31. Link, *Wilson: The New Freedom,* p. 306.

32. E. David Cronon, ed., *The Cabinet Diaries of Josephus Daniels* (Lincoln: University of Nebraska Press, 1963), pp. 35-37, 44-45; Link, *Wilson: The New Freedom,* pp. 306-307.

33. Short to Burton, April 3, 6, 1914, Burton Papers, Box 19; Oscar Straus, *Under Four Administrations: From Cleveland to Taft* (Boston: Houghton Mifflin Co., 1922), pp. 338-339.

34. Short to Burton, April 15, 20, 1914, Burton Papers, Box 19; *New York Times,* April 16, 17, 1914; Straus, letter in *ibid.,* April 17, 1914; Link, *Wilson: The New Freedom,* pp. 311-314.

35. Jessup, *Root,* II, pp. 264-268.

36. The founding of The Church Peace Union is exhaustively analyzed in C. Roland Marchand, *The American Peace Movement and Social Reform, 1898–1918* (Princeton, N.J.: Princeton University Press, 1972), pp. 338-355.

37. Jessup, *Root,* II, pp. 268-269; *New York Times,* April 19, 1914.

38. Link, *Wilson: The New Freedom,* p. 314.

39. *Washington Post,* December 11, 1912.

40. "Mr. Bryan's Visit in London," *Commoner,* VI (July 13, 1906), p. 14.

41. "The Hague Court," *ibid.,* VII (October 11, 1907), p. 2.

42. Mead to Henri La Fontaine, August 1, 1913, IPB Papers, General Correspondence (UNL), Box 7; Butler to Trueblood, November 8, 1912, APS Papers (SCPC), Box 6; Dutton to Bryan, July 24, 1913, 500.A3/15; J. Reuben Clark (chairman of the American preparatory committee) to Dutton, August 1, 1913, 500.A3/16.

43. J. Reuben Clark to Moore, September 18, 1913, 500.A3/28. A convenient summary appears in *AP,* LXXVI (January, 1914), pp. 10-11.

44. *New York Times,* November 27, December 5, 1913; Bridgman to Bryan, November 27, 1913, 500.A3/21; Bridgman to Wilson, November 27, 1913, 500.A3/27. "Call the Third Hague Peace Conference Without Delay," *Independent,* LXXVI (December 4, 1913), pp. 429-431; Scott to Holt, December 8, 1913, and Holt to Scott, December 16, 1913, Scott Papers; *AP,* LXXV (November, 1913), p. 224; resolutions and discussion in *LMC 1913,* pp. 8-9, 82-114, 184; Tryon to Suttner, November 26, 1913, Fried-Suttner Correspondence (UNL), Divers Correspondant (1894–1914) File: NYPS Minutes, December 23, 1913; NYPS Papers, Box 1; Short to Jordan, January 26, 1914, JPC, Box 1.

45. Root to Bryan, December 10, 1913, reproduced in *CEIP 1913–1914,* pp. 122-123.

46. Wilson to Bryan, January 19, 1914, Wilson Papers, Reel 305.

47. Van Dyke to Bryan, November 4, 1913, 500.A3/19; Moore to Bryan, January 19, 1914, 500.A3/29.

48. Bryan to Wilson, January 28, 1914, Wilson Papers, Reel 243.

49. Wilson to Bryan, January 29, 1914, *ibid.;* Moore to Van Dyke, January 31, 1914, 500.A3/19. The circular note is in *FR 1914,* pp. 4-5.

50. *AP,* LXXVI (March, 1914), pp. 49-50; platform in *LMC 1914,* pp. 8-9; "Third Hague Conference," *Independent,* LXXVII (February 16, 1914), p. 224; Scott to General E. H. Crowder, June 20, 1914, Scott Papers; *New York Times,* February 12, 19, 24, July 3, October 4, 1914.

51. Andrew D. White in *LMC 1914,* p. 103; Denys P. Myers in *ibid.,* pp. 116-117; declaration of business organizations in *ibid.,* p. 174; *AP,* LXXVI (April, 1914), pp. 73-74.

52. Although the army remained secondary to the naval question, Slayden and Oswald Villard personally expressed their concern about the pending Militia Pay Bill to President-elect Wilson on December 30, 1912, and Slayden sent Wilson a copy of the minority report of the Committee of Military Affairs on the bill. Slayden to Wilson, December 31, 1912, Wilson Papers, Reel 37. Mead attacked General Leonard Wood's military camps for college students, the newly formed Army League, and the reports of a military pageant at Wilson's upcoming inauguration. *New York Times,* July 20, 1913; and Mead to Wilson, January 1, 2, 1913, Wilson Papers, Reel 37.

53. See Hensley's address to the American Peace Society in *AP,* LXXVI (June, 1914), pp. 131-133.

54. Cf. Richard Hofstadter, *The Age of Reform: From Bryan to F.D.R.* (New York: Alfred A. Knopf, 1955), pp. 272-274.

55. *AP,* LXXIV (September and October, 1912), p. 207; LXXV (March, 1913), p. 51; *Peacemaker,* XXXII (Midsummer, 1913), p. 47; platform in *APC 1913,* p. 440; Holt to Suttner, February 28, 1913, Fried-Suttner Correspondence, Divers Correspondant (1894-1914) File.

56. *CR,* 63rd Cong., 1st sess., L, pp. 5830-5835, 5913-5918, and *ibid.,* 63rd Cong., 2nd sess., LI, pp. 479-480; *AP,* LXXVI (January, 1914), pp. 3-4; (April, 1914), p. 83; *New York Times,* March 16, 1914.

57. Wilson to Bryan, December 9, 1913, Wilson Papers, Reel 255.

58. *Annual Reports of the Navy Department for the Fiscal Year 1913* (Washington, D.C.: Government Printing Office, 1914), pp. 9-10; *New York Times,* December 5, 1915.

59. Jonathan Daniels, *The End of Innocence* (Philadelphia: J. P. Lippincott Co., 1954), p. 49, quotes Bryan.

60. *Cabinet Diaries of Josephus Daniels,* pp. 27, 35; Josephus Daniels, *The Wilson Era: Years of Peace, 1910–1917* (Chapel Hill: The University of North Carolina Press, 1944), pp. 411-414.

61. *Ibid.*

62. Bryan to Wilson, March 13, 1914, Wilson Papers, Reel 312.

63. Wilson to Bryan, March 16, 1914, *ibid.* Hensley, the acknowledged leader of the small-navy forces in the House, remained hostile to the administration's two battleship program the following month. *CR,* 63rd Cong., 2nd sess., LI, pp. 7041-7047, 7050.

64. Daniels, *End of Innocence,* pp. 121-122.

65. House Diary, December 2, 12, 1913, Edward M. House Papers (Yale University Library). House's disarmament scheme is told in *The Intimate Papers of Colonel House,* ed. Charles Seymour, 4 vols. (Boston: Houghton

Mifflin Co., 1926–1928), I, pp. 235-275. But neither Seymour nor other historians have related House's disarmament proposal to other disarmament suggestions which influenced Wilson's growing enthusiasm for the subject.

66. *AP*, LXXVI (August and September, 1914), p. 173.

67. Armin Rappaport, *The Navy League of the United States* (Detroit: Wayne State University Press, 1962), pp. 41-44; *CR*, 63rd Cong., 2nd sess., LI, pp. 7020, 8241-8245; Joseph L. Morrison, *Josephus Daniels: The Small-d Democrat* (Chapel Hill: The University of North Carolina Press, 1966), pp. 58-59.

68. Harold and Margaret Sprout, *The Rise of American Naval Power, 1776–1918* (Princeton, N.J.: Princeton University Press, 1939), p. 303.

69. Link, *Wilson: The New Freedom*, p. 324n20, lists many books and articles by scholars on this theme; also Dexter Perkins, *A History of the Monroe Doctrine* (Boston: Little, Brown and Co., 1955 edition), pp. 320-322. Hull in *ASJSID 1913*, pp. 75-96; David Starr Jordan, *America's Conquest of Europe* (Boston: American Unitarian Association, 1913), pp. 35-37; *NYPS 1913*, p. 16.

70. Slayden to Carnegie, November 17, 1910, Carnegie Papers, Vol. 182; Slayden's address in *Official Proceedings of the Twenty-First Annual Session of the Trans-Mississippi Commercial Congress, Held at San Antonio, Texas, November 22, 23, 24, and 25, 1910* (n.p.: n.p., n.d.), pp. 114-116.

71. *CR*, 61st Cong., 3rd sess., XLVI, p. 1461. Bryan to Wilson, November 5, 1913, Wilson Papers, Reel 180, enclosing letter from Slayden; Samuel Flagg Bemis, *The Latin American Policy of the United States: An Historical Interpretation* (New York: Harcourt, Brace and Co., 1943), pp. 194-196.

72. "Our Duty in Mexico," *Independent*, LXXV (July 31, 1913), pp. 235-236; "Idealism or Expediency in Our Policy Toward Mexico," *ibid.*, LXXVI (November 13, 1913), pp. 288-289; and "Intervention—Not Yet," *ibid.*, LXXVII (January 12, 1914), pp. 49-50; *AP*, LXXV (April, 1913), pp. 78-79; (October, 1913), pp. 207-208.

73. Butler to John Morley, September 30, 1913, Butler Papers, Morley File.

74. *New York Times*, November 8, 26, 1913.

75. *AP*, LXXV (December, 1913), p. 246.

76. *Ibid.*, LXXVI (April, 1914), p. 83.

77. The votes in the House and Senate were 337 to 37 and 72 to 13. Bartholdt and Root voted against the resolution, Burton privately denounced the intervention but for unknown reasons was absent on all votes, and Hensley supported it, presumably out of party loyalty. A few hours before the vote Slayden telephoned his wife that he was going to oppose the resolution, though he finally voted "present." *CR*, 63rd Cong., 2nd sess., LI, pp. 6957-6958, 7006-7008, 7014; Burton to Short, April 23, 1914, Burton Papers, Box 17; Ellen Slayden, *Washington Wife: Journal of Ellen Maury Slayden from 1897–1919* (New York: Harper & Row, 1963), p. 233.

78. *AP*, LXXVI (May, 1914), p. 112, gives a good summary of many of these meetings. Also, NYPS Minutes, April 24, 1914, NYPS Papers, Box 1;

Mead and Angell to Wilson, telegram, April 18, 1914, Jenkin Lloyd Jones to Wilson, telegram, April 26, 1914, Robert C. Root to Wilson, telegram, April 18, 1914, Wilson Papers, Reel 213.

79. The resolution, dated April 21, 1914, is reprinted in Federal Council of the Churches of Christ in America, *Annual Report 1914* (New York: n.d.), pp. 31-32. William H. Short was a leading promoter of the Federal Council resolution. Short to Burton, April 21, 1914, Burton Papers, Box 19.

80. Carnegie to Wilson, April 21, 1914, Wilson Papers, Reel 213.

81. Link, *Wilson: The New Freedom,* pp. 403-405.

82. Short to Burton, April 21, 1914, Burton Papers, Box 19.

83. On the public restraint, see Ellen Slayden, *Washington Wife,* p. 235.

84. Wise to Short, April 21, 1914, NYPS Papers, Box 7.

85. Typewritten petition of public meeting in Chicago, April 27, 1914, CPS Papers.

86. Holt's letter in *New York Times,* April 27, 1914.

87. *Ibid.,* April 26, 1914; also see Carnegie's letter in *ibid.,* April 27, 1914.

88. Arthur L. Weatherly in *APC 1913,* p. 150.

89. *Commoner,* March 8, 1912, p. 3, quoting Bryan's speech printed in Boise *Capital,* n.d.; *New York Times,* December 11, 1913.

90. *Ibid.,* March 27, 1914.

91. John Wesley Hill in *APC 1913,* p. 380. Also see Beals in *ibid.,* p. 179.

92. *Ibid.;* also, John Lewis (editor of *Toronto Star*) in *ibid.,* p. 429.

93. Edwin D. Mead, "England and Germany," *Atlantic Monthly,* CI (March, 1908), pp. 399-407; Charles E. Jefferson, "The Delusion of Militarism," *ibid.,* CIII (March, 1909), pp. 379-388; Kirchwey in *LMC 1909,* pp. 30-35; Frederick Lynch, "Peace and War in 1913," *Yale Review,* III (January, 1914), pp. 272-284; Robert C. Root to International Peace Bureau, April 11, 1912, IPB Papers, General Correspondence (separate folder); Mead to Henri La Fontaine, March 14, 1913, *ibid.,* Box 3; Lucia Mead to Suttner, March 16, 1914, Fried-Suttner Correspondence, Divers Correspondant (1894-1914) File; Dutton in *LMC 1914,* pp. 80-84; David Starr Jordan, "The World Peace Foundation: Work in 1914," *World Peace Foundation, Pamphlet Series,* IV, No. 7 (December, 1914), pp. 23-24.

94. *APS 1912,* pp. 15-16; *AP,* LXXIV (December, 1912), p. 254.

95. David Starr Jordan, "The Impossible War," *Independent,* LXXIV (February 27, 1913), pp. 467-468; David Starr Jordan, "Bankers as Peace Guardians," *World To-Day,* XXI (February, 1912), pp. 1787-1789.

96. Lynch, "Peace and War in 1913," pp. 272-276; Bartholdt in *APC 1913,* p. 104; Mead in *ibid.,* pp. 347-348; Jane Addams, "Peace on Earth," *Ladies Home Journal,* XXX (December, 1913), p. 27; Theodore E. Burton, "The Day of International Peace," *Saturday Evening Post,* CLXXVI (December 6, 1913), pp. 3-4, 68-70; Andrew Carnegie, "A Silver Lining to War Clouds," *World To-Day,* XXI (February, 1912), p. 1793.

97. Bernadotte E. Schmitt, *The Coming of the War, 1914,* 2 vols. (New York: Charles Scribner's Sons, 1930), I, pp. 59-76.

98. Nasmyth to Mead, March 29/April 11, April 24, 1913, Edwin and

Lucia Mead Papers (SCPC), Box 1; also Nasmyth to A. Gobat, April 2, 1913, IPB Papers, General Correspondence, Box 4.

Chapter 12

1. Richard Bartholdt, *From Steerage to Congress: Reminiscences and Reflections* (Philadelphia: Dorrance & Co., 1930), pp. 357-359; Scott to Root, August 1, 1914, and Scott to J. Loudon, December 19, 1914, James Brown Scott Papers (Georgetown University Library); *AP*, LXXVI (August and September, 1914), pp. 177, 180-181.

2. Edwin D. Mead, "The World Peace Foundation: Work in 1914," *World Peace Foundation, Pamphlet Series*, IV, No. 7 (December, 1914), p. 8.

3. *AP*, LXXVI (October, 1914), p. 211.

4. *Ibid.*, p. 207.

5. See the report of French peace advocate, Theodore Ruyssen, in *ibid.*, LXXVI (November, 1914), pp. 236-238; and Edwin D. Mead, "World Peace Foundation: Work in 1914," *World Peace Foundation, Pamphlet Series*, IV, No. 7 (December, 1914), p. 8.

6. CPS Executive Committee Minutes, October 8, 1914, CPS Papers (Chicago Historical Society), Vol. II; Frederick Lynch, *Through Europe on the Eve of War: A Record of Personal Experiences; Including an Account of the First World Conference of The Churches for International Peace* (New York: The Church Peace Union, 1914), pp. 13-16.

7. *Ibid.*, pp. 25-26, 37-56.

8. *New York Times*, August 5, 1914.

9. *CR*, 63rd Cong., 2nd sess., LI, p. 13929. Also see Charles E. Jefferson, "The Nemesis of Armaments," *Independent*, LXXIX (August 17, 1914), p. 247.

10. Jordan's statements in *New York Times*, October 11, November 26, September 23, 1914. Also see the editorial in *AP*, LXXVI (October, 1914), p. 199. Trueblood told Hull that "one of your and my best friends [Edwin D. Mead?] wrote this editorial." Trueblood to Hull, October 4, 1914, William I. Hull Papers (SCPC), Box 2.

11. Lynch to Carnegie, September 3, 1914, Andrew Carnegie Papers (LC), Vol. 225.

12. *New York Evening Post*, September 24, 1914; Scott to Joachim Grieg, November 6, 1914, Scott Papers.

13. *New York Times*, September 23, 1914.

14. Edwin D. Mead, "The World Peace Foundation: Work in 1914," *World Peace Foundation, Pamphlet Series*, IV, No. 7 (December, 1914), p. 13; typed copy of William H. Short's statement in *New York Press*, August 30, 1914, provided by Frederick W. Short.

15. Jordan to Upton Sinclair, October 15, 1915, JPC (HI), Box 4.

16. Jordan to Erving Winslow, December 22, 1914, *ibid.*, Box 2; Lynch to Carnegie, September 3, 1914, Carnegie Papers, Vol. 225; Carnegie to Wilson, November 23, 1914, Woodrow Wilson Papers (LC, on microfilm), Reel 64.

17. Edwin D. Mead, "The German Point of View," *Everybody's Magazine*, XXXI (October, 1914), pp. 525-526; Hull in *LMC 1916*, pp. 77-81; Jefferson in *ibid.*, pp. 82-86; George W. Nasmyth, "What I Saw in Germany," *Independent*, LXXX (October 19, 1914), pp. 91-92.

18. Charles E. Beals, *Benjamin Franklin Trueblood—Prophet of Peace* (New York: Religious Society of Friends, 1916), pp. 14-15; Beals in *AP*, LXXVIII (December, 1916), p. 328; *ibid.*, LXXVII (May, 1915), p. 105.

19. Mead to Hull, November 4, 1914, Hull Papers, Box 2; Mead to Hull, March 19, 1915, *ibid.*, Box 3.

20. Lucia Mead to Miss Trueblood, April 18, August 2, 1915, APS Papers (SCPC), Box 6; Lucia Mead to Jordan, August 24, 1918, JPC, Box 9; Lucia Mead to Addams, July 13, 1919, Jane Addams Papers (SCPC), Box 7.

21. Albert E. Pillsbury to Mead, April 29, 1924, and Lynch to Mead, June 5, 1924, Edwin and Lucia Mead Papers (SCPC), Box 1, congratulated Mead on his recent recovery. Edwin D. Mead, "The President and the Big Navy," *Unity*, CLXXI (December 14, 1931), pp. 208-210; and Edwin D. Mead, "The Moral of the Navy League Flurry," *ibid.* (December 21, 1931), pp. 223-225, exemplify Mead's later condemnation of large armaments and the Navy League.

22. *New York Times*, November 25, 1915.

23. Louise Whitfield Carnegie, preface to *Autobiography of Andrew Carnegie* (Boston: Houghton Mifflin Co., 1920), p. v.

24. Quoted in Arthur S. Link, *Wilson: The Struggle for Neutrality, 1914–1915* (Princeton, N.J.: Princeton University Press, 1960), p. 7.

25. Scott to Joachim Grieg, November 6, 1914, Scott Papers.

26. Moore to Baldwin, June 9, 1919, Baldwin Family Papers (Yale University Library), Box 117.

27. Baldwin to Moore, June 16, 1919, *ibid.* Also see George G. Wilson in *ASIL 1916*, p. 104.

28. *ASIL 1915*, p. 55.

29. Root in *ASIL 1920*, p. 21.

30. C. Roland Marchand, *The American Peace Movement and Social Reform, 1898–1918* (Princeton, N.J.: Princeton University Press, 1972), pp. 166-167.

31. *New York Times*, May 14, 1916; *AP*, LXXVII (August, 1915), pp. 186-187; and Call in *ibid.*, LXXVIII (January, 1916), pp. 10-13.

32. *Ibid.*, LXXVII (May, 1915), pp. 105-106.

33. *Ibid.* (August, 1915), pp. 188-189.

34. *Ibid.* (June, 1915), pp. 143-144.

35. Scott to Jackson H. Ralston, June 16, 1915, reproduced in *ibid.* (November, 1915), pp. 239-241.

36. *Ibid.* (June, 1915), pp. 144-145.

37. *CPS 1915*, pp. 12, 15-18; Lochner to Lucia Mead, October 9, 1914, Mead Papers, Box 1; Jenkin Lloyd Jones to Jordan, January 22, 1915, JPC, Box 3; *AP*, LXXVII (March, 1915), pp. 68-69.

38. Lochner to Butler, January 4, 1915, Nicholas Murray Butler Papers

(Butler Library, Columbia University), Lochner File; Scott to Addams, December 31, 1914, Woman's Peace Party Papers (SCPC), Addams File.

39. *Detroit News,* November 20, 1915.

40. Henry S. Haskell to Lochner, n.d. [November, 1915], Ford Peace Plan Papers (LC), Box 3; Call to Lochner, November 22, 1915, Louis P. Lochner Papers (State Historical Society of Wisconsin), Box 52; Lochner to Call, November 28, 1915, and Lochner to Henry C. Morris, November 28, 1915, CPS Papers, Vol. II; Jenkin Lloyd Jones in *AP,* LXXIX (February, 1917), pp. 61-62.

41. Jordan to John Mez, February 18, 1915, JPC, Box 3.

42. Jordan to Henry S. Pritchett, November 23, 1915, *ibid.,* Box 5. To his wife, Jordan spoke openly of the endowment's "cowardice and incompetence." Jordan to Jessie Jordan, November 23, 1915, *ibid.*

43. Bartholdt to Lochner, November 24, 1915, Lochner Papers, Box 52. Also see John Mez to Jordan, December 9, 1915, JPC, Box 5.

44. Call to Trueblood, July 30, 1915, APS Papers, Box 6.

45. *New York Times,* December 13, 1915.

46. Call to Trueblood, September 29, October 30, 1915, APS Papers, Box 7.

47. Kirchwey to Butler, July 20, 1915, Butler Papers, Kirchwey File; Dutton to Butler, October 6, 1915, *ibid.,* Dutton File; *New York Times,* December 13, 1915.

48. On Kirchwey's pacifist leanings, see his article, "How America May Contribute to the Permanent Peace of the World," *Annals of the American Academy of Political and Social Science,* LXI (September, 1915), pp. 230-234; and Kirchwey to Spencer, July 2, 1917, Anna Garlin Spencer Papers (SCPC), Box 1. *AP,* LXXVIII (December, 1916), pp. 320-321.

49. Call to Hull, December 9, 1916, Hull to Call, December 18, 1916, Call to Hull, December 19, 1916, January 3, 1917, APS Papers, Box 6; *AP,* LXXIX (June, 1917), p. 165.

50. *Ibid.* (March, 1917), pp. 69-70.

51. *Ibid.* (April, 1917), pp. 99-100.

52. Executive Committee Minutes, April 27, 1917, APS Papers, Box 1.

53. Quoted remarks and other information come from Report of the Committee on Organization, November 23, 1914, pp. 57, 60, Annual Meeting of the Board of Trustees, November 24, 1914, pp. 59a, 62. Special Meeting of the Board of Trustees, October 11, 1915, pp. 93-96, Annual Report of the Finance Committee for the Financial Year Ending September 30, 1915, pp. 107-108, Special Meeting of the Board of Trustees, October 11, 1915, pp. 93-96, Special Meeting of the Board of Trustees, June 3, 1916, pp. 118, 120, and Report of the Committee on Organization, presented at Special Meeting of the Board of Trustees, January 8, 1916, p. 99, WPF Files (WPF).

54. Special Meeting of the Board of Trustees, October 11, 1915, pp. 93, 94-95, and Report of the Committee on Organization, presented at Special Meeting of the Board of Trustees, January 8, 1916, p. 99, *ibid.;* "Annual Report, 1915," *World Peace Foundation, Pamphlet Series,* V, No. 6, Part II (December,

1915), pp. 11-15; Butler to Frederick P. Keppel, May 28, 1915, JPC, Box 4; *New York Evening Post,* January 25, 1915; *New York Times,* May 10, 1915; *CEIP 1915,* pp. 70-72; *CEIP 1916,* pp. 61-62.

55. Annual Report of the Finance Committee for the Financial Year Ending September 30, 1915, pp. 101-106, WPF Files.

56. On the founding of the League to Enforce Peace, see Warren F. Kuehl, *Seeking World Order: The United States and International Organization to 1920* (Nashville, Tenn.: Vanderbilt University Press, 1969), pp. 181-192; Ruhl J. Bartlett, *The League to Enforce Peace* (Chapel Hill: The University of North Carolina Press, 1944), pp. 25ff; and Sondra R. Herman, *Eleven Against War: Studies in American Internationalist Thought, 1898–1921* (Stanford, Calif.: HI, 1969), pp. 72-78.

57. Special Meeting of the Board of Trustees, July 12, 1915, pp. 86-88, Special Meeting of the Board of Trustees, January 8, 1916, p. 115, Special Meeting of the Board of Trustees, June 3, 1916, p. 121, and Annual Meeting of the Board of Trustees, December 1, 1917, p. 141, WPF Files. For fears that the League to Enforce Peace might be "captured by the militarists," see W.H.P. Faunce to Jordan, October 23, 31, 1916, JPC, Box 7.

58. Jordan to Jessie Jordan, November 30, 1914, *ibid.,* Box 2; Jordan to Jessie Jordan, November 26, 28, 1915, *ibid.,* Box 5.

59. For cautious approval of the League to Enforce Peace, see Jordan to Gerald Stanley Lee, April 21, 1916, and Jordan to Short, May 1, 11, 1916, *ibid.,* Box 6. Jordan to Albert L. Guérard, September 3, 1919, *ibid.,* Box 11.

60. Jordan to Jessie Jordan, November 6, 1916, *ibid.,* Box. 7.

61. Special Committee on Improvements in the Form of the World Peace Foundation Organization, January 8, 1916, pp. 109-114, and Special Meeting of the Board of Trustees, January 8, 1916, p. 17, WPF Files.

62. Charles Herbert Levermore, *Samuel Train Dutton: A Biography* (New York: The Macmillan Co., 1922), pp. 166-170; Dutton to Butler, October 6, 1916, Butler Papers, Dutton File; Revised Minutes of the Adjourned Annual Meeting, December 2, 1916, pp. 129-130, WPF Files; Dutton to Jordan, December 13, 1916, JPC, Box 7.

63. Carnegie to Short, November 2, 1914, NYPS Papers (SCPC), Box 3.

64. *New York Times,* December 12, 1914.

65. *NYPS 1915 and 1916,* pp. 9-12.

66. *New York Evening Post,* January 7, 1915; Bartlett, *League to Enforce Peace,* pp. 30-33; *New York Times,* November 7, December 27, 1915.

67. Holmes to Short, November 4, 1915, NYPS Papers, Box 4.

68. Michael Wreszin, *Oswald Garrison Villard: Pacifist at War* (Bloomington: Indiana University Press, 1965), p. 46.

69. For striking examples of veteran peace advocates' disillusionment with the smug nationalism, intolerance, materialism, and general decline in moral standards in post-war America, see Jefferson to Mead, October 20, 1924, Mead Papers, Box 1; Edwin D. Mead, "Boston Memories of Fifty Years," *Fifty Years of Boston: A Memorial Volume,* ed. Elisabeth M. Herlihy (Boston:

Goodspeed's Bookstore, 1932), pp. 18-20; and, less stridently, Lucia Mead, *Law or War* (New York: Doubleday, Doran & Co., 1928), pp. 140-146, 237-242.

70. Slayden in *AP*, LXXIX (July, 1917), pp. 204-205; Charles E. Jefferson, "What We Must Do?" *Independent,* XC (May 26, 1917), p. 374; Lawrence W. Levine, *Defender of the Faith, William Jennings Bryan: The Last Decade, 1915–1925* (New York: Oxford University Press, 1965), pp. 37-92; William B. Hixson, Jr., *Moorfield Storey and the Abolitionist Tradition* (New York: Oxford University Press, 1972), pp. 82-87; Jordan to Henry S. Pritchett, December 24, 1917, JPC, Box 8.

71. Dole in *AP*, LXXIX (August, 1917), pp. 242-243; Wreszin, *Villard,* pp. 68-71; Holmes to Lucia Mead, October 6, 1917, Mead Papers, Box 1.

72. For prewar views, see above, pp. 117, 125, 166, 168-169, 189. On some lawyers' sympathy for collective security, see *ASIL 1917*, pp. 118-124. Professor of international law, George Wilson, actively participated in the League to Enforce Peace.

73. Kuehl, *Seeking World Order,* pp. 191-192; Herman, *Eleven Against War,* pp. 72-77.

74. Kuehl, *Seeking World Order,* pp. 215, 219; Hull to Call, December 18, 1916, APS Papers, Box 6. For attempts to find a mid-way position, see Lucia Mead in *LMC 1915,* pp. 46-47; Lucia Mead in *LMC 1916,* pp. 137-139; and Hixson, *Storey,* pp. 88-93.

75. Bryan in *LMC 1916,* pp. 144-147; Wreszin, *Villard,* p. 123.

76. Root to House, August 16, 1918, Elihu Root Papers (LC), Box 136; Chandler P. Anderson Diary, December 12, 1918, Chandler P. Anderson Papers (LC).

77. Philip Jessup, *Elihu Root,* 2 vols. (New York: Dodd, Mead & Co., 1938), II, pp. 315-319, contains excerpts from the Root-Bryce correspondence during the war; also see Bryce to Root, December 15, 1914, Root Papers, Box 118; Root to Bryce, April 12, 1918, *ibid.,* Box 136; and Root to Bryce, June 6, 1919, *ibid.,* Box 137.

78. Martin David Dubin, "Toward the Concept of Collective Security: The Bryce Group's 'Proposals for the Avoidance of War,' 1914–1917," *International Organization,* XXIV (Spring, 1970), pp. 288-318 (see especially p. 292).

79. Root's first amendment to the League of Nations Covenant quoted Bryce's definition of justiciable disputes verbatim, and Root acknowledged his indebtedness to the British group. *ASIL 1919,* pp. 50n, 52.

80. Anderson Diary, November 18, December 12, 1918.

81. Moore to Edward L. Conn, June 23, 1915, John Bassett Moore Papers (LC), Box 161.

82. For legalists' criticisms in the preceeding paragraph, see Kuehl, *Seeking World Order,* pp. 209-213, 248; *New York Times,* June 18, 1915, December 17, 1916; George W. Kirchwey, "How America May Contribute to the Peace of the World," pp. 230-234; Scott in *ASIL 1917,* pp. 101-107; Scott to Albert Shaw, July 7, 1915, and Shaw to Scott, July 17, 1915, Scott Papers; Moore to

Short, May 5, July 3, 1915, Moore Papers, Box 161; Alpheus H. Snow in *AP*, LXXVIII (July, 1916), pp. 203-207; and (November, 1916), pp. 303-304; Lansing to Wilson, May 25, 1916, Wilson Papers, Reel 79; also see Diary of Robert Lansing, September 18, October 27, 1918, Robert Lansing Papers (LC), Box 65; David Jayne Hill to Marburg, August 21, 1915, Theodore Marburg Papers (LC), Scrapbook No. 10.

83. Levermore to Andrews, February 3, 1917, Fannie Fern Andrews Papers (The Arthur and Elizabeth Schlesinger Library on the History of Women in America); Tryon in *LMC 1916,* pp. 108-122; Tryon to Moore, December 11, 1916, Moore Papers, Box 35; Dutton to Butler, January 16, 1917, Butler Papers, Dutton File.

84. *New York Times,* December 27, 1916.

85. *New York Times,* December 15, 17, 1916; Marburg to Wilson, May 22, 1917, Wilson Papers, Reel 360. Butler's articles were originally published in the *New York Times* under the pseudonym "Cosmos."

86. Wilson to Marburg, February 3, 1915, May 6, 1916, March 8, 1918, Wilson Papers, Reel 533; Taft to Marburg, June 6, 1916, Marburg Papers, Scrapbook No. 10; Kuehl, *Seeking World Order,* pp. 239, 254-255.

87. Ray Stannard Baker, *Woodrow Wilson: Life and Letters,* 8 vols. (New York: Doubleday, Page & Co., 1927–1939), VII, pp. 53, 203; VIII, p. 17; David Hunter Miller, *My Diary at the Conference of Paris, With Documents,* 21 vols. (n.p.: privately printed, 1924), I, p. 48n. On several occasions, for instance, Wilson ignored suggestions for inserting a provision into the Covenant calling for periodic conferences on international law.

88. House Diary, January 13, 27, 1918, Edward M. House Papers (Yale University Library); Wilson to House, March 22, 1918, *ibid.*

89. House Diary, June 1, 1918.

90. Wilson's extraordinary prejudice against conservative legalists and the legal profession is documented in my study, "The United States and the Origins of the World Court to 1920," *Political Science Quarterly* (forthcoming).

91. For recent interpretations of the League issue in the United States, see Kuehl, *Seeking World Order,* p. 300ff.; Ralph A. Stone, *The Irreconcilables: The Fight Against the League of Nations* (Lexington: University of Kentucky Press, 1970); Gene Smith, *When the Cheering Stopped: The Last Years of Woodrow Wilson* (New York: Morrow, 1964); Herman, *Eleven Against War,* especially pp. 78-85, 201-216; and Roland N. Stromberg, "Uncertainties and Obscurities About the League of Nations," *Journal of the History of Ideas,* XXXIII (January-March, 1972), pp. 139-154.

Conclusion

1. Michael Arnold Lutzker, "The 'Practical' Peace Advocates: An Interpretation of the American Peace Movement, 1898-1917" (Ph.D. Dissertation, Rutgers University, 1969), ch. 5.

2. Cf. Robert H. Wiebe, *The Search for Order, 1877–1920* (New York: Hill and Wang, 1967), pp. 140-159.

3. Much of the material here and in the following pages is excerpted from my essay, "An Interpretation of the American Peace Movement, 1898–1914," *Peace Movements in America,* ed. Charles Chatfield (New York: Schocken Books, 1973), pp. 32-33.

4. Cf. Wiebe, *Search for Order,* pp. 159-163 (cf. note 2).

5. See Paul A. C. Koistinen, "The 'Industrial-Military Complex' in Historical Perspective: The InterWar Years," *Journal of American History,* LVI (March, 1970), especially pp. 831-835.

6. Interpretations of the American peace movement for post-1920 decades include Charles Chatfield, *For Peace and Justice: Pacifism in America, 1914–1941* (Knoxville: University of Tennessee Press, 1971); Robert H. Ferrell, "The Peace Movement," in *Isolation and Security,* ed. Alexander DeConde (Durham, N.C.: Duke University Press, 1957); John K. Nelson, *The Peace Prophets: American Pacifist Thought, 1919–1941* (Chapel Hill: University of North Carolina Press, 1967); Charles L. DeBenedetti, "American Internationalism in the 1920s: Shotwell and the Outlawrists" (Ph.D. Dissertation, University of Illinois, 1968); Robert Domenic Accinelli, "The United States and the World Court, 1920–1927" (Ph.D. Dissertation, University of California, Berkeley, 1968); and Lawrence S. Wittner, *Rebels Against War: The American Peace Movement, 1941–1960* (New York: Columbia University Press, 1969).

Index

Abbott, Lyman, 33, 56, 77, 106, 183-185, 284, 299

abolitionism, *see* antislavery

Acorn, The, 25

Adams, Samuel, 81

Addams, Jane, 171; anti-imperialism of, 71, 82; pacifism of, 188, 198, 249; response to World War, 239

Adelphi College, 243

Advocate of Peace, 2-3, 27, 35, 43, 51, 123, 136, 222, 234; and First Hague Conference, 93, 96-97, 99; chronicles growth of peace movement, 171-173; and Taft treaties, 174; and CEIP, 194, 196; and military preparedness, 218; and World War, 237-239, 242

Aguinaldo, Emilio, 82

Alabama claims, 100

Alaska boundary question, 109

Aldrich, William F., 271

Always Arbitrate before You Fight: An Appeal to All English-speaking Folk, 97

American Anti-Imperialist League, *see* Anti-Imperialist League

American Association for International Conciliation, *see* Association for International Conciliation

American Bar Association, 155-156, 301

American Board of Commissioners for Foreign Missions, 55, 72

American Civil War, 1-3, 6-11, 17, 32, 59, 70

American Conference on International Arbitration, 126-127, 294

American Federation of Labor, 21

American Journal of International Law, 164, 303

American Neutral Conference Committee, 247

American Peace and Arbitration League, 169, 184, 187

American Peace Congresses, 129-130, 131, 136, 140, 142-143, 167, 171, 186-187, 209-210

American Peace Society (APS), 2-3, 5-9, 21, 26-27, 100-101, 112, 115, 123, 135-136, 140, 187, 191, 207-208, 215, 232, 253, 256-257, 282, 285, 288, 295, 309; reaction to Venezuelan boundary dispute, 33-34; and Olney-Pauncefote treaty, 43; and Cuban crisis, 51-54; and Anglo-American arbitration, 67, 94; and anti-imperialism, 84-86, 280; and First Hague Conference, 92-93; relation to CEIP, 144-145, 193-196; reorganization of, 150; federative tendencies of, 172-173; and military preparedness, 182-184; response to World War, 237-243, 251

American Purity Alliance, 265

American Scandinavian Society, 141

American School Peace League (ASPL), 130, 134; origins of, 136-138; New York branch of, 140; and WPF, 191-192, 243; and League to Enforce Peace, 250

American Society for the Judicial Settlement of International Disputes (ASJ-SID), 130, 164, 169, 302

American Society of International Law (ASIL), 130, 156-158, 160, 163, 169, 236-237, 301-302

American Union Against Militarism, 247

Ames, Charles G., 3, 12, 32, 308; anti-imperialism of, 85; and election of 1900, 89; and First Hague Conference, 106

Ames, Lucia True, *see* Mead, Lucia Ames

Anderson, Chandler P., 156, 163

Anderson, George W., 295

Andrews, Fannie Fern: and origins of ASPL, 136-138; response to World War, 244, 250

Angell, James B., 156

Angell, Norman, 203-204, 226, 229, 230,

327

Miles, James B., 2
Miles, Nelson, 57
military preparedness, 9, 34-35, 37; and imperialism, 66, 73-74, 93; and post–1900 peace movement, 130, 181-187, 200, 209-210, 217-221, 232-233, 303, 317; Taft on, 165, 169-170, 305. *See also* arms limitation
monetary questions, 40, 90
Monroe Doctrine, 30-33, 41-42, 76, 155, 179, 209, 221
Monroe Doctrine League, 41
Montague, Andrew J., 300
Montenegro, 99
Moore, John Bassett, 189; and Olney-Pauncefote treaty, 43; and Panama, 125; and Hay treaties, 126-127, 294; and Venezuelan debt decision, 155; and ASIL, 156; legal outlook of, 157, 188; as counselor in State Department, 163, 216; and Taft treaties, 176; and World War, 236, and League to Enforce Peace, 252
"Moral Equivalent of War, The," 137, 236
Morley, John, 73, 80
Morrow, William W., 156
Mott, John R., 295-296
Mott, Lucretia, 4
Moxom, Philip S., 43, 56
Mugwumps, 27, 38, 43, 53, 84-85, 89, 133, 198-199, 286
munitions interests, 200, 260
Muraviev, Count Michael, 96

Nasmyth, George W.: and Cosmopolitan Clubs, 136; on eve of World War, 228-229; reactions to World War, 243; and League to Enforce Peace, 244, 250; and WPF, 246, 296
National Arbitration and Peace Congress, *see* American Peace Congresses
National Arbitration Committee, 37-39, 41-44, 52, 273
National Arbitration Conference, 37-38, 49
National Arbitration League, 5
National Citizens' Committee, 174
National Council of Women, 24, 26, 49, 106
National Education Association, 137
National Equal Rights Party, 4
National Peace Congress, *see* American Peace Congresses
National School of Superintendents, 137

National Woman's Christian Temperance Union, *see* Woman's Christian Temperance Union
navalism, *see* military preparedness
Navy League of the United States, 183-184, 187, 195, 220-221
Netherlands, 99, 102, 123, 216, 231
Neutral Conference for Continuous Mediation, 247
neutralization, 76-77, 275
New England Free Trade League, 32
New England Magazine, 23, 34, 67
New England Peace and Arbitration Congress, 166-167
New Granada, *see* Colombia
New York American, 166
New York Journal, 41
New York Peace Society (NYPS), 149, 171, 195, 197-198; origins of, 130, 138-141; and international peace commission, 166; and CPS, 172; and military preparedness, 185; and anti-Japanese sentiment, 186; and Panama Canal tolls, 213; and Third Hague Conference, 215; and World War, 246-247
New York State Bar Association (NYSBA): and international tribunal, 102-103, 153-154
New York Sun, 41
New York Supreme Court, 154
New York World, 42, 44
Nicholas II, Czar, 83, 92-99, 102, 105-106, 116
Nobel Peace Prize, 167
North American Gymnastic Union, 213
North Carolina Peace Society, 184
Northwestern University, 172
Norway, 40, 45, 114, 271
Nye Committee, 260
Nys, Ernest, 164

Olney, Richard, 31, 36, 38-46, 273
Olney-Pauncefote arbitration treaty (1897), 28, 36-46, 54, 58-59, 63, 69, 93-94, 98-99, 102, 104, 126, 165, 175, 255-256; terms of, 271
Outlook, The, 33
"Open Door," 76-77
Oppenheim, Louis, 164

Pacific Banner, 25
Paine, Robert Treat, 27, 308; and Anglo-American arbitration, 28-29, 43, 94-95, 269; and Venezuelan boundary